POLICE DIVERSITY
Beyond the Blue

Tara Lai Quinlan

First published in Great Britain in 2025 by

Policy Press, an imprint of
Bristol University Press
University of Bristol
1–9 Old Park Hill
Bristol
BS2 8BB
UK
t: +44 (0)117 374 6645
e: bup-info@bristol.ac.uk

Details of international sales and distribution partners are available at policy.bristoluniversitypress.co.uk

British Library Cataloguing in Publication Data
A catalogue record for this book is available from the British Library

ISBN 978-1-4473-4794-1 hardcover
ISBN 978-1-4473-4795-8 paperback
ISBN 978-1-4473-4798-9 ePub
ISBN 978-1-4473-4796-5 ePdf

Cover design: Anonymous
Front cover image: Getty/kali9
Bristol University Press and Policy Press use environmentally responsible print partners.
Printed and bound in Great Britain by CPI Group (UK) Ltd, Croydon, CR0 4YY

FSC
www.fsc.org
MIX
Paper | Supporting
responsible forestry
FSC® C013604

Contents

List of tables

List of interview subjects

The interviews used in this volume are on file with the author. Below are a list of subjects giving ethnicity, gender, sexuality, rank, jurisdiction and the year the interview took place.

Subject	Ethnicity	Gender	Sexuality	Rank	Jurisdiction	Interview year
Interview Subject 1	Black	Male	Straight	High-ranking leader	UK	2019
Interview Subject 2	White	Female	Straight	Police Chief	US	2020
Interview Subject 3	White	Male	LGBTQ+	Police Chief	US	2020
Interview Subject 4	White	Male	Straight	Police Chief	US	2020
Interview Subject 5	Black	Male	Straight	Police Chief	US	2020
Interview Subject 6	Latino	Male	Straight	Police Chief	US	2020
Interview Subject 7	Black	Male	Straight	High-ranking leader	UK	2020
Interview Subject 8	Latino	Male	Straight	Police Chief	US	2020

About the author

Tara Lai Quinlan is Associate Professor in Law and Criminal Justice at Birmingham Law School, University of Birmingham. Dr Quinlan's research and teaching focus on criminal law and criminal procedure, policing, diversity and disproportionality in the criminal justice system, and counter-terrorism. She is a qualified lawyer (New York).

1

Understanding and defining police diversity

This book examines police diversity in the UK and US. While this volume proposes police diversity as one of the tools valuable in reforming UK and US police, it does not offer police diversity as a panacea for all that is ailing in policing. Rather, it provides a nuanced understanding about the benefits and limitations of police diversity through the lens of street police culture – that is the culture of patrol officers who comprise the majority of officers in the UK and US police organizations – and in doing so offers a new way of understanding police diversity in both jurisdictions. From the outset, it argues that comparison of these two distinct police jurisdictions is possible because knowledge and lessons to be drawn from police diversity are not of limited relevance solely to their country-specific cultural contexts. Rather, this volume asserts that using the theoretical framework of street police culture provides a cohesive understanding of the ways police diversity is created, supported and challenged in both locales.

Prior volumes on police diversity have mostly overlooked street police culture, and have not used it to understand the history or state of police diversity in the UK and US. They have not considered the ways street police culture shapes policing experiences, particularly for officers from traditionally marginalized groups. This book asserts that police diversity cannot be meaningfully understood without employing the street police culture theoretical lens. It is the street police culture framework which provides a generalizable and overarching mechanism for evaluating police diversity in the UK and US.

At the core of this volume's examination of police diversity is a street police culture with norms originating in White, working-class male perspectives on masculinity, violence, aggression, tolerance and offending, among others. It asserts that street police culture strongly influences the character of policing institutions and the behaviours of officers on the streets, and is a very difficult influence for officers to resist. It examines the ways most police officers assimilate in whole or in part into street police culture norms, while others may reject some or all aspects of street police culture. It considers how street police culture places particular pressures on officers from traditionally marginalized groups who, the research undertaken for this volume suggests, often do not feel empowered to push back against street police culture norms. However, the research conducted for this book also reveals that street police culture shapes the experiences of officers from traditionally under-represented backgrounds in very specific ways, often different from those of their majority group colleagues, and can create differences in their experiences of equality, diversity and inclusion on the job, including discrimination and different terms and conditions of employment in ways they may or may not be aware of. This volume explores how under certain conditions, minority group officers can feel empowered to reject aspects of street police culture, show less hostility toward and alienation from some minority communities, and can conduct policing in ways different from their majority group colleagues.

While this book examines police diversity in its particular UK and US cultural contexts, it argues that the analysis provides many similarities in the ways police culture shapes experiences of diversity in police institutions, and in turn, influences on policing practices on the streets. The volume therefore, for the first time in police diversity research, comparatively examines the ways street police culture shapes the goals, roles and impacts of police diversity in the police services in the UK and US. The book's methodology examines a wealth of empirical research from a broad array of interdisciplinary literature from fields including criminal justice, criminology, law, organizational behaviour, cognitive psychology and critical race theory, coupled with analysis of eight elite police leader interviews conducted in both jurisdictions.

To engage in this analysis, the book adopts a conceptualization of diversity focused on groups traditionally under-represented in policing, whose existence in the institution poses challenges for established street police culture norms – racial and ethnic, gender, sexual orientation, gender identity and education minorities. It explores the ways these historically marginalized groups not only experience policing, but also the ways they challenge or assimilate into street police culture, and uses the theoretical framework of representative bureaucracy to consider how this might impact how they conduct policing on the streets. Indeed, representative bureaucracy theory provides a way to consider how some police from traditionally marginalized backgrounds, as a result of their lived experiences and the discrimination they face in policing, may feel representative of their communities of origin and/ or other marginalized communities, which has to date been under-researched in UK and US policing. Ultimately, the book argues that street police culture requires officers from these groups to adapt, refute, distance themselves from, and otherwise navigate street police culture norms, which in turn impacts policing more broadly. In particular, this volume asserts that these disparate internal experiences of street police culture for diverse officers within police institutions influences external policing practices and police legitimacy with policed communities, particularly for traditionally marginalized groups.

The book is a particularly important study of police diversity given the long-troubled relations between UK and US police and the traditionally marginalized communities they serve, including many communities of colour, women, in LGBTQ+ and other minority communities. The severity of these tensions has been illustrated in recent decades with well-publicized UK and US police killings of people of colour, and particularly Black people, including Chris Kaba (London, 2022), Patrick Lyoya (Grand Rapids, MI, 2022), George Floyd (Minneapolis, 2020), Breonna Taylor (Louisville, 2020), Dalian Atkinson (London, 2016), Philando Castile (Falcon Heights, MN, 2016), Eric Garner (New York, 2014), Michael Brown (Ferguson, MO, 2014), Mark Duggan (London, 2011), Sean Rigg (London, 2008), and many others. Given increased academic and public interest on this subject, this volume serves an important function of providing theoretically and empirically informed discourse through the lens of police culture for the first time to comparative debates about police diversity and its implications.

Police are not just blue

The lens of this book challenges established approaches to police diversity research. Not only does it use street police culture and representative bureaucracy theories as overarching frameworks but, contrary to most books, it also considers police diversity in intersectional and multi-layered ways.

Most volumes on police diversity adopt a singular lens of police institutions and the policing experience, either to criticize or support policing (Johnson, 1976; Reiner, 1978; Alexander, 2010; Vitale, 2017). Such perspectives tend to view police and policing institutions as a cohesive entity known as 'the police' focused on exercising state power through social control (Johnson, 1976; Sim and Tombs, 2009). These approaches tend to see 'the police' as a monolith with a single set of shared beliefs and approaches to policing, all looking and acting the same while wearing blue police uniforms. To some extent this perspective is understandable, given that street police culture normalizes particular shared values among officers which they are all expected to uphold. Yet this lens regards 'the police' as an entity comprised of straight White male officers. Even if this approach in passing notes the existence of ethnic minority, women, LGBTQ+ and college-educated officers, it does not interrogate the differences experienced by officers from traditionally marginalized groups once they join the police, who are frequently explicitly and implicitly confronted with discrimination, bias, different terms and conditions of employment, and street police culture norms which do not comport with their own beliefs and lived experiences.

Rather than adhere to the dated singular policing framework, this volume both acknowledges the embedded history and influence of straight White men in UK and US policing, and argues that policing must be understood by considering the differences in perspectives and lived experiences of police officers from diverse backgrounds, and endeavours to do so. This book seeks to highlight the ways largely immutable personal characteristics of officers – including race, gender, sexual orientation and gender identity – have produced multi-layered experiences of and approaches to policing. Instead of ignoring differences among police officers as most police diversity volumes have traditionally done, this volume embraces the richness and variation of police officers through a much closer analysis of police diversity than provided in most existing police diversity literature. In doing so, this volume offers for the first time a much needed layer of nuance to craft a more complex picture of UK and US police diversity. While painting such a complicated picture of police diversity is rare in policing research, it is unprecedented in comparative analyses of police diversity in the UK and US, making this book the first to undertake this endeavour, and an important contribution to the field.

Street police culture literature

The existing literature on street police culture provides the theoretical underpinning for this volume's analysis of police diversity, and will be briefly introduced here before being more fully developed in Chapter 2.

All institutions, from workplaces to universities to social clubs, have distinct cultures. Institutional cultures have a significant influence on both individual and institutional practices (Griffith et al, 2007). Like other institutions, police services have distinct organizational cultures shaping policies and practices at the individual and institutional levels (Chan, 1997). Within the same police institution there can be multiple organizational cultures, including those related to leaders, middle managers and street-level officers (Reuss-Ianni, 1983). Yet it is street police culture which has proven highly influential in UK and US policing (Manning, 1997).

Street police culture refers to the norms and beliefs of patrol officers, a role that all officers experience at least early in their careers, and which proves instructive and enduring in terms of how they understand what it means to be an officer. The particular values which form street police culture are the product of the straight White working-class men who have traditionally constituted the majority of police in these jurisdictions (Loftus, 2009). Street police culture is defined by numerous characteristics, including aggression, violence, repression, bias, stereotypes, toxic masculinity and warrior mentality, among other traits (Cockcroft, 2003; Bowling et al, 2019). While street police culture can be shaped by local, state or national culture and agency-specific aspects, the key street police culture traits are remarkably consistent across jurisdictions including the UK and US (Chan, 1997; Bowling et al, 2019).

Because policing institutions and the policing practices of individual officers are so heavily influenced by street police culture, as discussed further in Chapter 2, this volume uses street police culture as the overarching theoretical framework for understanding police diversity. This book argues that the nuances and complexities of police diversity in the UK and US cannot be understood without rigorously examining street police culture, making it a highly original contribution to the police diversity field.

Most volumes on police diversity omit or downplay references to street police culture, either due to lack of familiarity with the theory, lack of understanding of, or scepticism about, the ways it remains extremely influential on all aspects of policing. For example, Waddington (1999) and Rowe (2004) famously reject the value of the concept of police culture in understanding policing. Waddington (1999) asserts that the influence of police culture is overblown, and argues that, to the extent it is impactful, it is beneficial to policing because it promotes camaraderie in a very difficult job. Similarly, Rowe (2004) is sceptical about the value of police culture in understanding policing, asserting police culture is not a singular, monolithic structure which all officers adopt, and therefore arguing it is unhelpful to apply negative street police culture traits such as deviance, cynicism and racism to all police officers. He argues the concept of police culture is often used in a generalized and stereotypical manner against police, and that even where police hold such negative police culture attitudes, this may be disconnected from how they engage in policing in practice.

Yet despite how significant a role street police culture plays in shaping police institutions, police practices and police experiences, it has never been used as an overarching framework for a volume on police diversity until now.

Even volumes attuned to discussing issues of bias in policing largely only mention street police culture in passing rather than delving into the complex ways it influences policing institutions, policies and practices. For example, in the UK context, Bowling and Phillips (2002) argue that street police culture, with its negative stereotypes of people of colour, is an important aspect of understanding police practices directed at communities of colour, although they caution that police culture is not the only explanation for police racism. Moreover, they argue that these racist police culture attitudes inevitably impact the way police engage in policing on the streets. Similarly, Webster (2007) recognizes the value of the police culture in understanding behaviours among lower level UK officers, and resistance to what they perceive as political pressures from police leaders to be anti-racist. Webster (2007) also recognizes the ways police culture helps us understand racism by police who negatively stereotype people of colour, but argues that overly culture-focused explanations may overlook larger social, structural and institutional aspects of policing.

In the UK context, the Casey Review (Casey, 2023) examined the standards of behaviour and internal culture of the London Metropolitan

Police Service (London Met Police), the UK's largest police service, following the murder of Sarah Everard by a serving London Met Police officer, finding that the institution was institutionally racist, sexist and homophobic. The report even went so far as to conclude that officers from traditionally marginalized groups were frequently subjected to bullying, racism, sexism and homophobia, but it did not draw on literature on street police culture, nor did it draw on literature offering how this biased police culture could be changed.

In the US context, much of US policing literature similarly neglects reference to street police culture, or downplays its influence on police institutions, police officer experiences and police practices. Ray, Ortiz and Nash (2017), for example, find that aspects of police culture may contribute to officers of colour not being fully integrated into police departments, and continue to structure police institutions as 'racialized social systems' reflecting larger racial inequalities, but do not use the concept as the analytical framework for analysis of policing. Similarly, Todak, Huff and James (2018) and Sklansky (2022) both acknowledge in passing the challenges posed by street police culture for creating and maintaining police diversity, but neglect to delve into the details of the ways police culture impacts on police experiences.

Even where police literature acknowledges widespread stereotyping of racial, ethnic, gender or other minority groups, they have neglected to tackle how addressing police culture might reduce such biases. For example, in *Suspect Race* (2014), Glaser examines the social psychology behind racial profiling by police, arguing that while prejudice remains common in law enforcement, it is only a relatively small influence in police profiling. Rather, he argues stereotyping is far more influential on police profiling. Glaser focuses on the science of profiling, but does not examine the ways police culture normalizes and reinforces racial stereotypes. Similarly, while the President's Task Force on 21st Century Policing (White House, 2015) emphasized that police negatively stereotype racial, ethnic and other minorities, and raised the potential greater diversity has for changing this culture and these stereotypes, it did not readily connect these practices to the police warrior culture it so heavily criticizes, a topic discussed further in Chapter 2.

Existing police diversity literature

Although police diversity has been a topic of interest in the UK and US for decades, these discussions generally lack robust theoretical and empirical analysis situated within the context of broader academic literature on police culture. Because police diversity literature has largely shied away from such structural analyses of how police culture impedes the equality, diversity and inclusion of officers from traditionally marginalized backgrounds, this volume fills an important research gap.

For example, while discussions of police diversity have existed in US literature for decades, they have largely failed to engage with structural analysis using street police culture theory. For example, Forman's 2017 account of the movement in Black communities from 1948 to 1978 to reduce anti-Black police violence by lobbying for more Black officers, while highlighting tensions and difficulties for Black police officers, does not situate the analysis in an understanding of how police culture shapes their experiences. Similarly, while the US Commission on Civil Rights (USCCR, 1981) investigated tense relations between communities of colour, particularly Black communities, and large US police departments, following urban uprisings in the 1960s and 1970s, while acknowledging the need for police diversity to quell tensions, it did not address the ways embedded street police culture within police institutions prevents applicants of colour from joining or remaining in police forces.

There are clear parallels with this approach in the UK. For example, Lord Scarman's report following the 1981 Brixton uprisings – which saw Black people in Brixton, London clash with the London Met Police over perceived racist policing – while it acknowledged racist police incidents, attributed these to isolated incidents by a few officers rather than being structurally driven by street police culture within the police institution (Scarman, 1981). Scarman looked to police diversity as one means to ease tensions with Black communities but did not consider the ways street police culture might impede police departments from engaging in meaningful equality, diversity and inclusion.

By contrast, Lord Macpherson's enquiry into the London Met Police's handling of the racist murder of Black teenager Stephen Lawrence, for the first time found that the police were institutionally racist, and acknowledged that racist street police culture contributed to stereotyping and biased policing of Black people (Macpherson, 1999). While Macpherson strongly urged UK police to increase police diversity to improve relations with Black communities, it did not evaluate the ways street police culture could impede the hiring and retention of officers of colour. This volume takes forward some of the ideas raised by Macpherson in this regard. However, rather than treating street police culture as a minor part of the police institution, this book fills a significant research gap by foregrounding street police culture as the overarching, highly influential mechanism shaping policing generally, and the ability of police institutions to create and maintain police diversity in particular.

A limited amount of police diversity literature has analysed the importance of street police culture in relation to police legitimacy, particularly in traditionally marginalized communities, but failed to examine the ways representative bureaucracy theory may motivate some officers to improve legitimacy and disproportionate policing outcomes with marginalized communities. Indeed, existing police diversity literature has shied away from applying representative bureaucracy to policing to examine how members of traditionally marginalized groups may feel allegiance with their communities of origin and police differently as a result.

One such volume is Bowling and Phillips' book, *Racism, Crime and Justice* (2002). While it does not focus primarily on police diversity, instead focusing on racism throughout the criminal justice system of England and Wales, they do argue that the Peelian notion of policing by consent, discussed further below, is compromised if police fail to reflect the diversity of policed populations. Similarly, the UK-focused book, *Policing, Race and Racism* (Rowe, 2004), identifies the need for increased police diversity for multiple reasons, including building greater trust and confidence with communities of colour, increased cooperation of witnesses and victims and increased crime reporting, among others. These reflections are consistent with US police research connecting the concepts of police representation and police legitimacy (USCCR, 2000; Weitzer and Tuch, 2006; The White House, 2015), as discussed in Chapter 3 of this book.

This volume introduces a further layer of analysis, for it not only considers the ways police diversity can enhance police legitimacy, but it also introduces the question of how representative bureaucracy theory may explain why diverse officers may be incentivized to improve legitimacy in historically marginalized communities.

Further, existing police diversity literature has also not considered the ways street police culture theory and representative bureaucracy theory interact in practice in policing institutions. This volume fills this gap by showing that street police culture impedes the ability of officers from marginalized groups to meaningfully engage in representative bureaucracy, or ensures they contend with negative departmental consequences if they do so, and can their drive experiences of bias within police institutions.

For example, Rowe (2004) examines the UK's history of voluntary police diversity initiatives, changes in laws facilitating greater recruitment of officers of colour, and briefly touches on the departmental experiences of officers of colour, but does examine how they might police differently from straight, White male colleagues, or how their experiences are shaped by street police culture. Along similar lines, Bowling, Reiner and Sheptycki's (2019) UK-focused book, argues that police diversity is important both as a matter of fairness, and because representation matters to policed communities, but does not produce the nuances of how and why police from marginalized backgrounds might experience police institutions differently. Neither text delves into the nuances of street police culture or the ways it generates negative experiences for officers from traditionally marginalized backgrounds and how they might respond by engaging in representative bureaucracy. This volume, therefore, fills a gap in adopting and applying these two theoretical lenses to the experiences of diverse officers from UK and US police services.

Only a few articles have begun the process of using street police culture for understanding the nature of the experiences and challenges for officers in increasingly diverse UK and US police services. For example, writing two decades ago, Paoline (2003) introduces a framework for conceptualizing police culture, its origins, what it prescribes, and its outcomes for policing. He engages briefly with diversification of policing, arguing that greater diversity in policing could introduce a broader array of perspectives and lived experiences, and reshape police culture socialization patterns. However, Paoline does not take this analysis further by exploring the application of this approach in depth, as this volume aims to do.

More recently, Zempi's article (2020), examining the lived experiences of bias and discrimination of 19 police officers within one English police force, recognizes the importance of police culture in creating an environment where officers from traditionally marginalized groups are regarded as outsiders and subjected to different terms and conditions of employment. Similarly, Hasan's article (2021), chronicling the lived experiences of ten current and former UK female officers of colour, is one of few empirical examinations which, much like this volume, foregrounds the impact of police culture on stereotypes, racism and sexism experienced by officers, in this case focused on her sample of Black and Minority Ethnic (BAME) women in UK policing. While both articles are important contributions to literature for the UK officers they interviewed, neither applied the lessons learned on a larger scale, including whether they might apply in the US.

Some more radical volumes on policing do not engage with the nuances of street police culture as applied to diverse officers, asserting that all police adhere to the same beliefs, meaning police diversity is of little value (Alexander, 2010; Vitale, 2017). Indeed, they reject the notion that police diversity can change discriminatory policing practices disproportionately impacting communities of colour, arguing policing is incapable of reform because it was designed to oppress marginalized communities, particularly communities of colour. For example, Alexander's book (2010) asserts that 'cosmetic' efforts to diversify criminal justice institutions by making them look more representative of communities of colour have in actuality pacified communities of colour with a 'racial bribe' which furthers inequality and division, rather than achieving racial justice. She argues that US policing is inherently structured to produce and reproduce a cycle of mass incarceration of people of colour, and this framework cannot be rehabilitated with diversity or similar means.

Similarly, Vitale's book (2017), a cornerstone of the defund policing movement, argues that US policing's origins in colonialism, slavery and capitalism mean the institution is inherently exploitative and reinforcing of inequalities, particularly racial inequalities. Vitale argues that policing reforms including increasing diversity are not effective because officers of colour act in ways similar to, or even worse than, their White counterparts in relation to policing communities of colour. Vitale asserts that policing is so inherently flawed that it must be abolished, and communities empowered and funded to address harms in fairer and more restorative ways.

While Alexander, Vitale and others make a strong case doubtful about any efforts to reform policing, they do not engage with the theories of street police culture and representative bureaucracy discussed earlier or their practical applications to the lived experiences of diverse police officers and police leaders discussed throughout this volume. Thus, while their texts assert important challenges interrogating the very purpose of policing, their solutions for defunding policing are more theoretical then practically based. Indeed, while their subsequent work has pointed to successful US pilot defund programmes in relation to mental health, drugs and domestic violence, they have yet to engage meaningfully with the practicalities of dealing with pressing public safety issues including homicide, terrorism and other serious violence-related concerns. Until there are meaningful alternative interventions offered to address serious public safety issues in UK and US communities, defunding the police in whole will not be readily achievable. Working within this practical reality, this volume offers theoretically informed analysis of the importance of attending to diverse experiences of policing within UK and US police institutions that seem likely to remain funded for decades.

Representative bureaucracy theory and policing literature

This volume also draws significantly on the representative bureaucracy theory, a concept essential to understanding the ways street police culture creates unique and significant challenges for the lived experiences of police officers from traditionally marginalized groups. Most volumes on police diversity have failed to incorporate representative bureaucracy theory into their analysis, but this book argues it is key to understanding the complexities and nuances of UK and US police diversity.

Representative bureaucracy theory originates in public administration theory, and as applied to policing asserts that police have potential to act as advocates of their communities of origin if certain conditions are met, as discussed further in Chapter 8 (Mosher, 1982; Wilkins and Williams, 2008; Trochmann and Gover, 2016). The theory asserts that passive bureaucratic representation in civic institutions means bureaucrats from traditionally marginalized groups have numbers mirroring the composition of local minority communities. Active bureaucratic representation means that, under certain conditions, these minority bureaucrats can consciously or unconsciously actively represent the interests of their communities of origin, resulting in individual and government agency behaviours which reflect the interests of those communities (Mosher, 1982; Wilkins and Williams, 2008; Trochmann and Gover, 2016). Where active bureaucratic representation takes place, this can increase legitimacy of government agencies, and increase beneficial outcomes to these communities (Meier and Stewart, 1992; Riccucci et al, 2014; Riccucci and Van Ryzin, 2017; Ryzin et al, 2017; Lucero et al, 2022; Keiser et al, 2022).

While public administration and political science have tended to embrace representative bureaucracy theory as core to understanding the motivations and experiences of public officials from traditionally marginalized groups, police literature has been more reluctant to engage with the concept. Those volumes that do consider the reasons historically under-represented officers might experience policing or conduct policing practices in particular ways have largely failed to have robust theoretical underpinning to the analysis.

For example, Rowe (2004) fails to engage with representative bureaucracy theory, and in passing argues that officers of colour do not necessarily feel strongly connected to their communities of origin, and that to expect them to do so is naive and treats people of colour as one-dimensional, seemingly arguing that they have more commonalities with than differences from their White colleagues. Similarly, Bowling et al (2019) also neglect representative bureaucracy theory, but assert that police from traditionally marginalized backgrounds, such as women and people of colour, generally do not police in ways different from their White male colleagues, and fail to examine a wide array of empirical evidence to further explore this assertion, something missing from police diversity literature that this book seeks to address. Ultimately, they allow that more evidence of differences in policing outcomes for officers from traditionally marginalized groups may develop with greater numbers of diverse officers.

Very few works in the field of policing have squarely analysed the relevance of representative bureaucracy theory, but those that do are fairly sceptical of the concept, preferring to view all police as a monolith of approaches, values and ideas grounded in street police culture. For example, Wilkins and Williams (2008) argue that police culture precludes officers of colour from feeling representative of their communities of origin. Todak et al (2018) similarly assert that there is only limited evidence of representative bureaucracy in policing, although they did not conduct an empirical examination of the phenomenon.

Similarly, Forman (2017) does not engage with representative bureaucracy theory, but does reflect on the significant discrimination faced by Black officers in US police departments between 1948 and 1978 given their small numbers compared to majority White police departments. Forman is sceptical about whether Black officers had racial solidarity with Black communities, questioning whether Black officers really felt more allegiance or racial solidarity with Black communities than White officers. While Forman finds Black officers had better rapport with Black communities compared to White officers during this period, he also observes the degrees of aggression some Black officers displayed toward Black communities. While Forman attributes this hostility to class divisions in Black communities, with Black officers aggressively policing poor Black people, and to notions of protecting Black communities from offenders who would plague those communities with crime and violence, he does not explore the ways police culture placed pressure on Black officers to conform to biased policing attitudes or practices, at the risk of further ostracization from White officers.

This volume is the first in police diversity scholarship to apply representative bureaucracy theory to policing and to provide in-depth analysis of its value in considering how street police culture and conscious or unconscious active representative motivations may create the statistically significant differences in the lived experiences and policing outcomes borne out of research on police officers from traditionally marginalized groups.

Defining key concepts in equality, diversity and inclusion

Prior volumes on police diversity have, for the most part, not critically engaged with the theories behind the concepts of equality, diversity and inclusion to better understand the meaning and implications of UK and US diversity in police institutions. While these notions are used interchangeably in some policing literature, a review of literature discussed below illustrates that these ideas are not synonymous, and have distinct meanings in relevant literature and different applications for policing. After first defining these key terms, then engaging with these concepts throughout the volume, this provides much richer, more in-depth and better understandings of the experiences and impacts of police diversity. It also allows for easier comparison across the two distinct jurisdictions by drawing similarities between the approaches to police diversity in different police institutions in both countries.

Defining equality

Legal scholars assert that equality can be conceptualized in two distinct ways – formal equality and substantive equality. Formal equality is the approach most commonly associated with lay notions of equality. Formal equality focuses on evenhanded treatment for all individuals and groups (Prasad et al, 2006). It emphasizes ensuring that individuals or groups are all treated in the same way in employment, housing, health and other service provisions (Fredman, 2008, 2016). Formal equality perspectives aim for uniform fairness in treatment and decision-making, but do not take into account the unique characteristics or challenges faced by individuals, such as personal backgrounds, lived experiences, group inequalities, historical disadvantages or structural inequities that might impact or shape the experiences of individuals (Prasad et al, 2006). Indeed, formal equality approaches prohibit treating individuals or groups of individuals differently from one another based on their membership in a traditionally marginalized group, such as race, ethnicity, gender, religion, age, pregnancy, marital status, disability, sexual orientation or similar, or characteristics which subject groups to oppression (Fredman, 2008, 2016).

In both the UK and US, equality laws generally adopt formal equality approaches (McCrudden, 1982; Prasad et al, 2006). In the UK, formal equality approaches are enshrined in its equality legislation, including the Equality Act 2010. In the US, formal equality approaches are enshrined in the US Declaration of Independence, which sets out that 'all men are created equal', and the 14th Amendment to the Constitution's 'equal protection of the laws' provision, as well as in the constitutions of all US states, and many city ordinances which adopt similar formal equality language.

While formal equality provides a minimum standard for conceptualizing equality laws and frameworks, critics argue these approaches have limited effectiveness (Quinlan, forthcoming). Sceptics assert these largely reactive visions of equality require victims to proactively bring enforcement actions if they are treated in discriminatory ways. Indeed, marginalized community members bear the burden of proving they have not been treated equally to others based on their race, ethnicity, gender, religion, age, pregnancy, marital status, disability, sexual orientation or other protected characteristics, in relation to hiring, termination, terms and conditions of employment or provision of other goods and services. Although it is well established by legal scholars that formal equality has benefits, it results in very slow changes in the treatment of traditionally marginalized groups because it fails to address underlying drivers of inequalities (Fredman, 2008, 2016). Focusing exclusively on formal equality approaches in fact impedes achievement of more robust diversity because the model obstructs the introduction of the type of more widespread equality measures which address systemic inequalities, to be discussed later, giving employers and society more generally the sense that equality has been achieved and additional measures are unnecessary (Wrench, 2005). Formal equality will, therefore, only ever be limited in its impacts on achieving equality in the workplace and beyond (Prasad et al, 2006).

In contrast to formal equality measures, substantive equality approaches extend beyond just treating individuals or groups identically. Substantive equality adopts a structural view of discrimination, its effects, and its solutions (Noon, 2010). Substantive equality explicitly declines to treat all individuals and groups identically, but rather emphasizes that groups who have been subject to historic inequalities or continue to face oppression in employment, housing, health and other areas require additional support to achieve equal opportunities. This approach recognizes that protected group membership including race, ethnicity, gender, religion, age, pregnancy, marital status, disability, sexual orientation or similar characteristics can subject individuals and groups to structural social inequalities which require ameliorating (Fredman, 2008, 2016).

To address systemic inequalities where they are detected, substantive equality approaches are proactive measures which compel employers and other service providers to treat disadvantaged groups more favourably than advantaged groups regarding hiring, termination, terms and conditions of employment, admissions and other service provisions (Fredman, 2008). Such approaches are aimed at providing benefits to groups with structural disadvantages to give them opportunities to put them closer to an equal footing with those who have structural advantages in a particular context (Fredman, 2008; Noon, 2010).

Substantive equality measures in employment, for example, take into account protected group membership as highly relevant criteria in employment decisions (Davies and Robison, 2016). This approach extends beyond existing formal equality limitations by mandating equal employment outcomes to redress disadvantages for BAME candidates and other traditionally marginalized groups. The substantive equality approach recognizes protected group membership can disadvantage applicants in occupations such as policing, and makes it a highly relevant employment criteria (Noon, 2010).

In the UK, substantive equality approaches are generally prohibited. In the US, the 14th Amendment to the Constitution has been interpreted to permit substantive equality approaches in government agencies, private businesses and non-governmental organizations since the 1950s, and many have been required to implement substantive equality approaches related to race, ethnicity and/or gender (see, for example, *Brown v Board of Education; Griggs v Power Duke Co.; Green v. County School Board of New Kent County, VA*). However, since the late 1970s, the US Supreme Court has repeatedly narrowed the scope of permissible substantive equality programmes in government hiring, government contracting and higher education not because they are no longer needed, but arguably due to the changing political climate in the US (see, for example, *Bakke v. California; City of Richmond v. Croson; Adarand Constructors v. Pena; Grutter v. Bollinger*).

Prior volumes on policing offer varying views of equality, with most tending to limit diversity aspirations to those falling within the formal equality framework (for example, Rowe, 2004; Bowling et al, 2019). Others reject the notion that policing should aspire for greater diversity given, arguing instead that all police officers will only ever be state agents for social control (Sim and Tombs, 2009; Alexander, 2010; Vitale, 2017).

This volume argues achieving greater police diversity is imperative for three essential reasons. First, it can improve fairness for the experiences of under-represented officers despite the challenges of street police culture. Second, it can increase police legitimacy in local policed communities. And third, it argues for the first time in a police diversity book based on in-depth understandings of the theories of street police culture and representative bureaucracy, that greater police diversity may reduce disproportionate policing outcomes toward traditionally marginalized groups.

This volume asserts that the lagging police diversity in most UK and US police services, and its significant internal and external repercussions, show that formal equality alone is not working, and is insufficient for achieving these aims. This book, therefore, makes an important original argument in the UK and US police diversity context by arguing that as a matter of great urgency, significantly improved equality is imperative to the functioning of contemporary policing, and all measures, including substantive equality measures such as affirmative action/positive discrimination, must be used to achieve it.

Defining diversity

Works on police diversity have naturally examined the concept of diversity, however, the term is often poorly defined and inconsistently applied across the relevant literature. Diversity can be contemplated in a variety of aspects of life. People often discuss diversity in terms of different experiences, ideas and perspectives. Diversity is also evaluated in relation to the composition of institutions including schools, workplaces and social settings. This volume focuses narrowly on diversity in the workplace as the focal point for its discussion.

In the context of workplace diversity, varied stakeholders may define the term differently. Employers, employees, unions, advocates, academics and others may all frame diversity differently according to their positionality in relation to particular workplace composition outcomes. While diversity clearly has legal implications in the workplace, it is not inherently a legal term with a prescribed legal meaning (Prasad et al, 2006). As such, workplace diversity has more often than not been primarily a voluntary, employer-led endeavour focused on recruiting and retaining individuals from minority, traditionally under-represented and/or legally protected groups (Prasad, 2001).

Scholars differ on the precise scope of what constitutes diversity in the workplace. Some argue workplace diversity should be interpreted very broadly, meaning inclusion of people from different legally protected groups, along with diversity of physical traits, cognitive abilities and personality types including leadership styles (Thomas, 1992). Such an expansive approach regards all differences as meriting equal attention when it comes to diversifying the workplace, consistent with the sort of formal equality approaches discussed above. However, it does not account for the role some traits may play in creating more severe disadvantages, or the impact of systemic inequalities, for some individuals over others (Jones and Stablein, 2006).

By contrast, other scholars argue workplace diversity efforts should focus on those groups that have been historically disadvantaged (Prasad et al, 2006). This argument asserts that traditionally marginalized groups, including racial and ethnic minorities, women, LGBTQ+ individuals, persons from poor and lower socio-economic backgrounds, among others, should be the primary focus for workplace diversity initiatives and attention. It asserts that the same structural inequalities seen in society manifest within organizations (Konrad et al, 2021). Proponents of this argument assert that regardless of whether traditionally marginalized groups receive legally protected status, their employment participation should be subject to workplace support measures (Prasad et al, 2006). Significantly, workplace diversity should not be defined and analysed without contextualizing in relation to larger economic and social structures of power, power relations and social inequality (Prasad, 2001; Jones, 2004; Pringle and Ryan, 2015; Konrad et al, 2021). This approach is consistent with notions of substantive equality discussed in the preceding section.

Moreover, some types of diversity have greater resonance in certain countries and cultural contexts than others (Prasad et al, 2006). This can be a result of historic, legal and representational differences among groups in different jurisdictions, or different norms and values. Indeed, critical diversity scholars argue diversity policies should therefore address multiple levels of inequality and oppression to attend to the broadest possible array of diversity needs (Pringle and Ryan, 2015). Some argue diversity should be evaluated through three interconnected layers: the macro, which involves the larger historic, socio-economic, socio-political structures; the meso, which focuses on considerations relating to the particular field or profession; and the micro, which contemplates the individual objectives and interpersonal relations of a workplace (Syed and Ozbilgin, 2009). Others assert diversity must be analysed through an intersectional approach, which recognizes multiple and linked forms of oppression – a concept discussed later in this volume (Crenshaw, 1989; Riad and Jones, 2022).

Yet critical scholars argue that simply addressing equitable workplace representation is not enough. They assert that robust diversity approaches must also assess the conditions and quality of experiences for under-represented groups in the workplace. Issues of workplace power dynamics, anti-oppression, inclusion and support of traditionally marginalized groups must also be factored in (Prasad et al, 2006). Research shows that where members of traditionally marginalized groups believe they are not welcomed and perceive that their workplaces do not value diversity, their potential for success is impeded (Bond and Haynes, 2014). Moreover, perceived biased or hostile workplaces create performance anxieties which can lower the self-esteem of under-represented groups, negatively impacting performance (Payne and Cameron, 2010).

Thus while some volumes discussing police diversity, including Rowe (2004) and Forman (2017), do acknowledge the challenges of discrimination and different terms and conditions of employment for officers from diverse backgrounds, particularly for officers from ethnic minority backgrounds, still they have not tended to probe more deeply into the nuanced aspects of the experiences of diverse officers, or drivers of their exclusion and ostracization in UK and US police services. By contrast, Hunt (1984), Heidensohn (1992), Herbert (2001), Colvin (2015, 2020) and others have probed more deeply into the exclusion and ostracization of female officers and LGBTQ+ officers within police institutions, although they tend not to adopt an intersectional approach to these examinations. This volume, therefore, adopts an intersectional analysis of police diversity focused on the experiences of groups historically disadvantaged and discriminated against in the policing field.

Defining inclusion

Earlier volumes on police diversity have not traditionally wrestled with the tensions posed by notions of inclusion in police institutions. Inclusion broadly defined extends beyond mere representation, and instead refers to valuing individual differences, including skills, lived experiences, lifestyles, appearances, language skills and communication styles, among others (Prasad et al, 2006; Chavez and Weisinger, 2008). Yet inclusion is not without controversy in workplaces. Rather, inclusion broadly defined is in tension with the notion of cultural assimilation, meaning cultural distinctions are surrendered for the adoption of dominant cultural practices (Prasad et al, 2006). The idea of cultural assimilation is that in return for acceptance within a workplace, individuals should voluntarily abandon their distinct cultural differences to integrate into the work culture (Prasad et al, 2006). Criticism of this approach to cultural assimilation is a prominent theme in this book, which clearly reflects that police services in both the UK and US expect officers from diverse backgrounds to provide the benefits of diversifying police departments, yet reduce their agency to operate in ways consistent with their own distinct cultures. Indeed, police departments in both jurisdictions expect officers from traditionally marginalized backgrounds to adopt the dominant street police culture norms to gain acceptance and integration into the workplace rather than lean into the unique attributes that make them different from the norm.

This creates significant challenges for members of traditionally marginalized groups, who feel pressured to assimilate into established workplace cultures (Prasad et al, 2006). Indeed, under-represented groups may not feel empowered to maintain their own cultural identities or wear with pride their cultural differences. Research has found it fairly commonplace for employers to emphasize 'sameness' among employees as a means to ensure group coherence (Jones, 2004). This is certainly proven true in the case of police institutions, an issue explored in greater detail in Chapter 2.

Rather than promoting assimilation, employers with more developed inclusion perspectives seek to help traditionally marginalized group members retain their cultural differences rather than strip them away wholesale and apply pressure to adopt the majority workplace culture (Prasad et al, 2006). Researchers assert that to accomplish this, employers must therefore provide under-represented groups with necessary situational and environmental factors to support performance once in their roles, including those tailored to their particular needs (Wang, 2003). Indeed, scholars and activists argue that recognizing, promoting and supporting differences among employees is essential to creating truly diverse and inclusive workplaces (Jones, 2004). This cultural pluralism approach holds the greatest potential to expand and help evolve workplace cultures to include a broader array of perspectives and lived experiences, including those of traditionally marginalized groups (Prasad et al, 2006). Where employers demonstrate that they value differences and champion diversity and inclusion, research shows traditionally marginalized group members can thrive (Opotow, 1997; Wang, 2003). This book adopts this cultural pluralism approach to diversity and inclusion when analysing UK and US police diversity, favoring celebration of what differences can bring to policing, rather than suppression of distinctions.

Defining colour-blindness

Rather than embracing pluralistic inclusivity approaches, police workplaces in both the UK and US tend to adopt colour-blind perspectives to equality, diversity and inclusion in practice, as discussed later. Colour-blindness means workplaces emphasize 'blindness' to or ignoring of race, ethnicity and colour (Pincus, 2003). Colour-blindness proponents argue an individual's racial group, ethnicity or colour are irrelevant to employment, and do not impede their opportunities for success in the workplace (Bonilla-Silva and Dietrich, 2011). Yet colour-blindness has not traditionally been a theoretical lens addressed in volumes on police diversity in the UK or US context, and this volume seeks to correct that omission, for the concept is important in police diversity analysis.

Superficial colour-blind rhetoric is rooted in formal equality, and does not account for the ways traditionally marginalized groups have experienced inequalities, discrimination or denials of opportunities. Colour-blind approaches focus on success in a workplace as matters of individual achievement, not substantive equality programmes designed to provide additional support to historically under-represented groups (Collins, 2003). Where individuals from traditionally under-represented backgrounds are unsuccessful in workplaces such as policing, colour-blindness proponents assert this is the result of lack of skills, hard work, cultural assimilation and integration, rather than structural inequalities or group-based challenges or disadvantages (Bonilla-Silva and Dietrich, 2011).

Colour-blindness proponents view the approach as a very positive one for individuals from traditionally marginalized groups. Indeed, the analysis asserts that if differences among individuals are not readily acknowledged, discrimination will not occur (Prasad et al, 2006). While well-intentioned, scholars argue this approach is naive to presume that simply ignoring differences can overcome entrenched inequalities and discrimination shouldered by groups and permeating institutions (Prasad et al, 2006).

Rather than ignore distinctions among officers from a variety of backgrounds, this volume's cultural pluralism approach to diversity asserts that differences in perspectives, approaches and styles should be acknowledged, embraced and supported by police institutions, rather than drowned out. Indeed, this volume argues that precisely because some officers feel pride in their differences from straight White male officers and established police culture norms, they engage in policing in ways that are different, and at times statistically significantly different from majority group officers.

Defining intersectionality

In understanding the experiences of diverse police officers in the UK and US and their impacts on policing institutions and outcomes, police diversity volumes should endeavour to adopt an intersectional approach, which is generally lacking in both theoretical and empirical analyses of police diversity.

Intersectionality refers to contemplating diversity, oppression, marginalization and lived experiences in multi-layered, intersecting ways, rather than singularly. The concept of intersectionality originated with the work of Black feminist lawyer Kimberlé Crenshaw, who objected to the ways legal and social analysis viewed oppression through a singular and often mutually exclusive lens (Crenshaw, 1989, 2013). Crenshaw and other critical race theorists believe law, criminal justice and other aspects of social and political life must think of and respond to oppression multidimensionally, rather than treating singular identities, experiences and tools of oppression as all-encompassing (Crenshaw, 2013).

Intersectionality considers not just a single characteristic such as race, gender, sexual orientation or countless others, but instead the ways multiple personal characteristics combine to shape an individual's experiences (Crenshaw, 1991). Thinking about these multiple bases of identity develops richer and more nuanced understanding of individuals' circumstances within police institutions and other workplaces. This book endeavours to draw on an intersectional approach to understanding the experiences and impacts of UK and US police officers with a diverse array of personal characteristics.

Rather than simply being an abstract academic concept, intersectionality is a tool for studying, understanding and better responding to different forms of societal inequalities and oppressions (Collins, 2015). However, in the contexts of UK and US policing highlighted in this book, analysis of marginalization has been lacking in both scholarly work and in addressing inequalities in the field of practice. Consideration of police diversity from an intersectional perspective has therefore largely not been part of conversations about how to frame or address inequalities in UK and US policing, with most theoretical and empirical literature examining diversity and lived experiences through singular categories of race, gender, sexual orientation, class, religion, and others.

Only a few exceptional pieces of police diversity research have examined lived experiences of police officers through an intersectional lens. Zempi's (2020) UK-based research focused on 19 UK police officers from traditionally marginalized groups, for example, is one of few policing studies adopting this approach. Indeed, Zempi's research aims to extend beyond mere examination of institutional racism to utilize the concept of intersectionality to better understand experiences of bias and discrimination involving racism, sexism, homophobia, among others.

Like Zempi, Hasan's study of ten current and former UK female officers of colour (2021) similarly addresses the need to conceive of police diversity in complex, multifaceted ways. Hasan advocates adopting an intersectional approach to understanding the lived experiences of female officers of colour in policing, whose encounters with bias in police institutions can often best be understood through the combined effects of racism and sexism, rather than simply conceiving of biases as defined by either one or the other.

This volume seeks to highlight inequalities for officers from a variety of different backgrounds, and wherever possible consider these experiences and inequalities intersectionally. However, one significant barrier to this effort is the lack of available data in both the UK and US studies which adequately capture officers' multi-layered personal characteristics. Where intersectional data are available, they have been incorporated into this volume. However, this research illustrates the significant shortcomings of UK and US policing research in considering experiences and impacts of diversity through intersectional lenses, and appeals to policing researchers for greater incorporation of intersectional narratives and analysis into future policing research projects.

Benefits of comparative criminal justice research

This study compares police diversity in the UK and US, arguing that understandings developed in one jurisdiction have applicability to the other because street police culture unites police institutions in both locales. When it comes to criminological research, comparative study has often been lacking. Indeed, most policing research tends to focus on a single jurisdiction. In particular, US criminological research has often operated in a vacuum without considering the relevance of theories, policies and practices stemming from other jurisdictions (Zimring, 2006). This volume, therefore, fills a significant gap in policing research by offering a comparative analysis of police diversity in both jurisdictions.

This book follows a long established albeit minority tradition of comparative criminological study between the UK and US (Miller, 1977; Garland, 2001; Newburn and Jones, 2007). Yet the benefits of comparative criminological research on policing and other topics are well documented. Indeed, scholars increasingly argue comparative criminological research is key for theoretical advancement of criminology, and institutional progression of criminal justice policies (Messner, 2014). Cross-cultural criminological research has traditionally been used to either test the generalizability of an existing theory developed in one cultural context for applicability to another, or to create a new theory generalizable across different cultural contexts (Bennett, 1980). This volume adopts the former approach by drawing on existing police culture literature to apply it across jurisdictions.

Moreover, comparative criminology research is important because it is highly influential in the development of criminal justice rhetoric, agenda-setting and policy making across jurisdictions (Garland, 2001; Zimring, 2006; Newburn and Jones, 2007; Nelken, 2010). This volume asserts that some of the solutions to problems plaguing policing in the UK and US lie in addressing highly problematic police culture and its impacts on police diversity. Furthermore, comparative analysis is valuable for exploring similarities and differences between two countries' approaches to police and policing (Nelken, 2010; May, 2011). Additionally, comparative criminological examination serves as a mirror to better understand a single country's criminal justice practices within larger social contexts (Nelken, 2010; May, 2011). This volume asserts that understanding the nuances of police diversity, and in turn ways to improve diversification in both jurisdictions, is enhanced by comparing their respective experiences.

This book argues that because extensive literature by Chan (1997), Reiner (2010), Bowling et al (2019) and others has clearly documented that street police culture exists in both nations, using this theoretical lens allows for a broader and generalizable discussion about police diversity in both UK and US cultural contexts, despite different historical, political and institutional differences in each country.

Geographic policing variations and criminal justice policy transfer

Despite the overarching theoretical lens of police culture and a rich minority tradition of comparative criminological study across jurisdictions, it is important to acknowledge some of the structural differences in UK and US policing before addressing whether this study lends itself to comparative examination.

Naturally, both the UK and US have significant social, cultural, historical, political and economic differences in which policing and police diversity operate. Indeed, the population demographics, numbers of police departments, police department size, police organizational structures and composition of police departments, among other factors, mean that in many respects police departments in the UK and US are very different from one another. When it comes to comparing UK and US policing, the different cultural contexts mean particulars of law, politics, economics, history and culture influencing their respective approaches to policing vary (Klockars et al, 2004).

Indeed, while England and Wales have 43 police forces with significant central oversight, the United States has over 18,000 relatively autonomous police forces, a majority of which are smaller forces with less than 100 officers. In the UK, the London Met Police is the nation's largest, followed by West Midlands, Greater Manchester and West Yorkshire police services. These largest urban UK police services are also the country's most diverse (Home Office, 2022). By contrast, the smallest UK forces, including Cumbria, Durham, Wiltshire and Warwickshire, are among the most rural and least diverse (Home Office, 2022). Similarly for US policing, large cities with over 500,000 people have the most diverse police forces, including New York City, Los Angeles and Philadelphia (BJS, 2022). Like the UK, the smallest police forces tend to be in rural areas, and are the least diverse (BJS, 2022). Both UK and US jurisdictions, therefore, see the most heterogeneous police services in the largest, most diverse urban areas, and the most homogeneous forces in rural areas, with far fewer officers of colour, women, LGBTQ+ officers and officers with college degrees.

While the structures, sizes, oversight mechanisms and autonomy of UK and US police forces vary greatly, this book argues that the lens of police culture offers a unifying theoretical underpinning through which experiences of police diversity are best understood. While police diversity operates in unique cultural contexts in each country, it is also important to note a long tradition of comparative study of policing between the two nations which has historically been undertaken for a variety of reasons, as discussed further later. Scholars argue that despite differences in policing contexts between the UK and US, comparisons between these jurisdictions is particularly feasible at the level of theory and abstraction, where similarities between jurisdictions such as the UK and US can emerge (Klockars et al, 2004). This volume embraces that approach by focusing on broader, overarching similarities between UK and US policing which help illustrate commonalities in experiences of police diversity.

In addition to sharing influential police cultures, a number of general parallels in the development and operations of UK and US policing further facilitate the comparative study undertaken in this volume. Significantly, the British model of policing was heavily developed according to the principles generally attributed to Sir Robert Peel (Peelian principles), the former UK Prime Minister who as Home Secretary helped established the London Met Police. At the core of these Peelian principles were notions of garnering public respect and approval, impartiality, service to the public and minimizing the use of force (Lentz and Chaires, 2007).[1] The core tenets include police responsibility for preventing crime; requiring public approval/legitimacy to carry out their duties; applying restraint in the use of physical force; and maintaining a good relationship with the public (College of Policing, 2014). Although Peelian principles were more aspirational than reality-based, it is well documented that they were particularly influential in the development of the first US police departments in Boston, New York and other large US cities (Miller, 1977; Reiner, 1992; Lentz and Chaires, 2007). The Peelian influence means that UK and US police departments arguably share some similarities in their organizing principles and early origins (Miller, 1977), even as various police institutions in both jurisdictions have developed their own characters, approaches and operations.

Moreover, in the last several decades, scholars have reflected on the degree to which criminal justice rhetoric, policies and practices can transfer between jurisdictions (Jones and Newburn, 2021). The US has been a particular focus of this research given its significant influence on criminal justice policy in the UK and elsewhere (Jones and Newburn, 2006, 2021). Scholars assert that while terminology, rhetoric and other 'soft' aspects of criminal justice policies can transfer from one jurisdiction to the other, it is more difficult for the 'hard' nuts and bolts aspects of specific criminal justice policies to be implemented from one jurisdiction to the other in practice (Jones and Newburn, 2021).

In the policing context, this means the terminology, rhetoric and other superficial aspects of US policing policies, including broken windows policing, zero tolerance policing, hot spot policing, 'three strikes and you're out' and neighbourhood watch, have gained traction in the UK (Young, 2003; Jones and Newburn, 2006; Andreas and Nadelmann, 2006; Lacey 2008), they have not necessarily been imported wholesale from the US into the UK's different jurisdictional context.

Research is clear that the soft policy transfer of criminal justice terminology and rhetoric among jurisdictions also places particular emphasis on the importance of policy makers intent on shaping criminal justice policy change (Jones and Newburn, 2021). The original empirical research for

---

[1] While these principles are attributed to Peel, they were likely developed by the first London Met Police Commissioners, Charles Rowan and Richard Maybe (Lentz and Chaires, 2007). Nonetheless, they remain popularly known as 'Peelian principles'.

this study has therefore focused on a small sample of UK and US police decision-makers to assess their perspectives on police culture, and how it influenced the development and implementation of particular police diversity experiences, policies and practices in their respective jurisdictions, as well as efforts to reform police culture and improve police diversity. As will be discussed later, access to elite policy makers to probe their views on police development, implementation and change is often limited in criminological research (Noaks and Wincup, 2004), and therefore is a particularly novel contribution of this book.

With respect to cross-jurisdictional engagement among UK and US police jurisdictions generally, and for the elite police leaders accessed for this study, it is significant that a number of US police leaders interviewed herein spent time in the UK, and similarly UK police leaders spent time in the US to share ideas, knowledge, techniques, ideas and approaches, and identify areas for collaboration. Some interview subjects, including Interview Subjects 1 and 4, frequently travelled to the US and UK, respectively, to gather information and adopt strategies learned from their work in the other jurisdiction. Thus, at both a theoretical and a practical level, consideration of the issue of police diversity from a comparative perspective is a valuable lens through which to explore this topic.

Despite the unique cultural contexts in which policing in the UK and US are situated, comparative analysis is valuable and insightful for understanding police diversity. Indeed, by using the overarching theory of street police culture to develop insights about diverse policing experiences, this book presents a generalizable theory that deepens knowledge about the way police diversity operates and its implications for police and policing in each jurisdiction.

Original police leader interviews

To develop its rich understanding of the complexities and implications of diversity in UK and US policing, this book surveys a vast array of existing theoretical and empirical literature. It also offers unique insights by drawing from the lived experiences of eight diverse police chiefs and/or high-level police leaders in the UK and US interviewed specifically for this book. These notoriously difficult to access elite subjects were willing to share their insights about police diversity and police culture because of their belief in the project of diversifying policing (Noakes and Wincup, 2004). They were selected not as a random or representative sample of all police chiefs in the UK and US. Rather, they were selected specifically because they were well-known police leaders who had invested time, policies and resources through their leadership of their own organizations to creating meaningful diversity in their policing institutions and mitigating the effects of police culture, particularly on marginalized groups. These leaders were accessed through the author's personal contacts in law and law enforcement. This volume provides original data about police diversity and police culture in practice from those individuals who have been groundbreaking in diversifying UK and US policing.

Each of the police chiefs or leaders interviewed for the book forged new ground in policing in their respective departments as they climbed through the ranks (although importantly they did not necessarily become chiefs in the departments where they began their careers). Three American male police chiefs of colour forged new paths in helming American police departments. One American male police chief of a large urban department forged new ground as someone from a very poor, working-class background. One female American police chief helmed several large urban police departments. One American male police leader was one of few openly gay men in American policing. Two British police leaders of colour led departments, organizations or divisions where few people of colour had ever been leaders. All of these remarkable individuals offered candid insights and reflections over many hours of conversation about all aspects of policing, from their reasons for joining the profession to challenges they faced given their diverse backgrounds, to the difficulties of police culture, to the struggles for police reform. As a result, this book offers unparalleled insider perspectives on police diversity and police culture in practice in UK and US policing.

Elite interviews

The semi-structured interviews conducted for this study offer unique insights because they come from elite police leaders – six current/former police chiefs and two high-ranking police leaders who were not police chiefs – all of whom are notoriously hard to access in policing research. Rarely does research on policing have access to the viewpoints of police leaders because they are generally concerned about maintaining confidentiality given the sensitive nature of their roles. One of the few pieces of research which have accessed police leaders include Reiner (1978). In fact, of the 15 police leaders contacted for this volume, only eight consented to interviews, with the remainder declining based on concerns about confidentiality and significance of their roles.

Because elites are so inaccessible, they are often excluded from qualitative or quantitative social science research in policing and other disciplines, creating a fairly significant gap in gathering data on elite beliefs, knowledge and attitudes. Indeed, understanding the perceptions, strategies and beliefs of powerful decision-makers who hold sway and create policies is important because these perspectives cannot typically be gleaned from books, records or official documents (Richards, 1990). Scholars argue that elites, particularly political elites, are often omitted from research because their numbers can be relatively small, and because they can be particularly difficult to access (Lilleker, 2003; Savage and Williams, 2008; Harvey, 2010).

The definition of elite research subjects generally refers to those who hold 'top salaries' or 'strategic positions' within an organization or agency (Harvey, 2010). However, identifying individuals who occupy these roles can be a fluid process and can change over time (Savage and Williams, 2008; Harvey, 2010). Rather, understanding the mindset and rationales of top officials requires discussions with them about their motives and beliefs. This information is important not for the objective truth of their articulated beliefs or rationales, but rather to better assess the ways governments and agencies adapt to social and political changes (Aberbach et al, 1975; Richards, 1990). Studying political elites can, therefore, shed light on relationships among elites, how elites analyse and interpret problems, how they prioritize policy issues, interpret policy problems, engage in policy decision-making processes, and their objectives and strategies for engaging in and undertaking certain policy responses (Aberbach et al, 1975). Research suggests qualitative interviews with open-ended questions are a particularly effective way to gain insights about the thinking of elite decision-makers (Aberbach et al, 1975; Richards, 1990; Harvey, 2010).

For this study, a key reason for undertaking elite interviews of police chiefs and police leaders is the lack of research about their perspectives on police diversity and police culture. There has, to date, been little police diversity research based on elite interviews and none has used police culture as a theoretical lens. There is thus a gap in the literature about the values, beliefs and decision-making processes of elites when it comes to police diversity and police culture. And most police diversity literature is not focused on elite perspectives of diversity from diverse police leaders. Given the profound influence of police leaders on diversity policies in policing in the UK and US, it is essential to understand how elite decision-makers think and what factors they consider when making key policing policy diversity decisions, as well as their views on the potential impacts of diversity on policing outcomes. This method thus allows the elite interview data to be situated within larger theoretical literature and social trends.

Small interview sample size

The qualitative interviews conducted for this volume are drawn from the small, elite sample of eight UK and US police chiefs and police leaders described earlier. While large sample sizes have traditionally been viewed as the most straightforward means to achieve data saturation, there are increasingly different views emerging when it comes to small sample sizes in qualitative research (Roy et al, 2015). Researchers argue that data saturation is the point in data collection and analysis when new information produces 'little or no change to the codebook' (Guest et al, 2006: 65), or where no new theoretical insights emerge from the data (Low, 2019).

While traditionally debates around adequacy of sample size in achieving saturation are grounded in the perceived lack of rigour in qualitative research more generally (Marshall et al, 2013), in recent decades a number of studies have pointed to the need to assess the quality, intensity and richness of data obtained through qualitative research, rather than just the numerical tally (Roy et al, 2015; Young and Casey, 2019). For example, Young and Casey (2019) assert that qualitative data saturation does not have a singular numerical determinant, but rather the study purpose and conditions can determine when qualitative interviews research a saturation point. Similarly, Roy et al (2015) assert saturation can be determined by the intensity of the research. Indeed, researchers including Roy et al (2015) argue that quality of interviews is as important a consideration as quantity to achieve saturation, and that the depth, richness and context of the data are essential considerations (Roy et al, 2015). They caution against the traditional, positivist assumption that the larger the sample size the more scientifically robust it is. Here, the extremely high quality data drawn from a very intense set of interviews undertaken with a rich sample of elites at the highest levels of policing allowed the study achieve saturation despite the small sample size.

Another means researchers use to gauge saturation in qualitative interviews is assessing at what point all of the themes used for thematic data analysis have been identified. Thematic analysis is a common method of qualitative data analysis used for coding information which draws out important themes from the data (Boyatzis, 1998; Attride-Stirling, 2001; Feredey and Cochrane, 2006; Bryman, 2008). Rather than being objective, thematic data analysis is an inductive method that is inherently subjective, requiring the researcher to faciltitate data coding and identification of key themes (Hsieh and Shannon, 2005). Saturation using this method is achieved when themes across a data set significantly repeat (Bryman, 2008; Longhofer et al, 2012). Guest et al (2006: 65) found most themes had been identified in the first six interviews. Francis et al (2010) similarly found the first six interviews established the vast majority of research themes in the data. Hennink, Kaiser and Marconi (2016) also found that the first six interviews were generally sufficient to establish the key data themes. McCracken (1988) argued that conducting more than eight in-depth interviews was unnecessary and wasted resources, given that themes were identified.

Here, the eight in-depth interviews conducted for the study quickly identified key themes which then consistently repeated across the sample.

More than eight interviews became unnecessary to gain further insights into the views of elite police leaders on police diversity and police culture as saturation was demonstrably achieved.

Book overview

This book is divided into three sections designed to examine police diversity through the lens of police culture. Chapters 1–3 establish the theoretical underpinnings for the book by setting out key theoretical concepts in the book's exploration. Chapter 1 of the volume has started with an examination of the key theoretical concepts defining the book's analysis. Notions of equality, diversity, inclusion, intersectionality and colour-blindness were explored. Moreover, the chapter evaluated the benefits and challenges of comparative, cross-jurisdictional police research between the UK and US. It also assessed the ways the unique elite police leader interviews undertaken for the volume, despite being a small sample size, provide significant understanding of police diversity throughout the volume.

Chapter 2 explores the theoretical concept of police cultures generally, and street police culture in particular, which is the underpinning theoretical concept for the book. The chapter considers the origins of street police culture, and the way it impacts experiences of policing for all officers, but particularly for officers from traditionally marginalized backgrounds. It further sets out challenges in changing street police culture which are explored in more depth in Chapter 9.

Chapter 3 begins by examining the concept of government legitimacy generally, and develops understandings of the ways it is developed and sustained. The analysis then turns to focus on these aspects of police legitimacy. It considers the significant histories of strained police legitimacy in both the UK and US. Moreover, it offers original analysis not previously addressed in police diversity literature by analysing the ways government legitimacy generally, and police legitimacy in particular, are tied to perceptions of diversity among the public, a notion referred to as passive bureaucratic representation, as well as examining ways active bureaucratic representation can improve legitimacy in traditionally marginalized communities. Finally, it considers the ways increased diverse police representation can impact communities' trust and confidence in the police.

Chapter 4 examines the experiences of police officers of colour, and the pressures they face amid street police culture which negatively stereotypes and results in disproportionate policing of many communities of colour. It explores the pressures faced by officers of colour to assimilate into street police culture and stereotyping models of policing, and the consequences for resisting those pressures. The chapter also considers some of the unique experiences of female officers of colour compared to their male counterparts, who face both racism and sexism in the role.

Chapter 5 explores the ways hegemonically masculine street police culture impacts the experiences of women officers, and the ways masculinity as defined and highly regarded in street police culture impacts their experiences and challenges in the role. The chapter also considers the intersectional challenges for female officers of colour faced with street police culture's particular views of masculinity and racial stereotyping, and considers the ways their experiences are different from those of White female officers.

Chapter 6 considers the ways heteronormative and hegemonically masculine street police culture shapes the ways LGBTQ+ officers experience policing. The chapter evaluates how heteronormativity and hegemonic masculinity influence and create the pressures LGBTQ+ officers experience given street police culture's prescriptive views of gender, masculinity and heterosexuality. It further evaluates commonalities and distinctions in the experiences of gay and bisexual men, lesbian and bisexual women, and transgender officers in the UK and US, which are significantly shaped by differing stereotypes of gender, masculinity and heterosexuality imposed by street police culture.

Chapter 7 examines the under-researched topic of the impacts of social class on policing. It explores the origins of UK and US policing as a working-class institution, and the way street police culture developed from traditional working-class perspectives of gender, race, violence and aggression. It considers the tensions created within working-class police institutions developed to police working-class populations, and the mechanisms working-class officers use to distance themselves from these target populations. The chapter then evaluates efforts to professionalize UK and US policing into a middle-class occupation with the introduction of education requirements, and considers whether officers with increased education levels can mitigate some of the most challenging aspects of street police culture.

Chapter 8 analyzes the theory of representative bureaucracy, considering the ways it developed in relation to public sector employees, examining the differences between passive and active representation, and why it holds potential for bureaucrats to engage in policies, procedures and practices benefitting their communities of origin. It then applies these theories to police institutions, and evaluates challenges for police officers of engaging in active bureaucratic representation. The chapter then considers the empirical evidence illustrating the ways officers from traditionally marginalized groups have engaged in active bureaucratic representation. Finally, the chapter evaluates the benefits of diversity for majority group officers by analysing the impacts of intergroup contact theory, and the ways it can potentially help reduce biased attitudes and other negative aspects of street police culture.

Chapter 9 concludes by reviewing key theoretical arguments made in the book. It also looks forward at the future of police diversity in the UK and US, and identifies areas for further research.

2

Police culture

This book examines comparative experiences of UK and US police diversity through the theoretical lens of police culture. This chapter defines and evaluates the police culture concept, setting the stage for examination of the ways street police culture impacts the experiences of police officers generally, and particularly for officers from traditionally marginalized backgrounds. The chapter foregrounds the key questions posed throughout the volume: What are the impacts of street police culture on UK and US policing? How are experiences of street police culture different for officers from diverse backgrounds? How might street police culture impact policing outcomes? Can street police culture norms be shifted with sufficient diversity?

This chapter begins by defining street police culture. It examines key research, important findings and key debates around the concept of police culture (for example, Chan, 1997; Waddington, 1999; Loftus, 2009; Reiner, 2010; Cockcroft, 2013). Next, it reviews empirical literature about the impact of street police culture on diverse police officers, and suggests their experiences of street police culture can differ from those of majority group officers (Holdaway, 1997a; Brown, 2015; O'Neill and Holdaway, 2015). It considers the particular pressures faced by diverse officers to conform to a street police culture traditionally shaped by straight White male norms, and contemplates the risks posed if they do not assimilate. The chapter then considers whether diverse officers in the UK and US can play roles in changing these established police culture norms. It contemplates the ways street police culture is imparted and reinforced in UK and US policing, including through academy training and police unions. It queries whether diverse police officers can shift established police culture values to include the experiences and values of different officers (Skolnick, 2008). Finally, it discusses some of the impediments to changing street police culture, and foregrounds the discussion of this subject explored further in Chapter 9, the book's conclusion.

Defining police culture

Police culture refers to the organizational culture of the police workplace. While it is well established that all organizations and all workplaces develop distinct cultures, the study and analysis of the role of street police culture is controversial in policing research. While many researchers find policing cultures influential in policing agencies (Loftus, 2009), others are more sceptical of their significance (Waddington, 1999). A common understanding of police culture is the informal norms, attitudes and values that can shape police behaviour in police organizations (Chan, 1997; Reiner, 2010).

Like many workplace cultures, however, police cultures can vary across different policing agencies (Cockcroft, 2013). There can also be multiple police cultures within the same organization, particularly for street officers, middle management and senior leaders (Reuss-Ianni, 1983; Manning, 2007). Moreover, while police cultures are not static and can evolve over time, numerous factors impact the speed and rate of change (Loftus, 2009).

Research suggests the core of police culture is about identification with the street police officer rather than the management or leadership officer, and this is most influential on the behaviours of police on the streets (Hunt, 1984; Reuss-Ianni, 1983). Indeed, the inherently discretionary nature of street policing in the UK and US means there are significant opportunities for street police culture to influence behaviours in practice (Manning, 1997). This does not necessarily make street police culture entirely deterministic of all police decision-making and behaviour on the job, but it does prove to be a significant influence in practice (Chan, 1997).

While street police cultures may vary across agencies and countries, certain core tenets of street police culture share similarities across jurisdictions including the UK and US (Reiner, 2010; Loftus, 2009). Empirical research in the UK and US shows street police culture is often characterized by aggression, violence, competition, authority, hierarchies, dominance, paranoia, insularity, intolerance, masculinity, racism, sexism, homophobia and stereotyping, among others (Hunt, 1984; Haarr and Morash, 1999; Miller, 1999; Sklansky, 2007; Seklecki and Paynich, 2007; Loftus, 2009; Reiner, 2010).

The development of street police culture norms was shaped by those who traditionally comprised the police services. In most cases, street police cultures in the UK and US were initially shaped by the norms, values and beliefs of the straight White males who historically formed the majority of police in most of the UK and US (Miller et al, 2003). Thus the concept of street police culture is embedded with straight White maleness and traditionally reflects straight White male values (Haarr and Morash, 1999; Bolton and Feagin, 2004; Holdaway and O'Neill, 2004). For much of policing history, street police culture in the UK and US has tended to be characterized by its straight White male homogeneity (Sklansky, 2006; Reiner, 2010).

Street police culture in UK and US policing follows the 'warrior model'. The police warrior model refers to policing which embraces its quasi-military structure, prioritizing and rewarding violence, aggression, conflict, use of force and escalation over particular people and populations (Holdaway, 1997a; Loftus, 2009). Following this military-like model, warrior-officers tend to see themselves as enforcers at war against criminals and potential criminals (The White House, 2015; Richardson, 2015).

Police warrior culture drives a wedge between police and the communities they serve. Warrior police are more often disconnected from the communities where they operate, and frequently feel animosity toward targeted communities, which are disproportionately poor and ethnic minority (Reiner, 1978; Stoughton, 2014). Warrior police perceive a lack of shared values with the communities they police. One illustration of the prevalence of the warrior police mentality was a 2017 Pew survey of over 7,000 US officers across many different departments, which found 59 per cent of officers polled believed people in the neighbourhoods where they worked shared some of their values and beliefs, while only 11 per cent believed community members shared all of their values (Pew Research Center, 2017: 51).

The distance between warrior police and policed communities means officers are less invested in those communities, can more easily engage in aggressive policing tactics and violence, and do not fear repercussions from the largely marginalized populations (Conti and Doreian, 2014). The same Pew survey found that 56 per cent of officers believed being aggressive in certain neighbourhoods was more effective than being courteous. Moreover, 44 per cent of officers surveyed believed that hard, physical tactics were necessary to deal with some people or populations (Pew Research Center, 2017: 54). This warrior street police culture tends to view poor, ethnic minority and other traditionally marginalized groups as more deserving of these aggressive policing than others (Reiner, 2010; Stoughton, 2014).

Minority officers and street police culture

Research suggests all police officers feel significant pressure to adopt street police culture norms (Goldstein, 1977; Bowling et al, 2019). Officers who do not adopt, or indeed challenge, street police culture can be made to feel uncomfortable or alienated from their peers, or even met with open hostility (Dowler, 2005; Jones and Williams, 2015). For people of colour, female, LGBTQ+ and other officers from traditionally marginalized groups, the pressure to adopt street police culture approaches is particularly acute (Holdaway, 1997a; Pogrebin et al, 2000). Given the core tenets of street police culture tend to contain explicit and/or implicit racist, sexist, homophobic, classist aspects, it is unsurprising that it can make UK and US racial minority, female, LGBTQ+ and other under-represented officers uncomfortable, alienated and stressed about fitting into policing institutions that continue to be composed of a majority of straight White males (Holdaway, 1997a; Miller et al, 2003; Dowler, 2005; Seklecki and Paynich, 2007; Jones and Williams, 2015).

Research in both the UK and US over a number of years illustrates the intense pressure that officers from traditionally marginalized backgrounds feel to adopt street police cultures. For example, Holdaway's 1997 study of 59 Black and Asian officers in the UK found it was often easier to just go along with street police culture than challenge it, even when it stereotyped ethnic minorities and led to racial jokes and banter (Holdaway, 1997b). For these officers, the only way to do their jobs was to play along with police culture, for the racism on the job was inescapable. Many officers in Holdaway's study reported they would be ostracized if they pushed back or rejected the racism in street police culture.

Similarly in the US, Pogrebin et al (2000) found that African American officers in a large urban police department felt significant pressure to assimilate into mainstream street police culture norms, even where those norms were explicitly racist against African Americans. The study observed that the risks of not adopting these approaches were severe, including being isolated and ostracized by fellow officers. Black female officers in the study, in particular, felt pressure to 'not make waves' and avoid being controversial by simply conforming to street police culture.

The experiences of officers in these UK and US studies feeling significant pressure to adopt street police culture norms are consistent with some of the first-hand accounts provided by police leaders interviewed for this book. Indeed, diverse police leaders interviewed discussed some of the approaches they adopted and observed for dealing with street police culture norms that did not necessarily reflect their own values. For example, Interview Subject 3, an LGBTQ+ police leader, reflected on these pressures to adopt police culture and not be seen to give preferential treatment to officers' communities of origin:

> I think members of minority groups across the board, including a lot of the Black and Hispanic[1] officers, for example, that I worked with, felt that they had to go out of their way to actually not be particularly decent to the communities that they came from to prove that they weren't giving anybody any special treatment.

---

[1] While the term Hispanic was at times used by individuals interviewed for this manuscript, and is often used in official statistics, the term Latino is preferred by the author and used throughout.

Similarly, Interview Subject 6 talked about the pressures he faced as a Latino officer to adopt street police culture norms, which were antithetical to his community-focused upbringing:

> So the dilemma occurs though when I bring my values of a boy scout serving and that, what my mum taught me, into a profession that's overly cynical and destructive. I teach this, I preach it. You have to be careful with your audience but when I walk in with 38 years of experience at high level they listen, and when they listen and they're honest I'm going to say some things that maybe they're not prepared to hear but need to hear. So my conflict was who I was coming in to an organization that was bent on changing me. This need – and it's basic, it's basic peer pressure but this need to belong and if we want to extend it more in to the hierarchy of need and how we get to that point where that's what motives you, it's the need to be accepted by the group that you're with, you conform. That's where I think, number one, problems start.

Along similar lines, Interview Subject 1 was active in the ethnic minority officer association in his UK police department, and was criticized by White officers for doing so:

> A [BAME][2] support organization ... was considered quite radical and of course people didn't know what it was or what the organization was going to deal with, so it was seen as quite threatening by some people and they were saying 'Well why do you need to do this? Is it a union?', so some people saw it as a threat. The whole idea was to provide support and discourage [BAME] officers leaving because they have had support provided.

Taken together, the existing police research and interviews conducted for this book illustrate the difficult positions in which all officers, but particularly those from traditionally marginalized groups in policing, face in relation to adopting or shunning police cultures within their respective policing institutions. While the pathways and strategies for officers are not singular, research suggests there can often be parallels in the dilemmas faced by minority groups in relation to police culture.

---

[2]   While the term BAME refers to Black and Minority Ethnic persons and is frequently used in UK policing research and official UK statistics, the term people of colour is preferred by the author. It is used interchangeably with BAME and non-White throughout the manuscript.

Despite the intense pressures for officers from traditionally marginalized backgrounds to assimilate into street police cultures, there may be some evidence of important racial differences in adopting the warrior police mentality. Callousness was a measure more likely associated with officers who endorse using aggressive or physically harsh tactics in certain communities and situations, more likely to have reported a recent physical confrontation, more likely to have fired their weapon on the job, and report being more angered by the job (Pew Research Center, 2017: 57). While 62 per cent of White officers agreed they had grown more callous on the job, only 32 per cent of Black officers felt the same, compared to 51 per cent of Latino officers (Pew, 2017: 56). These results suggest that there may be some racial differences in the way officers of colour view and police communities, particularly marginalized communities, a theme explored further in subsequent chapters of this book.

Police academy training embeds street police culture

Research suggests that academy training is typically officers' first exposure to street police culture. The police academy training is the earliest opportunity for socialization into the police role and away from the civilian identity (Fielding, 1994). In this setting, more senior officers train new recruits in the norms and expectations of street policing, and regale recruits with stories (Paoline, 2003). The police academy, therefore, plays a central role in embedding and reinforcing street police culture in recruits, which is later reinforced during field training and on the job (Rambaut and Bittner, 1979; Fielding, 1994).

Police academy training involves embedding written rules and procedures, and unwritten policies and practices including street police culture. Uniformity, cohesion, and loyalty are emphasized (Paoline, 2003). Part of this process involves immersion in the unwritten aspects of street police culture in terms of 'the language, the behaviors, the symbols, and the rituals' warrior police officers need on the streets (Nolan, 2009: 253). Imparting these unwritten aspects of street police culture involves lessons on mechanisms including '[r]itualistic forms of voice, gait, posture, demeanor, language, and dress' (Nolan 2009: 253).

Police academy training conveys understandings of power dynamics, with recruits learning to obey authority and, in turn, learning to exercise control of populations on the streets (Conti, 2009). This training focuses on managing conflicts with civilians in the classic street police culture ways, including through aggression, physical tactics and violence, rather than resolving disputes verbally (Herbert, 2001). The street police culture knowledge transfer in the police academy is contextualized in a quasi-military model requiring obedience and degradation of cadets, which breaks police recruits down and rebuilds them as adherents to street police culture (Nolan,

2009; Conti and Doreian, 2014). Scholars argue this quasi-military tactic indoctrinates police in approaches and practices that are undemocratic, lessons which they take with them into the field of practice (Conti and Doreian, 2014). Police academy socialization therefore begins the process of creating loyalty among officers, while simultaneously creating animosity toward civilians previously discussed (Sherman, 1980; Conti and Doreian, 2014).

Loyalty and the blue wall of silence

One defining feature of street police culture is loyalty to fellow officers (Skolnick, 2002). The concept of loyalty among officers is first introduced in the police academy and is repeatedly reinforced throughout an officer's career (Skolnick, 2002), advocating that officers be loyal to each other and not the civilians they police (Herbert, 2001). The notion of loyalty among officers is emphasized as a way to guard police against threats to their safety, given both the dangers police face on the job and the scrutiny the activities of police officers face (Skolnick, 2002). Yet the officer camaraderie and loyalty emphasized in police culture simultaneously creates and reinforces alienation from policed communities (Sherman, 1980; Conti and Doreian, 2014), typical of street police culture discussed earlier.

On the job, loyalty can manifest in a number of different ways. On the positive side, it can mean officers feeling personally connected to one another on and off the job, and providing each other with emotional and physical support (Skolnick, 2002). Loyalty can also have negative aspects, including the so-called 'blue wall of silence', an unwritten 'code of silence' among police officers against reporting misconduct that is embedded in street police culture (Martin, 1980; Skolnick, 2002; Westmarland and Conway, 2020). The blue wall of silence can include failing to report misconduct by fellow officers, providing false information or making false reports, refusal to provide information to a police misconduct inquiry, or otherwise engaging in cover-ups of prohibited, illegal or unethical policing activities (Skolnick, 2002).

Studies show the blue wall of silence obstructs misconduct investigations and impedes accountability (Knapp, 1973; Independent Commission on the LAPD, 1991; Mollen, 1994; Morris 2002). Scholars argue the blue wall of silence creates a 'no snitch' culture where a stigma is associated with being a 'rat' or 'snitch', making officers worried that they will not be backed up in dangerous situations if they are viewed as disloyal (Westmarland and Rowe, 2018). Critics argue the blue wall of silence is an illustration of the hegemonic masculinity character of street police culture (Nolan, 2009), as discussed in further detail in Chapter 5.

This aspect of street police culture is concerning given that research shows it is commonplace for officers to break established rules, guidelines and the law on the job (Klockars et al, 2004; Westmarland and Conway, 2020). Studies evidence that policing as an occupation provides a multitude of opportunities for misconduct, given its highly discretionary nature, work in private settings without direct supervisor observation, often in front of fellow officers or witnesses from traditionally marginalized groups who might be portrayed as unreliable (Klockars et al, 2004; Nolan, 2009). With all these opportunities for misconduct, with minimal supervision and the pronounced blue wall of silence, violations of rules, guidelines and the law frequently go unreported (Klockars et al, 2004; Westmarland and Conway, 2020).

Studies of police show the street police culture places expectations and pressures on officers to both engage in misconduct and adhere to the blue wall of silence when witnessing misconduct of fellow officers. For example, a study of 2,698 full-time officers from 21 different US states by the National Institute of Ethics (Trautman, 2000) found that 46 per cent (532) had witnessed misconduct by another officer but declined to take action. Of these 532 officers, 236 (44 per cent) stated they declined to take action because they feared ostracization or being blackballed by fellow officers (Trautman, 2000). More recently, a Pew survey, in 2017, found 53 per cent of officers believed most officers would not report a fellow officer driving while intoxicated, with only 22 per cent saying they would report the cover-up (Pew Research Center, 2017: 33).

Interestingly, there may be some racial differences in police officers breaking departmental rules and, in turn, adhering to the blue wall of silence. For example, the Pew survey of American police officers found racial differences in encouraging fellow officers to break departmental rules, with 63 per cent of White officers compared to 43 per cent of Black officers and 47 per cent of Latino officers saying they would advise a colleague to break departmental rules to do the moral thing (Pew Research Center, 2017: 33). It is unclear whether these racial differences are the result of feeling less embedded in the policing institution, being more resistant to wholesale adoption of street police culture, or other reasons, as explored further in Chapter 4.

Police unions reinforce street police culture

With these many, complex aspects of street police culture, it is helpful to consider the roles of police unions in reinforcing it. Indeed, research suggests that police unions play an essential role in setting the tone and conditions of policing, yet their function in reinforcing street police culture and impeding police reform is only infrequently analysed. In both the UK and US, the vast majority of police officers are represented by police unions. In the UK, while police are legally prohibited under the Police Act 1996 from joining trade unions, the Police Federation of England and Wales is effectively a union (dubbed a 'representative organization' or 'professional association') representing over 130,000 police officers across all 43 police forces in England and Wales (Police Federation, 2022). In the US, roughly 55 per cent of the nation's more than 700,000 police officers are union members across more than 18,000 law enforcement agencies, a proportion of union membership that has remained relatively consistent in recent decades (Walker, 2008; DiSalvo, 2020). Union representation is particularly high among officers in the largest US police departments in major cities including New York, Chicago and Los Angeles (Walker, 2008).

Police unions resemble traditional trade unions in many ways – advocating for their members on a variety of issues including wages, promotion, retirement, discipline, and other conditions and benefits of employment. This makes police unions similar to other unions as a 'vehicle of working class consciousness' (Reiner, 1978: 166). However, police union contracts often extend protections beyond those afforded to other public sector employees in significant ways, making police unions very unusual compared to other unions. Indeed, scholars observe that police unions bargain around a large number of matters related to police conduct and working conditions including schedules, promotions, performance quotas, discipline, internal misconduct investigations, termination and reinstatement, and right to representation/counsel before making statements regarding incidents of misconduct on the job (Fisk and Richardson, 2017). These aspects bargained for in police union contracts set police unions apart in significant ways from other public sector unions.

Moreover, police unions also play an important and unique role in exercising social control on behalf of the state, a decidedly undemocratic activity for a traditional union, and an illustration of the inherent street police culture of the profession. The nature of policing, and by extension police unions, is to maintain society's economic, political and ideological status quo (Reiner, 1978; Thomas and Tufts, 2020). The police as an institution are charged with enforcing laws, controlling and repressing dissent, including strikes by organized labour (Gilroy and Sim, 1985; Berry et al, 2008). Police are tasked with this role and use force where required to maintain social order (Walker, 2008; Reiner, 2010). Unlike other public employees, police institutions are authoritarian in nature, hierarchical and quasi-military, core components of street police culture as discussed above (Gilroy and Sim, 1985; Thomas and Tufts, 2020). Thus, while police are indeed public sector employees, their societal function in both the UK and US makes them inherently aligned with power and power structures of the state, which is distinct from most public sector unions. These aspects of the police role make the street police culture inherently conservative compared to other UK and US workers' unions (Reiner, 1978, 2010).

Research in the UK and US further illustrates the ways police unions frequently oppose reform measures including civilian oversight boards, court decisions imposing restrictions on police practices, reform-minded police chiefs, grassroots movements for criminal justice reforms including Black Lives Matter, greater local control over police departments, and efforts to discipline or terminate officers found to have engaged in misconduct (Wilson and Buckler, 2010; Fisk and Richardson, 2017; Sklansky, 2022). In the US, unions have asserted their opposition to these sorts of policing changes in numerous ways, from filing lawsuits, public news conferences, efforts to defund publicly funded reform agencies, to refusing to agree to reform measures proposed as part of the collective bargaining process negotiating union contracts (Wilson and Buckler, 2010). These views were reflected in interviews conducted for this book, where diverse police leaders – including Interview Subject 3, a gay US police leader – noted the impediments to shifting street police culture posed by police unions.

Numerous examples from the late 2010s and early 2020s illustrate the ways police unions have impeded efforts to increase scrutiny on police officers, sometimes in conflict with other public sector unions. For example, some American police unions have broken with other public sector trade unions over condemnations of police misconduct, including disproportionate police killings of Black civilians (Nolan, 2020). Indeed, heads of many American police unions have been particularly vocal in condemning criticism of biased policing (Namako, 2015; Hager and Li, 2020). Police union leaders have also loudly condemned the Black Lives Matter protests over the police killings of George Floyd and other Black people (McCrone, 2017; Hager and Li, 2020). Indeed, there are also lengthy histories of American police unions opposing or blocking programmes seeking to diversify policing, including resisting hiring of LGBTQ+ officers and affirmative action programmes for women and ethnic minorities, alienating officers from traditionally marginalized backgrounds (McCormick, 2015; Firestone, 2015).

Like other aspects of this book, research suggests the lack of diversity in police union leadership may impede efforts to shift police unions beyond their support for street police culture and opposition to police reform efforts (Sklansky, 2022). The lack of diversity in police union leadership undoubtedly influences the tone, tenor and content of police unions' messaging, but also the directions of their advocacy on policing issues. Research indicates that policing institutions have traditionally not been focused on the value or importance of diversity among their membership or leadership (Berry et al, 2008). Indeed, the evidence suggests most American police unions have traditionally been, and continue to be, predominantly led by straight White men (Hager and Li, 2020; Sklansky, 2022), with the same proving true in the UK. Some research suggests many police unions have historically showed bias both against officers of colour and in assertions of highly racialized views (Thomas and Tufts, 2020). For example, research on the 'Blue Lives Matter' movement, which began in the US in 2014 as counter to the Black Lives Matter movement, found that the assertions that 'blue' lives required protection as much as Black lives, undermined social justice advocates' demands for accountability for racialized violence targeting Black people (Thomas and Tufts, 2020).

The anti-reform posture and racialized discourse of many police unions was evident in discussions with diverse police leaders interviewed for this book. For example, Interview Subject 1, a UK police leader of colour, was told police unions represent the interests of all officers equally, and met with derision when he objected to that view and asserted the need to join the National Black Police Association to assert his rights, as discussed in Chapter 4.

Thus, while police unions serve functions similar to other labour unions, the significant street police culture influence on UK and US policing makes police unions significantly different from other public sector unions. Further, the research suggests the police role in maintaining the status quo on behalf of the state, and the limited scope of police representation for all police officers, particularly those from traditionally marginalized groups, requires further attention in policing research.

The guardian policing model

While street policing culture is distinctly warrior in character and has long been dominant in UK and US policing, it is by no means the only approach. The most prominent alternative is the guardianship model, which is fundamentally opposite from the core tenets of street police culture in most respects (The White House, 2015). Guardian policing offers a different set of values, focusing on building and enhancing police legitimacy, community trust and confidence, mutual respect, and police sense of belonging to the communities they serve (Eisinger, 1980; Skinner, 2020; Chaffin, 2020; Villa, 2021). Guardian policing de-emphasizes street police culture's violence, escalation and hostility toward communities, instead emphasizing support, consideration, trust and being neighbourly (Rahr and Rice, 2015; Skinner, 2020; Chaffin, 2020).

The guardianship policing model better reflects the way most police actually spend their time. Contrary to popular culture portrayals that police are constantly in danger from chasing 'bad guys', police spend most of their time performing social service functions (Bittner, 1974; Punch, 1979), for which street police culture makes them ill-equipped. Indeed, street police occupy most of their shifts addressing child welfare, homelessness, drug abuse, mental health crises, local business issues, neighbourhood and domestic disputes, not pursuing criminals. Given the reality is that police spend most of their time as a 'secret social service' (Bittner, 1974), there is much less justification for the aggression and use of force emphasized with street police culture.

While warrior-like street policing continues to dominate UK and US policing, there are indications that a vocal minority of officers and police leaders embrace the guardianship policing model, including some interviewed for this manuscript, and there are also some promising signs of shifts in UK and US policing. For example, the national 2017 Pew study of over 7,000 police officers across American police departments asked officers about their commitment to the core tenets of the two respective policing models. While 62 per cent of police officers surveyed saw themselves equally as enforcers and protectors, and 8 per cent of officers in the same study saw themselves primarily as community enforcers, 31 per cent saw themselves primarily as community protectors (Pew Research Center, 2017: 24). This suggests about one third of American police officers surveyed saw their roles primarily as community guardians rather than warriors. While there are not any UK studies polling officers on their views of community enforcement versus community engagement, qualitative evidence from the UK interviews conducted for this study, and evidence from other research conducted by this author, suggest similar percentages of UK police officers may also subscribe to the guardianship based approach.

Moreover, this tension between warrior street policing and guardian cultures has become prominent among some policy makers in the US as part of criminal justice reform efforts. Most significantly, the President's Taskforce on 21st Century Policing (White House, 2015), comprised of community, policing and academic leaders, strongly recommended the adoption of the guardianship model and moving away from warrior policing. The UK, on the other hand, has yet to have a similar reckoning with warrior street police culture, and requires more significant efforts for policy makers, community, police and academic experts to coalesce around embracing guardian police culture.

Changing street policing culture

Culture change in policing is very difficult to achieve. It is the subject of much discussion but less empirical research. A number of policing scholars are sceptical of police culture's ability to change given its embeddedness in the profession (Holdaway, 2013). Holdaway (2013) argues the core tenets of street police culture are too firmly entrenched in police organizations regardless of significant shifts in the field. Others take a different view, arguing that police culture can shift, albeit incredibly slowly (Chan, 1997; Quinlan, 2021).

Efforts to change street police culture will always be challenging. One particularly difficult aspect is that empirical research suggests that straight White male officers whose norms street police culture generally embodies, tend to resist efforts to reshape police cultures (Felkenes and Schroedel, 1993; Loftus, 2009). Nonetheless, resistance is no reason street police culture should not and cannot change. It simply means that change is difficult and time consuming.

Changing street police culture's inherent warrior nature to a guardianship model is no easy feat. This has been observed by Obama's President's Task Force on 21st Century Policing (White House, 2015), which noted that moving from warrior to guardianship police culture is necessary but difficult. Scholars have long debated how exactly to accomplish police culture change. Chan (1997: 61) and others argue that the only way to fundamentally change police culture is if the nature and structure of police work are transformed. New policing approaches must be continually reinforced, otherwise police culture will easily default to the deeply embedded and long-held traditional attitudes and ways of conducting policing. In the context of police warrior culture practices, this requires guardianship approaches to be reinforced at all layers of the policing organization. Indeed, to change street police culture from its warrior focus toward guardianship policing, all aspects of policing require revamping to reflect the changed priorities, including police recruitment, academy training, field training, performance evaluation and metrics, discipline and promotion, among others.

Countless factors can impact the nature and rate of police culture change (Loftus, 2009). This book argues that street police cultures are compelled to change as a result of significantly changing the composition of police services from primarily straight White males, to more balanced compositions including significant representation of officers from traditionally marginalized communities. Analysis of the degree to which greater representation from traditionally marginalized groups can change street police culture norms is assessed in Chapter 3, considering evidence from Kanter (1977), Meier (2019) and others who have suggested there are tipping points or a critical mass in terms of representation that can facilitate organizational shifts in workplace culture.

Research suggests changes in police force composition to achieve culture change are unlikely to occur through voluntary diversity programmes, which have not proven highly successful in radically altering the composition of the personnel of police services (Walker, 1989). Rather, swift police composition change has been most successful through implementation of compulsory affirmative action/positive discrimination programmes, and these have been particularly impactful in the US (Walker, 1989; Quinlan, forthcoming). While the extent to which the composition changes achieved under compulsory affirmative action/positive discrimination programmes have changed street police culture in these departments requires more empirical analysis, this book argues these diversity increases in departments have resulted in changes in policing in practice. Indeed, the impacts of having greater diversity in a police workforce in terms of policing outcomes is examined in depth through the theoretical lenses of representative bureaucracy and intergroup contact theory in Chapter 8.

Police cultures may also change as the result of compulsory, court-ordered consent decrees and settlement agreements mandating changes in policies, practices and procedures brought as a result of class action lawsuits filed by multiple plaintiffs, or 42 U.S.C. §14141 pattern and practice lawsuits filed by the US Justice Department, as seen in many large American police departments including the New York City Police Department, Los Angeles Police Department, New Orleans Police Department, Ferguson (Missouri) Police Department, and Oakland Police Department, among countless others. These settlement agreements and court monitoring orders for a period of years can require a wide variety of measures which can be used to reshape street police culture, including compulsory trainings (de-escalation, bias, communication skills, and so on), changes in hiring and promotion procedures, altering composition of elite units, instituting new evaluation metrics, support measures for officers from traditionally marginalized groups, officer residency requirements within the service area, use of body-worn cameras to increase accountability, compulsory data collection, and many other measures.

Some practitioners are optimistic about the ability to change police culture (White House, 2015). The research undertaken for this book reflects that a number of police leaders interviewed expressed optimism about the ability of street police culture to change over time, asserting that as policing becomes more diverse, it is inevitable that it changes and evolves as its composition changes. For example, Interview Subject 2, a female police leader, argued that in her decades of policing, she had observed changes in street police culture as the increasing composition of women helped change perspectives in American police departments:

Q: Have you seen a shift in the culture of policing as you've been in policing a long time?

R2:   Oh, absolutely, so as more and more women came into the scene women became definitely more accepted. … If you want to have a culture shift you first have to truly change how people think. If they truly – this is like my story of sharing with you about diversity. Never dawned on me about equity but you change my thinking and you will actually have a culture change, so that's what you want to do.

Interview Subject 2 later went on to reflect on the benefits of intergroup contact of officers from diverse backgrounds (an idea discussed further in Chapter 8) on improving street police culture:

Q: So do you think diversity is a key component to shifting culture? How so?

R2:   I do. I think getting people – because it forces people in to the same sandbox to play and once you get people in to that sandbox – maybe you have to force them in to the sandbox but once you get them in there they start for the most part appreciating, oh, you know, you're not so bad. There is just a human nature element that when you start to work together and see the value that people bring to the table then you're more embracing and when you see that you start to change your thinking about stuff. That is the true culture shift there.

Numerous other leaders, including Interview Subjects 5 and 6, believed they could create street police culture change through setting different department priorities, practices and standards for their officers, such as valuing and rewarding community engagement and partnerships rather than alienation and hostility with communities. Others, such as Interview Subject 3, believed they could also facilitate street police culture change through hiring senior police leaders and ensuring supervisors were aligned with their values of serving as police guardians not police warriors. All of the police leaders interviewed for this book believed that increased police diversity was an important means to shift perspectives away from established and long-entrenched street police culture norms toward a broader set of values, practices and ways of thinking in policing. As discussed further in Chapter 9, all of the police leaders interviewed for the book emphasized that street police culture change is thoroughly possible but can only occur gradually rather than instantaneously.

Conclusion

Street police culture is the overarching theoretical underpinning for this book's examination of UK and US police diversity. To set the stage for this exploration of police diversity in both jurisdictions, this chapter has defined the concept of street police culture and its core aspects as seen in both the UK and US jurisdictions. This chapter has illustrated that while police organizations can have several different cultures, and police cultures can vary across different institutions, research including the original interviews conducted for this volume has established that core tenets of street police culture are most revered and most embedded in UK and US policing. Street police culture characteristics have remained remarkably consistent over time, emphasizing the warrior aspects of policing including aggression, violence, machismo, hegemonic masculinity, loyalty, bias and alienation from communities, among other aspects. These street police culture norms remain some of the most difficult to change in policing, as reflected in the book's interviews with police leaders. Yet change is possible and increasing, as policing becomes more diverse, as explored throughout the chapters of this book, and the public demand reforms to ensure greater police accountability and legitimacy. The guardian model of policing presents an alternative set of police culture norms that have been growing among some police leaders and in some police agencies. Indeed, the police leaders interviewed for this book all believed street police culture change was not only possible, but many believed they had modelled ways to move their respective departments away from the established street police culture norms, albeit in gradual ways. All believed that police diversity was an integral part of the street police culture change process in both the UK and US.

3

Police legitimacy, culture and representativeness

This chapter examines the key concept of institutional legitimacy for public institutions generally, and police departments in particular. It offers theoretically informed definitions of legitimacy for public institutions, and identifies the component parts required for legitimacy. It considers the factors which influence its development and maintenance in communities. It then applies these requirements to police institutions, illustrating the particular aspects of police department legitimacy, and why it is essential for police efficacy. The chapter explores the lengthy histories of poor police legitimacy in many UK and US communities, particularly in communities of colour. It evaluates the ways poor legitimacy has been developed and maintained by UK and US police institutions, to the detriment of community relations and police effectiveness. It considers the ways police misconduct, both the incidents themselves, and police institution mishandling of incidents, negatively impacts police legitimacy.

Significantly, the chapter offers an important theoretical contribution to existing police diversity literature by connecting the concepts of police diversity and police legitimacy through the theory of representative bureaucracy. The chapter examines the ways passive bureaucratic representation, meaning mere perceptions of greater diversity in traditionally majority group institutions, can improve public perceptions of legitimacy, particularly in traditionally marginalized communities. It applies this theory to police institutions, and offers examples from empirical research supporting the symbolic representation thesis by showing data reflecting improved police legitimacy with increased perceptions of diversity, particularly in minority communities. Another important theoretical contribution to police diversity literature from the chapter is its examination of the degree of minority group representativeness required to improve legitimacy, and ultimately change organizational culture. Drawing on theoretical research exploring the concept of whether a 'critical mass' of diversity is required to shift organizational culture, it applies these theories to police institutions. The chapter concludes by arguing that the only way to rapidly achieve the sufficient degrees of representativeness to improve legitimacy in some key minority communities is through positive discrimination/affirmative action, an argument explored in further detail in Chapter 9.

Legitimacy of public institutions

The concept of legitimacy is grounded in the exercise of power by an individual, an institution, the state or others, and involves whether the exercise of that power has consent, support or justification in the eyes of those subject to that power (Beetham, 2013). While legitimacy has been the topic of much debate among moral, political and legal philosophers, the concept is multi-dimensional. Beetham (2013) asserts the exercise of power has three components considered when evaluating legitimacy: (1) adherence to established rules; (2) whether those rules are justified by shared values of the power holder and those subjected to that power; and (3) whether the subordinate consents to those power dynamics.

Applying these aspects to the legitimacy of public institutions in the eyes of the public, scholars assert it is essential to consider the establishment of rules and adherence to those procedures when assessing institutional fairness (Tyler, 2003). The sense of shared values and ethics between the public and the public institution gives the institution moral authority encompassing a shared sense of right and wrong (Hough et al, 2010). This shared set of values is communicated to the public through the actions of the public institution (Hough et al, 2010). In general, many communities of colour in both the UK and US have traditionally been less trusting of public institutions compared to their White counterparts (Bobo and Gilliam, 1990).

Defining police legitimacy

Scholars have applied Beetham's theory of institutional legitimacy to police services (Tyler and Fagan, 2008; Hough et al, 2010). Police legitimacy refers to how legitimate the public perceive the police to be (Tyler and Fagan, 2008). For police to be viewed as legitimate, they must establish and adhere to procedural rules; share values supporting those rules with the public; and have the public consent to police authority to exercise its power according to those rules (Beetham, 2013).

Legitimate police are entitled to exercise their power through giving commands and taking actions which the public feel obligated to follow (Tyler and Fagan, 2008). The public's perception of a police agency's legitimacy is rooted in the belief that police have moral authority to dictate appropriate behaviour (Hough et al, 2010). If a police institution is viewed as acting fairly, it has moral authority. But where the police force is perceived as acting unfairly, either through police misconduct or failing to follow police procedural rules, it has less moral authority (Hough et al, 2010). Procedurally unfair experiences with the police, through either disrespectful treatment or unfair decision-making, make constituents feel the police do not respect them, eroding their respect for police and the law more generally (Jackson et al, 2012). When community members do not see the police as legitimate, they feel less obligated to follow police directives or obey the law (Hough et al, 2010). Moreover, where the public see the police as less legitimate, they are less likely to cooperate with them, report crimes or provide tips about criminal activities (Tyler and Fagan, 2008). Thus, strained police legitimacy not only negatively impacts community relations, but also police efficacy and operational success.

People from traditionally marginalized groups, including racial and ethnic minorities, women and people from lower socio-economic status neighbourhoods in both the UK and US, have for many decades generally viewed police as having lower levels of legitimacy (Congressional Research Service, 2018; Henry and Franklin, 2019; HM Government 2021). As discussed below, research shows a variety of ways police exercise power in disadvantaged communities, including historic and ongoing over-policing and under-protecting, overt police racism, killings of civilians, and disproportionate policing outcomes such as stop and searches, are all drivers of disparities in levels of legitimacy between majority and minority groups in both jurisdictions (Bowling and Phillips, 2002; Weitzer and Tuch, 2006; Henry and Franklin, 2019). As a result of these differences in levels of police legitimacy, studies have endeavoured to better understand ways to improve legitimacy in marginalized communities, as addressed later in this chapter.

Poor police legitimacy in many UK communities of colour

Before considering ways police diversity interacts with police legitimacy, it is important to consider the ways police legitimacy has been strained in a number of communities, often for many years. This is particularly evident in UK and US communities of colour, where the evidence base of these effects across time has been well documented.

Police legitimacy has long been problematic in many UK Black and Minority Ethnic (BAME) communities. For many, this dates from at least the Windrush arrivals in 1948. Throughout the 1940s and 1950s, all White police forces had tense police relations with West Indian communities, with police accused of failing to protect Black communities against racialized violence yet aggressively policing them (Whitfield, 2004). Negative views of homogeneous police forces persisted during the 1950s and 1960s, with many BAME communities distrusting police they believed unsympathetic to their victimization while criminally stereotyping them (Webster, 2007). These police legitimacy strains dissuaded most ethnic minorities from applying to police services, with the first BAME officers only hired in the late 1960s (Whitfield, 2004).

By the early 1970s there were small increases in BAME officers, and BAME communities became more vocal about their over-policing and under-protecting (Bowling and Phillips, 2002). Yet by the mid-1970s, research established that police were instrumental in propelling false stereotypes that Black people were more likely to engage in criminality than Whites (Hall et al, 1978). Data also evidenced widespread racial bias in UK police services, with many officers expressing negative views of ethnic minorities (Holdaway, 1996; Bowling and Phillips, 2002). The few serving BAME officers received little particular support despite the unique challenges faced, and were expected to assimilate into frequently stereotyping police cultures (Cashmore, 2002). Police recruitment also remained colour-blind, with no special efforts to recruit BAME candidates (HMIC, 2001).

Strained police legitimacy in many BAME communities became more visible in the early 1980s with the 'Brixton riots' in Black communities in London and elsewhere (Webster 2007). Lord Scarman's (1981) enquiry concluded they were motivated by perceptions of unfair policing. Scarman (1981: 122–123) also found some officers were racist, and called for better screening out of bigoted police. Scarman (1981: para. 4.1) observed, 'A police force which fails to reflect the ethnic diversity of our society will never succeed in securing the full support of all its sections'. Accordingly, Scarman recommended 'vigorous action' to increase BAME police diversity to improve legitimacy. But Scarman neglected to make specific hiring recommendations, set hiring targets, or propose changing equality laws, leading to limited impact.

Government failed to make major changes responsive to Scarman, instead simply establishing a BAME recruitment working group resulting in minimal BAME officer increases (Cashmore, 2002). Further 1985 uprisings in London and Liverpool, sparked by policing of Black communities, prompted government calls for positive action to increase BAME officer representation, but little else (Holdaway, 1996). The few BAME officers routinely encountered racial prejudice, including fellow officers' racist language, which, coupled with BAME community perceptions of disproportionate policing, drove poor police legitimacy and reluctance to apply for police jobs (Cashmore, 2002).

Police failed to significantly increase BAME officers or improve many BAME communities' trust throughout the 1990s. Research shows police did not prioritize combatting low police legitimacy levels or bias against BAME police officers (Bowling and Phillips, 2002). Data evidenced continued police–BAME community tensions, with national surveys showing Black and Asian respondents less likely than Whites to see police as polite or to be satisfied with police interactions (Skogan, 1994). By 1996, both the Commission for Racial Equality (Oakley, 1996) and Her Majesty's Inspectorate of Constabulary (HMIC, 1997) called for police to be more representative of policed communities. Yet the small numbers of BAME police applicants remained less likely than Whites to receive interviews or offers, or be appointed after probation, while BAME officers were twice as likely to resign or be dismissed as White officers (Bland et al, 1999). Research found prejudice, ignorance, marginalization and lack of supervisor support prompted BAME officer resignations (Holdaway, 1996).

Strained police legitimacy in many BAME communities gained national attention after the 1993 racist murder of Black teenager Stephen Lawrence. Lord Macpherson's (1999) enquiry concluded institutional racism and stereotyping of Black people within the London Metropolitan Police Service (London Met Police) shaped the flawed Lawrence murder investigation. Many testifying officers acknowledged that disparities in policing outcomes such as stop and searches were partially attributable to discrimination. Macpherson (1999: 47.1) further found UK police institutionally racist, and recommended all police services be mandated 'to increase trust and confidence in policing amongst minority ethnic communities'. Macpherson advised aggressive hiring of BAME officers and establishing BAME recruitment goals.

Government responded with ten-year BAME hiring targets for police services and enhanced recruitment in BAME areas (Home Office, 1999). But even these lacklustre efforts faced resistance from some police leaders (Murji, 2014). Research showed many police remained hostile toward and stereotyped ethnic minorities, evidencing persistent police culture bias (Bowling and Phillips, 2002). These dynamics ensured many BAME community members continued to distrust police, and a 2000 government survey found unfair policing perceptions and racist fellow officer fears deterred BAME applications (Stone and Tuffin, 2000). Indeed, BAME officers in Smith et al's 2015 study reported increases in misconduct allegations in the 2000s following a backlash from the Macpherson report (1999), as BAME officers sought to change biased aspects of police cultures.

The 2000s saw little improvement in poor police legitimacy in many BAME communities, and only slight increases in the numbers of BAME officers. Police–community tensions continued to discourage BAME applications, with some community members fearing being labelled as 'traitors' for joining (HMIC, 2001). BAME officers also reported that fellow officers' racism influenced biased policing in BAME communities (Cashmore, 2002). Some ethnic minority officers also expressed reluctance to join BAME officer associations, fearing ostracization for lack of police culture assimilation (O'Neill and Holdaway, 2007).

Tensions worsened when a 2003 BBC undercover report, *The Secret Policeman*, showed embedded police prejudice shaped how some officers policed BAME people (Daly, 2003). Police-led research indicated the documentary's racism depictions deterred BAME applicants, yet government merely responded with plans to help forces voluntarily meet BAME recruitment targets (ACPO, 2004). Simultaneously, both the Morris Inquiry (2004) investigating poor police legitimacy in London BAME communities, and the public Commission for Racial Equality (2005), called for positive discrimination for BAME police candidates. But government refused to adopt these recommendations.

By the tenth anniversary of the Macpherson Report, a House of Commons committee (2008) lamented poor BAME police diversity progress, concluding BAME officer recruitment and retention disparities, and tense BAME community relations, fuelled poor police legitimacy. Government nonetheless abandoned national police recruitment targets in 2008 (Home Office, 2008). The decision contravened extensive evidence that improving trust and confidence in UK BAME communities required increasing police diversity (Macpherson, 1999; Runnymede Trust, 2009). These actions were also taken despite strenuous objections from many BAME communities, BAME officer associations, and the public Equality and Human Rights Commission (Home Office, 2008). Government simultaneously refused to implement positive discrimination to increase BAME officers, despite successes in Northern Ireland, the Netherlands, the US and elsewhere.

Lack of police diversity and decades of poor police legitimacy in many BAME communities again gained national attention in 2011, when the police killing of Black British Mark Duggan sparked uprisings in London and elsewhere. As with prior 'riots', researchers concluded they were largely driven by perceptions of biased policing (Lewis et al, 2011). Political leaders acknowledged that greater diversity could improve police legitimacy (House of Commons Home Affairs Select Committee, 2013). Contemporaneous research showed many BAME communities still distrusted police and believed them biased, impeding applications (Holdaway, 2013).

For decades government has thus paid mere 'lip service' to police diversity in England and Wales (House of Commons, 2016: 31). Despite the growing BAME population feeling over-policed and under-protected, racial and ethnic police diversity remains bleak. Data show large numbers of BAME people distrust police and are less likely than Whites to believe police treat them with fairness and respect (HMIC, 2016). These negative police legitimacy perceptions, coupled with low BAME officer numbers and disproportionate policing activities such as stop and search and deaths in custody, have continued to deter many BAME police applicants.

Poor police legitimacy in many US communities of colour

Like the UK, many US police departments have long and well-documented histories of strained police legitimacy, particularly in communities of colour. Although police killings of people of colour, particularly Black people, in cities across the US in the 2010s and 2020s are most present in memory, including Tyre Nichols (Memphis, 2023), Patrick Lyoya (Grand Rapids, MI, 2022), George Floyd (Minneapolis, 2020), Breonna Taylor (Louisville, 2020), Philando Castile (Falcon Heights, MN, 2016), Eric Garner (New York, 2014), Michael Brown (Ferguson, MO, 2014), data show there are over 1,000 police killings in the US annually (*Washington Post*, 2023). For young men of colour, particularly young Black men, US police violence is one of the leading causes of death (Edwards et al, 2019). Data also show that Black women and men, and Native American women and men, are also significantly more likely to be killed by US police than White women and men (Edwards et al, 2019). Given the volume of police violence in communities across the US, the fact that there are over 18,000 autonomous US police departments (as discussed in Chapter 1), and the local and state oversight rather than a unified system of national control over-policing, it is more difficult to succinctly track the evolution of strained police legitimacy in communities of colour across the US in this volume.

One illustrative US case study of poor legitimacy particularly in communities of colour is the New York City Police Department (NYPD), America's largest police force, which has suffered tension with many communities of colour for decades. While problems between the NYPD and communities of colour have been troubled for years, as discussed elsewhere in this volume, tensions became prominent in the 1980s. In 1981, for example, a report by the US Commission on Civil Rights (USCCR), raised concerns about troubled relations between American police departments like the NYPD and ethnic minority communities (USCCR, 1981). Among other recommendations, the report recommended hiring more officers of colour, but recognized that unfair hiring practices disqualifying minority applicants in the NYPD and other departments, and perceptions of racism within departments, continued to keep numbers of officers of colour low (USCCR, 1981).

Shortly after the report, New York and other American cities were hit with the crime and violence stemming from the crack cocaine epidemic, which saw New York City's poor and ethnic minority communities over-policed and under-protected. By the early 1990s, New York City's murder rate hit an all-time high, with large proportions of murder victims and perpetrators hailing from poor and ethnic minority communities, but the NYPD failed to get a handle on the violence (Bowling, 1999; Skolnick, 2008). But in 1994, the new Police Commissioner Bill Bratton launched a 'war on crime' concentrated in poor and ethnic minority communities, applying tactics including increased numbers of police officers, aggressive use of stop and frisks, using COMPSTAT computerized mapping of crime data, and the introduction of zero tolerance policing (Manning, 2001; Fagan et al, 2011). Zero tolerance policing in New York City was particularly invasive in poor and ethnic minority communities, and was a practice inspired by James

Q. Wilson and George Kelling's 'broken windows' theory, which posited that high volumes of arrests for low-level 'quality of life' offences including subway fare evasion, vagrancy, panhandling and vandalism, would deter more serious crime in poor and ethnic minority communities (Wilson and Kelling, 1982; Bowling, 1999). By the late 1990s, New York City's rates of violence and homicide had declined dramatically at the expense of aggressive policing of poor and ethnic minority communities. While Bratton and his supporters credited the war on crime, critics argued that many factors, including demographic shifts in the population and the decline of crack cocaine use, drove the drops (Bowling, 1999; Manning, 2001).

The NYPD's war on crime made New York City's ethnic minority communities feel singled out for disproportionate police targeting. Numerous incidents of police brutality directed at Black men in the 1990s and 2000s illustrated the strains with the NYPD, generating outrage and coalescing anger at the police. The 1997 assault with a plunger of Haitian American immigrant Abner Louima by NYPD officers in a Brooklyn police precinct angered ethnic minority communities. The 1998 killing of unarmed African immigrant Amadou Diallo in the vestibule of his apartment, and later acquittal of the officers involved, set off a firestorm of protests against the NYPD. A subsequent *New York Times* poll found that 89 per cent of Blacks, and 81 per cent of Latinos believed there was 'absolutely no excuse' for shooting Diallo (Barry and Connelly, 1999). In 2000, African American Patrick Dorismond was killed by undercover officers during a drug sting, and a contemporaneous Quinnipiac University poll of New York voters found 72 per cent of Blacks and 53 per cent of Latinos disapproved of the performance of the NYPD (Quinnipiac University Polling Institute, 2000). The 2006 killing of African American Sean Bell at a Queens strip club on his wedding day would later be added to this list.

Academic research confirmed the depths of strained relations between the NYPD and New York City's communities of colour. One study found that the Louima, Diallo and Dorismond incidents had profoundly increased negative views of the NYPD in Black and Latino communities, and had worsened already strained ethnic minority relations (Weitzer, 2002). Another study found that a significant number of ethnic minority New Yorkers believed the NYPD engaged in racial profiling, which undermined their support for the police force (Tyler and Wakslak, 2004).

Just as in the UK, stop and search (known as 'stop and frisk' in the US) also played a crucial role in mistrust of police in many of New York City's ethnic minority communities. Persistent complaints and community anger at stop and frisk prompted then-Attorney General Elliot Spitzer to undertake an examination of all 175,000 NYPD stop and frisks conducted from 1998 to 1999 (New York Attorney General's Office, 2000). The examination confirmed community complaints, as it found disproportionality in the

NYPD's stop and frisk practices, with Black people comprising 50.6 per cent of stops but only 25.6 per cent of the population, and Latino people constituting 33 per cent of stops but only 23.7 per cent of the population (New York Attorney General's Office, 2000). The report was the first quantitative analysis showing clear disproportionality of the NYPD's stop and frisk practices, and lending support to community over-policing claims.

Despite the evidence of severely strained legitimacy and complaints about unfair policing in ethnic minority communities, the NYPD continued its war on crime through the 2000s, and particularly its aggressive use of stop and frisk policing. While minority communities loudly voiced concerns about the NYPD's mistreatment and disproportionate targeting, the true scale of the invasive stop and frisk practices would not be examined for another decade. In 2008, ethnic minority communities launched a class action lawsuit contesting what they asserted was racial profiling of Black and Latino men by the NYPD (*Floyd v. City of New York*, 2008). During the course of the lawsuit, the NYPD's own figures would later reveal that 4.4 million stops were made between January 2004 and June 2012, over 80 per cent of which were Black or Latino people (*Floyd v. City of New York*, 2013).

By this time, the NYPD's poor legitimacy with communities of colour was clearly evidenced. For example, a 2012 poll of New Yorkers showed that 77 per cent of Black people felt the NYPD favoured Whites over Blacks, and 56 per cent of Blacks felt the NYPD had harassed innocent people using stop and frisk (Grynbaum and Connelly, 2012). In 2013, it appeared that public sentiment across New York had finally turned against the NYPD's large-scale use of racially disproportionate stop and frisk, with a poll of New York voters showing 67 per cent of Black people and 58 per cent of Latino people disapproved of the tactic (Quinnipiac University Polling Institute, 2013). That same year, the federal court concluded that the NYPD had unconstitutionally racially profiled Black and Latino men for more than a decade (*Floyd v. City of New York*, 2013). By the time newly elected Mayor Bill DeBlasio assumed office in 2014, he and returning NYPD Police Commissioner Bratton were compelled to reassure the public that targeted stop and frisk in ethnic minority neighbourhoods would be reduced, and relations with New York City's ethnic minority communities would be improved (Weiser and Goldstein, 2014). Yet Eric Garner's death at the hands of police in a widely circulated video did little to dispel perceptions that the NYPD continued to engage in racial profiling of Black and Brown people (Fagan and Ash, 2017).

Simultaneous with the clear evidence of the NYPD's systematic use of racial profiling to target Black and Latino men across New York City, leaked reports in 2011 revealed that the NYPD had also targeted Muslim communities, particularly Muslim communities of colour, for a campaign of undercover spying, infiltration and entrapment with its counter-terrorism programme since the 9/11 attacks under the guise of counter-terrorism policing (Apuzzo and Goldman, 2011). For New York City's Muslim communities of colour, the revelations compounded distrust in police and further strained already low levels of legitimacy in many of these communities (CLEAR, 2013). These negative perceptions of the NYPD's profiling practices have persisted in more recent years, with studies repeatedly showing racial and ethnic minority and lower-income communities viewing the NYPD as less legitimate, and stop and searches being one key driver of these strained legitimacy perceptions (Henry and Franklin, 2019).

While the case study of NYPD profiling and strained legitimacy with ethnic minority communities is by no means unique to New York City, it is illustrative of profound tensions between police and communities across the US. While addressing poor police legitimacy will require solutions tailored to the particular needs of each jurisdiction, this volume seeks to offer a broader perspective and present research that will be helpful in crafting policies and practices that hold promise to improving police–community relations.

Police misconduct impacts police legitimacy

As seen repeatedly in both the UK and US, police legitimacy is strained when police exercise of power is perceived as lacking procedural fairness through a variety of actions, including over-policing, under-protecting, police killings, disproportionate policing outcomes, as well as all types of police misconduct and perceived institutional mishandling of these incidences. Research suggests that where the public perceives police as violating departmental policies or legal rules, and they perceive police organizations as failing to hold officers to account for these harmful or illegal activities, this can further impede police legitimacy, particularly in traditionally marginalized communities.

When police violate established policies and laws, this reduces police legitimacy in the eyes of the public (Terrill and Paoline, 2015; Headley et al, 2020). Where there are community perceptions that incidences of police misconduct are persistent and rarely addressed, particularly those impacting traditionally marginalized groups, this reinforces negative public perceptions that police institutions and police cultures are racist, misogynist, and bullying, among other negative aspects discussed in Chapter 2. Racial and ethnic minorities tend to view police misconduct as more problematic and racially biased compared to their White counterparts (Weitzer and Tuch, 2006; Weitzer et al, 2008; Cochran and Warren, 2012; Headley et al, 2020).

It is not simply the perceived occurrences of police misconduct which tarnish police legitimacy. How misconduct incidents are handled by police departments is also essential to assessments of legitimacy. Research suggests that when police incidents of misconduct are not addressed adequately in the eyes of impacted communities, this can often be perceived as a lack of desire by the institution to hold offending officers to account (Greene, 2007). Where misconduct incidents are severe or frequent, the public can view police institutions as only paying lip service to addressing bad police behaviour, but not having the inclination to undertake institutional reforms to stop police misconduct from occurring (Punch, 2009).

Studies have found that where police services engage in appropriate, transparent and accessible handling of police misconduct, this functions to both ensure accountability and reinforce a visible communal commitment to rule of law in the eyes of the public (Greene, 2007). However, where institutional handling of police misconduct fails to fulfil these important functions, police legitimacy is reduced (Bayley, 2002; Weitzer and Tuch, 2006; Greene, 2007; Walker, 2007).

One of the ways tensions are exacerbated around police misconduct is where communities and institutions have differing views on how to address it. Research suggests many ethnic minority communities view police conduct through the lens of the 'rotten barrel', meaning they perceive misconduct as an institution–wide phenomenon (Weitzer and Tuch, 2006). This perspective ties into notions of police institutional cultures, particularly street police culture, as biased against people of colour, as discussed in Chapter 2.

By contrast, it is commonplace for many if not most police services to regard police misconduct through the lens of the rotten apple, meaning attributable to an isolated few 'bad apple' police officers, rather than laying blame on an entire police institution or street police culture (Weitzer and Tuch, 2006). UK and US research suggests most police departments tend to adopt the bad apple approach by firing offending officers when incidents of misconduct arise (Weitzer and Tuch, 2006; Punch, 2009). This focus on individual wrongdoers avoids addressing systemic issues of racial, gender, sexual orientation and other types of biases in policing (Casey, 2023). But this approach does little to dissuade an already sceptical public that police misconduct is taken seriously, and will be adequately rooted out. Indeed, without addressing systemic institutional and cultural problems within policing institutions when misconduct arises, police services are viewed as weak and ineffective at stemming misconduct.

A variety of mechanisms to reduce police misconduct and increase accountability are key to police legitimacy. Sufficient police service oversight is viewed by communities as an important accountability tool (Congressional Research Service, 2018). This can be accomplished through departmental investigative units, external local or national government agencies, or civilian–led review boards (Congressional Research Service, 2018; Headley, 2022). However, external police accountability bodies vary in their legal authority, investigative powers, transparency and abilities to change police service policies and practices (Headley, 2022).

The ability of citizens to bring complaints against police either to the department itself or to one of the external government or civilian bodies described earlier is another accountability tool. The enactment of government-driven changes in departmental policies or rules, either through government initiative or in response to lawsuits, settlements or consent decrees, can provide further mechanisms for police accountability, as discussed in Chapter 9.

Connecting institutional legitimacy and diversity

One of the growing areas of research about ways to improve police legitimacy among historically over-policed and under-protected groups is the impact of perceptions of police diversity. While increasing police diversity has long been seen as a means to improve police–community relations, including a demand from communities themselves (USCCR, 1981; Macpherson, 1999; Forman, 2017), empirical evidence supporting this theory for policing in particular has not been well developed until more recently.

Yet the interactive effects between public perceptions of diversity and increased positive community attitudes toward public institutions generally has a robust empirical basis. Symbolic representation theory posits that the mere presence of visible, representative diversity within an institution can have tangible impacts on public attitudes toward that institution (Riccucci et al, 2014; Riccucci and Van Ryzin, 2017; Keiser et al, 2022). When it comes to legitimacy of institutions, the established body of research shows that the presence of passive bureaucracy – that is, representativeness in public institutions – can positively impact the public's opinions of institutional fairness and legitimacy. This has been shown to be particularly true for traditionally marginalized groups in both the UK and US, who, as discussed earlier, have often held lower levels of trust and confidence in public institutions for decades (Bobo and Gilliam, 1990; Lim, 2006; Marks and Stout, 2011; Riccucci et al, 2018; Keiser et al, 2022).

The reasons minority groups often more positively perceive more diverse institutions is they believe that bureaucracies which are more inclusive have bureaucrats who better understand their concerns, share their values, understand their lived experiences, can better represent their interests, and will engage in policies and practices beneficial to their communities (Bobo and Gilliam, 1990; Marks and Stout, 2011; Keiser et al, 2022). These effects are particularly evident at the local level, in relation to trust and confidence in local-level bureaucrats (Bobo and Gilliam, 1990; Meier and Stewart, 1992; Meier, 1993; Lucero et al, 2022).

There is thus clear evidence that minority groups in both the UK and US have less trust in a variety of public institutions than do their majority group colleagues. As discussed above, this holds true with the police as well.

Efforts to improve legitimacy in police agencies has thus examined whether the theory of symbolic representation shows similar promise for police. Evidence from empirical research in the UK, US and other jurisdictions in recent decades has found similar positive effects of symbolic representation for police organizations as shown for other public agencies. This increasing body of empirical research has evidenced the ways perceptions of police diversity by the public positively impact their views of police legitimacy, particularly in communities where police–community relations have traditionally been strained, including racial and ethnic minority groups, women and lower-income communities. An increasing number of studies in the US and other jurisdictions have shown that where police visibly increase diversity, police legitimacy improves as diversity perceptions increase (Weitzer and Tuch, 2006; Sklansky, 2006; Marschall and Shah, 2007; Fridell, 2008; Theobald and Haider-Markel, 2009; Gustafson, 2013; Marks and Stout, 2011; Cochran and Warren, 2012; Nanes, 2018; Muibu and Olawole, 2022; Stauffer et al, 2022; Huber and Gunderson, 2023).

Specifically, empirical studies support the notion that increasing police diversity in majority White police departments can improve police legitimacy in policed communities. Fridell (2008) found that greater diversity in police departments conveyed a sense of equality to the public. Other research suggests people see racially diverse policing as fairer and more trustworthy (Weitzer and Tuch, 2006). While mostly White police departments can struggle with earning and maintaining the trust and confidence of diverse communities, police departments that are viewed as more representative see enhanced police credibility and respect from community members (Sklansky, 2006).

For ethnic minorities in particular, their perceptions of police legitimacy can hinge on how inclusive they view their local police institutions to be (Marschall and Shah, 2007; Nanes, 2018). Studies show that, for ethnic minority community members, interactions with ethnic minority officers in majority White departments tend to improve perceptions of police legitimacy (Theobald and Haider-Markel, 2009). For ethnic minorities, encounters with ethnic minority officers are viewed as more legitimate (Cochran and Warren, 2012). Research suggests police organizational diversity can reduce conflict with local communities (Gustafson, 2013). Moreover, police services seen as more racially diverse are seen as more accountable to the communities they serve (Stauffer et al, 2022). There is also some evidence that ethnic minority officers are more inclined to embrace non-traditional policing strategies (Black and Kari, 2010), which can mean more community-focused guardianship approaches, and less traditional hard street police culture tactics. Research also indicates that having an ethnic minority police chief improves positive views of the police in communities of colour (Marks and Stout, 2011), and having a female police chief also improves legitimacy perceptions (Huber and

Gunderson, 2023). More racially diverse police institutions are also seen as more accountable and more legitimate, particularly where officers of colour comprise larger proportions of a police service (Stauffer et al, 2022).

Street police culture, diversity and legitimacy

The long and troubling history of strained police legitimacy between UK and US police and their respective communities, particularly traditionally marginalized communities, begs the question about the extent that these tensions are driven in part by the core tenets of street police culture, which are grounded in biased attitudes toward historically oppressed communities, including ethnic minorities, the poor and LGBTQ+ people, and alienation of police from the policed.

As discussed in Chapter 2, street police culture is, by nature, racist, misogynist, homophobic, intolerant and insular (Bowling et al, 2019). It advocates distance and separation from local communities, and promotes using aggressive tactics to police in disproportionate and unequal ways (Cockcroft, 2013). Because street police culture is a driver of the over-policing and under-protecting approaches that have contributed to decades of poor police legitimacy in many UK and US communities, consideration must be given to how street police culture might be shifted as one significant way to improve police legitimacy. Indeed, if policing was less driven by values which disrespect certain segments of the UK and US populations, positioning police in opposition to these communities, and more tied to guardianship approaches where police build trust, respect and partnership with local communities, it follows that trust and confidence in police could be improved.

While efforts to shift street police culture within police institutions lack a robust empirical evidence base, as discussed later, a growing body of research has begun to establish clear connections between perceptions of diversity and improved police legitimacy.

The changing demographics of police departments hold great promise for changing police cultures, particularly street police culture. While increased diversity is not a singular solution to changing troubling aspects of street police culture, it certainly holds promise for institutional culture change (Sklansky, 2006). Evidence reflects differences in the ways officers from traditionally marginalized backgrounds can view their policing role, including being champions of their communities of origin and speaking out about structural racism in policing (Kelly and Farber, 1974; Boyd, 2010; Pew Research Center, 2017; McCarty et al, 2019; Gau and Paoline, 2017), and how they approach and make decisions on the job, including reluctance to stop and search, racially profile, or harass marginalized communities, compared to their majority group colleagues, a subject explored in more significant depth in Chapter 8.

Part of the analysis of how diversity can change street police culture revolves around the degree of minority group representation required in a police service to facilitate that cultural shift, a topic discussed further in the next section.

Degree of police representation required

The evidence is clear that there are profound tensions between communities, particularly communities of colour, and the police in both the UK and US. In many areas the strained police legitimacy is severe, and impedes effective policing. While this volume does not argue that police diversity is a panacea to reforming policing, it does assert it is part of the tools required to improve police legitimacy and unequal policing outcomes. Given the growing body of evidence supporting the symbolic representation thesis, which connects increased levels of visible police representativeness with higher levels of police legitimacy, one of the considerations is the degree of police representation of traditionally marginalized groups that may be required to meaningfully diversify UK and US police forces.

Ideally police force representation should mirror the composition of the communities they serve. This delivers the positive benefits of symbolic representation (also known as active bureaucratic representation or representative bureaucracy) discussed earlier and further in Chapter 8. While UK and US communities are diverse and multifaceted, it is particularly important that traditionally marginalized groups historically subjected to over-policing and under-protecting are well represented within UK and US police services. Indeed, as discussed throughout this volume, the poor police legitimacy and disproportionate policing outcomes for many ethnic minority communities are a matter of particular concern and, therefore, require striving for proportionate representation of the largest ethnic minority groups, including many communities of colour, in UK and US police services.

One of the persistent questions in this analysis, however, is the degree of police representativeness required for the presence of minority group officers to result in meaningful change. Meaningful change could range from active bureaucratic representation by minority group officers, or wider institutional changes such as shifting the tenets of problematic street police culture. Meier (1993, 2019) and Meier and Stewart (1992) argue that for mere active bureaucratic representation to occur, no threshold figure of representation is needed. They argue that given that individual bureaucrats – from teachers, to local government workers, to police officers – use their discretion to assess and explicitly or implicitly engage in representative bureaucracy, they are making these decisions all the time (Meier, 2019).

Yet in the context of fundamental organizational culture change for policing or other agencies, the empirical evidence in this area has not been well developed in either the UK or US. Nonetheless, some of the limited research suggests there may be a diversity threshold of representation at which point organizational culture may change in police services, although this requires significantly more empirical testing.

While there is no definitive answer about the degree of police representativeness, that is, the 'critical mass' (Meier, 2019) required in a police service to sufficiently shift street police culture norms, there are some clues in the available evidence. Kanter's early studies of female representation in American corporate departments considered how being a minority group in majority straight White male environments impacted the experiences of women and the overall organization (Kanter, 1977). While observing the negative impacts on women having so little representation in their workplaces, Kanter (1977) considered what ratio might change the negative experiences of women and other minorities, and contribute to changing the culture of the organization. Kanter (1977) described the so-called skewed ratio where one minority group feels tokenized when they make up 15 per cent or less of the workforce while a majority group comprises 85 per cent of more. At a more balanced ratio of 40 per cent minority and 60 per cent majority, the minority group does not feel tokenized.

One important caveat is provided by Meier (2019), who has argued that the critical mass required for minority group members to engage in active representation varies depending on the level of the bureaucrats in public institutions. Meier (2019) asserts that a critical mass above 15 per cent and closer to 25 per cent among supervisory and leadership-level bureaucrats is necessary for representative bureaucracy to occur.

Subsequent research has applied this theory to policing to consider whether there may be a tipping point in terms of the critical mass of police representation required to make traditionally marginalized officers feel on better footing in police departments and help shape the institutional culture. Kanter (1977) found that when minority groups make up 15 per cent or less of an organization, they feel highly visible and feel they attract disproportionate attention and feel like novelties. This creates work conditions where minority group members like women are subjected to greater scrutiny than their male peers (Kanter, 1977). This heightened visibility of minority group officers in majority straight White male workplaces creates heightened efforts to avoid mistakes and increased fears of failure, given that greater visibility makes them subject to greater scrutiny (Kanter, 1977; Wertsch, 1998). Under this scrutiny, the fear of making mistakes is intense and places particular pressure on minority group members.

Additional research has carried forward Kanter's (1977) hypothesis to consider what police force composition should look like in relation to women, people of colour and other traditionally marginalized groups.

Krimmel and Gormley (2003), Archbold and Schulz (2008), Rabe-Hemp (2007) and others have applied Kanter's hypothesis to policing, and have found that where women or other minorities remain under the 15 per cent threshold suggested by Kanter, they will continue to experience negative impacts of their minority status, and the organizational culture will remain intact. For example, Krimmel and Gormley (2003) found that female officers in departments with 15 per cent or fewer female officers had lower self-esteem, higher levels of depression, lower levels of job satisfaction, and were more likely to change jobs. In their study of racial differences in police killings of Black people across multiple American police forces, Nicholson-Crotty et al (2017) found that 35–40 per cent representation was the threshold where Black officers may feel less pressure to adopt street police culture norms, including those which discriminate against Black citizens. Nicholson Crotty et al (2017) suggested that Black officers who achieve the 35–40 per cent representation in a police service may feel more empowered to be active representatives of Black communities (a notion explored further in Chapter 8).

Similarly, Headley (2022) argues that organizational changes can be realized when traditionally under-represented groups in policing achieve at least the 40 per cent threshold. Research by Stauffer et al (2022) suggests that perceptions of improved police legitimacy among female citizens and communities of colour represented a significant proportion of the police force, specifically over 45 per cent. Taken together, this research suggests the possibility that representation of minority groups of 35–45 per cent may be a threshold for organizational culture change, but this requires significantly more empirical testing.

If we accept that taking forward Kanter's hypothesis and subsequent empirical research applying this theory may help set appropriate diversity goals in UK and US police services at the 35–45 per cent level, many if not most large British and American police departments fail. Indeed, most UK and US police departments fall far short of 35–45 per cent representation of officers from traditionally marginalized groups.[1]

---

[1] Such figures also fail to adequately factor in intersectional representation where officers belong to multiple traditionally marginalized groups. Researchers, including Meier (2019), have observed the importance of intersectionality within the critical mass thesis, but acknowledge the difficulty of analysing the levels of representation among bureaucrats taking into account multiple protected characteristics or oppression factors, in significant part because data are rarely collected about individuals in relation to these multiple characteristics. Thus, the degree of critical mass required from an intersectional characteristic analysis is difficult to assess, and requires further empirical examination to determine how intersectional representation impacts required critical mass thresholds for active bureaucratic representation.

These shortcomings in achieving 35–45 per cent representation are particularly evident when examining police service representation at all levels of the police institution, where very few police services have 35–45 per cent representation in supervisory and leadership roles, as discussed in later chapters of this book. Indeed, Meier (1993, 2019), Meier and Stewart (1992) and others argue that although the critical mass of managers is lower at around 25 per cent given their decision-making power, most UK and US departments do not hit that target.

The shortcomings in achieving the 35–45 per cent representation is illustrated from UK and US police data on both gender and race. For example, while many larger British and American police departments, particularly those in urban areas, are comprised of more than 15 per cent women, few reach the 35–45 per cent balanced threshold that Kanter (1977) and Crotty (2017) hypothesize would make women feel like they are no longer tokens and can shift the institutional culture (Home Office, 2022; BJS, 2022).

Similarly when it comes to race, while some larger British and American police departments surpass the 15 per cent threshold for officers of colour, only a small number of large American police departments in majority people of colour cities, including Baltimore, Detroit, Dallas, Washington DC, among others, reach the over 35–45 per cent threshold required to reduce tokenization of minority group officers, and again, hold potential to change the institutional cultural norms (BJS, 2022). In the UK, Britain's largest police departments – the London Met Police and West Midland Police Service – both in cities (London and Birmingham, respectively) approaching majority people of colour citizenry – fall far short of proportionate representation and do not begin to approach the 35–45 per cent representation threshold to reduce the tokenization of officers of colour (Home Office, 2022). These shortfalls in representation lend support to the argument that affirmative action (i.e., positive discrimination) is necessary to more rapidly and meaningfully increase representation of minority groups, as argued later in this volume and elsewhere (Quinlan, forthcoming).

Thus while Kanter's initial research (1977) and subsequent studies by Nicholson-Crotty et al (2017), Stauffer et al (2022) and others in policing has hypothesized about potential representation targets which could improve the experiences of officers from traditionally marginalized groups and potentially reshape street police culture, most UK and US police departments are years if not decades away from reaching those important representational thresholds. Without further empirical research testing these hypotheses in both the UK and US, there remains a lack of adequate guidance about precisely which representation targets will help improve experiences of officers from traditionally marginalized groups, and legitimacy in traditionally marginalized communities.

Conclusion

This chapter offered novel considerations and understandings about police diversity by analysing the ways police diversity and police legitimacy are interconnected. Beginning with theoretical definitions of government institutional legitimacy generally, it applied these theories to police institutions in particular to consider the factors required for policed communities to view police as legitimate. Next, it explored the negative consequences of poor police legitimacy for police–community relations and police effectiveness, as has been the case in many parts of the UK and US for decades. Moreover, the chapter applied the theory of representative bureaucracy, offering original insights about the ways just numerical diversity – that is, passive bureaucratic representation – can nonetheless have positive effects on perceptions of institutional legitimacy for government institutions including the police. It also considered the ways mere passive representation can turn into active bureaucratic representation, and in doing so can improve legitimacy with potentially positive effects on changing street police culture norms. The chapter concluded by considering whether there is a required minimum threshold or critical mass of diversity to change street police culture in police institutions, something which has not been explored in depth in prior volumes on police diversity.

4

Racial and ethnic minorities in policing

This chapter considers the ways street police culture shapes the experiences and expectations of racial and ethnic minorities in police services, focusing on officers of colour in the United Kingdom and United States. As discussed in preceding chapters, street police culture is grounded in norms developed by the straight White male officers who have historically comprised UK and US policing, and reflects their traditional perspectives on masculinity, race, crime, violence, danger and aggression, among others. This chapter considers the perspectives officers of colour bring to the policing role through their lived experiences, which can potentially be similar to, or quite different from, those of their White counterparts. It also assesses the ways perceptions of them by fellow officers, supervisors and department leaders, developed and reinforced through the lens of street police culture, can impact their experiences of policing. The chapter further considers the ways policies and practices which seem, on the face of it, to be neutral and applied to all officers may, in fact, be applied in different ways to officers of colour, and have disparate impacts on their experiences of policing in the UK and US.

This chapter evaluates the ways officers of colour experience the policing role through triangulating a variety of relevant evidence. First, it relies on key theoretical evidence on race and racism, intersectionality, police culture and representative bureaucracy. It evaluates the ways race and racism within police institutions, and embedded in street police culture, can place pressures on officers of colour to assimilate into or conform with negative stereotypes of people of colour, including from their countries of origin. It also explores the ways negative police culture stereotypes of people of colour can be applied to officers of colour themselves by fellow officers and supervisors in their own departments, resulting in negative, and sometimes deadly, consequences. The chapter further considers the vastly under-researched intersectional experiences of female officers of colour who are often subjected to street police culture stereotypes about race and gender. Moreover, the chapter examines the ways officers of colour may seek to resist conforming with or assimilation into street police culture norms, including informal support networks or joining affinity associations. It also explores the ways officers of colour may seek to challenge street police culture influences through active bureaucratic representation, as discussed further in Chapter 8.

Second, it applies these key theories to several sources of empirical data. Specifically, it applies the theoretical frameworks to original interviews with five US and UK male police chiefs/leaders of colour. The theoretically informed analysis of these in-depth elite interviews provides robust insights into the ways officers of colour who have remained in policing institutions throughout their entire careers, beginning in low-level positions and rising to elite leadership positions, were shaped, informed and defined by race and racism, police culture and representative bureaucracy. Further, these theoretical frameworks are applied to official UK and US government data on hiring, evaluation, promotion, discipline, termination and voluntary departure of officers of colour to contextualize the readily apparent disparities in both jurisdictions. Finally, the chapter utilizes the underlying race and racism, police culture and representative bureaucracy theories to provide original insights about numerous empirical studies. Taken together, these theoretical and empirical data are triangulated to provide robust and detailed analysis of the experiences of officers of colour in UK and US police institutions.

Officers of colour in the UK

Before analysing the ways officers of colour contend with street police culture norms on the job, it is essential to set the scene to understand how non-White officers have come to populate UK policing. In sum, the UK has long struggled with police diversity. Although historians have unearthed that John Kent and Robert Branford were the first Black Britons to join the UK police services in the 1840s, these pioneers do not alter the profound struggles with diversity of the police services of England and Wales. Indeed, most agencies operated without Black and Minority Ethnic (BAME) officers until the late 1960s, and even then hired very few (Whitfield, 2004). In 1965, there were only three officers of colour in the entire UK, despite the ethnic minority population totalling 2 per cent of the population (Cashmore, 2001). During the 1970s, the few BAME officers worked in police services that helped drive Black criminality stereotypes (Hall et al, 1978), and were simply expected to assimilate into stereotyping police cultures (Cashmore, 2002). BAME officers received no special support for their unique placement in UK police services. Moreover, police recruitment efforts did not target BAME communities, and instead were colour-blind (HMIC, 2001).

In 1981, fewer than 1 per cent of officers were BAME across a total of 116,590 officers in England and Wales (Whitfield, 2004). Riots against policing practices in Black British communities occurred in 1981 and 1985 (Lea and Young, 1984; Holdaway, 1996), yet government declined to engage in widespread recruitment of BAME officers (Murji and Cutler,

1990; Cashmore, 2002). By 1989, 1 per cent of officers were BAME out of 123,726 officers (Whitfield 2004; Home Office, 2010, 2014, 2019).

The 1990s saw some BAME officer number increases. By 1995, ethnic minority officers made up 1.7 per cent of all officers in England and Wales, compared with at least 5.2 per cent of the population (Oakley, 1996). Yet BAME candidates and officers faced serious hurdles, being less likely to receive interviews, offers or appointments after probation, but twice as likely to resign or be dismissed as Whites (Bland et al, 1999). Indeed, while 23 per cent of White officers held ranks above constable, only 10 per cent of ethnic minority officers did (Oakley, 1996). Research found prejudice, ignorance, marginalization and lack of supervisor support prompted BAME officer resignations (Holdaway, 1996). The 1993 racist murder of Black teenager Stephen Lawrence and subsequent Macpherson enquiry (1999) identified the strong need for increased BAME officer numbers. The Home Office (1999) responded with ten-year BAME police hiring targets and more recruitment in BAME areas, which some police leaders resisted (Murji, 2014). In 1999, 2 per cent of officers were BAME out of a total of 123,841 (Home Office, 2010, 2014, 2019).

In the 2000s, there were small increases in BAME officer numbers, but government research showed police mistrust deterred many BAME applications (Stone and Tuffin, 2003). In addition to these legitimacy concerns, some BAME people feared being labelled 'traitors' in their communities for joining the police services (HMIC, 2001), an issue also seen in the US (Alex, 1969), and one that continues to feed pressures and insecurities for officers of colour. During this period, fairly clear evidence of the influence of street police culture stereotypes was evident in the experiences of officers of colour, including how they were often viewed by fellow officers. Research evidenced that many UK police remained hostile to, and stereotyping of, ethnic minorities (Bowling and Phillips, 2002), and many BAME officers feared fellow officers' racist policing of BAME communities (Cashmore, 2002). Other BAME officers expressed fears of ostracization for joining BAME officer associations, a common sentiment among officers of colour including those interviewed for this volume (O'Neill and Holdaway, 2007). By 2010, 4.6 per cent of the total 141,647 officers were BAME (Home Office, 2010). Yet, as indicated by previous research, BAME officers made up 5 per cent of constables but only 3 per cent of the higher ranks of chief inspector or above, with not a single BAME chief constable (Home Office, 2010). The composition of BAME officers in 2010 was 40 per cent Asian, 22 per cent Black, 28 per cent Mixed Race, and 11 per cent Chinese or Other (Home Office, 2010).

In the early 2010s, the police killing of Black British Mark Duggan sparked further uprisings in London and elsewhere prompted by perceived police racism and anti-BAME bias (Lewis et al, 2011). In response, many UK police leaders urgently called for rapidly increasing police diversity, including through positive discrimination, a sentiment many continue to echo today (Evans, 2013; Boffey, 2014; Dodd, 2020). Yet the UK government refused to take any urgent BAME recruitment action. Indeed, while equality and diversity initiatives had been introduced following Macpherson's calls for greater diversity in UK policing (1999), by the 2010s it was clear they had not sufficiently worked, and they were largely abandoned (Smith et al, 2015). Attrition among officers of colour, which has been a persistent problem from the outset, continued during this period, as it does today, as discussed further later in this chapter. Contemporaneous research from this period in the UK showed ongoing BAME community distrust of police and views that police were inherently biased against BAME people, sentiments that continued deterring BAME candidate applications to join the police services (Holdaway, 2013).

Today, there are 8.4 per cent (11,966) BAME officers in England and Wales, out of a total of 147,430, of which 3.8 per cent are Asian (including Chinese), 2.6 per cent are Mixed Race, 1.3 per cent are Black, and 0.7 per cent are Other. BAME officers are concentrated in the UK's urban sectors, with the highest concentration of BAME officers in London at 17.3 per cent, compared to a London population that is 46.3 per cent BAME. The large urban centre in the West Midlands has 14 per cent BAME officers, compared to a BAME population of 38 per cent. The lowest proportions of BAME officers are in rural communities such as Cumbria, Devon and Cornwall, and North Wales Police, which each have around 1 per cent BAME officers (Home Office, 2024).

This book argues that the embeddedness of street police culture ensures that racism, stereotyping, pressures and different terms of employment for UK BAME officers persist today. Studies, including interviews with Subjects 1 and 7 carried out for this volume, consistently find that BAME officers continue to feel stereotyped by fellow officers and supervisors, and subjected to closer scrutiny than their White colleagues in relation to hiring, probation, discipline and promotion (Smith et al, 2015; Zempi, 2020). Some BAME officers, including Interview Subject 1, report that, when seeking promotion, they face not being supported by their supervisors, which some attribute to stereotypes about their skills or 'fit' within the organization (Zempi, 2020). Others, such as Interview Subject 7, report having the goal posts changed for them in relation to the criteria they must satisfy before being promoted, while White colleagues do not face the same shifting standards. As a result of these pressures, stereotypes and perceived differential treatment, it is unsurprising that BAME officers consistently resign from the police services at higher rates than their White colleagues (Home Office, 2024). As discussed in the next section, there are significant parallels between these findings, which suggest continued negative influences of police culture norms and stereotypes, and the similar experiences of BAME officers in the US.

Officers of colour in the US

Like the UK, many officers of colour in the US have long faced negative stereotypes, resistance and different terms and conditions of employment compared to their White colleagues. While those aspects are largely similar, it is noteworthy that the history of police diversity in the US is more deeply rooted compared to the UK. Indeed, diversity in the US police departments dates back to at least 1861, when the first African American officers began working in Washington DC (Kuykendall and Burns, 1980). Throughout the late 1800s, African American officers worked in a number of large American cities including Chicago, Galveston, Philadelphia, Charleston and New Orleans. In 1890, there were approximately 74,629 'watchmen, policemen and firemen', approximately 2 per cent of which were Black (Kuykendall and Burns, 1980: 4). These figures continued climbing in the early 1900s (Kuykendall and Burns, 1980), and the first African American female officer was appointed in Los Angeles in 1916, with Chicago, Indianapolis, Pittsburgh and New York City also hiring at least one African American female officer before 1920 (Taylor Greene, 2000). While the 1920s saw declines in the overall numbers of BAME officers (Kuykendall and Burns, 1980), other urban departments hired their first Black female officers in this decade, including Washington DC, Toledo and Detroit (Taylor Greene, 2000).

Yet the 1930s continued to see declines in BAME officer numbers, which continued well into the 1940s (Kuykendall and Burns, 1980). It was not until the post–Second World War era of the 1950s that BAME officer numbers started increasing again, when African Americans represented roughly 2 per cent of all US police officers (Kuykendall and Burns, 1980) and 3.6 per cent of urban police forces (Bolton and Feagin, 2004; Conti and Doreian, 2014). It is noteworthy that many southern US police departments hired few if any African American or other ethnic minority officers during the Jim Crow era of legalized segregation which spanned from the 1890s to the 1960s (Walker et al, 2017). Moreover, there is little readily available documentation about the history of Latino, Asian or Native American officers in US police departments during this pre-1960s period.

Figures from 1960 indicate African American officers made up 4 per cent of all American officers (Kuykendall and Burns, 1980; Walker et al, 2017). Research has found that the 1960s US Civil Rights Movement saw African American communities demand more African American officers to ease racial tensions and improve police–community relations (Bolton and Feagin, 2004; Conti and Doreian, 2014; Forman, 2017). Decades of demands for equal opportunities from local communities, culminating in the

Civil Rights Movement, led to the implementation of a variety of federal equality and anti-discrimination laws, including the 1964 Civil Rights Act, which afforded greater protections for the rights of ethnic minorities and women, and improved their chances of entering professions including policing (Townsey, 1982). In response to the urban 'riots' in African American communities in the mid-1960s, the Kerner Commission (1967) called on American police departments to hire more African American officers to improve community relations. This resulted in a number of urban departments recruiting more ethnic minorities and women from the mid-1960s (Townsey, 1982), although as discussed later in this chapter, their experiences, challenges and terms and conditions of employment were often very different from those of White men.

By the 1970s, African Americans accounted for 6.4 per cent of officers across the US (Raganella and White, 2004), while women accounted for around 1.5 per cent (Townsey, 1982). Research suggests that through at least the 1970s, many US police departments not only remained largely White, but even more diverse police departments remained racially biased and heavily segregated. Officers of colour faced pressures and obstacles others did not face. Not only were officers of colour denied advancement opportunities and assignment to specialized units, as discussed further below, but they were also often assigned to exclusively patrol ethnic minority neighbourhoods (Teahan, 1975). This meant that well into the 1970s, many African American officers were primarily assigned to police African American neighbourhoods, without being given any other assignment opportunities or options (Bolton and Feagin, 2004). Perhaps it was assumed that African American officers wanted to patrol in their communities of origin. Or perhaps they were stereotyped within police services as being only interested in or able to police in African American neighbourhoods.

African American officers also faced overt racism within many US police departments during this period. For example, some White officers were unwilling to partner with African American colleagues, and objected to supervising Black officers or being supervised by Black officers (Teahan, 1975; Conti and Doreian, 2014). Teahan (1975) further found that a number of White police officers displayed higher levels of prejudice and lower positive feelings toward Black people than Black officers. Moreover, some Black officers were even prohibited from arresting White offenders during this period, further displaying overt institutional-level racism within some departments (Martin, 1994). While there were increasing numbers of Black women officers in the 1960s and 1970s, they remained under-represented in US policing and rarely advanced beyond the role of police officer (Taylor Greene, 2000). That said, by 1975 a number of urban US police departments saw increasing representation of officers of colour, with Atlanta (30 per cent), Detroit (22 per cent), Newark (22 per cent), Columbus (14 per cent) and Berkeley (15 per cent) having the highest percentage of Black officers, while numbers of other officers of colour or Black women officers were not similarly tracked (Lewis, 1989).

Bolstered by the energy of the Civil Rights Movement and the legal changes it brought about, the 1970s and 1980s saw the first lawsuits to compel police departments to hire people of colour, and to give them the same opportunities as White officers. For example, minority officers sued the Mobile City Police Department to end racial segregation in patrol car assignments and neighbourhood patrol assignments (*Allen v. City of Mobile*, 1972). As a result of some of these lawsuits, compulsory and voluntary affirmative action hiring plans for ethnic minority and women officers were implemented in many US police departments (Townsey, 1982). Researchers attribute the subsequent increases in ethnic minority representation across many urban US police departments to these affirmative action programmes. For example, by 1980, many large urban departments, including New York City, Chicago, Philadelphia, Detroit, Baltimore, Washington DC, Cleveland, and Boston, among others had more than 10 per cent Black officers (Walker, 1983), while women accounted for around 3.5 per cent of all officers (Townsey, 1982). Yet despite these often legally driven increases in police diversity in many US police departments, they failed to adequately mirror ethnic minority representation across most urban populations. For example, research from this period by Walker (1983) and others found that most large urban areas had 25 per cent or higher representation of Black people in the population, yet no urban centre mirrored the Black population in their respective police departments. Similarly, while most large urban centres had Latino populations well over 10 per cent, no large metropolitan police departments reflected their Latino populations (Walker, 1983).

Yet, as the 1980s progressed, there were growing numbers of voluntary, and more importantly compulsory, affirmative action programmes. Researchers argue these compulsory programmes in particular were responsible for significant increases in Black and Latino officer representation throughout the 1980s (Townsey, 1982; Walker, 1989). By 1988, the majority of large urban police departments had 10 per cent or more Black officers, albeit most still failed to proportionately represent their Black populations (Walker, 1989). Latino officers similarly became better represented in many large urban police departments, but most still failed to mirror their Latino populations (Walker, 1989). And by the 1990s, there were approximately 7,260 Black female officers across US policing agencies, representing around 2 per cent of all officers (Taylor Greene, 2000). Indeed, in some cities, particularly those with majority Black populations including Washington DC, Detroit, Baltimore, Atlanta, Cleveland, New Orleans, Newark and

Compton, Black female officers actually outnumbered White female officers in the 1990s (Taylor Greene, 2000).

Many US police departments increased their Black and Latino officer composition as a result of voluntary or compulsory affirmative action programmes (Walker, 1989), often mandated as a result of court-ordered consent decrees following lawsuits by US Department of Justice investigation or lawsuit. Research shows that affirmative action was instrumental in helping American police departments become more diverse. For example, Gustafson's sample of 180 American police departments found compulsory affirmative action programmes were much more effective in increasing ethnic minority representation across the police departments analysed (Gustafson, 2008). Lewis (1989) examined hiring of Black officers across 46 of America's largest police departments, and found that compulsory affirmative action programmes were instrumental to making departments more representative of their Black populations. Lewis further found that given the resistance to hiring Black officers in police departments, compulsory affirmative action programmes were necessary to achieve the desired representation. Stokes and Scott (1996), Sass and Troyer (1999) and Lott (2000) all found that compulsory affirmative action programmes were essential to increasing ethnic minority police force representation in the US in the 1980s and 1990s.

By 2002, Black officers made up 11.7 per cent of all US officers and 38.1 per cent of officers in urban American departments (Reaves and Hickman, 2002). And by 2013, 27 per cent of full-time police officers were from ethnic minorities: 12 per cent African American, 12 per cent Latino; and 4 per cent were Asian, Pacific Islander, American Indian or multiracial (BJS, 2013). The most recent data available from the US Bureau of Justice Statistics (BJS, 2022) shows that in 2020, US policing had continued to diversify, as set out in Table 4.1.

Yet Sklansky (2006) argues that despite increases in US police diversity, figures vary significantly across US police departments. While a few large

Table 4.1: Composition of American police departments by race, 2020

	White	African American	Latino	Other (including Asian, Native American and Mixed Race)	Unknown
Total	69%	12%	14%	4%	1%
Large departments (1,000,000+)	47%	16%	30%	7%	0%
Small departments (less than 10,000)	86%	6%	5%	2%	1%

Source: BJS, 2022

American departments, such as Washington DC, Detroit, Atlanta and Baltimore have become majority minority officers, consistent with being majority ethnic minority cities, most of the other 18,000 US departments remain primarily composed of White officers (BJS, 2022). Furthermore, it is important to note that in most large urban police departments like the New York City Police Department (Guajardo, 2014) and Los Angeles Police Department, racial diversity is concentrated in the lower tiers of the force, with the leadership roles remaining mostly White (BJS, 2022), a trend which will be discussed in further detail later in relation to promotions and leadership diversity. These demographics lend further evidence to the argument in Chapter 2 about the entrenched nature of street police culture as a result of the continued homogeneity in terms of officer diversity.

Evaluating representation intersectionally based on the limited intersectional data available, representation of US female officers of colour[1] has also continued to grow in recent decades, and certainly exceeds non-White female officer representation in the UK. According to the BJS (2022), while 61 per cent of all US state and local police officers are White males, 7 per cent were White females, 3 per cent were Black females and 3 per cent were Latina females.[2] However, despite these increased percentages, female officers of colour remain largely under-represented in most American police departments compared to the representation of women of colour across the population of major US cities, with exception of some large cities with large Black and Latino populations, including Detroit, Washington DC, Chicago, Philadelphia and New York, where women of colour, particularly Black women, are better represented in policing than elsewhere in the US (Taylor Greene, 2000; BJS 2022). Moreover, Black women have served as police chiefs in large American cities including New York City, Philadelphia, Columbus, Louisville, Seattle and Portland, Oregon. But on the whole, female officers of colour remain under-represented in most US police agencies and, where they are present, remain concentrated at the lower ranks of US police departments, with a lack of representation at supervisory and leadership levels in most American police agencies. And once again, these diversity statistics showing increases in representation of female officers of colour do not illustrate the experiences of those women in the role, or the police culture pressures they face within police institutions, as detailed in the next section.

---

[1] Given their smaller numbers, female officers of colour remain not just significantly under-represented in US police departments, but also significantly under-researched by policing researchers. Many US police departments and researchers fail to collect or publish studies with data showing the composition and experiences of female officers of colour.

[2] Numbers for Asian and Native American female officers are not consistently recorded.

Officer of colour experiences

This book has previously established that street police culture norms originate in traditional straight, White, male, working-class views of race, gender, violence, loyalty, tolerance and numerous other perspectives. While officers of colour may vary in terms of their cognisance, processing and acceptance of different sets of experiences and terms and conditions of employment in policing institutions, the reality for many officers of colour is that their experiences can potentially be similar to or quite different from those of their White counterparts.

Part of this assessment is in the perspective of the officers themselves, and some may consciously or subconsciously be aware of differences in treatment but ignore them. Others may be very cognisant of their different treatment from White officers. This may cause some to lean into police culture norms, and try to perform in ways deemed acceptable within the street police culture framework. The assimilation into street police culture is a practical reality faced by many officers of colour. When they assimilate and act according to street police culture norms like their White colleagues, this feeds scepticism among community members and academics that their presence in the police service makes any difference. However, the interviews conducted for this book, triangulated with the official government statistics and empirical research study data, illustrate that officers of colour frequently do not have the same experiences as their White colleagues, often in very concerning ways. Indeed, the data analysis conducted for this book suggests officers of colour face a host of explicit discrimination, racist language, stereotypes, aversive racism,[3] social isolation, ostracization, and different terms and conditions of employment compared to their White colleagues. The differences in terms and conditions of employment can include differences in assignments, lower rates of promotion, different evaluation criteria, greater rates of internal discipline and termination, higher rates of voluntary resignation and higher levels of stress, among others.

Because some UK and US officers of colour experience the policing role differently from their White colleagues, the data analysed for this book show this can in turn lead to different adaptations and coping mechanisms on the job. The results of these differences for some include not socializing with White colleagues, joining officer of colour affinity groups and quitting the police service. Significantly for this book, this can also result in officers of colour explicitly or implicitly becoming active bureaucrats, meaning engaging in practices which benefit or represent the

---

[3]   Aversive racism is an explicit or implicit type of racism or bias which stereotypes or regards people of colour as unskilled and unqualified for their roles (Turner and Pratkanis, 1994).

interests of communities of colour. This can range from fostering better community relations, partnering with communities of colour, engaging in less racial profiling and using force less frequently and with less severity against people of colour.

To be clear, this chapter does not propose that there is a singular set of experiences for officers of colour in the policing role in the UK and US. However, it does highlight what the data analysis for this book reveals – that while not all ethnic minority officers experience or report experiencing these types of challenges on the job, many do. Moreover, it is notable that despite the differences in the structures and compositions of UK and US police services, the experiences of officers of colour across both jurisdictions show remarkable similarities.

Assimilation into police culture

The data discussed in this chapter show clear evidence of a number of different types of racial disparities impacting the experiences of officers of colour in UK and US police services. One aspect of challenges faced by officers of colour in both jurisdictions is the tensions over dealing with and assimilating into street police culture, as introduced in Chapter 2. As discussed earlier, street police culture is largely characterized by violence, insularity, authority, hierarchy, competition, masculinity, racism, sexism and homophobia, among others (Haarr and Morash, 1999; Bowling et al, 2019; Quinlan, 2021).

One of the particular obstacles for officers of colour, who are increasingly joining UK and US police departments, is that these core tenets of street police culture have not necessarily changed with their arrival (Conti and Doreian, 2014). Instead, many argue street police culture often remains fairly static because it is so deeply embedded in officers and so difficult to change (Chan, 1997; Quinlan, 2021).

Contending with often biased street police culture norms creates added challenges for officers of colour and others who join policing from traditionally marginalized groups. Research on officers of colour in both the UK and US has found significant pressures to assimilate into street police culture (Holdaway, 1997b; Macpherson, 1999: 6.28; Cashmore, 2001; Bolton, 2003; Pogrebin et al, 2000). Some ethnic minority UK and US officers describe their degrees of assimilation into street police culture as a litmus test from White officers to gauge their loyalty and trustworthiness (Holdaway, 1997a; Holdaway and Barron, 1997; Pogrebin et al, 2000). These pressures can make officers of colour and others from under-represented backgrounds feel uncomfortable, alienated and stressed about fitting in to their respective police departments (Dowler, 2005; Jones and Williams, 2015). This presents officers of colour with a difficult choice – either adopt street police cultures which often negatively stereotype people of colour and others, or refuse to do so and risk isolation, alienation and lack of support from White officers, who often form the majority of the police department (Holdaway, 1997a; Miller et al, 2003; Dowler, 2005; Jones and Williams, 2015).

Some research frames the pressure on officers to adopt street police culture as compelling them to subvert their racial identities by emulating White colleagues (Holdaway, 1997a; Cashmore, 2002; Smith et al, 2015). For example, officers in Cashmore's 2002 survey of 100 UK ethnic minority officers reported pressure to act more 'White', meaning embracing White officers' ways of thinking and acting on the job. A decade later, Smith et al's 2015 study of UK officers of colour similarly found many of their White colleagues refused to accept their cultural differences or different approaches to doing things at work. These officers of colour were made to feel 'it is wrong to be different', and were urged to more closely mimic the practices of their White colleagues. These studies are consistent with earlier UK studies including Holdaway's (1997b: 23) research on 59 current/former Black and Asian officers across five UK police forces, where one respondent explained the dilemma for officers of colour this way:

There are some aspects of [police culture] that aren't very savoury but by and large it tends to indoctrinate you, well brainwash. Because the police culture, it applied even to me. I found myself regurgitating and spewing it up at home. It was like I was a third person. I could actually see myself making all these comments, thinking, 'Well, that's not quite right'. I found myself doing it. I mean, specifically, I started picking people, putting them into little compartments. I found myself thinking 'Well, that's not quite right, perhaps coming from an ethnic minority myself and having experiences at first hand, I should know better' but I found myself doing it. (Holdaway, 1997b: 23)

This pressure to assimilate was evidenced in interviews conducted for this book. For example, Interview Subject 1 was active in the ethnic minority officer association in his UK police department, and was criticized by White officers for being so:

A [BAME] support organization … was considered quite radical and of course people didn't know what it was or what the organization was going to deal with, so it was seen as quite threatening by some people and they were saying 'Well why do you need to do this? Is it a union?', so some people saw it as a threat. The whole idea was to provide support and discourage [BAME] officers leaving because they have had support provided.

The UK studies about the pressures faced by officers of colour to adopt street police culture parallel similar studies in the US. For example, Pogrebin et al (2000) found that African American officers felt tremendous pressure from other officers to adopt street police culture even though it was frequently racially biased in stereotyping African American people. This pressure was very acutely felt by African American female officers in the study, who were a double minority in the department as a result of both race and gender.

Racial hostility and racism

Because street police culture is embedded with racialized bias and discrimination including explicit and implicit racism, stereotypes and racially disproportionate practices, these aspects are inherent to the operations of police institutions in the UK and US. Sometimes this can manifest in explicit and implicit racial hostility and racism experienced by officers of colour in both jurisdictions. Many factors can shape the extent of these experiences for officers of colour, including their prior lived experiences of racial hostility and racism, their own views, their adoption of racialized aspects of street police culture norms, the explicitness or severity of the racial hostility and racism they experience, and the support they have from other officers – officers of colour and White allies alike. Yet research suggests these experiences of racial hostility and racism can be instrumental differences in how officers of colour experience the job, and whether they decide to stay in the position.

Acts of racial hostility and racism can vary in frequency and severity, and may be more explicit when officers are more junior compared to when they are serving in leadership ranks. The scope of racial hostility and racism can run the spectrum from explicit racial epithets and racial stereotypes, assaults and bullying, to less explicit or seemingly implicit/unconscious racially tinged banter, jokes and microaggressions. Regardless of the form of racial hostility or racism, research suggests the significance of these experiences for officers of colour cannot be overstated, as each incident can take a toll on them in terms of feelings of inclusion and belonging, mental and physical health and well-being.

Research evidences that racial hostility and overt racism have been the experiences of ethnic minority officers as long as they have been members of British and American police forces. Research dating from the 1960s (Alex, 1969) through to the present day in both the UK and US has chronicled the ways many ethnic minority officers experience racial hostility from some White officers and managers (Sullivan, 1989; Haung and Vaughn, 1996; Holdaway, 1997a; Bland, 1999; Cashmore, 2000, 2002; Toch, 2002; Home Office, 2005; Smith et al, 2015). For example, Alex's 1969 study of 41 Black officers in the New York Police Department (NYPD) in the 1960s found most had experienced explicit discrimination for fellow officers. Numerous subsequent American studies show parallel findings (Sullivan, 1989; Haung and Vaughn, 1996; Toch, 2002). For example, Bolton and Feagin's 2004 study of 16 Southern US departments found non-White officers experience racial animus from colleagues and managers, with 96 per cent of African American officers surveyed finding racial prejudice and discrimination regularly impacted their experiences in their respective police departments. Bolton's (2003) interviews with 50 Black officers in the US South found Black officers reported racism permeated the atmosphere of their respective departments, making them feel like outsiders (Bolton, 2003). Jollevet (2008) also found 99 per cent of 224 African American police executives reporting witnessing racial discrimination in their careers.

Given the relative consistency of racial bias and intolerance in street police culture across jurisdictions, it is unsurprising that data show many similar experiences with racial hostility and racism for officers of colour in the UK. Study after UK study has consistently found non-White officers experience overt racial hostility from fellow officers and supervisors (Holdaway, 1997a; Cashmore, 2000, 2002; Morris, 2004; Home Office, 2005; Holdaway, 2010; Smith et al, 2015). Cashmore (2002), for example, found that officers of colour had to become 'case-hardened', that is tough, highly motivated and resilient given the habitual overt racism they experienced on the job. A further example comes from Holdaway's 2010 study, including interviews with leaders of the UK Black Police Association, which found that many officers felt racism in the UK police workplace was so significant that it meant they could not necessarily trust their White colleagues.

Racial animus in police departments can take numerous different forms. Research in both the UK and US suggests the most common behaviours reported by non-White officers include racialized verbal abuse, racial jokes and cartoons, racial and ethnic slurs and epithets, and derogatory language used by White officers toward their non-White colleagues (Holdaway, 1997a; Cashmore, 2002; Bolton, 2003; Bolton and Feagin, 2004; Home Office, 2005). Holdaway found that for Black and Asian officers in the UK, racialized banter and jokes by White officers were commonplace, which for some minority officers were easier to laugh along with rather than challenge. Indeed, some officers found it made more sense to simply accept racial banter and jokes as part of the job, rather than risk their job (Holdaway, 1997a). Similarly, Cashmore's 2002 study of ten BAME officers across three police services in England found that the vast majority had endured severe racial and ethnic taunting on the job, particularly as new officers, which they characterized as particularly vicious due to their ethnicities. Research by the UK Home Office (2005: 31) found that 72 per cent of officers surveyed had encountered racist officers in their police forces. BAME officers in the Home Office's 2005 study believed that any declines in use of racist language by officers were cosmetic rather than because racist attitudes had changed. Indeed, they asserted that overt racism by White officers had simply 'gone underground' for fear of disciplinary action, not because White officers were any less racist (Home Office, 2005). More recently, Casey's report on the London Metropolitan Police Service (London Met Police) found 36 per cent of Asian officers and 35 per cent of Black officers had experienced bullying, rates that were higher compared to their White colleagues, and which Casey remarked were important differences to acknowledge in relation to their membership in traditionally under-represented groups.

In my interview with Interview Subject 1, a former high-level UK police leader of colour, he recounted that he was repeatedly subjected to explicit racial jokes, taunts and bullying, particularly in the earlier stages of his career: 'With my shift colleagues it wasn't bullying, it was done in jest, but there were people who would use the jest as a form of bullying. And senior people as well'. Yet when he reported the incidents, officers closed ranks and did not support him, turning him into the problem as opposed to the problematic racist and their racist behaviour:

A number of the incidents I reported of overt racism, there was a closing of ranks and this is my direct personal experience. I would report things, and nobody had heard anything in terms of the canteen or what was said, but I felt I became the problem immediately for having reported something that was wrong. Instead of people saying yes, let's get to grips with that. … The fact that they felt able to do that and it was important that they were supported in doing that, but that's not how I was treated when I saw wrongdoing, and so huge pressures in order to do it. Of course there were a number of occasions where I just felt, well, I'm just up against everybody here, I'm just not going to win this battle and the good thing is there are often one or two allies, either senior or junior, but one or two allies who kept me going.

Interview Subject 1 further reflected on the importance of White allies in his struggles to fight against the racism he encountered on the job:

R1:   [B]ut in an organization that was inherently racist, and institutionally racist, the allies were all important. And the point being that not everybody was racist. There was a lot of racism but not everybody was racist. You couldn't make that assumption and fall into the same trap, but the allies made the biggest difference.

Q: Because it helped you get that sense of belonging?

R1:   It did, yeah. Well, even if you didn't have that sense of belonging, and I don't think I did … but the point is that the allies are the people who kept me in the organization in a way.

Despite the pervasiveness of both explicit and implicit racial hostility in police departments across the UK and US, most incidents go unreported. Because street police culture normalizes racism in UK and US police services, it places pressure on officers of colour to accept racial hostility and racism as acceptable behaviour within policing. Further street police culture tenets of the blue wall of silence whereby police protect one another and form a united front, as discussed in Chapter 2, also mean that officers of colour are under pressure not to report racial hostility or racist incidents they experience on the job. Indeed, as observed in Baroness Casey's report on the London Met Police (2023), officers of colour who report discrimination are often ignored, or even worse, racism complaints are weaponized and turned into misconduct complaints against reporting BAME officers.

It is, therefore, unsurprising that the data from UK and US police services over many decades support this assessment, consistently showing the reluctance of officers of colour to report racist incidents. Alex (1969), Holdaway (1997a), Cashmore (2002), Bolton (2003) and many other studies have found in both the UK and US, a majority of non-White officers chose not to report incidents and not to vocalize their views about racism, civil rights or other racial equality topics, to avoid hostility from White officers. Studies repeatedly show that despite non-White officers acknowledging the racial animus they experience from White officers on the job, they fear retaliation, including assignments, as well as implications for career advancement (Bolton, 2003), and that these concerns about retaliation and impact on careers are well founded.

For example, Cashmore's 2001 UK study found ethnic minority officers not only did not want to hurt their careers by raising objections to racism by other officers, but they also feared the consequences of being unable to rely on White colleagues for help in dangerous situations on the job. An Asian officer observed:

If I call for assistance, that means I need somebody there now, not in ten minutes. I need to know that I'm going to get it. If I've taken somebody to task for a racial remark or whatever, months or weeks later, that same bobby might be the one who's called out for me … it would put some doubt in your mind. (Cashmore, 2001: 654)

This sentiment was echoed by diverse police leaders interviewed for this study. For example, Interview Subject 1 experienced significant incidents of racism throughout his UK policing career, but was reluctant to report incidents perpetrated by his supervisors for the sake of continuing on in the service:

> So I've described a lot of the experiences, the bad experiences in my career. But also how I overcame them, and that was an issue of some things I challenged and some things I didn't. Sometimes I would call people out, and sometimes it wasn't appropriate, when they were more senior. Some of it was about survival.

Again, these data reflect very real concerns about career prospects for reporting racist incidents, but also about retaliation that could place in jeopardy the safety of officers of colour.

Intersectional discrimination and female officers of colour

The underlying values of street police cultures embedded in UK and US policing include not only racial bias, discrimination and disproportionality, but also sexism, classism, ableism, homophobia and other forms of bias. When evaluating experiences of racial hostility and racism for officers of colour, adopting an intersectional lens illuminates the ways the street police culture norms shape the experiences of female officers of colour in ways which are unique from those of male officers of colour. Given the levels of the combination of different forms of biases inherent in street police culture, it is important to understand the intersections of the ways female officers of colour experience the combination of racism and sexism on the job. Unfortunately, the intersectional analysis of the combined experiences of racism and sexism endured by female officers of colour is extremely limited by the lack of UK and US policing research considering the ways these multiple forms of oppression impact their lived experiences. Yet the data that do exist show the ways contending with both racism and sexism in departments with largely male majorities make the plight of female officers particularly difficult in UK and US policing.

One of the first investigations of the intersectional experiences of discrimination for female officers of colour was Martin's (1994) interviews with White and Black male and female officers across five American police departments. Martin found that of the 31 Black female officers interviewed, 7 per cent had experienced gender discrimination, 13 per cent had experienced race discrimination, 48 per cent had experienced both gender and race discrimination and 32 per cent said they experienced neither. Thus, nearly half of Black female officers experienced the combination of racial and gender discrimination, and all told 68 per cent had experienced some form of discrimination on the job.

Similarly, Pogrebin et al (2000) interviewed all 21 Black female police officers in a large urban US police department, who formed just 1.5 per cent of the force. They found that 100 per cent of their participants had experienced discrimination on the job, although it was not always clear whether it was race or gender discrimination, or both. Pogrebin et al (2000) found that gender discrimination seemed to manifest in three particular areas: questioning professional abilities (that is, aversive racism), job performance and supervisory duties. Some of the participants described being left pornographic material, being excluded from mainstream communication, being left without back-up when calling for aid on the radio, and similar forms of harassment.

They found that the African American women in their study experienced overt sexism equally from White and African American male officers. The research hypothesized that because the extent of gender discrimination was so severe for Black female officers, perhaps this was attributable to both White and Black male officers' desires for masculine back-up on the job in certain circumstances, which they stereotyped that female officers could not provide.

The UK context sees strong parallels with the US in the experiences of racism and sexism for female officers of colour. While there are even fewer of such studies than in the US, the small amount of research suggests intersectional racial and gender discrimination is a significant part of the policing experiences of ethnic minority women in UK policing. One important study was Holder et al's interviews with 16 women officers including 11 Black and Asian female officers of colour in a police service in England and Wales, conducted in 2000. All of the non-White female officers in the study reported experiencing racism, and the majority reported experiencing both racism and sexism within the police service. Respondents reported that the racism they experienced on the job as women of colour was particularly distressing and personal in nature, and often occurred independently of sexism. Some Black women officers reported explicit sexual harassment based on stereotypes linked to their identification as Black women.

More recently, Zempi's 2020 UK-based research focused on 19 UK officers from traditionally marginalized groups included several female officers of colour. Their lived experiences indicated the often difficult interactions with co-workers and supervisors in police services which often left them feeling targeted by racism and misogyny, including being differently treated from other male officers of colour and White female officers. Along similar lines, Hasan's 2021 UK-based research focusing on the lived experiences of ten current and former UK female officers of colour found the significant influence of street police culture in their lived experiences of being subject to racial and sexist stereotypes, and discrimination in UK police services. Hasan strongly advocated for further intersectional research to be undertaken into the lived experiences of female officers of colour in policing, who in both the UK and US represent a small minority of policing institutions.

The findings of intersectional racism and sexism experienced by female officers of colour in the UK and US are remarkably consistent across the Martin (1994), Pogrebin et al (2000), Holder et al (2000), Zempi (2020) and Hasan (2021) studies. While many officers of colour experience racism on the job, the experiences of female officers of colour across these two jurisdictions suggest a unique combination of very difficult experiences. Experiencing these multiple layers of intersectional bias at work creates particular stresses and obstacles for female officers of colour in UK and US police departments, which are different from those of White men, men of colour and White women. Yet police institutions rarely address the needs of female officers of colour based on their unique intersectional experiences of discrimination, and policing research rarely examines these lived experiences. This is an area where both much further empirical research and policy development are required.

General assignments and special assignments

Because street police culture normalizes racism and racial hostility generally, experiences of racialization for many officers of colour in both the UK and US are not limited simply to explicit racist harassment and racialized jokes. As with other workplaces, discrimination against officers of colour can take the form of more implicit biases, including differences in the terms, conditions or quality of opportunities in their policing roles. Although these more subtle aspects of discrimination are not typically the focus of most policing research, the limited UK and US data reflect disproportionality over a number of decades in the ways many officers of colour are treated on the job compared to their White colleagues.

Studies in both the UK and US reflect that for officers of colour, the quality of their assignments, and opportunities to pursue special assignments including in elite squads such as firearms, narcotics, special protection, counter-terrorism and other selective positions, are often more limited compared to their White colleagues (Holdaway, 1997a; Bland et al, 1999; Cashmore, 2001; Bolton, 2003; Guajardo, 2014; Bury et al, 2018; Zempi, 2020; Casey, 2023).

One problem showing differences between officers of colour and White officers is the disproportionate assignment of non-White officers to roles considered less desirable in policing institutions, an issue of concern to ethnic minority officers for decades. Townsey (1982), for example, looked at 1979 American policing figures, and found disparities in the assignments of Black and White officer assignments, with Black male officers not only better represented in patrol than their White counterparts (66 per cent to 63 per cent), but also represented at lower rates in coveted special assignments including investigations (12 per cent to 13 per cent) or traffic (4 per cent to 6 per cent) or technical roles (2 per cent to 4 per cent). Subsequent studies of police departments such as the NYPD illustrate similar trends. For example, Fyfe and Kane's 2006 study of the NYPD found that African Americans, Latinos and Asians were under-represented in the force's elite divisions, including the aviation, emergency service, harbour, highway patrol and mounted units, compared to their White colleagues. More recent studies of the NYPD have shown these trends persist (Guajardo, 2014).

In the UK, government data have long established that non-White officers serve in special assignment positions at lower rates than their White counterparts. Bland et al (1999) was one of the first UK studies to show ethnic minority officers were under-represented in desirable special assignments including traffic, investigations, training, tactical units, firearms, among others. In 2021, UK government data showed that BAME officers were under-represented in some of the largest and most prestigious special policing assignments in England and Wales policing including the Firearms Unit, Intelligence, Road Policing, Serious and Organised Crime Unit, and Witness Protection, among others (Home Office, 2022; see Table 4.2). This disparity was also reflected in Baroness Casey's report on the London Met Police (2023), who remarked that members of the Firearms Unit and other special squads were over 90 per cent White male. While there is not extensive research on this subject, both UK and US studies show that issues of under-representation of officers of colour in prestigious special units and

Table 4.2: Police officer specialist assignments in England and Wales by race, 2020–21

	Total officers	BAME	White
Road policing	3,853	3.6%	96.4%
Firearms Unit	3,549	4.2%	95.8%
Intelligence	4,475	4.9%	95.1%
Advanced public order	1,224	8.7%	91.3%
Airports and Ports Unit	687	7.6%	92.4%
Dogs section	962	1.8%	98.2%
Mounted police	198	0%	100%
Custody	2,119	6.5%	93.5%
Serious and Organised Crime Unit	2,499	6.2%	93.8%
Witness protection	466	3.6%	96.4%

Source: Home Office, 2021

assignments can be part of their lived experiences of discrimination and inequality on the job.

These differences can be a particularly frustrating area for officers of colour, who have highlighted over the decades in multiple studies the barriers they perceive to obtaining these posts. For example, in Alex's 1969 study of 41 Black officers in the NYPD in the 1960s, officers of colour reported experiencing discrimination that prevented them from obtaining prestigious special assignments, roles often needed for career advancement and promotions. Forty-five years later, Guajardo's 2014 study of ethnic minority officers in the NYPD similarly found officers of colour perceived discrimination as creating barriers for obtaining these important positions. Similarly, Wilson and Wilson's 2014 study of 62 African American officers across nine US police departments found that 81 per cent believed they were not provided with sufficient opportunities for special assignments within their respective departments, which negatively impacted their potential for promotion and overall career advancement. National studies of American police officers, including the Pew Survey (2017) of over 7,000 American officers, similarly reflect frustrations with assignments and lack of assignment opportunities, with 53 per cent of Black officers and 19 per cent of Latino officers believing White officers are treated better in their respective department in terms of assignments and promotions (Pew Research Center, 2017: 21).

In the UK, a significant amount of research has not been undertaken in this area, but it has been observed by policing researchers, and more recently by Baroness Casey's report (2023), that prestigious specialist units are often described as 'closed shops' where only those within established networks or who are perceived as fitting into established policing norms and culture are invited to join (Bury et al, 2018: 5). Baroness Casey found that specialist police units were 'well resourced, with elitist attitudes and toxic cultures of bullying, racism, sexism and ableism, normal rules do not seem to apply or be applied' (Casey, 2023: 190). The dominance of aggressive, street police culture in these specialized units that Casey found were 90 per cent White male meant they were not only viewed as positions unavailable to officers of colour and female officers, but those non-White males and women who obtained these roles had a very difficult time keeping them (Casey, 2023). Casey found that non-White and female officers were often treated in subordinate ways to White male officers in these units, and frequently had their competence and commitment to street police culture questioned by fellow officers (Casey, 2023). Given the prestigious nature of specialist squads, the exclusion of officers of colour from these roles, or the obstacles created making it more difficult for them to remain in these roles, create problems for officers of colour both in terms of their ability to succeed in the role, and in terms of their career advancement.

Promotions

Given the explicitly and implicitly racialized and often biased attitudes inherent in street police culture in both the UK and US, it is unsurprising that officers of colour have experiences of disproportionality in a number of aspects of their employment. One significant example that has seen some degree of empirical research involves officers of colour and promotions. Indeed, one of the most significant differences in the experiences of officers of colour and White officers are the different rates of promotion and representation at supervisory and leadership ranks. Across departments in both the UK and US, distinct rates of promotion and representation beyond the ranks of patrol officer (the equivalent of constable in the UK) for non-White and White officers has long been a source of frustration for officers of colour.

These disparities have been reflected in policing research for decades. From the early days, police research showed disparities in the promotion of non-White officers to supervisory and leadership positions. In the US context, for example, an early study of racial differences by Townsey (1982) found significant Black officer under-representation, with White officers three times more likely to occupy ranks above patrol officers compared to their Black counterparts. Townsey (1982) also found that White women were more than three times more likely than Black women to occupy supervisory positions including command, supervisory and investigative positions.

While Townsey's research was carried out 40 years ago, American police data continue to reflect poor, and often extremely low representation of non-White officers in supervisory and leadership positions in many US police departments at both middle management and senior leadership levels. The most recent Bureau of Justice (BJS, 2022) statistics available show that, across American police departments, intermediate supervisors (positions below chief but above sergeant) were 80 per cent White, 10 per cent Black, 7 per cent Latino, and 3 per cent Other (including Asian American, Native American, or Mixed Race) (BJS, 2022). Sergeants were 75 per cent White, 10 per cent Black, 10 per cent Latino, and 4 per cent Other (including Asian American, Native American, or Mixed Race) (BJS, 2022). Given the numbers of Black, Latino, Asian and Native American patrol officers, they continue to be vastly under-represented in these types of supervisory and management positions across most American police departments.

These under-representation trends are also apparent at the individual force level. For example, Guajardo's 2014 study of employment data for the NYPD found diversity decreased as rank increased, with few very ethnic minority officers holding positions higher than sergeant (see Table 4.3).

Regarding the experiences of female officers of colour in the NYPD, Guajardo's 2014 study found even more significant under-representation. Out of 2,511 higher level leadership positions in the NYPD (lieutenant

Table 4.3: NYPD leadership figures

	White	Black	Latino	Asian	Native American
Bureau chief	7	1	1	0	0
Assistant chief	15	2	2	0	0
Deputy chief	44	3	3	0	0
Captain	340	24	40	11	0
Lieutenant	1,104	128	233	41	3
Sergeant	2,413	656	836	234	8
Patrol officer	10,559	3,956	6,524	1,357	28

Source: Guajardo, 2014

to bureau chief), there were 117 White women (4 per cent), 54 (2 per cent) Black women, 51 (2 per cent) Latina women, 6 (0.2 per cent) Asian women, and 0 (0 per cent) Native American women. Among 9,594 lower level supervisory and specialist positions (detective to sergeant), there were 483 (5 per cent) White women, 461 (4 per cent) Black women, 411 (4 per cent) Latina women, 29 (0.3 per cent) Asian women, and 3 (0.03 per cent) Native American women.

The lack of representation in the NYPD, particularly at the supervisory and higher ranks, is replicated at police departments across the US. Few American police departments have achieved racial representation proportionate to their ethnic minority populations. Chapter 3 discusses the ways proportionate police representation is extremely important for police legitimacy, particularly with traditionally marginalized populations. This lack of diversity, including at senior leadership ranks, thus poses problems for police legitimacy, effectiveness and community relations.

Yet the vast under-representation of non-White officers in upper ranks of police departments is not a uniquely American problem. Like the US, ethnic minority officers in the UK are also concentrated in lower rank positions such as constables (equivalent of US patrol officers), and have consistently been under-represented in the supervisory and managerial ranks of the 43 forces of England and Wales. For example, one of the first studies to document this statistically significant difference was by Bland et al (1999), who found that officers of colour often struggled to be promoted, finding that it took on average 12 months longer to reach the rank of sergeant compared to White colleagues. A House of Commons Home Affairs Select Committee (2016) report years later found similar trends, observing that England and Wales police services continued to fail to promote BAME officers at similar rates to White officers. Moreover, a 2018 Police Foundation study of officers in

England and Wales found that while over 5 per cent of constables were ethnic minority, officers of colour made up less than 4 per cent of supervisory and middle management ranks and less than 1 per cent of police chiefs. The study also found that female officers of colour occupied less than 1 per cent of supervisory or leadership positions across the 43 forces of England and Wales in 2018 (UK Police Foundation, 2018).

Today, the most recent UK data show that officers of colour are significantly under-represented at supervisory and leadership ranks, comprising 0 per cent of chief constables, 7 per cent of chief officers, 4 per cent of chief superintendants, 5 per cent of superintendents, 6 per cent of chief inspectors, 5 per cent of inspectors, 6 per cent of sergeants (Home Office, 2023b). Where officers of colour are promoted, they remain concentrated in the lower policing ranks, particularly at the sergeant and to a lesser extent inspector and chief inspector ranks. UK government data show officers of colour continue to be promoted at rates lower than their representation across the police services, as reflected in Table 4.4.

The data from both the UK and US are therefore clear that officers of colour have consistently been under-represented at the supervisory and leadership ranks compared to their numbers in patrol officer roles, and are far from representative of the large metropolitan areas where many of them serve.

Table 4.4: Proportion of England and Wales promotions of officers of colour, 2009–23 (excluding London Met Police Service)

Year	BAME promotion rate
2009–10	4.7%
2010–11	4.3%
2011–12	5.4%
2012–13	3.4%
2013–14	3.0%
2014–15	6.6%
2015–16	5.4%
2016–17	5.0%
2017–18	3.1%
2018–19	4.6%
2019–20	4.9%
2020–21	6.5%
2021–22	9.5%
2022–23	7.6%

Source: Home Office, 2024

The reasons for the under-representation of non-White officers in the supervisory and managerial ranks of police departments in the UK and US are complex and can be difficult to disentangle. Both UK and US research, however, appear fairly consistent that officers of colour view promotions processes as more unfair than White officers, which may significantly deter them from applying for promotions. This has been borne out in empirical research, where some US studies clearly reflect that non-White officers are much less satisfied with promotion processes, which some may perceive as more biased against them than White officers. For example, Bolton's 2003 interviews with 50 Black officers in the US South found that many believed there were systemic barriers which limited their ability to be promoted and advance their careers compared to White officers. Wilson and Wilson's (2014) subsequent study of 62 African American officers across nine police departments found 56 per cent believed the promotion processes in their department were unfair toward them. Similarly in the UK context, Casey's review of the London Met Police (2023) found that Black (59 per cent) and Asian (58 per cent) officers were more likely than White officers (51 per cent) to see the promotions process and career progression as unfair. Not all of the officers in these studies asserted that they viewed promotions procedures as unfair because they were explicitly biased against them, but there is an underlying sense in these studies that police institutions which measure success and career opportunities as contingent on demonstrating fitting into and adopting street police culture norms can pose barriers to promotion for officers of colour.

The ways these types of promotion barriers manifest can be both explicit and very subtle. Explicit deterrence can include telling officers of colour they are not permitted to apply for promotion. This was the situation for Interview Subject 1 interviewed for this volume, who recounted such an incident when he was pursuing a high-level promotion in another department:

> I had asked my boss at the time can I apply and he said 'No, it's not your turn' ... and that 'no, you can't'. So he goes on holiday and then I wait until his deputy is then in charge and said 'Yeah, I'll sign your reference. I'll give you a reference and sign your application'.

Interestingly, Interview Subject 1 did not attribute his supervisor's discouragement as explicit racism, but rather tinged with implicit bias.

Indeed, some officers of colour view implicit biases framed as friendly advice or a helping hand, and a means to assist officers of colour with navigating the internal departmental politics, as extremely discouraging when applying for promotion. In addition to the example above from Interview Subject 1 where he received the seemingly friendly advice not to apply for promotion, other examples of supervisors' implicit bias in promotions can include casting doubt on individual credentials (akin to aversive racism discussed earlier in this volume); stereotyping officers of colour as not working hard enough to deserve a promotion; not valuing individual lived experiences as people of colour as important to decision-making or skill development; not crediting positive community relations or relationship-building with communities of colour as part of the promotions process, among other examples.

And research has shown that lack of supervisory support is a common reason officers of colour do not apply for promotion. Whether it is attributable to explicit racism, implicit bias or other reasons, there is a perception from officers of colour that these aspects can readily factor into supervisory lack of support for promotion applications.

Other deterrents to officers of colour pursuing promotion fall squarely in concerns they will be compelled to further adopt street police culture norms and policing approaches they find problematic and racially biased. Given the significant under-representation of officers of colour at supervisory and managerial ranks in most UK and US police departments, officers of colour in some research studies have expressed fears they will be compelled to further assimilate into the street police culture norms. The discomfort with having to become the standard bearers for biased street police culture can therefore dissuade officers of colour from applying for promotions. This was reflected in Cashmore's 2002 survey of 100 ethnic minority officers across three English police forces, many of whom hesitated to apply for promotions because they did not want to be required to further support and reinforce the dominant street police culture beliefs.

Another aspect of this street police culture tension for officers of colour is being perceived as too closely tied to their communities of origin to be seen as legitimate leaders in the eyes of fellow officers and supervisors. Indeed, some officers of colour may be viewed by colleagues and supervisors as too obstinate in failing to assimilate into street police culture to warrant promotion. One Black police leader interviewed for this book (whose identifying information has been anonymized here) was subjected to explicit racial bias during an interview for a chief of police position when his ties to Black communities and distance from street police culture norms was explicitly discussed:

> In fact the first question is 'But you're black, you're going to be doing all these black things if you're the chief', and I laughed, because I'm relaxed, I said 'What do you mean "black things"', and he said 'Well, you know, going around the country, being black' and he was clumsy in the way that he said it, because these are ordinary people, so they weren't necessarily articulate. And so I laughed and rather than

being offended I laughed, and that was probably the best thing to do. (Anonymized Interview Subject)

Finally, officers of colour may be disinclined from applying for promotion because they do not want to be disconnected from engaging the communities they serve by rising into management ranks away from more day-to-day community relations. Cashmore's 2002 survey of 100 UK ethnic minority officers across three English police forces, for example, found that a number of interviewees would not apply for promotion because they did not want to become alienated from the communities they serve. This finding suggests further evidence to support the representative bureaucracy thesis introduced in Chapter 1 and discussed in more detail in Chapter 8, where it is argued that officers from traditionally marginalized backgrounds may feel connected to the communities they police, sometimes in more significant ways than officers from majority groups.

Internal discipline

Another way that street police culture normalization of racialized differences occurs in both explicit and implicit ways is in relation to internal discipline of officers of colour in both the UK and US. Indeed, studies over many decades in both jurisdictions show clear differences in experiences of officers of colour compared to their White colleagues in rates of internal discipline (Bland et al, 1999; Rojek and Decker, 2009; Hassell and Brandl, 2009; Bury et al, 2018). Studies since the 1970s in both the UK and US have been consistent in showing frequent disproportionality in the rates that officers of colour are subjected to internal discipline compared to their White colleagues (Bland et al, 1999; Hickman et al, 2000; Muir, 2001, Morris, 2004; Commission for Racial Equality, 2005; Fyfe and Kane, 2006; Rojek and Decker, 2009; Smith et al, 2015; NPCC, 2019).

One of the particularly influential factors on internal discipline in UK and US police departments is the broad discretion afforded to supervisors with regard to disciplining officers under their supervision. Indeed, police supervisors can choose to discipline officers in informal ways, such as speaking with an officer and requesting they refrain from the behaviour, or in more formal ways, such as initiating or approving an internal investigation or disciplinary proceeding (Hickman et al, 2000; Barton, 2003). Studies in both the UK and US repeatedly show that officers of colour are more often subjected to formal disciplinary proceedings compared to their White colleagues.

In US studies, Black officers in particular have often been subject to higher rates of internal discipline compared to their White colleagues (Hickman et al, 2000; Fyfe and Kane, 2006). For example, Hickman et al's

2000 analysis of all Philadelphia Police Department formal discipline data totalling 3,690 cases from 1991 to 1998 found Black officers were charged for the first time with violations of the disciplinary code at a higher rate (52 per cent) compared to White officers (40 per cent). Similarly, Bolton's 2003 study of Black officers in an American police department found they perceived they were disproportionately disciplined for behaviours that their White colleagues were not. Moreover, a study by Rojek and Decker (2009) examined 1,706 misconduct complaints against officers in a large Midwestern American police department composed of 37 per cent minority officers. Significantly, they found officers of colour accounted for 58 per cent of internal complaints raised from within the department, compared to 42 per cent for White officers.

In the UK there are far fewer large-scale studies of racial and ethnic differences of police internal discipline, but it has nonetheless been highlighted as an area of significant ethnic minority disproportionality (Muir, 2001; Morris, 2004; Commission for Racial Equality, 2005; Smith et al, 2015; NPCC, 2019). For example, the Morris Inquiry (Morris, 2004) into professionalism in the London Met Police found significant disproportionality in the rates at which officers of colour were subjected to formal internal discipline and investigations, compared to White officers. The report expressed serious concerns about the way officers of colour were managed, finding that some supervisors treated their behaviour differently because of race, and applied different standards to their conduct compared to White officers. Later, a House of Commons Home Affairs Select Committee (2016) report examining police diversity similarly chastised the police services of England and Wales for, among other things, disciplining BAME officers at higher rates than White officers.

Similarly, Smith et al's 2015 study of officers in the Greater Manchester Police also found significant disproportionality in internal discipline proceedings for officers of colour. They found that in the 2000s after the Macpherson Report, officers of colour were encouraged to report discrimination, but they often faced great scrutiny as a result of making complaints, including being subjected to internal disciplinary proceedings. Among officers of colour in the study, there was a sense that internal discipline proceedings were used to 'keep [officers of colour] in their place' (Smith et al, 2015: 568). The study also found the alleged misbehaviour of officers of colour was disproportionately referred for formal investigation compared to White officers whose similar conduct was often handled informally by supervisors. These findings were confirmed by research by the National Police Chiefs' Counsel (NPCC, 2019). More recently, Casey's report on the London Met Police (2023) found systemic bias in the internal misconduct system, with Black officers 81 per cent more likely to be in the system compared to their White colleagues.

The disproportionality findings of the UK studies on internal discipline proceedings echo the experiences of Interview Subject 7, a leader of colour involved in his own internal disciplinary matter, which saw him referred for a formal internal disciplinary investigation while his White colleague's identical behaviour was dealt with informally by his supervisor. Interview Subject 7 suggested that part of the problem, in his experience, was that his White supervisors might know White officers better given their socialization outside of work in pubs or playing sports, and their sense of shared interests. By contrast, Interview Subject 7 and many other officers of colour did not necessarily socialize with their White supervisors, and perhaps had customs or practices unfamiliar to, or misinterpreted by, White supervisors as showing a lack of shared interests or customs. Interview Subject 7's observations are consistent with the body of psychology research showing managers exhibit in-group member favouritism with those perceived to share similar interests, values and experiences, who are often given more flexibility or benefit of the doubt compared to out-group members in workplace settings (Rivera, 2012).

Perhaps because of the long history of documented racial disparities in UK and US police internal discipline proceedings, the processes for handling such internal departmental violations are often viewed as discriminatory by officers of colour. In the US, for example, the Pew Research study of over 7,000 officers across American departments found 62 per cent of Latino officers and 58 per cent of Black officers believed the disciplinary process in their department was unfair, compared to 49 per cent of Whites (Pew Research Center, 2017: 41). This meshes with other US studies, which have found Latino officers trust the internal disciplinary process less and believe it is more discriminatory compared to their White counterparts (DeAngelis and Kupchic, 2007). Overall, the research shows racial differences in views about the integrity of disciplinary processes and confidence in the processes.

The impacts of feeling disproportionately subjected to internal disciplinary procedures they view as discriminatory take a devastating toll on many officers of colour. Experiences of unequal internal discipline procedures can make officers of colour feel angry, hurt, isolated, distrusting, vulnerable and subject to profound injustice compared to their White peers (Smith et al, 2015). Studies have also documented retaliation against officers of colour who challenge the fairness of internal discipline procedures, including being transferred or terminated (Fyfe and Kane, 2006; Smith et al, 2015). Studies suggest these experiences can make BAME officers lose confidence not only in the internal discipline processes but in their police departments more broadly.

Indeed, disproportionate discipline is a driver of voluntary attrition among non-White officers in both the UK and US. For example, UK data show

Table 4.5: Rate of voluntary resignation (as percentage of all departures)

Voluntary resignations	BAME officers	White officers
2015–16	19%	15%
2016–17	22%	16%
2018–19	26%	17%
2020–21	27%	15%

Source: Home Office, 2016, 2017, 2019, 2021

that officers of colour have consistently voluntarily resigned from England and Wales policing at much higher rates compared to their White colleagues as reflected in Table 4.5, with studies indicating internal discipline is a contributing factor.

These findings are supported by the data obtained in the original interviews conducted for this book. As discussed earlier, the experience of Interview Subject 7 being subjected to the discriminatory internal discipline proceeding caused him to voluntarily resign from his police department. Interview Subject 1 also reflected on racial differences in voluntary resignations, observing that a number of BAME colleagues had voluntarily resigned during his career because they were exhausted at being treated differentially from White colleagues on internal discipline and other matters, and his own ability to cope amid being differentially treated:

> A lot of my [BAME] colleagues left the service, at sort of mid-ranking levels. ... BAME colleagues left with having nervous breakdowns. So the point being, that the coping mechanisms were things I didn't realize I had, but either way, yeah, they were essential really for me to get to where I did.

Terminations

The depths of the embedded racialization in street police cultures in the UK and US are a helpful theoretical lens through which to understand and analyse differences in the terms and conditions of employment and lived experiences of officers of colour in both jurisdictions compared to their White counterparts. Another important illustration of these police culture shaped differences relates to the rates at which officers of colour are terminated compared to their White colleagues in both the UK and US.

Indeed, studies over several decades have repeatedly shown that non-White officers in both the UK and US are terminated at higher rates than their White colleagues (Doerner, 1995; Fyfe and Kane, 2006; Home Office, 2022). For example, Fyfe and Kane's 2006 examination of all terminations

Table 4.6: Rate of England and Wales officer terminations by race, 2015–21 (as percentage of all departures)

Terminations	All terminations	BAME officers	White officers
2015–16	245	3%	2%
2016–17		4%	2%
2018–19		3%	1%
2020–21		3%	1%

Source: Home Office, 2016, 2017, 2019, 2021

of NYPD officers between 1975 and 1996 (n=1543) found that rates of termination were higher for non-White officers on probation compared to their White colleagues. Significantly, Fyfe and Kane's study found non-White officers were fired at a higher rate than their White colleagues for violating the department's administrative rules, which is consistent with the research previously discussed detailing the disparities in non-White officers being subjected to disciplinary proceedings, and resultant negative outcomes. Other US studies are consistent with Fyfe and Kane's research. Doerner's 1995 study of the Tallahassee Police Department, for example, similarly found Black officers were terminated at a much higher rate than their White colleagues, with 50 per cent of all Black leavers being involuntary terminated on field training, compared to only 17 per cent of their White colleagues.

In the UK there remains a lack of significant empirical evidence analysing racial and ethnic differences in terminations. However, limited government data illustrate consistent disproportionality for officers of colour in terms of rates of terminations as part of overall departure figures, compared to their White officers, as illustrated in Table 4.6.

Despite the relatively limited data, it is important to highlight the ways disproportionate rates of termination can weigh heavily on the minds of officers of colour in UK and US police institutions, and potentially impact their choices on the job.

Racial profiling practices

As discussed above, officers of colour face tremendous pressures to adopt street police culture norms, which proves extremely complicated for them given the aspects which stereotype people of colour and endorse racial profiling.

Across wider society, research is clear that in the UK, US and elsewhere, people of colour, and Black people in particular, have long been stereotyped as criminals (Eberhardt, 2004; Welch, 2007). These negative stereotypes have undoubtedly impacted UK and US policing practices in communities of colour (Alex, 1969; Hall et al, 1978, Holdaway, 1997a; Macpherson, 1999; Alexander, 2010; Paul and Birzer, 2017; Lammy, 2017). Numerous studies have seen these stereotypes applied by White officers to communities of colour and officers of colour alike. In the US, Alex's (1969) early study of Black officers in the NYPD found White officers negatively stereotyped them along with all Black people, although some regarded Black officers as exceptions to generally negative anti-Black stereotypes. Similarly in the UK, the London Met's Black Police Association submission to the Macpherson inquiry and research reporting experiences of officers of colour found that many believed White officers negatively stereotyped Black and Asian people generally, including Black and Asian officers (Holdaway, 1997a; Macpherson, 1999).

Notions that White officers stereotype communities of colour, including fellow officers, have persisted in subsequent research. For example, Bolton and Feagin's 2004 study of 50 African American officers across 16 Southern US departments found that most believed White officers stereotyped Black people. Wilson and Wilson's 2014 survey of 62 African American officers across nine small US police departments found 84 per cent believed their department engaged in racial profiling. Wilson et al's subsequent survey of 102 Black officers (2015) found 91.2 per cent believed their department engaged in racial profiling. A number of other studies in both the UK and US reflect concerns by officers of colour that their White colleagues not only hold negative stereotypes of Black, Brown, Asian and other ethnic minority people, but also that those beliefs shape how colleagues police the streets (Pogrebin et al, 2000; Cashmore, 2001; Barlow and Barlow, 2002; Bolton, 2003; LeCount, 2017).

The influence of stereotyping street police culture, White colleagues who profile communities of colour, directives from supervisors, and the need to fit in places tremendous pressure on officers of colour to similarly racially profile people of colour, even from their own communities. For example, Barlow and Barlow's 2002 study of African American officers in the Milwaukee Police Department found that 10 per cent admitted to engaging in racial profiling. Wilkins and Williams' interviews with officers of colour, in 2008, showed some felt that in adopting street police culture they became socialized in ways which made it easier to racially profile communities of colour, as one African American officer explained: 'Sometimes you have to do some degree of it [profiling] because that's one of the instincts that we have and that we pick up over the years if you stay in it [police profession] long enough. Profiling will come to you to a certain degree like anybody else' (Wilkins and Williams, 2008: 657).

These findings were replicated in the UK. Cashmore's 2001 study of ethnic minority officers, for example, similarly showed officers of colour acknowledging that they adopted street police culture norms and engaged in racial profiling of people of colour. One Asian officer in Cashmore's study reflected on the pressure he faced from White colleagues to racially profile ethnic minorities: 'If I'm being honest with myself, I've done it [racial profiling]. It's hard to understand the pressure you're under. If you're in a particular situation and things are slow, then you almost subconsciously find yourself targeting Blacks' (Cashmore, 2001: 652).

The reasons officers of colour engage in racial profiling are complex. The same concerns which motivate some ethnic minority officers to embrace street police culture hold true in decisions to racially profile communities of colour. Research from the UK and US suggests some officers of colour may feel under pressure to follow their White colleagues in racial profiling to gain acceptance (Cashmore, 2001; Bolton, 2003). Others may feel compelled to adopt racially disproportionate policing to avoid isolation from White colleagues (Dowler, 2005; Jones and Williams, 2015). Some may follow their supervisors' directives to racially profile ethnic minorities in particular neighbourhoods (Long, 2013). And others may feel compelled to hit performance targets such as arrest or stop and search quotas in disproportionately ethnic minority neighbourhoods (*Raymond et al v. The City of New York et al*, 2017).

A small amount of research points to ethnic minority officers' efforts to resist pressure to racially profile ethnic minorities. LeCount's 2017 study, drawn from US General Social Survey data from 1972 to 2014, looked at attitudes of White and Black police officers and citizens. This research found that many African American police officers did not embrace negative racial stereotypes of Black people in the same ways as their White colleagues, suggesting resistance to racialized police culture norms. But this is difficult to accomplish, and more research about the struggles and coping mechanisms for officers of colour in resisting pressure to racially profile is required.

Racially profiled on and off duty

Regardless of the personal struggles officers of colour may endure in the pressures to assimilate into street police culture and conduct racial profiling in minority communities, research suggests a number of officers of colour are racially profiled by other officers while off duty or out of uniform while working in plain clothes. This phenomenon has been documented in a few studies and reports, and some notable cases in the media, and speaks to the engrained nature of biases and stereotypes in street police culture in the UK and US.

Racial profiling of officers of colour by fellow officers has been documented for decades. Alex's 1969 study of Black NYPD officers showed they were questioned, harassed, assaulted and disbelieved by White officers when they were on assignments out of uniform. In subsequent decades, studies indicate the problem persists, particularly for Black police officers, who are often subjected to the same well-documented stereotypes of Black criminality discussed earlier when out of uniform (Eberhardt et al, 2004; Paul and Birzer, 2017). For example, Barlow and Barlow's 2002 survey of African American officers in the Milwaukee Police Department found that 69 per cent had been racially profiled at some point in their lives, many including since becoming officers. A survey by Colin (2014) of some African American NYPD officers, like Alex's study 45 years before, found 24 of 25 had been racially profiled by other officers while off duty.

The media is also replete with examples of officers of colour being profiled off duty or on duty in plain clothes. For example, in the UK, London Met Police Inspector Charles Ehikioya sued his own department when he was stopped by White officers while driving home from work. During the traffic stop, body camera footage showed fellow London Met Police officers accusing Ehikioya, who was not in uniform, of driving unusually and 'look[ing] like he had gone through a red light' (Croxford, 2020). When Ehikioya questioned their behaviour, his colleagues accused him of being 'obstructive' (Croxford, 2020). While the incident did not result in arrest, Ehikioya believed the officers had racially profiled him because he was Black.

The problem also occurs with alarming frequency in the US, amplified with the police use of firearms. For example, in 1995, Black Boston Police Department officer Michael Cox was working on duty in plain clothes when he was severely beaten by fellow officers who mistook him for a gang member (Lehr, 2009). In 2000, off-duty Black Providence, Rhode Island officer Cornel Young Jr was killed by two White colleagues while trying to break up a fight in a parking lot (Kelley, 2000). In 2009, off-duty Black NYPD officer Omar Edwards was shot and killed by White colleague Andrew Dunton while Edwards was chasing a burglar in street clothes (Kleinfeld, 2009). In 2016, African American Prince George's County, Maryland detective Jacai Colson responded in plain clothes to an incident and disabled an active shooter, but moments later was shot and killed by White fellow officer Taylor Krauss, who mistook Colson for the shooter (Wilkins, 2022). In 2019, African American Saint Louis Metropolitan Police Department officer Milton Green sued his department after he attempted to subdue a suspect fleeing a car crash while off duty. When Green drew his weapon, displayed his badge, and ordered the suspect to stop, he was shot by a White officer pursuing the suspect (*Green v. City of Saint Louis*, 2020). In each instance, the White on-duty officers were not prosecuted.

The problem of officers of colour being killed by fellow officers has caused some, but not enough, alarm in UK and US policing. One effort to understand the issue was undertaken in 2010 by the New York State Task Force on Police-on-Police Shootings. It found that while White officers are killed by other officers in the line of duty, most officers of colour are killed by fellow officers while they are off duty or on duty in plain clothes (NYS, 2010). The Task Force concluded that race was a factor which prevented White on-duty officers from recognizing officers of colour when out of uniform, and contributed to the mistaken identification of the officer of colour as a criminal. Yet despite the increased attention this issue has received in recent years, the problem persists, and is an added burden borne by officers of colour in both the UK and US.

'Traitors' and negative community reception

As documented throughout this chapter, the obstacles faced by officers of colour in UK and US police departments are significant. While on the one hand they are accused of disloyalty by fellow officers if they do not sufficiently assimilate into street police culture as discussed earlier, they are not necessarily embraced by their communities of origin either. In both the UK and US, studies and first-hand accounts show that officers of colour are viewed by some in their communities of origin as 'traitors' for joining the police (Alex, 1969; HMIC, 2001; Dodge and Pogrebin, 2001; Cashmore, 2002). For example, Alex's 1969 ethnography of Black officers in the NYPD found they often forfeited their community credibility as they were seen as supporting police oppression of Black people. Decades later, studies have shown these views persist. For example, Dodge and Pogrebin's 2001 US study found that Black officers were often viewed as part of the oppressive police organization, and that working for the police meant 'selling out' Black communities.

Views that officers of colour operate against the interests of communities of colour are also common in the UK. Cashmore's 2002 interviews with 100 ethnic minority officers across three English police forces found that many of their families had urged them not to join the police, or that their friends shunned them after they joined. Other accounts of experiences of BAME officers in the UK similarly show views that BAME police are 'traitors' to their communities for working for police services which marginalize and oppress communities of colour (HMIC, 2001; Fuller, 2019; Logan, 2020).

Community relations

While there are some negative community perceptions as discussed earlier, relations between officers of colour and communities of colour are multi-layered and complicated. No singular analysis can encompass all of the nuances of police–community relations given the myriad factors involved. Relations can vary by officer, neighbourhood, district, department, city, state and country. Yet it is valuable to briefly highlight a few of the major themes to better understand some of the issues involved.

In terms of approaches to the policing role, a number of studies have found non-White officers, particularly Black and Latino officers, view community engagement policing approaches more favourably than their White counterparts (Skogan and Hartnett, 1997; Weisburd et al, 2000; Paoline et al, 2015; Pew Research Center, 2017; Gau and Paoline, 2017). Some of these studies may reflect officers of colour embracing the guardian policing approaches discussed in Chapter 2, however more research is needed to better understand these dynamics. Research conducted for this book also reflected that all five of the police leaders of colour interviewed (Interview Subjects 1, 5, 6, 7 and 8) embraced guardianship policing approaches and spoke of the importance of community engagement as part of their policing philosophies – dynamics explored further in Chapter 8.

While the core tenets of street police culture discussed in Chapter 2 emphasize distance and alienation from communities, studies suggest there may be important racial differences between officers of colour and their White counterparts in terms of the value they place on positive community relations. In the US, a number of studies over the decades have illustrated these differences. For example, Teahan's 1975 study found White officers did not feel police–community relations were worthy of prioritizing, unlike their Black colleagues, who placed significant value on police–community relations. More recent US studies reflect similar views. For example, the 2017 Pew national survey of over 7,000 officers across many different departments found that while 69 per cent of White officers believed it was very important to understand the communities they police, 78 per cent of Latino officers and 84 per cent of African American officers believed the same (Pew Research Center, 2017: 50). Other US studies have found Black and Latino officers to be significantly less cynical and more inclined toward partnerships with communities than their White counterparts (Lasley et al, 2011; Gau and Paoline, 2017).

Not only are there differences in the ways many White and non-White officers prioritize or value community relations, but studies also reflect differing perceptions of the state of relations with White and non-White communities. Many studies reflect police perceptions that relations with White communities are generally positive. In the US, 91 per cent of all 7,000+ officers polled in the Pew study agreed that police relations with White communities are generally good or excellent. By contrast, 60 per cent of White officers, 60 per cent of Latino officers, and 68 per cent of Black officers in the study saw relations with Black communities as fair or poor (Pew Research Center, 2017: 53). Regarding Latino communities, assessments were more positive for White and Latino officers, with 76 per cent and 71 per cent, respectively, believing relations between police and

Latinos are excellent or good (Pew Research Center, 2017: 53). Interestingly, Black officers did not share these positive views, with only 46 per cent of Black officers believing relations between police and Latinos are excellent or good (Pew, 2017: 53). These findings were similar for Asian communities. While 91 per cent of White officers and 88 per cent of Latino officers said relations with Asians in the community are good or excellent, only 75 per cent of Black officers agreed (Pew Research Center, 2017: 17).

Indeed, many ethnic minority officers may feel they can relate well to ethnic minority communities. Bolton and Feagin's 2004 study of 50 African American officers across 16 Southern US departments, for example, found that many Black officers felt they could relate to the Black communities they policed, with all of them either being raised in or currently living in Black communities. White officers in the study, by contrast, often lacked understanding and knowledge of Black communities and stereotyped them, which led to problems with those communities.

Ethnic minority officers can view their roles as liaisons with their communities of origin. Some Black officers in the US, for example, take on responsibility for the well-being of Black neighbourhoods they police (Bolton and Feagin, 2004; Sun and Payne, 2004; Lasley et al, 2011). Some Black British officers have expressed similar views about serving as role models and liaisons for Black British communities. Several studies have found many Latino American officers feel strong ties to the Latino communities they police, and feel a responsibility to these communities (Irlbeck, 2008; Lasley et al, 2011). Certain ethnic minority officers may view themselves as having a duty to improve relations and legitimacy between police and ethnic minority communities.

Irlbeck's 2008 study of Latino officers considered their desire to engage with and aid Latino communities. In her research involving 34 Latino officers in Omaha, comprised of one Puerto Rican, one Spanish and 32 Mexican heritage officers, Irlbeck tested ideas about whether Latino officers identified as Latino and felt connected to Latino communities, prerequisites for representative bureaucracy. Irlbeck (2008) posited that officers who identified as Latino and felt connected to Latino communities would police in ways more sensitive to the needs of those communities. In her study, 74 per cent identified strongly as Latino, while 21 per cent identified as Latino and White simultaneously, and 6 per cent identified as White. Irlbeck (2008) found that 95 per cent of officers who grew up in Latino communities strongly identified as Latino. Irlbeck (2008) also found that 88 per cent of Latino officers had two Latino parents. Irlbeck concluded that because Latino officers are not a monolith, and in order to serve the needs of Latino communities, officers who desire to engage those communities should be assigned. Indeed, it should not be assumed that all Latino officers want to engage Latino communities, aid them or identify with them. Irlbeck (2008) sheds light on why a number of studies of Latino officers show closer results to White officers than Black officers.

These positive relations between many non-White communities and the non-White officers who patrol them leads to research showing non-White officers feeling particularly valued in those communities. For example, Wilson and Wilson's 2014 study of 62 African American officers across nine small police departments found 90 per cent felt valued by ethnic minority communities in particular. By contrast, ethnic minority officers do not necessarily feel as valued in White communities. In Wilson and Wilson's study, for example, 47 per cent of the African American officers believed they lacked support from White community members.

Further, Boyd's 2010 study of 609 patrol officers from the Indianapolis, Indiana and St Petersburg, Florida Police Departments found 54 per cent of White officers and 77 per cent of Black officers believed improving neighbourhood conditions was an important goal of policing. Boyd (2010) and others argue that many African American officers see themselves as having more responsibility for helping solve problems in policed American communities than their White colleagues. In particular, Boyd observed that African American officers may feel better equipped to assess and address problems and avoid obstacles to solving problems particularly in African American neighbourhoods, given their shared racial or ethnic background with community members.

Importance of police chiefs of colour

In both the UK and US, there have historically been very small numbers of police chiefs of colour. Indeed, non-White police chiefs have always been and continue to be a vast minority of all police chiefs in both jurisdictions. That said, the numbers of police chiefs of colour, particularly in the US, are growing. In both countries, the figures on non-White police leaders below the rank of police chief continue to increase, particularly in larger urban police departments in cities with populations over 500,000, which generally have higher compositions of ethnic minority officers, and thus larger potential pools of police chiefs. Yet, as discussed earlier, people of colour nonetheless remain under-represented at the upper echelons of police organizations and particularly at police chief level in both the UK and US compared to their representation at lower ranks of policing, and overall population demographics in larger urban areas. This section considers potential reasons for disproportionality and why having police chiefs of colour, in particular, is so important, a theme explored further in Chapter 9.

In the UK there has only been one non-White chief constable, Michael Fuller QPM, who served as chief constable of the Kent Police from 2004 to 2010 (Fuller, 2019). Fuller's book details the challenges of being the first and only police chief of colour in England and Wales, including experiences of institutional discrimination, explicit and implicit bias from fellow officers including several racist incidents, microaggressions, as well as hostility from the Black community for working in the police, some of whom labelled him a 'traitor' (Fuller, 2019). As already discussed, government data show that there have been no police chiefs of colour in the UK since Fuller (Home Office, 2023a).

In the US, there have been much higher numbers of non-White police chiefs compared to the UK. Nationwide, the Bureau of Justice Statistics (BJS, 2022) show 87 per cent of police chiefs are White, 6 per cent are Black, 4 per cent Latino, and 4 per cent Other (including Asian American, Native American, or Mixed Race). Notable examples of non-White police chiefs in recent years in large urban departments, particularly in cities with populations over 500,000, include New York City, Los Angeles, Philadelphia, Chicago, San Francisco, Oakland, Dallas, Atlanta and Columbus, among others. But despite the achievements of some officers of colour in becoming police chiefs of some of America's largest cities, their small numbers represent just a tiny fraction of all US police chiefs currently serving across 18,000 US police departments. Given the very limited numbers of US police chiefs of colour when compared to the entire body of US policing, it is overly optimistic to suggest that the few American police chiefs of colour represent a sea change. Yet their service has been and continues to be significant, particularly as the US visibly struggles with police legitimacy and efforts to reform policing and improve relations with ethnic minority communities; struggles the UK has not yet begun to seriously address.

What then are the impacts of police chiefs of colour? This is an important original contribution of this volume. From the interviews conducted for this book, the leaders of colour, in particular, were very switched on to the importance of being leaders of colour in traditionally White UK and US policing organizations. One such discussion comes from Interview Subject 1:

Q: [D]o you think that your background, as someone from a diverse background. Are you switched on to inclusiveness and belonging? Are you particularly switched on to those kinds of things, having experienced it yourself?

R1:   I would like to say yes … but I think in anything it's because of the positions I held and people drawing things to my attention or saying things like 'We don't feel we belong' that I became switched on to those issues, but I can't pretend that I was always alive to them. Other than when they said the things that they did, I said yeah … I've spent all my career not feeling that I belong and it was … new evidence as to why, what alienated you from an organization, why didn't I feel- And I'm asking myself that question, and then the point being if I could address those issues and I also thought well yes, when I've been a member of a team where people have included you, they've respected your views, you feel you can have influence over the direction of the organization, that people are interested in listening to your views and generally listening and responding to what you've said, how differently I felt to most of the organizations where I haven't been able to have that degree of influence or been respected for my views.

Leaders set the tone for what is and is not acceptable behaviour. Interview Subject 1 explained that, under his leadership, he made clear that he would not tolerate a culture of racist or misogynistic bullying of officers of colour and female officers. Interview Subject 1 tried to create an environment that was welcoming to a variety of officers from traditionally marginalized backgrounds, and the department was recognized with several diversity and inclusion awards. One of the ways Interview Subject 1 tried to instil this supportive culture was increasing hiring and retention of a more diverse police workforce beyond its traditional straight White male composition.

From the interviews conducted with three current/former police chiefs of colour and two senior police leaders of colour, as discussed throughout this volume, the original empirical data gathered here indicate that police leaders of colour can make significant differences in priority-setting, policy making, accountability and community relations, particularly vis-à-vis communities of colour and other traditionally marginalized groups (Interview Subjects 1, 5, 6, 7 and 8). Police leaders interviewed for this book repeatedly emphasized the importance of their own personal visibility in their departments and their communities as leaders of colour.

But these findings are not without controversy. There remains debate about the impacts of police leaders on policing generally in terms of the disconnect between police leadership and policing practices happening on the ground. As discussed in Chapters 1 and 2, there are a number of police, community leaders and academics who believe that all police are only blue, meaning they are subsumed by police culture regardless of their lived experiences of being people of colour. This volume argues such attitudes are a vast oversimplification that lacks requisite nuance, and grounding in a sufficiently wide breadth of theoretical and empirical literature.

The extremely tiny numbers of UK police chiefs of colour, and slightly larger but still very small numbers of US police chiefs of colour, mean understanding the impacts of non-White chiefs is fairly limited, and has not been subject to significant academic study. However, some American studies have shown ethnic minority leaders/chiefs can positively impact recruitment of diverse officers. Zhao (1998), for example, examined police leadership across US police departments, and found that the presence of an African American police chief significantly improved hiring of ethnic minorities. Zhao et al (2005) have also found that African American and Latino chiefs translate, respectively, to greater African American and Latino officer recruitment in their police departments.

While police chiefs of colour can change recruiting practices, studies do not speak as clearly to the other sorts of impacts they might have on departments. One significant question that arose as part of this research is whether having police chiefs of colour could change policies, practices and interactions between police and communities of colour. Sociological theory offers some guidance on this possibility, and asserts that leaders of colour may impact experiences for communities of colour under certain conditions, known as the representative bureaucracy theory (Mosher, 1982), a concept explored further in Chapter 8 in its application to policing. But generally speaking, representative bureaucracy requires a diverse leader to satisfy three conditions to make their policies and practices positively impact served communities: (1) adoption of organizational culture; (2) opportunities for discretion; and (3) value congruence between individual bureaucrats and their subordinates or communities they serve (Johnston and Houston, 2018; Hong, 2016).

Other studies suggest that larger numbers of diverse police leaders can improve the experiences of ethnic minorities in police departments and change departmental culture. Bolton's 2003 study of ethnic minority officers in an American police department found they believed the challenging atmosphere could be improved with more ethnic minority police leaders in the department, who again might, under the right representative bureaucracy circumstances, be inclined to take an interest in their well-being and in department disproportionality discussed earlier. This meshes with interviews conducted for this book. Interview Subject 6, for example, believed he was not empowered to make changes in departmental culture, atmosphere or priority setting until he became a district commander in a large urban US police department, where he deliberately changed practices to build stronger relations with communities of colour. He recounted that after one police use of force incident in a low-income community of colour in his district, he was intent on addressing community concerns, de-escalating the situation and retaining good community relations:

> If that happens today a town is going to burn down but here it didn't because … when I arrived there we practised this philosophy, as difficult as it is because the entire department wasn't practising it, but we were. We had built such solid relationships … that when the pastors came out [after the incident] who I'd met with all the time, and we had

thousands of people starting to gather by the way, the potential was there for an explosion but it didn't happen because for the first time what I did was bring the pastors into the crime scene and everyone was watching. It's being done now but [wasn't] years ago because I knew that if they saw me talking to them, that when I sent them back out they knew they were getting the right information so there's no confusion here. So I brought [pastors] them in. I had a fight with the homicide supervisor who didn't think I should have but it was my district and they [homicide] were there just visiting, that's what I used to say, and then it de-escalated because people were not going to allow anything to happen here because of the mutual respect that we had for each other.

While, interestingly, Interview Subject 6 did not attribute his perspective and practices in that moment to being a person of colour, subsequent parts of the interview suggested that his approach was shaped by growing up Latino in the US and experiencing discrimination himself.

But other studies show more scepticism about the ability of ethnic minority leaders to shift the atmosphere in police departments, particularly given the strong influence of street police culture, as discussed in Chapter 2. For example, Cashmore's 2002 study of ethnic minority officers in a UK police service found that there were so few police leaders of colour, and so much assimilation was required of them to become leaders, that they might not be able to make big differences in police departments. Thus, more research in the UK and US is required to probe more deeply into the impacts of leaders of colour, in particular, in departments in terms of setting institutional policies and practices which might change the experiences in relation to both lower level police officers of colour and relations with communities of colour.

Conclusion

While police are frequently stereotyped as a monolith with identical beliefs and approaches to policing, this chapter illustrated that, for officers of colour, their experiences on the job are much more complicated. This chapter analysed how street police culture shaped the lived experiences, and terms and conditions of employment for officers of colour in UK and US policing, highlighting the ways these can differ significantly from their White colleagues. It illustrated the multitude of ways street police culture makes it explicitly or implicitly acceptable for officers of colour to be subjected to different experiences on the job – from racial and ethnic jokes, microaggressions and stereotyping from colleagues and supervisors. It has illustrated the less favourable terms and conditions of employment for some officers of colour, including less favourable assignments, preclusion from elite and specialized police units, lower representation in supervisory and leadership ranks, higher rates of internal discipline, voluntary resignations and terminations compared to their White colleagues in both the UK and US. The chapter considered the ways street police culture's inherent racism pressured officers of colour to adopt biased street police culture norms, potentially internalizing some of these stereotypes and negative beliefs about their communities of origin, or risk alienation from colleagues if they refused to do so. It considered the mechanisms for support available to officers of colour through other colleagues of colour, White allies, supervisors and ethnic minority police associations. The chapter analysed the ways officers of colour might choose to take an active interest in the communities they serve, and particularly in their communities of origin and other oppressed groups, acting in representative bureaucratic ways and policing differently from their White colleagues. But the chapter also considered the heavy toll street police culture places on officers of colour in particular, and how this contributes to lower levels of job satisfaction and higher rates of attrition from the job in both the UK and US. Finally, the chapter concluded by considering the ways police leaders of colour can play important roles in setting institutional priorities, policies and practices, and being visible representations of diversity, which may contribute to improving the conditions of employment for officers of colour and relations with communities of colour.

5

Women in policing

Chapter 5 examines the ways hegemonically masculine street police culture shapes the experiences of female officers in the UK and US police services. It evaluates the ways these street police culture norms developed from traditional straight, White, male perspectives of masculinity, gender, sexuality, aggression, escalation, violence and danger, among other attributes. It considers how street police culture creates and reinforces certain types of gender frameworks, giving rise to particular stereotypes, expectations and lived experiences for both female and male officers in the policing role. Rather than being beneficial to policing, this chapter argues these heavily gendered perspectives create challenges for both female and male officers, make the experiences of female officers in both the UK and US more difficult, and policing less efficient. The chapter explores the ways female officers may choose to adopt gendered street police culture norms, and operate in the role in ways consistent with those expectations. By contrast, it also examines ways female officers may opt to resist gendered police culture norms by shunning them or engaging in active bureaucratic representation, a theme explored in more depth in Chapter 8. The analysis in this chapter triangulates multiple sources of data including original interviews with police chiefs/leaders, official government statistics, and data from multiple UK and US empirical studies on women in policing to derive original insights and analysis.

History of women officers in the UK

In the UK there is a long history of women's involvement in policing roles. The plight of women and their difficulties with the criminal justice system led the Women's Freedom League (WFL), suffragettes and other women's organizations to campaign for female officers to take over the work of policemen who were fighting in the First World War (Heidensohn, 1992). Beginning in 1914, there were over 5,000 Women Police Volunteers (WPV) backed by the WFL and other suffragettes working in cities across England to protect refugees and girls (Jones, 1986). The WPV promoted women's rights, sought to prove its reliability in cities and secure permanent paid police positions for themselves (Lock, 1979; Jones, 1986; Woodeson, 1993). The WPV members wore uniforms and were trained in giving evidence, rendering first aid, and even ju-jitsu (Lock, 1979).

Parallel to the WPV, also beginning in 1914, the National Union of Women Workers (later known as the National Council for Women) organized voluntary, part-time women's patrols, known as Voluntary Women Patrols (VWP), around military encampments to discourage loitering and amoral behaviour (Woodeson, 1993; Brown, 1998). The VWP were largely upper and middle-class women who were not seeking full-time employment (Lock, 1979). The VWP did not wear uniforms but had armbands and identity cards, and were more amateurish compared to the WPV (Heidensohn, 1992). The VWP were concerned with morality and sought to restrain the problematic behaviours of working-class women and girls in certain neighbourhoods (Lock, 1979; Woodeson, 1993).

In 1915, most of the members of the WPV started a new organization – the Women's Police Service (WPS), which flourished in towns and cities across England (Woodeson, 1993). WPS volunteers wore uniforms, were generally from middle-class backgrounds, and were often educated (Heidensohn, 1992). The policing of the morality of women and girls during this First World War period was significant given the demand for prostitution during the war (Jones, 1986). The WPS's presence aided local police in these efforts, although WPS members lacked power to arrest. In 1915 WPS powers were expanded in some areas, and WPS member Edith Smith became the first sworn female police officer with power to arrest, and was paid while working alongside the police in Grantham, England, working on issues related to women and children, including prostitution (Heidensohn, 1992; Woodeson, 1993).

At the end of the First World War in 1918, the right to vote was extended to women who met minimum property requirements (Heidensohn, 1992). WPS members hoped they would be absorbed as paid members of local police departments, but most were not (Woodeson, 1993). In London, a 1918 police strike led to the recruitment of 100 WPS members into the London Metropolitan Police Service (London Met Police) as Metropolitan Women Police Patrols. They wore uniforms but they lacked powers to arrest, and focused their work on women and girls (Heidensohn, 1992). They were initially met with hostility both from the Police Federation quasi-union and the public (Jones, 1986). Local authorities outside London were also encouraged to incorporate women police and, by 1920, eight of 60 counties had done so, with 311 female officers in post, again without powers to arrest (Heidensohn, 1992).

By 1922, however, significant cuts to public expenditures targeted women patrols (Heidensohn, 1992). Public support for police women put pressure to keep women patrols, and eventually a small core of patrols were retained, giving women officers better conditions, including the title of constable and powers to arrest (Heidensohn, 1992). Yet shortly thereafter the Geddes Committee on National Expenditure delivered a negative opinion of policewomen, leading many forces to cut women altogether, while others like the London Met Police cut the number of women from 112 to 24 (Jones, 1986). Still the issue of employing policewomen was left to local police department discretion, with many police services including Norfolk, Rutland, Essex and the whole of Wales operating without any women into the late 1920s (Lock, 1979).

By 1928, the Representation of the People (Equal Franchise) Act provided that all persons over 21 had the right to vote, including women. Elected women MPs and lobby groups including the National Council for Women continued to pressure for better conditions for women officers. In 1930–31, the Home Office and Parliament approved better conditions of service, pay and pensions for women officers (Heidensohn, 1992). Women's duties were specified as dealing with vulnerable populations and addressing moral hazards, including responsibilities for finding missing women and children, working with the homeless, taking statements from women and children, and dealing with female prisoners (Jones, 1986). Women officers' roles would remain designated and focused on sexual and moral issues related to women and children, laying the foundation for modern policing roles which continue to find women officers disproportionately focused on roles involving morality and working with vulnerable populations (Heidensohn, 1992; Jones, 1986).

During the early 1930s, the Police Federation union opposed the hiring of policewomen, lobbied for halting their recruitment and refused to represent them (Lock, 1979). While the 1930s saw policewomen's ranks grow, their presence in policing was established as separate police departments within jurisdictions, with separate administration, rank and promotion structures (Jones, 1986). By 1939 just 45 of 183 police forces in Britain were employing women, many of whom were not sworn officers (Heidensohn, 1992). There remained significant resistance to sworn policewomen at the Home Office and local police levels, which negatively impacted recruitment and retention (Lock, 1979; Jones, 1986).

In 1939, the government created another separate policing entity for women, the Women's Auxiliary Police Corps (WAPC), whose members were paid but lacked police powers. WAPC members provided support to sworn police officers, including clerical, administrative, driving, radio, canteen and interviewing functions. Advocates for increasing the numbers of policewomen did not look favourably on the WAPC, which they believed diverted actual sworn police jobs from women (Lock, 1979).

The Second World War saw increases in the numbers of policewomen (Jones, 1986). By 1944, policewomen numbered 335 across the UK (Lock, 1979). During this period the numbers of WAPC members swelled as women were given further responsibilities for keeping moral order around military camps, numbering over 3,000 full-time members by 1944 (Jones, 1986).

The WPS remained focused on women and children's issues, and women officers trained separately from their male counterparts.

Women's wartime contributions to regular and auxiliary policing were praised by police and government officials alike, resulting in slow but steady increases in their numbers. Women's regular and auxiliary representation doubled by 1959 (Jones, 1986). Yet the vast majority of women continued serving in specialized roles focused on women and children, rather than working on the same matters as their male counterparts. Women's roles in UK policing, therefore, remained highly segregated by gender and stereotyped, trends which arguably still persist today, as discussed further below. Despite these separate roles, by 1966, 4,000 of 95,000 sworn officers were women (Jones, 1986).

By 1970, there were 3,621 female officers (Heidensohn, 1992). By 1971 there were 3,884 female officers constituting 4 per cent of the police forces in England and Wales (Jones, 1986). Although they had the same basic training as men, they remained segregated into women's police departments, with different ranks, promotions and pay, which was just nine tenths of male officer pay (Jones, 1986). Women officers generally investigated any offences perpetrated by or against women and juveniles, including abuse, neglect and missing persons (Jones, 1986). These formalized differences in the roles of female officers remained institutionalized in UK policing into the early 1970s.

As in the US, the social changes of the Civil Rights Movement and Women's Rights Movement put pressure on British officials to address the equality demands of people of colour and women. One such change was in relation to the women's policing units in England and Wales. In 1972, for example, the London Met Police disbanded women's divisions and integrated women officers into the general department duties (Heidensohn, 1992). By 1974, women officers' salaries were made equal to male officers nationally (Jones, 1986). Some police departments began integrating more female officers into general patrol duties rather than keeping them segregated in specialist roles (Jones, 1986).

Significantly, in the 1970s, the UK also passed two major pieces of equality legislation impacting women in policing. The 1975 Sex Discrimination Act banned sex discrimination and called for integration in government agencies, including the police. This resulted in the dissolution of most separate women's policing departments in England and Wales, and integration of women officers into regular police departments, where they assumed general police duties, including patrol and night shifts (Jones, 1986). A number of departments retained work focused on women and children victims and offenders as specialist work (Jones, 1986), which as discussed below continues to be where disproportionate numbers of UK women officers are assigned. The second new law, the 1975 Equal Pay

Act, required men and women to be paid the same for the same work (Heidensohn, 1992). Despite these new legal protections, researchers argue that they were not highly successful in increasing numbers of women in UK policing, with some arguing European Union equality provisions have been more impactful in shaping the composition of UK police services (Jones, 1986; Heidensohn, 1992).

Notwithstanding political pressures and legislative changes during this period, UK police departments still retained many discriminatory structures. The London Met Police, for example, was sued for using employment quotas for women officers, artificially limiting women's numbers. Many British police departments also retained minimum height criteria for prospective officers, which negatively impacted disproportionate numbers of women from even joining the police services (Heidensohn, 1992). Despite these barriers to entry for women wishing to join UK police services, research suggests that, unlike the US, the UK did not see large numbers of lawsuits aimed at compelling hiring or integration of police services for women (Heidensohn, 1992).

In 1977, women made up 7 per cent of the police forces of England and Wales (House of Commons, 2001), numbering 10,430 by 1980 (Heidensohn, 1992). It was not until the 1980s that women's representation in British police forces began to dramatically increase due to changing laws and political pressures (Martin and Jurik, 2007). Research would later reveal the extent to which women were deliberately excluded from UK policing for decades, including during the 1980s. Brown (1998), for example, observed that the London Met Police in the 1980s had an informal quota restricting the numbers of women who were recruited and hired. Later, these informal quotas were applied to restrict the numbers of women in prestigious special assignments (Brown, 1998).

By 1987, women comprised roughly 10 per cent of the police service in England and Wales (House of Commons, 2001), numbering 12,829 in 1990 or approximately 11 per cent of England and Wales police, including 3,406 in the London Met Police, Britain's largest police force (Heidensohn, 1992; Brown, 1998). By 2000, 17 per cent of the England and Wales police officers were women (House of Commons, 2001), yet there were no female Chief Constables (Martin and Jurik, 2007). By 2010 women were 28 per cent of the police forces of England and Wales (Home Office, 2010). Yet women were vastly under-represented in the supervisory ranks, with women making up 27 per cent of the constable ranks, but only 14 per cent of the senior ranks of chief inspector or above (Home Office, 2010).

In 2020, there were 40,319 female officers constituting 31 per cent of the police forces of England and Wales (Home Office, 2020; see Table 5.1). While the largest proportion of female officers was found at the constable rank (33 per cent), 30 per cent of chief constables are women, 23 per cent

Table 5.1: Female representation in England and Wales policing

Year	All males	All females
1977	93%	7%
1987	90%	10%
2000	83%	17%
2010	74%	26%
2016	71%	29%
2020	69%	31%
2023	65%	35%

Source: Home Office, 2023

of chief superintendents, 29 per cent of superintendents, 26 per cent of chief inspectors. In the lower supervisory ranks, 25 per cent of inspectors and 24 per cent of sergeants were women (Home Office, 2020).

Female officers of colour in the UK have always made up a very small proportion of all police officers. Roughly 1.4 per cent of all UK patrol officers in 2007 were women of colour, but by 2018 this had increased to 2.5 per cent (UK Police Foundation, 2018). Ethnic minority female officers served in less than 1 per cent of supervisory or leadership positions across the 43 forces of England and Wales in 2018 (UK Police Foundation, 2018). Women of colour are more heavily concentrated in diverse urban areas and under-represented in smaller, rural areas (UK Police Foundation, 2018).

History of women officers in the US

Compared to the UK, female officers have been a smaller but more consistent presence in US policing. Beginning at the turn of the 20th century, women began entering policing in the US at a time when a new American era of women's rights and police reform were under way (Martin and Jurik, 2007). The first women to join American policing were charged with protection of women and children (Martin, 1980). Among the first women police officers in the US, Lola Baldwin was hired by the Portland Police Department in 1905 to patrol areas where women were at risk of being accosted (Archbold and Schulz, 2012). Alice Wells joined the Los Angeles Police Department in 1910, and later formed the International Association of Policewomen (Martin and Jurik, 2007; Archbold and Schulz, 2012).

During this so-called progressive era, the Women's Christian Temperance Union and police reformers were instrumental in pushing for increases in women officers, under the theory that they could reduce corruption in policing (Archbold and Schulz, 2012). Throughout the 1910s, the numbers of female police officers steadily increased and, by 1918, 220 cities and towns had female officers (Martin, 1980). The numbers of women officers grew in the 1920s, although they were typically better represented in larger urban departments with populations over 400,000 (Martin, 1980). In 1922, there were 500 female officers nationwide (Heidensohn, 1992).

As women's ranks grew in US police departments during the 1920s, they faced significant resistance from male officers, including high entry standards, quotas, separate promotion lists and different assignments (Martin, 1980). Yet with the Great Depression of 1929, female officers became a casualty of hard economic times, with police hiring freezes resulting in dramatic slowing of the numbers of women joining US police departments. Indeed, by 1930 there were only 1,534 female officers across the US (Martin, 1980; Martin and Jurik, 2007).

Moreover, hiring of women was inconsistent across US states and police departments. Some large states such as New York and Massachusetts actively recruited women to serve, while others such as Connecticut did not hire their first female officers until the 1940s (Heidensohn, 1992). Women's hiring was also subject to strict quotas and hiring standards, including education and age criteria (Heidensohn, 1992). While the Second World War era saw 1,775 female officers by 1940, after the war ended many female officers were laid off (Martin, 1980). By 1950 there were 2,610 female officers, and their ranks would continue to swell significantly throughout the 1950s (Heidensohn, 1992). By 1960, the numbers of female officers in the US reached 5,617, but women still constituted less than 1 per cent of all American police officers (Martin and Jurik, 2007).

While women were a growing presence in US police departments by the 1960s, they were not given the same opportunities as their male colleagues. Like in the UK, women continued to be steered into internal and nurturing roles. Women officers were mostly assigned to non–patrol roles, including working inside the station and being assigned to juvenile justice positions (Herbert, 2001). The first American women did not go out on patrol until 1968 in Indianapolis (Heidensohn, 1992). In addition to being limited in their job duties, during the 1960s women were rarely promoted. In fact, some had to take legal action for the right to be considered for promotion, including a female officer who sued the New York Police Department (NYPD) in 1961, eventually winning the right to take the sergeant's promotion examination (Heidensohn, 1992).

At the same time, police departments continued presenting significant barriers to entry for women by setting strength and agility tests and other physical requirements which excluded many women from policing (Seklecki and Paynich, 2007). These physical agility tests persisted until a variety of lawsuits ruled they were not accurate measures of the requirements of policing in practice, which forced many departments to open the police role to women more broadly (Martin, 1980; Seklecki and Paynich, 2007). Yet, in 1971, there were so few women in regular patrol assignments that they numbered around 12 across the whole of the US (Rabe-Hemp, 2009). By 1970, women officer numbers had increased to 11,234 (Heidensohn, 1992), but the barriers to entry and retention remained significant.

Most research suggests US policing did not open up broadly for women until the political pressures of the women's liberation movement of the 1960s and 1970s compelled it to do so (Martin, 1980). The groundswell of this political movement, coupled with a series of legal victories for women's equality, required that US policing adapt to the changing times (Martin and Jurik, 2007). Specifically, new laws created legal obligations and pressure on police departments to include more women and treat them equally on the job, in terms of both pay and working conditions (Heidensohn, 1992). The Equal Pay Act of 1963, for example, mandated the same pay for men and women performing the same roles, including in policing (Archbold and Schulz, 2012). Title VII of the Civil Rights Act of 1968 was an important piece of legislation for women in policing because it barred discrimination in the workplace on the basis of gender, race, sex, colour and national origin (Seklecki and Paynich, 2007). Because Title VII requires the elimination of past, present and future discriminatory practices, and redressing consequences of discrimination at the individual level, this mandated police employers to implement measures making the profession more hospitable to women (Potts, 1983). The Crime Control Act of 1973 also prohibited discrimination against women in any law enforcement agency receiving federal government funds (Martin, 1980). And the Revenue Sharing Act of 1972 and Justice Systems Improvement Act of 1979 limited federal funding to programmes that were not discriminatory, including police departments (Heidensohn, 1992).

This host of new laws formed the bases of numerous lawsuits in the 1960s and 1970s for women to have equal access to, and equal pay in, policing (Heidensohn, 1992). The US Department of Justice sued police departments in cities including Los Angeles and Philadelphia to provide equal opportunities for women, including promotions (Heidensohn, 1992). In these lawsuits, police departments were accused of advertising police jobs as male jobs, involving discouraging the hiring of female recruits, different pay rates for male and female officers, use of gender-specific employment classifications, and exclusion of women from patrol assignments (Potts, 1983). As a result of changes mandated in settlements of these lawsuits, and with larger numbers of women entering the American workforce, women grew their representation in US policing throughout the 1970s.

By the late 1970s, women officers made up roughly 2 per cent of officers nationwide (Martin, 1980). By 1978, this had risen to 4 per cent of officers in US police departments, which included 2.6 per cent White women and 1.6 per cent women of colour (Martin, 1991). By 1978, there were nearly

Table 5.2: Female representation in American policing

Year	All males	All females	White females	Black females	Latina females	Other (including Asian, Native American, Mixed Race) females
1975	98%	2%				
1978	96%	4%	2.6%	All non-White combined: 1.6%		
1980	96%	4%				
1987	92%	8%				
1993	91%	9%	6%	2%	0.7%	0.1%
2000	90%	10%	7%	3%	1%	0.3%
2003	89%	11%	7%	3%	1.3%	0.3%
2007	88%	12%				
2013	88%	12%				
2016	88%	12%	7%	3%	2%	0.4%
2020	88%	13%	7%	3%	3%	0.4%

Source: BJS, 1993, 2000, 2007, 2013, 2019, 2022; Martin, 1991; Martin and Jurik, 2007

1,000 female officers on street patrol (Rabe-Hemp, 2009). As set out in Table 5.2, the numbers of women in US policing steadily increased, including among women of colour.

As reflected in Table 5.2, in the late 1980s women's representation in US police forces continued to grow. But in the 1990s it became clear that women officers, like officers of colour discussed in Chapter 4, were more concentrated and better represented in large urban police forces in larger American cities, compared to serving in smaller or rural departments. In fact, the data reflect that a number of large urban police departments had nearly 20 per cent women officers by the late 1990s, compared to many small and rural forces, which had few if any female officers. By 1997, Detroit (22 per cent), Philadelphia (22 per cent), Washington DC (25 per cent), Chicago (19 per cent), and Los Angeles (17 per cent) all had significant female representation (BJS, 2007).

While women were becoming better represented in American police departments in the 1990s, they were not necessarily being treated as equals with their male colleagues. Martin (1990), for example, found that women officers were still more likely to have separate roles from male officers, being much more likely to occupy administrative and community assignments, while men were more likely to serve on tactical teams and patrol support units. By 2007, these and other large US police departments had generally

Table 5.3: American police officers by race and gender, 2020

White men	Black men	Latino men	Other men	White women	Black women	Latina women	Other women
61%	9%	12%	4%	7%	3%	3%	0.4%

Source: BJS, 2022

increased their numbers female officers: Detroit (27 per cent), Philadelphia (25 per cent), Washington DC (23 per cent), Chicago (19 per cent), and Los Angeles (19 per cent) (BJS, 2007).

Despite these gains, the overall percentage of women in US policing has remained fairly stagnant since the mid-2000s. While between 1987 and 2007, the proportion of female officers in the US grew from 8 per cent to 12 per cent (Pew Research Center, 2017: 22), women have remained at just 12 per cent of US policing since 2007, with Black (3 per cent), Latina (2 per cent), and Other (0.4 per cent) female representation remaining roughly the same since 2000 (BJS, 2022; see Table 5.3). These figures show a significant lack of representation in both major urban and rural areas, where women constitute at least 50 per cent of the population. As with representation of officers of colour discussed in Chapter 4, women are better represented in larger urban forces serving populations over 1 million, where 19 per cent of officers are female (BJS, 2022). By contrast, and like officers of colour, women are under-represented in small police departments serving populations fewer than 10,000 people, which are often fairly rural, where just 9 per cent of all officers are female (BJS, 2022).

Women's experiences in policing

This book has set out in prior chapters that street police culture norms stem from traditional straight, White, male, working-class views of race, gender, violence, loyalty, tolerance and numerous other perspectives. The challenges for male and female officers alike is that these street police culture norms create a distinctly gendered framework in which they operate and experience the role. For female officers in particular, this highly gendered policing institutional culture and framework creates a number of challenges, many of which are not experienced, or are experienced less acutely, by male officers.

Like officers of colour, female officers also experience significant differences in the terms and conditions of their UK and US police employment, including being subjected to sexual abuse and harassment, gendered assignments, lower rates of promotion, lack of proportionate representation in supervisory and leadership assignments, greater rates of voluntary resignation and higher levels of stress, among others. These effects are felt even more acutely for female officers of colour, who face the combined effects of both sexism and racism in the role.

Given that female officers in both the UK and US often experience policing differently from their male colleagues, the data examined in this volume illustrate that there are a variety of approaches female officers can take to dealing with the circumstances of their role. The gendered framework of policing means female officers can either embrace the street police culture norms, shun them or operate in a space in between. The extent to which female officers are aware of, or consciously contemplate, these gendered institutional dynamics is not always clear, but often comes to light in qualitative interviews. One of the significant contributions of this book is considering the degree to which female officers may become active bureaucrats in the role, meaning acting in ways differently from their male colleagues by explicitly or implicitly acting in ways which benefit the interests of female community members or others from disadvantaged communities. The types of behaviours female officers actively engage in can include de-escalation of conflicts, less use of force, and better communication with crime victims, and is explored in more depth in Chapter 8.

While this chapter does not argue that female officers are a monolith and all experience policing in the same ways, it argues that the overarching gendered structure of policing means that many UK and US female officers experience significant disadvantages and different terms and conditions of employment compared to their male colleagues.

Hegemonic masculinity theory

Hegemonic masculinity is the overarching theoretical lens for this chapter, which, in conjunction with theories of police culture, helps illustrate the challenges, parameters, confines and pressures women face in UK and US policing. Hegemonic masculinity refers to the notion that men are superior, women are inferior and heterosexuality is dominant, which reinforces men's power over women (Prokos and Padavic, 2002; Miller et al, 2003; Rabe-Hemp, 2009; Morash and Haarr, 2012; Schuck, 2014; Westmarland, 2017). Feminist discourse has long tracked the ways hegemonic masculinity has developed, been reinforced and is perpetuated in many societies, including the UK and US. Part of the long running analysis of hegemonic masculinity in UK and US societies is the way it shapes a variety of public and private institutions, including workplaces.

Applied to the UK and US policing fields, hegemonic masculinity means that, within the occupation, it is structured in ways which view, support and promote the superiority of men over women, with men holding disproportionate power to women, that male violence and displays of force are means to reinforce power and authority over women, and that heterosexual sexuality is the only form of legitimate sexual orientation. This means that police institutions explicitly and implicitly create policies, practices, and norms that place priority, emphasis and value on maintenance of hegemonic masculinity within police forces.

Empirical policing scholars have researched a variety of ways through which hegemonic masculinity is created and maintained in policing (Prokos and Padavic, 2002; Miller et al, 2003; Rabe-Hemp, 2009; Morash and Haarr, 2012; Westmarland, 2017). Whether they are aware of it or not, hegemonic masculinity theory means female officers are regarded according to gendered stereotypes and power structures which intrinsically subordinate them to men, and evaluate them according to parameters developed and maintained by male officers and leaders. Female officers are expected to operate according to the confines of these dynamics, and may be rewarded for doing so. By contrast, female officers can be disadvantaged or punished for operating in ways contrary to these hegemonically masculine structures.

As discussed earlier in this volume, hegemonically masculine street police culture sets the heavily gendered norms, expectations and standards by which officer performance is typically measured in UK and US police departments. This decidedly hegemonically masculine street police culture is grounded in traditional, White, working-class perspectives on masculinity, gender, sexuality, aggression, violence, conflict and other traits (Reiner, 2010).

Indeed, masculine police work is considered the valuable and desirable side of street policing – crime fighting, proactivity on the streets, and not shying away from conflict or dangerous situations (Hunt, 1984; Herbert, 2001; Westmarland, 2001; Prokos and Padavic, 2002; Martin and Jurik, 2007; Rumens and Broomfield, 2012; Mennicke et al, 2018). There is an inherent physicality associated with masculine police work, and this type of policing is associated with possessing the type of physical traits viewed as required for these tasks. The highly valued nature of masculine police work is reinforced on the job by performance metrics, promotion criteria and verbal and written supervisor approval which gauge success according to these so-called masculine police measures (Prokos and Padavic, 2002). Male officers are most readily associated with masculine police work, while female officers are generally viewed as less capable of these approaches. That said, as discussed further later in this chapter and in Chapter 6, some women can prove themselves to be good cops by showing they are highly capable of masculine policing.

In contrast to masculine policing, hegemonically masculine street police culture frames feminine police work as the less valuable and undesirable side of policing – work inside the police station, community relations, assisting vulnerable populations, and administration (Hunt, 1984; Herbert, 2001; Westmarland, 2001; Rabe-Hemp, 2009). Officers engaged in feminine police work are viewed as averse to violence, avoidant of crime fighting, and weak at policing the streets (Rabe-Hemp, 2009). Feminine police work is associated with being soft (lacking masculinity), being overly caring, compassionate, trusting, moral and naive about the people and communities who are policed (Hunt, 1984; Herbert, 2001). There is an inherent lack of physicality associated with feminine police work, and it is associated with those deemed as lacking physical traits necessary for masculine police work (Miller, 1999; Garcia, 2003). Unlike masculine policing, the low-value nature of feminine police work means it often goes unrecognized by supervisors and is difficult to measure in standard performance metrics and promotion criteria (Westmarland, 2001). Female officers are viewed as more capable or willing to engage in feminine police work, and male officers are stereotyped as less competent in these approaches. Many male officers may enjoy or excel at so-called feminine police work and may be explicitly or implicitly discouraged from engaging in such work because it is viewed as weak and effeminate. Indeed, as discussed later in this chapter and in Chapter 6, male officers who engage in feminine police work are often regarded with disdain by male colleagues.

Because hegemonic masculinity sets the limitations of acceptable behaviour for female officers in UK and US police services, their forms of gender expression within police institutions are fairly limited if they want to remain in the policing field. Viewed through the lens of the hegemonic masculinity theory, early research by Martin (1980), showing that female officers were compelled to adopt one of two female officer stereotypes. Indeed, Martin (1980) and subsequent research has asserted that female officers must either embrace street police culture and adopt aggressive masculine police work personas as *police*women, or adhere to the feminine police work personas as police*women* (Martin, 1980; Heidensohn, 1992; Morash and Haarr, 2012).

Yet more recent research interpreted through a hegemonic masculinity lens suggests that female officers' expressions of gender in policing are more nuanced and complicated than the masculine or feminine police work binary suggested by Martin (1980). Rabe-Hemp (2009), Schuck (2014) and others argue that, today, the socialization process into street police culture and police institutions is more complex for female officers. On the one hand, they are faced with gendered stereotypes rooted in hegemonically masculine police culture. On the other, despite the hegemonically masculine police culture norms, female officers may still have a degree of agency in their self-expression whereby it occurs along a continuum rather than according to Martin's (1980) strict gender expression binary. Some scholars thus argue that while masculine and feminine policing sit at opposite poles along the hegemonically masculine police culture structure, there may be a variety of different possible gender expressions in between (Heidensohn, 1992).

While more agency to express gender identity along a continuum sounds empowering, there can be severe consequences for female officers who do not fit in to either of the prescribed hegemonically masculine police culture stereotypes, a notion which meshes with earlier discussion in this book about the pressures faced by members of historically marginalized groups in policing (Chan et al, 2010; Kringen and Novich, 2017). And as just asserted, the two ends of the spectrum are not viewed with equal validity in policing. The hegemonically masculine street police culture means masculine policing is more highly valued than feminine policing, and the stronger a female officer's orientation is toward masculine policing, the more valued and supported she will be by colleagues and superiors within the policing institution (Barratt et al, 2014). Although female officers and some male counterparts may resist being forced to adhere to these gendered stereotypes, scholars assert that the policing institutions are so hegemonically masculine that remaining within them means that, to some extent, female and male officers implicitly consent that they will be required to operate within the confines of this gendered power structure, even if they do not explicitly recognize it (Chan et al, 2010).

Significantly, the process of self-identification for female officers within policing institutions can occur at both the conscious and unconscious levels. Some women officers explicitly adopt masculine policing traits and embrace the associated power this choice provides (Prokos and Padavic, 2002; Mennicke et al, 2018; Clinkinbeard et al, 2020). Interview Subject 1 observed this is the price many women pay for acceptance in policing: 'The aggressiveness is something that's revered [in policing]. And the macho culture. Which you see in women as well. ... If they want acceptance'.

Yet, understood through hegemonic masculinity theory, the reality is that even those female officers who embrace masculine policing do not necessarily have an easy time in the policing institution. They often risk ridicule or ostracization for being perceived as hypermasculine, and are frequently labelled as lesbians by male colleagues (regardless of whether this is their actual sexual orientation) (Clinkinbeard et al, 2020). This hegemonic masculine framework poses particular pressures for lesbian officers, as will be discussed in Chapter 6, who can feel compelled to adopt masculine policing approaches and personas to gain acceptance from male colleagues and ensure career progression (Miller et al, 2003; Panter, 2018).

Despite the advantages within the hegemonically masculine institution for female officers to embrace masculine street policing norms, some female officers may nonetheless (consciously or subconsciously) reject them, preferring to embrace so-called feminine policing traits (Prokos and Padavic,

2002; Morash and Haarr, 2012; Panter, 2018; Clinkinbeard et al, 2020). For some this could mean these female officers lean towards caring, empathetic and support policing roles in policing. For others this could mean carrying themselves in demonstrably feminine ways rather than adopting masculine personas (Panter, 2018).

Researchers suggest the rejection of compulsory displays of masculine gender expression and engaging with feminine policing approaches within the hegemonically masculine policing institution carries significant negative consequences for some female officers. Indeed, this approach is often labelled 'feminist' and troublemaking by some male colleagues and supervisors (Westmarland, 2001). Within the hegemonically masculine street police culture which downplays the value of these traits, such feminine policing approaches may risk isolation from fellow officers and limit female officers' personal development, assignments and career advancement (Westmarland, 2001; Clinkinbeard et al, 2020).

The process of self-identification within the hegemonically masculine policing institutions is even more challenging for female officers of colour. While some White female officers may feel empowered to challenge gender norms because they have a certain degree of power, influence and status within the organization as White people (Morash and Haarr, 2012; NIJ, 2019), female officers of colour who are generally double minorities within UK and US police services must contend not only with sexism within the hegemonic masculine structure, but also with the additional burden of racism. This can leave female officers of colour feeling particularly disempowered and lacking support not only from White male colleagues, but also from male officers of colour and White female officers (Morash and Haarr, 2012).

Physical stereotypes

The hegemonically masculine policing framework contains inherent associations of male officers with physically demanding masculine police work, and female officers associated with the non-physically demanding feminine police work. These highly gendered stereotypes of male and female physicality are embedded in UK and US street police cultures. Stereotypes have been varied in how they are applied in practice. Sometimes they are explicit and codified in law or department rules, which was fairly prevalent in UK and US police departments before the 1990s. Indeed, as discussed earlier, for years, in both the UK and US, these gendered stereotypes were codified and used to prevent women from joining the respective police jurisdictions due to minimum height, weight and physical agility requirements which were claimed to be required for policing, but in fact were associated with the particular, masculine type of policing. Yet most of the explicit physical requirements for entry into the profession which were used to prohibit women from joining the UK and US police services were struck down by British and American courts in the 1970s and 1980s (Potts, 1983; Martin, 1991).

Other physical stereotypes can be implicit, with men and women assumed to have particular physical strengths or shortcomings, and these beliefs being reinforced in institutional policies, practices or decision-making by police leaders and supervisors. While physical stereotypes prove challenging for both male and female officers, they create particular obstacles for female officers. These gendered perspectives on physicality remain deeply held in policing (Potts, 1983; Martin, 1991; Herbert, 2001; NIJ, 2019). Indeed, UK and US research suggests female officers continue to be stereotyped by male colleagues as physically ill-suited for police work (Herbert, 2001; NIJ, 2019). Research shows some male officers resist hiring female officers, believing they cannot handle the physical rigours of policing, such as adequately controlling a volatile situation or backing up male officers in a fight (Herbert, 2001; Seklecki and Paynich, 2007). These gendered stereotypes of the physicality required for the police officer role mean some male officers resent female colleagues (Martin, 1991; Rabe-Hemp, 2008; Garcia, 2003).

As a result of these hegemonic masculinity based stereotypes about female officers' physical abilities to engage in policework, studies reflect that they often believe they have to prove to male colleagues they can handle physical altercations to earn respect (Archbold and Schulz, 2008). Female officers report going out of their way to take control of their service calls before their male colleagues arrived, to show they could physically handle these aspects of policing (Wertsch, 1998; Archbold and Schulz, 2008). These research findings mesh with data collected for this volume. For example, Interview Subject 3, an American high-level LGBTQ+ police leader, reflected on the challenges he witnessed in female officers having to prove their physicality to male colleagues to be trusted and respected:

And it's really hard, because the idea that simply by hiring a more diverse group of police officers will solve that is not really the case. What happens instead is that the culture influences the officers who draws them in to that. So, you know, the notion that – and I see that is still the case often with women in policing. It's gradually changing, but a lot of the women that I worked with, I think felt like they had to go out of their way to prove just how tough and how they just would not take any shit from anybody and how they could be more macho than the guys that they were working around. There was tremendous pressure for that.

Not only do the gendered stereotypes about the physicality required for police work create obstacles for female officers, but stereotypes about their emotional strength for carrying out masculine police work are also significant. Martin and Jurik (2007), Heidensohn (1992) and many others have found that stereotypes about women's emotional capacity for the rigours of masculine policing's crime-fighting roles have frequently been used to excuse female officers' unequal representation across all aspects of the police services, including special assignments, training roles, supervisory or leadership positions. Heidensohn (1992) has characterized these emotionality stereotypes about female officers as a constant shadow that hangs over their experiences of policing, and these stereotypes are both explicitly and implicitly used to keep female officers from being fully integrated into all aspects of policing (Heidensohn, 1992).

Male resistance to female officers

Given the influence of hegemonically masculine street police culture in setting policing norms, values and approaches to the role, it is unsurprising that many female officers experience resistance from male colleagues. Rather than being a historical relic illustrated by Martin (1980) and others, more recent research suggests male resistance to female officers is still pronounced in many UK and US police services (Martin and Jurik, 2007; Rabe-Hemp, 2007; Miller and Lilley, 2014).

There are a number of theories about what particular aspects of hegemonic masculinity drive male officer resistance to female colleagues. Some argue that the embeddedness of hegemonic masculinity in policing institutions means the presence of women is resented because it represents potential changes to the long-established dominance of masculine policing. Indeed, research suggests female officers are often resisted for what they represent in terms of the evolving nature of policing (Herbert, 2001; Martin and Jurik, 2007). Research shows resistance can be driven by male officer frustration that the straight White male composition in police departments is being visibly reduced with the arrival of female officers and others from traditionally under-represented backgrounds in policing (Miller et al, 2003; Seklecki and Paynich, 2007).

Others argue that male officers often resent their female colleagues because they perceive them as threatening the hegemonically masculine character of street policing (Hunt, 1984; Prokos and Padavic, 2002; Stroshine and Brandl, 2011; Miller and Lilley, 2014). The rationale here is that female police officers will inevitably alter the hegemonically masculine street policing culture to be less ultra-masculinist, misogynist and homophobic in ways not palatable to many male officers, hence the resistance. Along similar lines, other research suggests male officers feel the presence of female officers threatens their authority and legitimacy to carry out aggressively masculine street policing, without which police appear weak to local communities (Martin and Jurik, 2007).

At an interpersonal level, another rationale is that women's presence in policing institutions interferes with male officers acting in ways which strengthen and reinforce their hegemonic masculinity. Indeed, male officers may resist female officers for their perceived interference with the male camaraderie and bonding that occurs when carrying out masculine policing practices. Male officers may resent female officers for being unwilling or unable to engage in the type of masculine policing which creates this fraternal policing bond centred around hegemonically masculine street police culture (Martin and Jurik, 2007; Bowling et al, 2019). Yet, this stereotype-driven resistance of female officers runs contrary to the ways police actually spend their time, which is typically 90 per cent on social service tasks rather than aggressive crime fighting (see, for example, Bittner, 1974; Herbert, 2001; Garcia, 2003; Martin and Jurik, 2007). Women's presence in police institutions may then serve to expose the fallacy that police work requires engaging in ultra-masculine policing to successfully do the job (Hunt, 1984).

The ways hegemonic masculinity manifests as male resistance to female officers can occur in a number of ways. Often resistance is overt – through hostility, negative interactions, sexual harassment and other forms of explicit gender discrimination (Martin, 1991; Heidensohn, 1992; Seklecki and Paynich, 2007; Martin and Jurik, 2007; Archbold and Schulz, 2008; Hassell et al, 2011). Resistance can also be subtle – including being made to feel unwelcome, marginalized and isolated, exclusion from social settings or informal work networks, being subject to rumours or jokes, being underestimated, being stereotyped, receiving undesirable assignments, extra scrutiny, differential rates of hiring and promotion, pushing toward caring and victim-focused roles, and steering away from patrol and special assignments, among others (Kanter, 1977; Martin, 1980; Hunt, 1990; Rabe-Hemp, 2007, 2009; Martin and Jurik, 2007; Seklecki and Paynich, 2007).

Gender bias in assignments

The hegemonic masculine street police culture can also drive differences in the types of positions to which male and female officers are assigned. As discussed above, while men are associated with masculine policing emphasizing crime fighting and violence, women are associated with feminine policing including working with children, vulnerable victims and domestic violence survivors, or in community engagement roles.

Research suggests these embedded street police culture stereotypes prevented women from being assigned to patrol alongside their male colleagues for much of modern UK and US policing history (Martin, 1980; Heidensohn, 1992; Westmarland, 2017). Indeed, the so-called masculine policing nature of patrol work was deemed too dangerous for women officers, and women were formally or informally banned from patrol assignments in many UK and US police departments well into the early 1970s (Martin, 1980; Jones, 1986; Potts, 1983; Rabe-Hemp, 2009). It was only with the UK's Sex Discrimination Act 1975 and the US 1968 Civil Rights Act, both of which prohibited institutional discrimination against women, including barring them from particular roles or assignments, that police institutions were legally required to integrate them into patrol work and pay them the same as male officers. Despite these legal requirements, in practice women continued to be steered away from patrol, or toward particular neighbourhoods or shifts, again with the notion that the work was too much masculine policing for women to handle (Martin, 1980).

While interestingly today female officers are overrepresented in patrol assignments in both the UK and US (Guajardo, 2015; Home Office, 2022), this may signal two potential problems driven by hegemonically masculine police culture discussed further later in this chapter. First, women may be disproportionately assigned to patrol assignments focused on so-called feminine policing roles working with community members, vulnerable victims and similar scenarios. Second, women may remain stuck in patrol assignments because they are not proportionately promoted to prestigious special assignments and supervisory positions given they are stereotyped as better suited to front-line feminine policing working in communities and aiding victims. Both explanations raise significant concerns about women officers continuing to be stereotyped according to gendered street police culture norms.

Steering women into 'feminine' assignments

Hegemonically masculine street police culture stereotyping leads women to continue to be disproportionately steered towards and overrepresented in feminine policing roles. Specifically, an abundance of research over 50 years indicates that women officers have long been working with vulnerable populations, including women, children, and victims of domestic violence (Bloch and Anderson, 1974; Kanter, 1977; S. Martin, 1980, 1991; Hunt, 1984; Brown, 1998; Heidensohn, 1992; C. Martin, 1996; Holdaway and Parker, 1998; Bland et al, 1999; Holder et al, 2000; Westmarland, 2001, 2017; Martin and Jurik, 2007; Rabe-Hemp, 2009).

Street police culture stereotypes female officers as more caring, sympathetic, supportive and better listeners than male officers, given that women are stereotyped generally this way in society (Brown, 1998; Westmarland, 2001).

Research from both UK and US policing evidence that these gendered assignments have long been in place. In the UK, some of the earliest studies reflected these patterns, which persist today. Heidensohn (1992), Martin (1996) and Westmarland (2001), for example, all showed that female officers were more often assigned to deal with female and child crime victims. Brown's 1998 survey of 510 male officers and 1,640 female officers across England and Wales also found female officers were disproportionately assigned to community relations roles. These early studies, along with more recent research (see, for example, Westmarland, 2017) found that this work was viewed as low status among male colleagues and supervisors, who again appeared to adhere to the gendered perspective, finding that only masculine policing had value.

Results of US studies show the hegemonic masculinity patterns of steering women toward so-called feminine police work, and its devaluation, are remarkably similar to those seen in the UK. Early US studies by Hunt (1984), Martin (1991), Bloch and Anderson (1974), and more recent studies including Wertsch (1998), Miller (1999), Rabe-Hemp (2007), and Archbold and Schulz (2008) found female officers were more often assigned to victim support and community engagement, youth services and administrative roles. These studies showed female officers being stereotyped as having better skills for those roles compared to male officers. All of this research also showed so-called feminine police work was not viewed as 'real' policing by male colleagues and supervisors, who highly valued masculine crime-fighting roles.

Exclusion from special assignments

The under-representation of women in prestigious special assignments is another illustration of the ways hegemonic masculinity permeates street police culture, and is a disparity which has persisted in the majority of UK and US police departments for decades. Highly coveted specialist postings, including homicide, special protection, narcotics, investigations, firearms, hostage rescue, tactical, mounted, traffic, canine and other prestigious units have traditionally been considered masculine policing and have remained dominated by men in a majority of UK and US police services (Heidensohn, 1992; Brown, 1998; Miller et al, 2003; Bolton and Feagin, 2004; Rabe-Hemp, 2009; Guajardo, 2015; Westmarland, 2017; Panter, 2018; Gaub, 2020; Casey, 2023).

Similar to the explicit and implicit ways women were previously banned from police work generally and specifically patrol positions as a result of hegemonically masculine street police culture, women have also been overtly and covertly banned from special assignments. Research shows women were historically banned or limited by strict quotas for these specialist positions in both the UK and US. In the UK, some special units had outright bans on female officers joining. The London Met Police, for example, prohibited women from becoming Authorized Firearms Officers until 1988 (Heidensohn, 1992). Other studies found prestigious specialist units in England and Wales police services including firearms, diplomatic protection, investigations and mounted units had informal quotas on the numbers of women who could be appointed (Brown, 1998). Most recently, Baroness Casey's review found the London Met Police's elite firearms and diplomatic protection squads remained 90 per cent male (Casey, 2023), further evidencing the persistent nature of the problem.

Beyond explicit and implicit prohibitions, female officers are often openly or covertly discouraged from applying for these special squads. Research indicates their male colleagues often resist them joining owing to the same embedded physical and emotional hegemonically masculine stereotypes applied to women suggesting they lack the ability to engage in the hard-charging, masculinist behaviours required for these specialist roles (Miller et al, 2003; Panter, 2018). One study even found female officer access to these prestigious special assignments can hinge on how brave female officers are perceived to be by colleagues and supervisors (Herbert, 2001).

When female officers do manage to join these elite units, they often face an array of negative behaviours from male colleagues driven by hegemonically masculine street police culture norms. Indeed, female officers on these squads are often met with explicit stereotyping about their physical and emotional attributes as previously described. Moreover, they also often encounter an array of egregious behaviours from male colleagues, ranging from severe sexual harassment, to overt sabotage, to lack of support (Westmarland, 2001, 2017; Archbold and Schulz, 2008; Panter, 2018; Casey, 2023). Isolation is a particularly common experience for women in these special units, given they remain largely insular domains of masculine policing to which women are made to feel unwelcome.

As a result of the array of negative behaviours female officers are often subjected to in elite special units, they generally have a higher attrition rates than men in these squads. Indeed, given that female officers were previously explicitly barred from these units, and many are still discouraged from applying and are continually stereotyped as less capable in these roles than male colleagues, it is unsurprising that they frequently voluntarily resign or are fired.

For female officers of colour in these elite positions, there are few studies illuminating the unique intersectional aspects of their experiences, which is an area requiring significantly more research. However, the small number of studies suggest the combination of racial and gender-based stereotypes often create significant barriers for women of colour to obtain or remain on special assignments (Pogrebin et al, 2000; Holder et al, 2000; Bolton and

Feagin, 2004). Significantly, Bolton and Feagin's 2004 study of Black female officers in the US found that the association of prestigious specialist roles with masculine policing meant they were more easily filled by Black male officers, while simultaneously excluding Black female officers. Similarly, Casey (2023) found there were very few women of colour in the London Met Police's specialist units. These are illustrative examples of the ways that female officers of colour who coveted these prestigious positions for experience and promotion purposes were frequently less able to obtain them compared to their White male, White female, and male officers of colour colleagues.

Promotions

The significant effects of hegemonical masculinity on women's experiences in UK and US policing are further illustrated in relation to promotions. Indeed, women in both jurisdictions have consistently remained under-represented in supervisory and management positions since the earliest days of integrated police forces, a pattern which persists today. While contemporaneous data show women are better represented now as supervisors and police leaders than at any other time in history, their representation typically falls short not only of their police force representation at more junior levels, but also of their shares of their respective local and country populations (Home Office, 2022; BJS, 2022).

In the US, women officers were largely barred from pursuing promotional opportunities until lawsuits in the 1960s and 1970s saw women in the New York Police Department (NYPD), Los Angeles Police Department (LAPD) and other departments eventually win the right to seek promotion and to take the sergeant's examination (Archbold and Schulz, 2012). Yet these cases only produced slow changes for female officers, as reflected in the data. By 1978, for example, female officers in the US comprised less than 1 per cent of all supervisory officers, with women of colour comprising just one fifth (20 per cent) of that very small number of female supervisors (Martin, 1991; Martin and Jurik, 2007). Women gradually increased their representation in supervisory positions as their numbers grew in US policing overall, comprising 3 per cent of all supervisors by 1986, while women of colour made up just 1 per cent of all supervisors (Martin, 1991; Martin and Jurik, 2007). Tellingly, a further trend emerged with women concentrated in the most junior level supervisory positions (Martin, 1991), a disparity which persists in many US police departments today.

By 2001, women made up 13 per cent of all US officers in medium and large police departments, but occupied just 10 per cent of all supervisory roles, and only 1.5 per cent of the highest leadership ranks, with many large

US departments lacking any women in top command positions throughout the early 2000s (Martin and Jurik, 2007). Shjarback and Todak's 2019 analysis of national data from 2,826 US state and local policing agencies found that, on average, 3 per cent had a female chief, 7 per cent had female officers in middle management, and 7 per cent had female sergeants or front-line supervisors.

By 2016, only 3 per cent of all US police chiefs, 8 per cent of mid-level supervisors and 10 per cent of sergeants were women (BJS, 2019). Again, women fared better in larger urban police departments, where they accounted for 9 per cent of all police chiefs, 13 per cent of mid-level supervisors and 14 per cent of sergeants (BJS, 2019). Women were worse off in smaller and rural departments, accounting for only 3 per cent of all police chiefs, 5 per cent of mid-level supervisors, and 6 per cent of sergeants (BJS, 2019).

The situation of women's promotions in UK policing appears better than in the US, although not because there is less hegemonic masculinity in UK street police culture. Rather, the better rates of representation of women in supervisory and leadership positions in UK police services seem to be attributable to the smaller numbers of police departments (43 police services in England and Wales), the smaller number of officers (147,430), and the larger proportion of women in policing (34.7 per cent) (Home Office, 2024).

Specifically, UK data show that although women are better represented in UK policing, and better represented in supervisory positions, they nonetheless lack proportionate representation at the supervisory and leadership levels of police leadership in England and Wales (Home Office, 2024), a trend which has persisted for decades.

According to Brown's (1998) analysis of England and Wales police data, in 1996 women made up 14 per cent of all police but were vastly under-represented in supervisory and leadership ranks: 1.6 per cent of chief superintendents, 1.5 per cent of superintendents, 2.3 per cent of chief inspectors, 3 per cent of inspectors, and 3.7 per cent of sergeants. In fact, the UK only saw its first female chief constable (that is, chief of police) in England and Wales in 1996 when Pauline Clare was appointed to lead the Lancashire Constabulary (Silvestri, 2006). By the mid-2000s, women remained significantly under-represented at the most senior ranks of UK policing, comprising only 8 per cent of officers at the rank of chief inspector or above (Silvestri, 2006). Today the picture has improved for women in England and Wales policing, who comprise 34.7 per cent of all officers, but at 51 per cent of the UK population continue to lack proportional representation at all levels of policing, including supervisory ranks (Home Office, 2024). Indeed, the data show women comprise 30 per cent of chief officers, 30.8 per cent of chief superintendents, 30.5 per cent of superintendents, 31 per cent of chief inspectors, 26.9 per cent of inspectors, and 27 per cent of sergeants (Home Office, 2024).

This book argues that a complex and multi-layered variety of factors have caused UK and US women's under-representation in supervisory police roles, but that they all relate to the overarching hegemonic masculinity of police institutions. While empirical research shows that both individual and structural factors shape promotion aspirations, decision-making and disparities, these seem clearly tied to the overarching explicit and implicit biases women face in UK and US policing, as discussed further below.

Promotions as individual decisions

The majority of policing literature on promotions ignores structural factors and the role of hegemonically masculine police culture. Indeed, most of the literature focuses narrowly on personal factors which lead women officers to opt into or out of the promotion process (see, for example, Holdaway and Parker, 1998; Whetstone, 2001; Todak et al, 2021), without considering the ways gender stereotypes, peer pressure, and lack of support can deter women from seeking promotion. Rather than addressing promotion disparities through structural means, this body of research proposes responses to these inequalities focused on ways to encourage individual women to be more confident in their promotion aspirations and efforts, including seminars, coaching and training to improve promotion application successes (Silvestri, 2006; Bury et al, 2018).

Examples of this type of individual-focused promotions research abounds in UK and US policing. Early American policing research from Kanter's pioneering study about US female officers found they were often isolated from their male counterparts and relegated to the so-called feminine policing roles discussed earlier, reducing their ability to get the necessary experience, training and recognition required for promotion (Kanter, 1977). Decades later, Bolton and Feagin (2004) found that female officers, particularly African American female officers, did not consistently have access to the same training opportunities to prepare them for promotions as their White male and White female colleagues, but did not consider the ways street police culture shapes those opportunities.

Other studies have found female officers had lower promotion aspirations than their male colleagues, but did not consider the ways gender stereotypes shape those aspirations. Gau et al (2013), for example, looked at data about officers across seven US police departments and found female officers have less desire to pursue promotions than their male colleagues. Similarly, Todak et al's 2021 study of 287 American patrol women across the US, found while 42 per cent aspired to be promoted, 72 per cent were not actively seeking promotion at the time of the survey. Yet again, these studies do not sufficiently interrogate how structural factors shape individual-level promotion aspirations and decision-making.

Indeed, numerous studies point to tensions between the policing role and family and caring responsibilities as drivers of female officers' decisions not to seek promotion, but do not sufficiently factor in the role of stereotypes of female officers lacking the disposition for the policing job as discussed earlier, as well as police institutions' lack of structural support for those with caring responsibilities. For example, Whetstone's 2001 survey of 149 policewomen in one US department found 40 per cent of women did not pursue promotions due to childcare concerns. Similarly, Silvestri's study of 30 British female police leaders found many expressed difficulty reconciling the demands of work, promotion requirements and family, with some seeing the tension between being a mother and a police officer as an 'irresolvable conflict' (Silvestri, 2006: 273). Todak et al's 2021 study of US patrol women across several departments also found 20 per cent were not pursuing promotions due to familial obligations.

Another troubling personal factor highlighted by research relates to officers in the UK and US believing they lack sufficient skills, experience or years on the job compared to male colleagues to be qualified for promotion (Holdaway and Parker, 1998; Todak et al, 2021). These types of studies often fail to probe more deeply into the stereotypes of female officers as being best oriented to so-called feminine policing, and lacking the skills for more highly valued masculine policing, and how they contribute to female officers' sense of self-worth and value within policing organizations. Holdaway and Parker's 1998 UK study, for example, found that more than 30 per cent believed they lacked the criteria for promotions, while their similarly situated male colleagues did not have similar doubts about their readiness for promotion. Similarly, 28 per cent of female officers in Todak et al's 2021 survey did not apply for promotion because they did not feel ready and wanted to wait until they had more experience. This finding is consistent with research outside of policing that shows women with equal qualifications to men will not apply for a promotion (or position) while their male counterparts will. Researchers speculate that these self-doubts stem in part from engrained social norms which make women feel they must be demonstrably prepared to earn a promotion, while men are more likely to feel entitled to a promotion (Babcock and Laschever, 2004), but again much of policing research on these individual factors does not delve into these larger structural drivers of inequalities in promotions.

The explicit and implicit ways hegemonically masculine UK and US police departments discourage women officers from pursuing promotions is evident from the research. Some studies show that female officers are actively discouraged from applying by male supervisors, who suggest their promotions would be tokenistic and would result in stigma from male colleagues (Archbold and Schulz, 2008). Other studies show that female officers feel discouraged from applying because their police departments have poor records of promoting women (Todak et al, 2021).

Female officers of colour, who face a combination of intersectional factors including racial and ethnic biases in street police culture, as discussed in Chapter 4, and hegemonically masculine aspects of street police culture discussed throughout this chapter, can be particularly discouraged from applying for promotions in UK and US police departments. And this is illustrated in the research. For example, female officers of colour have been shown to have particularly pessimistic views of the lack of fairness in the promotions processes within their respective police departments (Bolton and Feagin, 2004; Pew Research Center, 2017; Todak et al, 2021). This could be because they see the under-representation of both people of colour and women in supervisory and leadership ranks within their departments. A study by Todak et al (2021) supports this hypothesis, for it showed where female officers of colour do not see other women of colour being promoted or in supervisory or leadership positions, this can reinforce the notion that the promotion process is unfair and they will not be successful if they apply, discouraging applications.

The reluctance of female officers of colour to seek promotions could also be because their own experiences of unfair treatment with respect to race and/or gender in other aspects of the job – such as hiring, probation, assignments and evaluations – might lead them to believe the promotions processes will also be unfair. Evidence for this hypothesis is illustrated in research from the Pew survey of over 7,000 American police officers across numerous departments, which showed that 61 per cent of Black women officers, 44 per cent of Latino women officers, and 33 per cent of White women officers believed men were treated better than women regarding assignments and promotions (Pew Research Center, 2017).

Promotions as institutionally driven

While most police literature on promotions focuses primarily on individual drivers of promotions for female officers, UK and US disparities in promotions for women officers must see policing institutions structurally address the ways hegemonic masculinity and other biases contribute to these inequalities.

Despite the importance of evaluating personal promotion factors as drivers of women's promotion disparities in UK and US policing, there is a tendency to overemphasize them and pay too little attention to structural and institutional factors (Silvestri, 2006). Indeed, female representation in police leadership cannot be looked at in isolation from hegemonically masculine street police culture, and the ways it structures police institutions and police work to the explicit and implicit disadvantage of women. Institutional policies and practices impacting promotions must therefore not be evaluated as gender neutral when they, in fact, produce deeply disproportionate gender effects (Acker, 1990; Westmarland, 2001; Miller et al, 2003; Silvestri, 2006; Rabe-Hemp, 2009; Barratt et al, 2014; Mennicke et al, 2018; Clinkinbeard et al, 2020).

While there is a clear need to highlight how hegemonically masculine street police culture is a key driver of disparities for women in promotions and representation in UK and US police departments, this can be challenging to illustrate empirically. Yet a small number of studies have attempted to show how particular institutional policies disadvantage female officers in the promotions process. For example, Martin's groundbreaking study argued two structural factors limited US female officers' promotions – preference for veterans and incorporation of supervisors' evaluations (Martin, 1989). This study showed how the promotions processes had little understanding of the ways these policies reinforced women's inequality in the police institution. Indeed, women could not benefit from the preference for veterans for promotion because fewer had served in the military, which then had the effect of ensuring men were promoted under this preference at higher rates than women, reinforcing disparities.

Moreover, Martin's study, along with Wertsch (1998) and others, have found that incorporating supervisors' evaluations into the promotions process is particularly damaging for women in hegemonically masculine policing institutions. Indeed, these studies have found that supervisors' evaluations tend to be highly subjective. It is unsurprising that this disadvantages women in the promotions process because, as discussed earlier, hegemonically masculine street police culture norms frame policing in masculine and feminine ways, and stereotype women as being ill-suited for valued masculine police work, and better suited for devalued feminine police work. With the depths of these hegemonically masculine norms framing the evaluation process, it is clear how female officers can be significantly disadvantaged where promotions processes incorporate supervisors' evaluations.

The structural impediments to women's advancement in UK and US police institutions ensure they routinely hit a glass ceiling, meaning if women do progress, they can only do so to lower level supervisory positions, but remain stuck in terms of career advancement after a certain point and rarely achieve top positions. The UK and US data about women's representation in different positions bear this out (BJS, 2022; Home Office, 2023a). The notion of the glass ceiling for female promotions is also supported by the research, with several researchers suggesting female officers frequently encounter a glass ceiling and can only rarely achieve promotions to the highest levels of police leadership (Westmarland, 2001; Silvestri, 2006; Rabe-Hemp, 2008).

Because promotion disparities must be considered through the lens of hegemonically masculine policing norms, research must begin from that departure point, and think about how an array of policing policies, procedures and practices disadvantage female officers in the promotions process. This can include stereotyping, assignments, hostility, ostracization, sexual harassment, family leave and caring responsibilities, unequal pay, and a variety of other factors which may explicitly or implicitly prevent female officer promotions (Shjarback and Todak, 2019). Significant research and policy re-evaluation must therefore be undertaken in both the UK and US to address these structural issues. Moreover, suggestions of how to restructure promotions policies in positive and creative ways to reduce the impact of these structural issues must also be considered, such as proposals to make promotions processes opt-out only, meaning all women are automatically considered for promotion alongside their male colleagues rather than being required to affirmatively make the case for promotion, and should also be given due research attention (Todak et al, 2021).

Sexual harassment

Sexual harassment of female officers is commonplace in UK and US police institutions, and is illustrative of hegemonic masculinity's permeation of street police culture. Hegemonic masculinity prioritizes straight male sexuality above all others, and condones expressions of straight male sexuality. By contrast female sexuality is something to be routinely discussed, desired and controlled (Acker, 1990; Westmarland, 2001; Miller et al, 2003; Silvestri, 2006; Rabe-Hemp, 2009; NIJ, 2019). At the same time, LGBTQ+ and other 'alternative' sexualities are ignored, ridiculed, shamed and suppressed (Bernstein and Kostalac, 2002; Miller et al, 2003). Therefore, rather than sexual harassment being exceptional, it is normalized in hegemonically masculine police services. As illustrated by the research below, until street police culture is changed, sexual harassment will continue to be part of the routine experiences of female officers in particular in the UK and US.

As a result of the pervasive nature of hegemonically masculine street police culture in UK and US police services, sexual harassment is faced by the majority of female officers on the job (Hassell et al, 2011).[1] Women officers

---

[1]   Male officers also contend with sexual harassment in police departments, albeit in different and less frequent ways (Hassell et al, 2011).

face sexual harassment from colleagues, supervisors, suspects and members of the public. The nature of sexual harassment behaviours faced by female officers ranges from sexually explicit comments or jokes, sexual propositions, unwanted touching, sexual assault, stigmatization based on appearance, and being subjected to false rumours (Hassell et al, 2011). These entrenched behaviours are pervasive in the experiences of many female officers in UK and US police departments, but too frequently go unaddressed at both the individual and structural levels (Brown, 1998; Casey 2023).

The volume of sexual harassment faced by female officers in hegemonically masculine UK and US police departments is astounding, and likely under-reported. There are now decades of research in both jurisdictions showing the pervasive nature of sexual harassment of female officers. There are a multitude of studies evidencing frequent sexual harassment for female officers in the US. For example, Martin's 1991 study of US women officers found 63 per cent had experienced sexual harassment at work, with 25 per cent subjected to sexual propositions in exchange for benefits on the job. Similarly, Somvadee and Morash's 2008 survey of 117 American police women and sheriff's deputies found 84 per cent had been subjected to sexually suggestive stories or offensive jokes, 51 per cent had been subjected to sexist remarks, while 37 per cent were subjected to unwanted touching. Rabe-Hemp (2008) found most of the female officers in her survey across 12 US police departments had experienced sexual harassment and other discriminatory behaviours on the job. A national roundtable of American female police leaders convened by the US Department of Justice's National Institute of Justice found that sexual harassment was normalized in American police departments, and so commonplace that only the most egregious cases were reported, if any (NIJ, 2019). Findings from these studies about the frequency of sexual harassment for American female officers are typical for policing research on this subject, and have been reaffirmed in a variety of research over the past two decades by Texeira (2002); Dodge and Pogrebin (2001); Haarr and Morash (1999); del Carmen et al (2007); Hassell and Brandl (2009); Hassell et al (2011); and many others.

In the UK, female officers' experiences of sexual harassment in hegemonically masculine police services similarly span decades and parallel experiences of female officers in the US. For example, Brown and Campbell's 1995 study of 1,640 policewomen in England and Wales across six police departments found 88 per cent had been subjected to sexually explicit comments; 92 per cent had been subjected to comments on their appearance; 30 per cent reported being inappropriately touched or pinched; and 6 per cent had been sexually assaulted, with Brown's (1998) follow-up study finding similar results. Martin's 1996 UK study similarly found 78 per cent of the female officers interviewed in a single UK police service had experienced physical sexual harassment, and most felt they were largely blamed for being sexually harassed my male colleagues and supervisors. A study by the UK Home Office (2005) found that use of sexist language by both colleagues and supervisors was widespread and broadly accepted across UK police services. Westmarland (2017) found sexual harassment in UK police services remained common, that female officers felt particularly scrutinized about their appearance, and that female officers' bodies were a common topic of conversation. These decades of research on sexual harassment evidence the continued pervasiveness of the problem for female officers, and again illustrate the challenges in overcoming it given the embedded nature of hegemonic masculinity in street police culture. More recently, Casey's review of the culture of the London Met Police (2023) found many female officers had been subjected to bullying, far more than their male colleagues.

While the enduring nature of sexual harassment of female officers in UK and US police departments is clear evidence of hegemonically masculine street police culture, a smaller number of studies examining the ways female officers of colour experience sexual harassment show the intersectional ways it operates alongside the entrenched racial biases and stereotypes of street police culture, to alarming effects. Indeed, while it is a very under-researched area, these studies have examined experiences of sexual harassment for female officers of colour, documenting the combined effects of sexism and racism, creating very challenging intersectional experiences of oppression (Martin, 1990; Holder et al, 2000; Dodge and Pogrebin, 2001; Hassell and Brandl, 2009). And those effects are particularly severe for female officers of colour in both the UK and US.

Indeed, studies of female officers of colour in the US and UK show sexual harassment occurs frequently, often even more frequently than for their White female counterparts (Haarr and Morash, 1999). Studies by Felkenes and Schroedel (1993), Pogrebin et al (2000), Texeira (2002), including del Carmen et al's 2007 study of Black and Latina female officers in the US, and Holder et al's 2000 study of Black and Asian female officers in the UK, all found most female officers of colour had experienced multiple forms of sexual harassment, including sexual harassment by peers or supervisors; physical assaults; pressure to perform sexual favours for better working conditions; unwanted touching; unwanted looks or gestures; unwanted letters, telephone calls or sexual materials; and being pressured for dates from peers or supervisors. This research suggests that female officers of colour are forced to contend with two particularly invidious aspects of street police culture – hegemonic masculinity and racism.

For female officers of colour as both racial and gender minorities within most UK and US police departments, these embedded street culture norms make them more likely targets for sexual harassment as they are seen as more isolated, with fewer networks and support mechanisms because they often lack the support White male and female officers experience (Whetstone and

Wilson, 1999; Martin and Jurik, 2007). These studies suggest that female officers of colour are particularly concerned about retaliation if they object to the sexual harassment they face in policing institutions, and their double minority positionality often means these incidents are never reported.

Male allies

The importance of male allies in supporting their female colleagues in hegemonically masculine policing institutions is a key aspect to consider in analysing the experiences of female officers in UK and US police services. Because female officers remain in the minority in most police departments in both jurisdictions, they inevitably rely on male colleagues and supervisors for training, allyship, mentorship and social networks, among other aspects of the role. Where male allies are active in providing support to female officers in these ways, women have a better chance of success in UK and US policing. Without this support, female officers are further disadvantaged and isolated in policing institutions.

Some policing research has illustrated the importance of male allyship for female officers in hegemonically masculine police institutions. For example, studies indicate male allies may help facilitate the inclusion of female officers who are often viewed as outsiders in male-dominated police institutions (Kanter, 1977; Wertsch, 1998; NIJ, 2019). Male allies can help female officers move from outsiders to insiders because they are seen vouching for their credibility and work ethic with male colleagues (Kanter, 1977; Wertsch, 1998). Male allies can serve important functions as advocates for female officers' interests, as they frequently have broader access to conversations and spaces where important decisions are made in policing institutions (NIJ, 2019). Male allies may, therefore, play essential roles in supporting female officers in career progression to special assignments and promotions (Kanter, 1977; Wertsch, 1998).

The importance of male allies for female officers in hegemonically masculine policing institutions was reflected on by Interview Subject 1, a male leader of colour in the UK. He reflected on the similar hurdles faced by women and officers of colour, and the need for men to mentor women of all colours:

And of course there was also mentoring of female officers and staff as well, because a lot of them didn't know, they weren't in on the networks, so the mentoring was quite important to them and I've mentioned quite a few senior women ... because ironically they faced a lot of the same issues that I've faced. ... I've been able to help them. ... And I've never been blind to the fact that they've faced exactly the same issues that I've faced. Often from the same individuals but all the same problems that they've faced. I mean the support network was mainly for BME staff, but amongst the women there were the same issues there were generally so I've mentored women of all colours and I thought it was interesting that they had asked me to and it's how to navigate what was very difficult organization.

Some research suggests male allies provide support to female colleagues in the hegemonically masculine policing workplace at some risk of themselves being ostracized by other male officers for acting in ways different from stereotypical male roles in policing institutions (Martin and Jurik, 2007; Kurtz, 2008). Indeed, being closely aligned with female officers who, as discussed earlier, are stereotyped in street police culture as being less capable of masculine policing, could potentially create negative opinions of male allies by association. Yet little is known about the drivers of male support for their female colleagues, for this area is under-researched. One of few studies examining male officer motivations for supporting female colleagues suggested better educated officers become more frustrated with the hegemonically masculine structure of policing, are less prejudiced toward female colleagues, and are therefore bolder about challenging street police culture norms by supporting female colleagues (Kurtz, 2008).

Research shows particular challenges for building male allies for female officers of colour within police institutions shaped by hegemonic masculinity and racial biases. While studies indicate some White male officers view their White female colleagues as in need of protection and support, consistent with societal and police culture stereotypes about White womanhood, delicacy and fragility, these views do not typically translate to female officers of colour, particularly Black female officers, who are viewed with negative racial stereotypes (S. Martin, 1994; C. Martin, 1996; Pogrebin et al, 2000; Martin and Jurik, 2007). For example, S. Martin (1994) and C. Martin (1996) found that, in keeping with hegemonically masculine and racialized stereotypes embedded in police culture, White women officers were often put on pedestals and perceived as fragile in police institutions, while Black female officers were often stereotyped by male officers as being strong and tough, and not requiring protection. These findings are consistent with those of Pogrebin et al (2000), who similarly found White female officers being afforded protections on the job by their White male colleagues, while Black female officers were not afforded the same support. The adoption of these stereotypes by White male officers means White female officers tend to benefit from more allyship and support than women of colour, particularly Black female officers.

There is also very limited research on in-group racial allyship for female officers of colour from male officers of colour amid the backdrop of hegemonically masculine and racially biased street police culture. Several US studies have focused in particular on whether Black male officers provide allyship and support to Black female officers in police institutions (Pogrebin et al, 2000; Dodge and Pogrebin, 2001; Bolton and Feagin, 2004). These studies have found that relationships between Black male and female officers in hegemonically masculine police services can be very complicated, and illustrative of the interconnected ways intersectional sexism and racism can operate to create multiple aspects of oppression for Black women. Indeed, the research suggests that some Black male officers may deliberately distance themselves from their Black female counterparts because they feel insecure about their own positions as minorities in their departments, which, as discussed in Chapter 4, frequently mean they are subjected to a host of disparities and different terms and conditions of employment.

For example, in Pogrebin et al's 2000 study, their 21 Black women respondents did not feel supported by their Black male colleagues. The research found that they avoided supporting their Black female colleagues to protect their own positions in the department out of a desire to remain insiders in frequently biased police institutions (Pogrebin et al, 2000). Similarly, Dodge and Pogrebin's 2001 study found many of the Black female officers interviewed in one US police department did not find Black male officers particularly supportive. Some women interviewed again speculated that the pressures associated with Black men's own minority status within the department and fragile relations with White colleagues, as discussed in Chapter 4, were associations they may not want to jeopardize by providing visible support for Black women colleagues. In contrast to the first two studies, Bolton and Feagin (2004) found that many Black female officers reported that their experiences were more similar than different to those of their Black male colleagues, although they recognized that the hegemonically masculine nature of police institutions meant their Black male colleagues could more readily obtain special assignment and promotions opportunities that they could not. These interesting findings suggest significantly more research would be beneficial to better understand the intersectional needs for allyship and support for female officers of colour in UK and US policing.

Scrutiny and internal discipline

As discussed earlier, the hegemonically masculine street police culture deeply embedded within UK and US police institutions subjects female and male officers alike to gendered stereotypes and gendered notions of policing. Within this gendered framework, women officers are viewed with more scepticism in the policing role, as they are stereotyped as being less inclined to and competent in the core aspects of so-called masculine policing. This not only harms their chances for promotion as discussed above, but also subjects them to higher levels of explicit and implicit scrutiny from both colleagues and supervisors compared to male officers.

Data from studies over the past four decades indicate that many female officers in both jurisdictions feel they have to work harder, if not twice as hard, as their male colleagues to earn respect and acceptance from male colleagues and supervisors (Kanter, 1977; Holdaway and Parker, 1998; Wertsch, 1998; Archbold and Schulz, 2008; Stroshine and Brandl, 2011). Female officers' positionality within the hegemonically masculine policing institution and subjection to stereotypes means they are at an inherent disadvantage when it comes to levels of scrutiny. Because female officers are stereotyped as less physically and emotionally capable of carrying out the hard-charging masculine policing activities which are so valued in policing institutions, they are often automatically assigned a position of inferiority when it comes to competence on the important aspects of the job. Indeed, female officers are assumed to be more capable of so-called feminine police work, which is undersupported and undervalued in police institutions, and thus they are inherently disadvantaged by street police culture norms when it comes to assessments of their performance even before individual conduct is evaluated.

Given these heavily gendered dynamics, it is unsurprising that data reflect female officers' disadvantages. Not only do female officers feel they have to work harder to show their value and earn respect, but many report that if they do not undertake such efforts, they risk not being accepted by their male counterparts and could remain alienated outsiders (Kanter, 1977; Wertsch, 1998; Archbold and Schulz, 2008). Studies of female officers recount their feelings of perpetually needing to prove themselves to their male colleagues and supervisors, and to avoid mistakes to gain acceptance (Holdaway and Parker, 1998). Given the pressure to work harder and show their worth to male colleagues and supervisors, it is therefore unsurprising that female officers feel they are more often criticized than their male colleagues in both the UK and US contexts (Holdaway and Parker, 1998; Gustafson, 2008).

The problem of greater scrutiny is very acute for female offices of colour in the UK and US, who as double minorities feel particularly susceptible to both racism and sexism in the police workplace. In the UK context, female officers of colour report being more heavily scrutinized for the same behaviour as their White colleagues (Smith et al, 2015). Indeed, in Smith et al's 2015 study of female Black and Minority Ethnic (BAME) officers in the UK's Greater Manchester Police, they found BAME officers frustrated by feeling supervisors more negatively view their work, and feeling more often referred for formal investigations compared to White officers, whose behaviours supervisors dealt with more informally, an experience common for officers of colour, as discussed in Chapter 4.

While the policing research discussed earlier situates scrutiny of female officers' performance within the larger hegemonically masculine street police culture, there are additional factors which may make female officers subject to greater oversight and criticism than their male counterparts. For example, research suggests one reason is that because female officers and others from traditionally marginalized groups remain the minority in most UK and US police services, they are more visible than their male colleagues, who continue to form the overwhelming majority (Kanter, 1977; Shoenfelt and Mendel, 1991; Wertsch, 1998; National Center for Women & Policing, 1999; Prokos and Padavic, 2002; Archbold and Schulz, 2008; Rabe Hemp, 2008). As a result, female officers' work is often watched more closely and viewed more critically than that of their male counterparts (Kanter, 1977; Shoenfelt and Mendel, 1991; Wertsch, 1998; Holdaway and Parker, 1998; National Center for Women & Policing, 1999; Prokos and Padavic, 2002; Bolton and Feagin, 2004).

The combination of female officers operating within hegemonically masculine police institutions, the bifurcation of policing into valued masculine policing and devalued feminine policing, the belief that female officers lack competence in masculine policing, the increased levels of scrutiny that female officers find themselves under, and the fact that everyone errs at work from time to time, mean it is inevitable female officers will be perceived as making mistakes on the job. But the processes invoked when female officers make errors showcase the influence of hegemonically masculine street policing norms as female officers are subjected to differential treatment in these instances compared to their male colleagues in both the UK and US contexts.

The additional scrutiny female officers face in hegemonically masculine policing institutions means their mistakes are often judged more harshly and punished more severely compared to male colleagues. Research by Holdaway and Parker (1998), Bolton and Feagin (2004), Martin and Jurik (2007), Morash and Haarr (2012) and others in both the UK and US contexts illustrates these differences in treatment, finding that stereotypes of female skills and performance by male colleagues and supervisors result in the mistakes of one female officer being ascribed to all female officers, reinforcing negative views of female officers' performance.

The resulting scrutiny faced by female officers in hegemonically masculine policing environments unsurprisingly results in higher levels of internal discipline and voluntary dismissal compared to male colleagues in both the UK and US contexts. Indeed, a number of studies over the past three decades have showed consistency in this regard (Shoenfelt and Mendel, 1991; Martin, 1989; Holdaway and Parker, 1998; National Center for Women & Policing, 1999; Hickman et al, 2000; Prokos and Padavic, 2002; Bolton and Feagin, 2004; Martin and Jurik, 2007; Morash and Haarr, 2012; Bury et al, 2018).

Specifically, when it comes to matters of internal discipline, the influence of supervisor discretionary decision-making is an important part of this process, which often yields different results for female and male officers. The environment of hegemonically masculine street police culture means supervisors make discretionary discipline decisions with the influence of gendered stereotypes about women officers and their abilities and perceived dispositions for so-called masculine and feminine police work. If supervisors view female officers as less able to carry out highly prized masculine police work, they may make discretionary discipline decisions in ways that negatively impact female officers.

Indeed, supervisor discretion when it comes to internal discipline in UK and US police services means supervisors can opt to discipline officers informally through discussions and unwritten warnings, or formally through established disciplinary policies, which can include initiating an internal investigation or disciplinary case (Hickman et al, 2000; Barton, 2003). Studies repeatedly show double standards when it comes to disciplining female officers for behaviours on the job, reflecting that female officers are more often disciplined and terminated for the same behaviours for which male officers receive lesser punishments (Shoenfelt and Mendel, 1991; Martin and Jurik, 2007). And internal discipline can also be a way of retaliating and reinforcing hegemonically masculine norms against women who file discrimination, sexual harassment or excessive force complaints against their colleagues or supervisors, with internal disciplinary procedures, including false allegations, being used to punish, harass or retaliate against female officers (National Center for Women & Policing, 1999).

The implications for female officers of being subjected to internal discipline disproportionate to their male colleagues suggests the enduring nature of embedded hegemonic masculinity within street police culture continues to influence policing institutions. In relation to internal scrutiny and discipline, the effects of this can have significant consequences for their policing careers. Indeed, the increased levels of internal discipline for female officers can mar personnel records, sour relations with colleagues and supervisors, result in negative evaluations by supervisors, deter candidates from applying for promotions or specialist assignments, or lead to voluntary resignations, leaving female officers further disadvantaged compared to their male colleagues.

Resignations and voluntary departures

As reflected in this chapter, the hegemonic masculinity of street police culture shapes police institutions in a variety of ways which negatively impact the experiences of female officers, creating significant disparities in their experiences compared to male colleagues. One of the important culminations of the impacts of hegemonic masculinity on female officers in

Table 5.4: Rate of voluntary resignation in England and Wales (as percentage of all departures by gender)

Voluntary resignations	All	Female officers	Male officers
2016–17	2,035	36%	20%
2018–19	2,175	34%	22%
2020–21	1,996	43%	29%
2021–22	3,435	52%	38%
2022–23	4,561	60%	45%

Source: Home Office, 2022, 2023

UK and US policing is evidenced in the fact that they resign from policing institutions at higher rates than their male colleagues in both jurisdictions.

Hegemonically masculine policing environments create significant pressures for female officers which drive them out of police institutions at higher rates than their male colleagues in both UK and US police services. Research and official government statistics over many decades reflect consistently higher rates of attrition for female officers in both countries (Martin 1980, 1989; Dick and Cassell, 2004; NIJ, 2019; Home Office, 2023a). For example, Table 5.4 illustrates the trends in female officer resignations from UK policing from 2016 to 2023.

While hegemonic masculinity inevitably creates the environment and sets the pressures faced by female officers in UK and US police departments, they may or may not be cognizant of the way it explicitly influences their tenure in police institutions. This is reflected in the research, where women officers articulate that the reasons for leaving policing at higher rates than their male colleagues are multi-fold. Studies show that resistance, discrimination and harassment many female officers experience may be significant drivers of voluntary departures (Martin, 1989). Other female officers grow frustrated at having to work twice as hard as their male colleagues without receiving ample recognition from colleagues and supervisors (Kanter, 1977; Archbold and Schulz, 2008; Stroshine and Brandl, 2011). Studies by Wertsch (1998) and others have found that the higher visibility and closer scrutiny female officers feel compared to their male colleagues create significant stress for female officers, causing some to want to leave their departments. Some female officers find challenges of managing the job along with caring responsibilities and family commitments is a reason for voluntary resignations, particularly in light of institutional policies unsupportive of such familial commitments (Martin, 1989). Moreover, as stated above, the lack of confidence in the promotions process and lack of perceived promotion and special assignment opportunities may also be contributing factors. Others feel the stress of feeling the need to overachieve in light of performance pressures is a reason to quit the job. Recent research by the National Institute of Justice (NIJ, 2019), and others suggests some women are explicitly driven to quit policing by its toxic masculine culture that they believe does not adequately value the contributions of female officers.

One key aspect of decisions to leave a policing role for female officers and others can be lack of support from colleagues and supervisors. Many studies over a period of decades have shown that female officers in the UK and US can grow frustrated with the lack of support or encouragement from colleagues, supervisors and senior officers compared to male officers (Worden, 1993; Whetstone and Wilson, 1999; Holdaway and Parker, 1998). Women officers also frequently report insufficient institutional support mechanisms, including lack of suitable or size appropriate equipment, inadequate maternity leave policies, poor sexual harassment policies and insufficient childcare provisions. (Doerner, 1995; Polisar and Milgram, 1998; Holdaway and Parker, 1998; Seklecki and Paynich, 2007). This lack of support can interfere with the ability to perform, and negatively impact their views of the job, leaving some female officers to question remaining in the role.

A number of studies in both the UK and US also reflect that the perceived lack of support is particularly acute for female officers of colour, who often grow particularly frustrated with insufficient support mechanisms provided by the institution, supervisors and fellow officers (Smith et al, 2015). Studies in both jurisdictions have shown these frustrations are particularly felt by Black female officers. For example, Bolton's 2003 interviews of 50 Black officers in the US South found they were frustrated by a lack of support but reluctant to seek union support, believing it would not be supportive, a notion consistent with the discussion of police unions in Chapter 2.

Conclusion

This chapter has examined the experiences of female officers in UK and US policing through the lens of hegemonically masculine street police culture, and the ways it impacts their lived experiences and different terms and conditions of employment in the job. It charted the growth of female officers in both jurisdictions since early 20th century within hegemonically masculine UK and US police services. It illustrated that while female representation has grown significantly, particularly in the UK, the increases in representation of female officers have not been seamless, nor have they been uniform across all levels of policing. This chapter has examined the way street police culture's hegemonically masculine norms continue to set expectations about the performance of female officers and impact the ways many are treated by colleagues. The data analysed for this chapter show that female officers consistently remain marginalized in UK and US police departments in many respects. Indeed, rather than being treated as equals to male colleagues, the hegemonically masculine culture of policing institutions means female officers continue to be frequently subjected to different terms and conditions of employment including being steered toward so-called feminine policing assignments and away from postings to elite units, lower rates of promotion, and continuing to endure rampant sexual harassment in ways very different from their male counterparts, with little recourse and few options. Moreover, this chapter explored the choices often faced by female officers to either adopt misogynistic street police culture beliefs or resist them, and set out the consequences of doing so. This chapter further analyzed the particularly challenging lived experiences of female officers of colour, whose experiences of the multiple, intersectional oppressions embedded within street police culture, including racism and sexism, make their experiences in UK and US police services even more difficult.

6

LGBTQ+ officers in policing

This chapter focuses on the ways hegemonically masculine and heteronormative street police culture shapes the lived experiences of vastly under-researched UK and US officers from LGBTQ+[1] communities. As discussed in Chapter 5, the hegemonically masculine character of street police culture refers to the concept that men are superior and should dominate, that their power over women is inherent, and women are inferior to men. This chapter further builds on this analysis by considering the ways street police culture is also heteronormative, meaning heterosexuality is normalized, reinforced and supported over other sexual orientations. Taken together, the hegemonically masculine and heteronormative character of street police culture in the UK and US shapes the growing numbers of LGBTQ+ officers, a group who have traditionally been excluded from being open about their sexuality for most of policing history in both jurisdictions.

This chapter analyses the ways hegemonically masculine and heteronormative street police culture poses specific challenges for LGBTQ+ officers. Significantly, it explores the ways these pressures create similarities but also differences in the experiences of different groups of officers within the LGBTQ+ communities, including gay, bisexual, lesbian and transgender officers. The chapter also considers the ways hegemonically masculine and heteronormative street police culture creates some explicit and implicit similarities, and also many differences, for LGBTQ+ officers' experiences compared to those of their straight colleagues in both jurisdictions. The chapter analyzes how the limited available evidence drawn from theoretical and empirical research examined in this book, triangulated with insights from diverse police leaders interviewed for this volume, shed light on and provide further depth of understanding of the experiences and challenges of LGBTQ+ officers in both jurisdictions.

---

[1]   The term LGBTQ+ is used throughout the chapter to refer to gay, lesbian, bisexual, transgender and queer people. However, given the scarcity of data on LGBTQ+ police, at times data is limited to lesbian, gay and bisexual (LGB) or even simply gay and lesbian officers. Data collection for transgender officers in the UK and US is also extremely lacking, and rarely collected alongside data for LGB officers. Moreover, at present there is no policing research in this volume which identifies queer or non-binary officers.

Introduction: police and LGBTQ+ communities

The hegemonically masculine and heteronormative character of street police culture in both the UK and US is readily apparent from the decades of history about the contentious relationships between police and LGBTQ+ communities in both jurisdictions (Colvin, 2012; Jones and Williams, 2015). Unsurprisingly given the core characteristics of street police culture, police have traditionally been seen by many in LGBTQ+ communities as anti-gay (Colvin, 2012). Some have gone so far as to assert that the hegemonically masculine and heteronormative aspects of police culture mean that it is inherently in conflict with the values and ideologies of LGBTQ+ communities (Leinen, 1993; Burke, 1994). That said, others take a more nuanced position, arguing that there are numerous challenges for LGBTQ+ people in relation to policing, but that these constituencies are not fundamentally opposed.

Yet, the data clearly show decades of mistrust of police in LGBTQ+ communities. Indeed, there is clear evidence in both the UK and US that police have consistently over-policed LGBTQ+ communities in both jurisdictions (Colvin, 2012; Jones and Williams, 2015). In both locales there are lengthy histories of police harassing, arresting and inflicting violence on LGBTQ+ people (Colvin, 2012; Jones, 2015b). Police have consistently been the arm of the state responsible for enforcing discriminatory anti-LGTBQ+ laws. For example, police in the UK targeted LGBTQ+ communities with gross indecency and anti-sodomy enforcement, while police in the US used anti-sodomy laws, 'masquerading' laws targeting cross-dressing, so-called 'three article rules',[2] recreational drug use laws, and others to disproportionately target LGBTQ+ people and spaces where LGBTQ+ people congregated (Colvin, 2012; Jones and Williams, 2015; Mitchell, 2015). Given the lengthy police history of hostility, harassment and entrapment of LGBTQ+ communities, it is unsurprising that relations have long been fraught (Bernstein and Kostelac, 2002; Jones, 2015b).

Simultaneous with the street police culture-driven aggressive policing of LGBTQ+ communities in both the UK and US, they also have a long history of under-protection of LGBTQ+ communities from crime and victimization (Colvin, 2012). Research shows that LGBTQ+ people have frequently been reluctant to report crimes, including hate crimes, in both the UK and US, in significant part based on the belief that police lack the

---

[2]   The three-article rule was an informal rule used by police in places such as New York City to check if individuals were wearing three items of clothing aligned with their biological sex to deter so-called 'cross-dressing'. In practice, it was used by police to routinely harass and assault LGBTQ+ people in the streets and in bars, nightclubs and other social settings (Mitchell, 2015).

interest or inclination to investigate crimes victimizing LGBTQ+ people (Colvin, 2012; Jones, 2015b). Moreover, some LGBTQ+ crime victims fear subjecting themselves to further hostility, harassment and victimization by police if they report crimes (Jones, 2015b).

The background of often fraught relations between police and LGBTQ+ communities in the UK and US has presented unique challenges to researching LGBTQ+ officers in both jurisdictions. Early literature on LGBTQ+ officers was consistent in highlighting the significant homophobia, hostility and heteronormativity of police cultures in both the UK and US, to such an extent that discussion about LGBTQ+ officers, research and data collection were very rare and particularly challenging (for example, Jacobs (1966), Niederhoffer (1967) and Swerling (1978), all cited in Burke (1994)). However, a growing body of literature on LGBTQ+ officers in both jurisdictions makes this a rich and important area of focus for police diversity.

UK LGBTQ+ police

In the UK, the history of LGBTQ+ officers is not as well documented as it should be, in significant part because of the centuries of criminalization of same-sex relationships, particularly gay male sex, and the police role in enforcing those discriminatory laws. Tensions between police and LGBTQ+ communities, including LGBTQ+ officers, and policing institutions, are therefore an important part of the story of sexual orientation diversity in UK policing.

In England, LGBTQ+ sexuality was first criminalized in The Buggery Act 1553, and later all gay acts between men were made illegal under the Criminal Law Amendment Act 1885. Sex acts between men remained criminalized in the UK until the Sexual Offences Act 1967 decriminalized many of these activities. Yet the atmosphere in the UK remained often openly hostile toward same-sex relationships and sexual activities. Even while largely decriminalizing gay sex in the 1960s, the UK continued to single out LGBTQ+ people for harsh treatment. Numerous examples of the UK's anti-LGBTQ+ discrimination can be found in law and regulations, with LGBTQ+ individuals effectively being treated as second class citizens in the UK. For example, Section 28 of the Local Government Act 1988 prohibited local governments from the 'promotion of homosexuality' and remained in effect until 2003. Moreover, it was not until 2017 that the Alan Turing Law, that is, the Policing and Crime Act 2017, pardoned gay men who had been cautioned and convicted of engaging in gay sex under discriminatory anti-LGBTQ+ laws. As a result of the UK's longstanding *de jure* and *de facto* discrimination against LGBTQ+ people, and given the UK police role in enforcing discriminatory laws, the police have long been perceived as unfairly targeting LGBTQ+ communities for aggressive and hostile policing (Jones, 2015b).

Because gay male sex was criminalized in the UK into the late 1960s, and given the openly anti-LGBTQ+ sentiment in the UK even after decriminalization, UK policing had a very slow uptake of openly LGBTQ+ officers, particularly gay male officers. Yet even amid the hostile climate toward LGBTQ+ people both inside and outside policing, small numbers of openly LGBTQ+ officers became visible in the UK in the 1990s. Significantly, in 1990, James Bradley founded the Lesbian and Gay Police Association (now known as the National LGBT+ Police Network) to support gay and bisexual officers in the police services through promoting equal opportunities, providing advice and support for LGB applicants and officers, and promoting better police relations with gay communities (Burke, 1994; Jones, 2015b).

Yet efforts to recruit LGBTQ+ officers were not pursued for much of the history of UK policing. It was not until the Macpherson Report in 1999 that LGBTQ+ officers were first cited as a target demographic for England and Wales policing, as the Commission considered more broadly the nature of strained police relations with minority communities and embedded biases in police institutions and police cultures (Jones, 2015b). In the 2000s and 2010s, England and Wales policing engaged in a national marketing campaign targeting LGBTQ+ communities, recruited LGBTQ+ community liaison officers and invested in LGBTQ+ police affinity groups, among other measures (Jones, 2015b).

The experiences of transgender police candidates and officers in the UK similarly saw significant explicit discrimination for most of the UK's policing history. Under UK law, it was not until the 1999 European Court of Justice decision in *P v. S and Cornwall County Council* that it was held that a transgender woman could not be discriminated against in employment on the basis of gender reassignment, including in occupations such as policing. It was only after that case that the UK passed the Sex Discrimination (Gender Reassignment) Regulations 1999, which theoretically permitted the hiring of transgender officers in the UK police services. However, critics observe that the law in sections 7B(2) and 19 provided Genuine Occupation Qualifications, which permitted exclusion of transgender people from certain sex-specific roles, including where the position required individuals to perform intimate physical searches, or provide assistance in private residences (Little et al, 2002). These prohibitions were routinely applied to exclude transgender applicants from being hired in UK policing in the late 1990s and 2000s.

Several employment discrimination cases in the 1990s upheld the rights of police institutions either not to hire or to transfer transgender women for allegedly occupational necessity reasons.

Specifically, two cases involving police applicants who were discovered to be transgender after offers of employment had been made by UK police services upheld the rights of police institutions to discriminate against transgender people upon learning of the applicants' transgender status (see *M v. Chief Constable of West Midlands Police* (1996); *A v. Chief Constable of West Yorkshire Police* (1999)). A third case saw an officer who underwent gender reassignment surgery reassigned from police duties to a civilian position, a move that was upheld by the courts (see *Ashton v. Chief Constable of West Mercia Police* (1999)). In each case, police argued that transgender policewomen could not operationally fulfil all of their duties. Specifically, police pointed to the Police and Criminal Evidence Act (PACE) 1984, which required police of the same sex to search suspects, which police services asserted could not be done if transgender women were still considered men under law (Little et al, 2002). In each instance, the courts sided with the police that barring transgender officers from searching suspects was a legitimate business reason for discrimination.

In 2003, the UK introduced its first explicit anti-discrimination laws for LGBTQ+ people in the workplace under the Employment Equality (Sexual Orientation) Regulations 2003. This provided unprecedented legal protections for LGBTQ+ police officers. Some argue this legislation and the wider incorporation of LGBTQ+ protections into the Equality Act 2010 made LGBTQ+ people more welcomed and more protected in UK workplaces including policing (Jones, 2015b). The true impacts are unclear and have not been empirically examined. However, data show that by 2012 there were over 5,000 members of the UK's Gay Police Association (GPA), including not only LGBTQ+ officers but also community support workers and civilian staff (Colvin, 2012). In 2014, the GPA's funding was removed by the UK government, and in 2015 a new representative body for LGBTQ+ officers and support staff was founded, the National LGBT+ Police Network. Today, the Network represents LGBTQ+ officers and staff across all 43 police forces in England, Wales and Northern Ireland. Only recently did the Home Office begin collecting data on sexual orientation of officers in England and Wales, which in 2023 showed 4.8 per cent gay/lesbian officers and 3.1 per cent bisexual officers (Home Office, 2024).

US LGBTQ+ police

Like the UK, the history of LGBTQ+ officers is not well documented before more recent decades. As with the UK, US police departments similarly have long histories of explicit discrimination against LGBTQ+ applicants and officers. In fact, as recently as the 1960s and 1970s, a number of US police departments explicitly banned gay and lesbian applicants and openly serving officers (Belkin and McNichol, 2002). For decades, being LGBTQ+ was considered incompatible with being a police officer in ways that appear driven by street police culture norms (Mennicke et al, 2018).

In New York City in the 1980s, for example, the Police Benevolent Association (PBA), the NYPD's largest union, was outspoken in asserting that LGBTQ+ people should not be police officers, and activity engaged in efforts to block LGBTQ+ hiring (Firestone, 2015). In 1981, then PBA Vice-President Pat Burns told the New York City Council that the PBA opposed hiring of LGBTQ+ officers, and that there were no LGBTQ+ officers in the NYPD (Giordano, 1981). However, Burns was contradicted in the same hearing when Charles Cochrane became the first openly gay NYPD officer by declaring: 'I am very proud of being a New York City policeman and I am equally proud of being gay' (Giordano, 1981). Cochrane would go on to found the nation's first Gay Officers Action League (GOLA) in New York City in 1982 to promote equality, fairness and non-discrimination against LGBTQ+ officers. Around the same time, San Francisco reportedly had its first openly gay officer in 1980 (Sklansky, 2006).

Research suggests that, beginning in the mid-1980s, some large American police departments, particularly those serving large LGBTQ+ populations such as New York, Los Angeles and Seattle, began to more actively recruit gay and lesbian officers in response to new laws and discrimination lawsuits (Belkin and McNichol, 2002). However, other police departments aggressively sought to prevent LGBTQ+ officers from joining. Indeed, some US police departments went so far as to give applicants questionnaires querying if they were attracted to same-sex individuals, with an affirmative answer forming the basis for disqualification from employment consideration (Belkin and McNichol, 2002).

The first lawsuit against a US police agency challenging its policy barring gay and lesbian applicants was *Childers v. Dallas Police Department*, 1982. The case involved a civilian employee from another agency who sought to work in the Dallas Police Department's property room, but whose interview was terminated when he admitted to the police interviewer that he was gay and regularly violated Texas's anti-sodomy laws under Texas Penal Code § 21.06. After Childers was rejected for the role and subsequently interviewed by the same police supervisor, he was told he needed a high tolerance for homophobic jokes about him in the police department, and also that his sexuality created a potential security risk to the department. On appeal, the Fifth Circuit upheld the discrimination. The decision provided that Childers' admission that he regularly broke Texas law made him ineligible for the position and that gay and lesbian people were not a protected class under anti-discrimination laws. The decision further held that Childers posed a potential security risk to the department because he was gay, that he was making himself a target for harassment in the department, and that he would promote unrest among department employees.

Another Dallas Police Department case, *England v. State of Texas*, involved a lesbian police applicant who applied to the department in 1989, and admitted in her interview that she was a lesbian. She was informed by the interviewer that being a lesbian was considered a deviant sexuality, and that her sexuality violated Texas Penal Code § 21.06. When England sued, a state court judge ruled the police department's practice of screening for sexual orientation violated the state constitution, which banned sexual orientation discrimination in other Texas police departments and public institutions.

Despite the discriminatory anti–LGBTQ+ practices of a number of US police departments in the 1990s, research suggests that the period also saw steadily growing recruitment and increasing numbers of openly LGBTQ+ officers in some larger US police departments. Chicago saw its first openly LGBTQ+ officers in 1991, much later than some of the more progressive US police departments (Sklansky, 2006). But by the early 1990s, more US police departments recognized the importance of active campaigns to recruit LGBTQ+ officers. Indeed, Leinen (1993) and Miller et al (2003) found that during this period, police departments in Boston, Minneapolis, Madison, Seattle, Portland, Atlanta, Philadelphia, San Francisco, Los Angeles, New York City and Chicago all actively recruited LGBTQ+ officers. While there is only very limited data on the numbers of openly LGBTQ+ officers in US police departments at this time, it seems to reflect these recruitment efforts. For example, by 1993, an early survey conducted by RAND (1993) of six of the largest American police departments reflected in Table 6.1 found that most had few openly gay or lesbian officers, although all had fewer than 1 per cent of openly LGBTQ+ officers on their respective police forces.

While the 1990s was the first period of concerted growth for LGBTQ+ officers in US police departments, hostility, homophobia and discrimination remained commonplace for LGBTQ+ officers in the 2000s. Research shows at least 95 lawsuits and administrative complaints were filed by LGBTQ+ officers between 2000 and 2015, asserting claims ranging from failures to hire and promote, to harassment, death threats, assault, failure to provide back-up and differential assignments (Mallory et al, 2013). In many of these cases,

Table 6.1: Number of out gay or lesbian officers in six US urban police departments

Department	Total officers	Total out gay or lesbian officers	Gay or lesbian officers as percentage of all officers
Chicago	12,209	7	0.06%
Houston	4,100	0	0.00%
Los Angeles	7,700	7	0.09%
New York	28,000	~100	0.36%
San Diego	1,300	4–5	0.25%
Seattle	1,300	2	0.15%

Source: RAND, 1993

courts remained highly deferential to law enforcement agencies who argued that departmental security and morale were put at risk by the presence of gay and lesbian officers (Thompson and Nored, 2002; Mallory et al, 2013).

It was not until the United States Supreme Court in *Lawrence v. Texas* (2003) ended bans on same-sex sodomy that opportunities for LGBTQ+ officers began to grow significantly. Indeed, the decision ended anti-LGBTQ+ sex laws in a number of states including Texas, Florida, Idaho, Kansas, Michigan, Mississippi, Missouri, North Carolina, Oklahoma, South Carolina, Utah and Virginia, leading many states and municipalities to ban discrimination on the basis of sexual orientation in policing and other occupations (Colvin, 2009; Banks et al, 2015). By 2009, over 20 states and 100 municipalities barred discrimination on the basis of sexual orientation in policing and other occupations (Colvin, 2009).

In 2013, the Supreme Court in *United States v. Windsor* (2013) ended discrimination against same-sex couples in the provision of federal benefits, which helped further broaden civil rights protections for LGBTQ+ people. The subsequent United States Supreme Court ruling in *Obergefell v. Hodges* (2015), which struck down state-level same-sex marriage bans, further entrenched the prohibition on anti-LGBTQ+ discrimination under US law. While none of these decisions explicitly prohibited anti-LGBTQ+ discrimination in policing or other workplaces, they had significant impacts in increasing public pressures to protect the civil rights of LGBTQ+ people. It was not until the 2020 US Supreme Court decision in *Bostock v. Clayton County* (2020), that LGBTQ+ status was deemed a protected employment characteristic (falling under sex) in Title VII of the 1964 Civil Rights Act.

These legal decisions changed the legal landscape for LGBTQ+ people in the US, including prospective and serving police officers. They prohibited explicit bans on LGBTQ+ applicants and officers, and had the effect of helping broaden social attitudes toward LGBTQ+ people generally. While US policing has seen growing numbers of openly LGBTQ+ officers as a result of these wider legal protections, this does not mean homophobic workplace discrimination in American police forces has subsided. Rather, just as explicit and implicit discrimination against officers of colour and female officers persists in US policing (as detailed in Chapters 4 and 5, respectively), so does anti-LGBTQ+ discrimination, as discussed further later in the chapter.

Hegemonically masculine street police culture

As introduced in Chapter 5, policing institutions are heavily gendered spaces, with specific gender beliefs and norms shaping the organizational structures, policies and practices of police services in the UK and US. Street police culture is hegemonically masculine, involving structuring and controlling of gender and sexuality in particular ways (Herbert, 2001). Specifically, hegemonic masculinity places heterosexual maleness, aggression and control at the top of a gender and sexuality hierarchy, which is characterized by dominance over women and women's bodies, and denigration of LGBTQ+ or alternative sexualities (Herbert, 2001; Miller et al, 2003; Rabe-Hemp, 2009; Broomfield, 2015; Westmarland, 2017). Within the hegemonically masculine policing culture, straight male sexuality is revered, while female sexuality, gay male sexuality and other so-called deviant sexualities are meant to be controlled (Bernstein and Kostelac, 2002; Miller et al, 2003). Straight male officers are bonded over the explicit or implicit hegemonically masculine aim of subordinating and controlling these non-normative sexualities (Myers et al, 2004; Mennicke et al, 2018). Policing reinforces and maintains hegemonic masculinity through a street police culture which uses displays of control, aggression and violence to enforce its particular norms around sexualities (Bernstein and Kostelac, 2002; Miller et al, 2003; Rabe-Hemp, 2009; Morash and Haarr, 2012; Westmarland, 2017).

The hegemonically masculine character of street police culture frames police work in extremely gendered respects. This particular type of gender hierarchy is performed and reinforced through daily practices and cultural codes which define policing according to a masculine and feminine dichotomy (Herbert, 2001). Masculine police work is defined by proactive crime fighting, violence and engaging in conflict on the streets (Herbert, 2001; Westmarland, 2001; Martin and Jurik, 2007; Mennicke et al, 2018). It is considered the most important part of policing, and is the criteria against which police officers are measured and evaluated (Prokos and Padavic, 2002). Male officers are readily associated with masculine police work, while female officers are viewed as less competent at it. While some female officers may choose to aggressively pursue masculine police work and earn the respect of their male colleagues, as discussed later, male officers who shy away from masculine police work are often viewed with disdain by other male officers (Miller et al, 2003; Charles and Arndt, 2013; Broomfield, 2015; Collins and Rocco, 2018).

By contrast, hegemonic masculinity in street police culture also creates so-called feminine police work, which is defined by community engagement, administration and work with vulnerable populations (Prokos and Padavic, 2002; Miller et al, 2003; Myers et al, 2004; Rabe-Hemp, 2009; Morash and Haarr, 2012; Schuck, 2014; Westmarland, 2017). It is not highly valued in policing, and is not work against which most officers are typically evaluated (Westmarland, 2001; Prokos and Padavic, 2002). Officers who perform feminine police work are viewed as unable to engage in the 'real' police work of masculine policing, and are considered weak (Herbert, 2001). Female officers are generally associated with feminine police work and are perceived as having a penchant for it. But male officers who choose to engage in feminine police work are viewed as 'soft' and effeminate by their masculine policing colleagues (Charles and Arndt, 2013; Broomfield, 2015).

Not only does hegemonic masculinity create and reinforce heavily gendered notions of police work, but it also establishes standards of acceptable expressions of gender and sexuality for both male and female officers in the police workplace. For many LGBTQ+ officers, this creates particular complexities for gender and sexual orientation expression (Miller et al, 2003; Broomfield, 2015). For lesbian and bisexual female officers, hegemonic masculinity can give rise to pressures to be demonstrably masculinist in their gender expressions to gain acceptance from peers and supervisors (Mennicke et al, 2018). By adopting masculinist rather than feminist gender expressions, some argue this can provide a different avenue for lesbian and bisexual female officers, who can potentially gain broader acceptance than heterosexual female officers or gay male officers within the hegemonic masculinity police department framework (Miller et al, 2003; Colvin, 2012; Collins and Rocco, 2018; Panter, 2018).

By contrast, for gay and bisexual male officers, hegemonic masculinity can similarly create pressures to be visibly masculine in terms of gender expressions, again to gain support and acceptance from peers and supervisors (Mennicke et al, 2018). This may mean acting in masculine ways or not disclosing their sexual orientation to colleagues. The risks for gay and bisexual male officers can involve being stereotyped as unable to adhere to the aggressive tenets of so-called masculine policing (Miller et al, 2003; Charles and Arndt, 2013; Broomfield, 2015; Collins and Rocco, 2018). In response, some gay and bisexual male officers may engage in aggressive masculine policing to ensure they are accepted and respected by colleagues and supervisors (Broomfield, 2015). Some gay and bisexual male officers may see the alternative of being stereotyped as preferring or being predisposed to so-called feminine policing as not worth the increased risk of ostracization from supervisors and colleagues, and therefore overcompensate with masculinist policing approaches (Charles and Arndt, 2013; Broomfield, 2015).

For transgender officers, particularly transgender female officers, the hegemonically masculine nature of street police culture can similarly create significant challenges within policing institutions. Research suggests transgender officers face particular pressures to adhere to the binarily constructed gender roles discussed earlier. Indeed, transgender officers may or may not consider themselves to fit neatly within the entrenched gender dichotomies commonplace in UK and US police departments, leading their fellow officers to actively resist their presence because they may not adhere to the narrowly defined gender expressions traditionally accepted within policing (Panter, 2018). This often very challenging situation for many transgender officers may reflect conflations of gender and sexual orientation expectations by fellow officers (Panter, 2018), but nonetheless can make their lived experiences in UK and US police services painful and strained.

Heteronormative street police culture

Not only is street police culture distinctly hegemonically masculine, but it is also heteronormative, meaning it operates in a manner where heterosexuality is normalized and privileged above other forms of sexuality (Dwyer, 2008). Specifically, heteronormativity privileges, standardizes, promotes, prefers and values heterosexuality over other sexualities, including LGBTQ+ sexual identity, while non-heterosexual sexualities are regarded as incorrect or unacceptable (Berlant and Warner, 1998; Herz and Johansson, 2015). Heterosexuality is placed at the very top of a sexuality hierarchy while all non-normative sexualities and sexual lifestyles, including LGBTQ+, pansexual, polyamory, BDSM and others, are viewed as abnormal, fringe and unimportant, and are blocked or discouraged (Berlant and Warner, 1998; Dwyer, 2008). These non-normative sexualities are viewed as expressions and activities that should not be conducted in the public sphere, and must be confined to private spaces (Berlant and Warner, 1998).

In the context of heteronormative street police culture in UK and US policing, this means police institutions are generally strongholds of sexuality hierarchies whereby heterosexuality is normalized, planned for and expected. By contrast, in most UK and US police departments, non-heterosexual identities, sexual practices or sexual lifestyles are often negatively regarded as odd, abnormal and fringe. Because street police culture privileges heterosexuality in policing, this normative sexuality provides another means through which police are united, so long as their sexual identities fit in (Myers et al, 2004; Galvin-White and O'Neal, 2016; Mennicke et al, 2018). This inevitably creates significant challenges for police officers whose sexual identities, practices or lifestyles are non-normative, as it tends to position them as sexual outliers, and can serve as the basis of for discrimination and alienation from colleagues (Burke, 1994; Colvin, 2009; Jones, 2015b).

The combination of street police culture's hegemonically masculine and heteronormative structural frameworks creates social and sexuality hierarchies that heavily influence gender and sexual orientation expressions in UK and US policing. Indeed, hegemonic masculinity and heteronormativity establish and reinforce acceptable expressions of gender and sexual orientation which are, by nature, ultra-masculine and aggressively heterosexual (Dwyer, 2008; Colvin, 2015). Because gender and sexuality expression generally occur simultaneously with awareness of dominant social mores (Miller et al, 2003), these normative frameworks make it more challenging in policing for those who operate outside these norms. For those who are not ultra-masculine and aggressively heterosexual, which can include LGBTQ+ officers, female officers, pansexual, polyamorous and others, the ways hegemonic masculinity and heteronormativity structure police workplaces can make gender and sexual orientation expression particularly challenging, creating sources of significant tension and stress.

Resistance to LGBTQ+ officers

Because street police culture sets the hegemonically masculine and heteronormative norms for policing institutions, it is unsurprising that evidence suggests that many UK and US police services can be difficult if not outright hostile environments for many LGBTQ+ officers. Although this area remains under-investigated, research reflects the inherent anti-LGBTQ+ sentiments of UK and US policing. Several studies have captured this, with officers in both jurisdictions routinely expressing anti-LGBTQ+ views (RAND, 1993; Bernstein and Kostelac, 2002; Miller et al, 2003; Myers et al, 2004; Blackbourn, 2006; Colvin, 2015; Miller and Lilley, 2014). Gay and bisexual men appear to be particularly disliked by police in this area of research (Burke, 1994; Miller and Lilley, 2014).

The drivers of negative police views about LGBTQ+ people generally, and gay and bisexual men in particular, are deeply rooted in the hegemonically masculine and heteronormative straight male norms of street police culture. These ultra-masculinist, uber-heterosexual perspectives are relatively fragile and, some theorize, may make straight male officers feel their maleness and heterosexuality is threated by LGBTQ+ people, and gay and bisexual men in particular. This has been borne out in some policing studies where straight male officers vocalize that being seen as explicitly tolerant of gay male sexuality somehow calls into question their own male heterosexuality (Burke, 1994; Herbert, 2001; Miller and Lilley, 2014).

The strongly hegemonically masculine and heteronormative norms of street police culture serve to constantly reaffirm heterosexual maleness as the ideal type among police officers. Researchers, therefore, argue that expressing anti-LGBTQ+ sentiments, particularly against gay and bisexual men, is another way to bond and to reaffirm commitment to a particular type of masculinist policing (Burke, 1994; Bernstein and Kostelac, 2002; Miller et al, 2003; Myers et al, 2004; Galvin-White and O'Neal, 2016). Martin and Jurik's 2007 US-based study found that straight male officers were hostile to LGBTQ+ police because they perceived them as threatening to straight male street police culture norms. Research by Myers et al (2004), Martin and Jurik, 2007, Colvin (2015), and Mennicke et al (2018) has found that the presence of gay and bisexual male officers, whom they perceive as outsiders to street police culture norms in UK and US police services, challenges the relative comfort and perceived social cohesion many straight male officers find in departmental homogeneity.

The overtly anti-LGBTQ+ sentiment created by hegemonically masculine and heteronormative street police culture can be very challenging for LGBTQ+ officers, and negatively impact their experiences on the job (Myers et al, 2004; Colvin, 2015). These aspects of police culture can make LGBTQ+ officers particularly fearful, uncomfortable, alienated, stressed about fitting in, and generally impeded compared to their straight male colleagues (Dowler, 2005; Hassell and Brandl, 2009; Jones and Williams, 2015; Collins and Rocco, 2018). Such anti-LGBTQ+ attitudes can also result in significant differences in the terms and conditions of employment for many LGBTQ+ officers, including disparities in assignments and promotions compared to their straight colleagues, as discussed later in the chapter (Blackbourn, 2006).

In practice, the forms of resistance to LGBTQ+ people and LGBTQ+ officers by fellow officers can range from explicit homophobic statements, less desirable assignments, poor performance evaluations, denials of promotions, refusing to partner with LGBTQ+ officers, refusing to be supervised by LGBTQ+ officers, starting rumours, harassments, and ostracization, among many others (Belkin and McNichol, 2002; Bernstein and Kostelac, 2002). Some of these significant challenges faced by LGBTQ+ officers in UK and US police services are discussed later.

Staying closeted or coming out in policing

Given street police culture's decidedly hegemonically masculine and heteronormative character, decisions about whether to come out at work are complex for LGBTQ+ officers. Naturally, there are inherent risks in disclosing one's sexual orientation in police institutions with entrenched explicit and implicit histories of hostility toward LGBTQ+ people. Yet there are also risks embedded in not being able to live openly according to one's sexual preferences, and having to hide aspects of oneself in the workplace. In both scenarios, LGBTQ+ officers face a degree of subordination – either by the institution itself or through self-subordination as they navigate working in heteronormative policing institutions (Collins and Rocco, 2018).

This inherent tension in the decision to come out in a policing service is one very important and very significant difference in the experiences of LGBTQ+ officers compared to their straight colleagues. Unlike personal characteristics which are more readily visible, such as race or gender, an LGBTQ+ officer's sexuality may not be readily apparent to police colleagues, given at least the appearance of free will in making the disclosure. Yet this can be challenging for LGBTQ+ officers because police institutions are shaped by hegemonically masculine and heteronormative street police culture which, by default, assumes that all officers are heterosexual unless or until they affirmatively disclose their LGBTQ+

status. Contending with this dynamic is one key reason LGBTQ+ officers are often referred to as invisible minorities within policing, meaning their marginalized status may not be readily apparent to colleagues and supervisors until or unless they disclose their sexual orientation (Galvin-White and O'Neal, 2016).

As with any sexual orientation disclosure decision for an LGTBQ+ individual, it is a deeply personal one. For LGBTQ+ officers working within hegemonically masculine and heteronormative police institutions, the determination about if, when and how to tell colleagues and supervisors is a highly individualized choice, and often a very stressful one (Burke, 1994; Miller et al, 2003; Galvin-White and O'Neal, 2016). Both institutional and individual factors can influence decisions to be 'out' in a police department, including perceived hostility or support for LGBTQ+ people and communities, presence of LGBTQ+ police associations, an officer's length of service, and feelings of support for individuals from colleagues and supervisors on the job (Miller et al, 2003; Galvin-White and O'Neal, 2016; Mennicke et al, 2018). And these disclosures can have a major impact on the policing role, as they can significantly shape an officer's future in the position, as well as their job satisfaction, work motivation, stress levels and interpersonal relationships on a police force (Colvin, 2009). Indeed, many LGBTQ+ officers fear being differentially treated at work after coming out (Hassell and Brandl, 2009; Collins and Rocco, 2018) and, as will be discussed later, some of these fears may be well founded based on the evidence from both UK and US policing contexts.

Decisions by LGBTQ+ officers about whether to be open about their sexual orientation within policing institutions are not necessarily straightforward. Indeed, such determinations can occur along a spectrum in both their personal lives and workplace contexts for many police officers (Miller et al, 2003; Colvin, 2009; Rumens and Broomfield, 2012; Jones, 2015b). Some officers choose to be closeted both at work and at home, passing for heterosexual in both their public and private lives, and keeping their LGBTQ+ status hidden from colleagues and friends alike (Burke, 1994; Miller et al, 2003; Charles and Arndt, 2013; Collins and Rocco, 2018).

Other LGBTQ+ officers choose to remain closeted at work only, splitting knowledge of their sexual orientation between their public and private lives (Burke, 1994; Myers et al, 2004). This means LGBTQ+ officers separate their work and home lives and, within the hegemonically masculine and heteronormative police institutions, they are simply assumed to be straight. This non-disclosure and presumption of heterosexuality can lead to LGBTQ+ officers leading 'double lives' (Burke, 1994; Miller et al, 2003; Collins and Rocco, 2018). Research suggests this type of pressure can be extremely taxing. Indeed, Burke (1994), Rumens and Broomfield (2012), Broomfield (2015), Galvin-White and O'Neal (2016), Miller et al (2003), Collins and

Rocco (2018) and others have found extreme stresses for LGBTQ+ officers leading these double lives, also referred to as 'counterfitting'.

This additional stress of not being out in the policing organization can compound the usual police officer pressures, resulting in additional anxiety, fear, stress, anger, worry and depression for LGBTQ+ officers (Galvin-White and O'Neal, 2016). Numerous studies illustrate the ways these psychological effects are particularly pronounced for closeted LGBTQ+ officers. For example, in Jones's 2015b survey of 836 LGB officers in England and Wales, 21 per cent of officers were closeted, fearing discrimination, bullying/harassment, isolation and significantly differential treatment if they disclosed their sexual orientation at work. Similarly, in Charles and Arndt's 2013 study of 14 LGB officers in the police and sheriffs' offices in the American Midwest, 11 were out to most people at work and in their personal lives, while three reported that they were either not out or out to very few at work. The three closeted gay male officers discussed the ways homophobic street police culture and witnessing homophobic incidents and discrimination at work discouraged them from coming out.

Support from fellow officers can be a valuable contributing factor to decisions for LGBTQ+ officers to come out in hegemonically masculine, heteronormative police institutions. Some studies show LGBTQ+ officers elect to share their sexuality with fellow LGBTQ+ officers only, but keep it hidden from straight colleagues as a means to build support and solidarity (RAND, 1993; Miller et al, 2003; Rumens and Broomfield, 2012; Charles and Arndt, 2013). Within workplaces where LGBTQ+ officers are only out to one another, there can be an unspoken code among them not to out each other at work (Galvin-White and O'Neal, 2016). Other studies reflect that some LGBTQ+ officers are only out to their patrol partners, with whom they spend lots of time and establish trust, while remaining closeted to most of their peers, supervisors and senior leaders (RAND, 1993; Miller et al, 2003).

Some LGBTQ+ officers stay closeted initially on the job, wanting to first establish their reputations as good police officers adept at the masculinist policing so highly prized in hegemonically masculine, heteronormative street police culture before coming out. A number of studies reflect that for officers who established their reputations as a 'good cop' first and came out to colleagues and supervisors later on, many felt a level of support after coming out (RAND, 1993; Belkin and McNichol, 2002; Miller et al, 2003; Charles and Arndt, 2013; Collins and Rocco, 2018).

Research suggests the pressures of adhering to hegemonically masculine, heteronormative norms in street police culture before coming out is particularly acute for gay male officers. Indeed, studies evidence that some gay and bisexual male officers weigh heavily the need for developing their masculinist policing reputations first, so there could be few doubts about their skills to be effective officers before coming out (Miller et al, 2003; Rumens and Broomfield, 2012; Charles and Arndt, 2013). In many instances, when LGBTQ+ officers finally do come out after an established period as an officer, they and their colleagues and supervisors may focus on their proven track record of masculine police work to help make the adaptation smooth (Belkin and McNichol, 2002). In such instances, an LGBTQ+ officer's past performance as a hardworking cop who adheres to the hegemonically masculine, heteronormative ways of policing can be more significant in calibrating their acceptance by other officers than their disclosure of their sexual orientation (Belkin and McNichol, 2002). This was echoed by Interview Subject 3, who made it a point of establishing his reputation as an active, tough, street-wise cop before coming out in his police service years later.

Within hegemonically masculine and heteronormative police institutions, personal health, safety and security are significant factors influencing LGBTQ+ officers' decisions to come out. Some officers reported not coming out because they worried about fellow officers physically or verbally assaulting them, ostracizing them or failing to back them up on service calls (Miller et al, 2003). Some studies reflect that LGBTQ+ officers' observations of homophobic discrimination, slurs, harassment and negative treatment of LGBTQ+ community members by police, and ill-treatment of other LGBTQ+ officers who previously came out, deterred them from doing so (Hassell and Brandl, 2009; Colvin, 2009; Rumens and Broomfield, 2012; Colvin, 2015).

Another aspect of safety concerns for LGBTQ+ officers revolves around being forcibly outed by colleagues. It is unsurprising that in hegemonically masculine and heteronormative police institutions with long histories of homophobia and discrimination, threats to out LGBTQ+ officers carry very real security considerations. Studies by RAND (1993), Colvin (2015), Collins and Rocco (2018) and others all demonstrate how realistic this concern is for serving LGTBQ+ officers. For example, of the 243 UK LGTBQ officers surveyed by Colvin (2015), 34 per cent reported being outed by a colleague against their wishes. Colvin's study found 35 per cent of gay male officers and 37 per cent of lesbian officers reported being outed by colleagues, supervisors or others at work. Similarly, 17 per cent of the 836 LGB officers in Jones's 2015 study were outed by a colleague.

The pressures on closeted LGBTQ+ police officers working within the confines of hegemonically masculine and heteronormative police institutions add significant emotional and relationship costs due to not being able to be public about their sexual orientation. Street police culture norms often pressure many closeted male officers to engage in discussions about heterosexual sexual conquests to avoid isolation and questions about their sexuality (Miller et al, 2003). Others feel forced to fabricate opposite-sex partners to satiate curiosity from colleagues about their love lives. For example, some of the lesbian officers and one bisexual female officer in Galvin-White et al's 2016 study fabricated male romantic partners to remain closeted and minimize sexual harassment from male colleagues. Similarly, Interview Subject 3 also felt the need to imply or fabricate female paramours to avoid suspicion of being gay at work.

Unsurprisingly, many LGBTQ+ closeted officers report high levels of stress from keeping their sexual orientation a secret from colleagues and hiding their relationships with their partners (Miller et al, 2003). This is consistent with the experience of Interview Subject 3 interviewed for this book. As a closeted gay man during the early parts of his career, he struggled with the pressures and stresses of not disclosing his sexual orientation to colleagues and supervisors:

> I have talked about this on several occasions. And I'm hoping that there is a lot less of this, that people, I think people certainly in [redacted] and other metro areas, I think you can be an out LGBT person and have very different experience now than what I experienced then. I think not being out, but being [closeted] … I think a lot of people over time began to suspect that something was not right here because you're the one that never has a girlfriend with you at occasions, or uses the various ambiguous pronouns. And so I think that it's a lot better now in a lot of places. I think that there are still, frankly, a lot of places where it is not better [for LGBTQ+ officers].

Taken together, Interview Subject 3's experiences coupled with the existing literature illustrate the ways hegemonically masculine, heteronormative street police culture sets the norms of acceptable sexualities in UK and US police services.

Being out in policing

For LGBTQ+ officers who choose to come out at work in hegemonically masculine, heteronormative police institutions, research suggests they perceive the benefits of disclosure to outweigh the costs (Rumens and Broomfield, 2012; Colvin, 2015).

Studies show the rates of officers being out at work are steadily increasing. In Colvin's 2015 survey of 243 LGBTQ+ officers in England and Wales, 71 per cent were out to everyone at work, including their colleagues, supervisors and subordinates. In Jones's 2015b survey of 836 LGB officers in England

and Wales, 41 per cent said they were out at work from their first day on the job. Broomfield's 2015 study of 20 gay male officers in England and Wales found nearly all were out in their respective departments. Many of the officers in Broomfield's study did not express difficulty with coming out at work, and felt policies, practices and training were sufficiently advanced as to help them easily integrate as out gay men in their departments.

Research suggests that LGBTQ+ officers being out at work can result in a range of different experiences. Studies show that being out at work can result in significant differential treatment for LGBTQ+ officers in a number of respects including stereotyping, bullying, harassment, poorer assignments, failure to be promoted, exclusion from mentorship, networking and social events, negative performance evaluations, formal complaints and firing, among others (Burke, 1994; Miller et al, 2003; Hassell and Brandl, 2009; Colvin, 2009; Rumens and Broomfield, 2012; Colvin, 2015). Some LGBTQ+ officers feel more heavily scrutinized by heterosexual officers after coming out, and find that many times straight officers can try to exclude, subordinate, establish boundaries with or otherwise remind LGBTQ+ officers of their status as minorities due to their sexual orientation (Miller et al, 2003).

Studies indicate that being out at work can prove particularly challenging for gay and bisexual male officers given the hegemonically masculine and heteronormative nature of street police culture in both the UK and US (Jones and Williams, 2015; Zempi, 2020). Indeed, research suggests that out gay and bisexual male officers are often stereotyped as lacking the skills to carry out masculine policing, and its requisite displays of aggression and toughness. An early study about LGB officers in the UK by Burke (1994), for example, found that LGB officers felt conflicted between their sexual identities and the hegemonic masculine values of street police culture upheld by their peers. Indeed, research has found that the masculinity of gay male officers is often questioned by straight male officers if they are out at work (Miller et al, 2003). Some gay officers overemphasize their toughness and strength to avoid being negatively stereotyped (Miller et al, 2003; Myers et al, 2004; Broomfield, 2015).

Some research based on qualitative interviews with LGBTQ+ officers asserts that out gay male officers often have more difficult experiences in policing than out lesbian female officers (Zempi, 2020). Such findings seem due to the pressures of hegemonically masculine and heteronormative street police culture, which remain particularly acute for out gay and bisexual male officers (Jones and Williams, 2015; Broomfield, 2015; Zempi, 2020). For example, Broomfield's study of 20 out gay male officers in the UK found that many clung to hegemonically masculine street police culture norms because they believed that effeminate gay men were the antithesis of 'traditional masculinity and effective policing' (Broomfield, 2015: 80). For these officers, being an ultra-masculine police officer was an essential part of their policing identity as a good cop, while being an effeminate or camp gay man made officers the subject of ridicule and scorn (Broomfield, 2015).

Indeed, research suggests that proving their skills as good police can be one way to mitigate the effects of anti-LGBTQ+ bias on LGBTQ+ officers, particularly for gay men (Belkin and McNichol, 2002; Miller and Lilley, 2014). This was the experience of Interview Subject 3, an American LGBTQ+ police leader, who described his need to prove himself on the job this way:

> I think that there are still, frankly, a lot of places where it is not better [for LGBTQ+ officers]. I think that gay men in particular in policing have always had more of a challenge than lesbians have, for weird reasons that don't entirely make sense either, but I think part of that, in terms of a formative for me, was I think that I became inappropriately and unnecessarily aggressive in my approach to policing. I felt, I mean I think that there really was some truth to the idea that I continually felt that I had to compensate and prove that there would be nothing that I wouldn't get involved in or couldn't do as a gay man.

Like gay male officers, some research has found that openly trans female officers challenge accepted hegemonically masculine and heteronormative expressions of gender expression within police institutions (Panter, 2018). This research indicates that trans female officers are often negatively stereotyped by their straight male colleagues for seemingly rejecting the most valued aspects of policing – their maleness – and instead focusing on the least valued aspects of policing – their femaleness (Panter, 2018). In this way, trans female officers are associated with negative stereotypes of feminine policing, as discussed earlier and in Chapter 5.

Unlike gay male, trans female and straight female officers, some research indicates that out lesbian and bisexual officers can be stereotyped by straight male colleagues as embracing street police culture norms, including aspects of masculine policing, such as aggression and toughness (Colvin, 2012; Galvin-White and O'Neal, 2016; Panter, 2018). This suggests lesbian officers may often be stereotyped by some straight male officers as being better suited to masculine street policing compared to their gay male, trans female and straight female officers (Burke, 1994; Panter, 2018). On the other hand, out lesbian and bisexual female officers may also be negatively viewed by straight male colleagues and supervisors, and treated in discriminatory ways, for deviating from binary expressions of gender and sexuality embedded in street police culture (Rabe-Hemp, 2009; Galvin-White and O'Neal, 2016).

For LGBTQ+ officers of colour, decisions about being out at work create a particular set of intersectional needs, which require addressing not only their lived experiences as officers of colour with all the accompanying racial disparities as discussed in Chapter 4, but also the additional challenges around overt LGBTQ+ identities in hegemonically masculine and heteronormative police institutions and cultures. While the subject is vastly under-researched, the data suggest LGBTQ+ officers of colour can face particularly harsh consequences given the weight of contending with these intersectional oppressions. One of few studies to explore this issue, Miller et al (2003), found that within the study's cohort, the vast majority of closeted officers were officers of colour, suggesting that the calculus about coming out may be particularly fraught for these officers with the added pressures of street police culture's racism, racial biases and racialized stereotypes within police institutions.

Given the research showing significant disparities in the treatment of officers of colour in both UK and US departments, when coupled with research on the disparities experienced by LGBTQ+ officers, it is unsurprising that LGBTQ+ officers of colour express particular concerns around being out and potentially subjecting themselves to intersectional discrimination and ostracization when they are part of two visible minority groups (or in the case of lesbian officers of colour, three visible minority groups). Miller et al's 2003 study found that the additional challenges faced by LGBTQ+ officers of colour were likely due to the White privilege enjoyed by White LGBTQ+ officers, meaning they are more accepted into the culturally White policing institution than their non-White colleagues. Because there is very little research in this area, and the experiences of LGBTQ+ officers with intersectional identities require much more empirical study.

Bias in assignments

Research suggests that the hegemonically masculine and heteronormative street police culture within UK and US policing produces notable and commonplace differences in the lived experiences of discrimination in hiring, firing, promotion and conditions of employment for LGBTQ+ officers in both jurisdictions. Indeed, studies suggest between 25 per cent and 66 per cent of LGBTQ+ officers face discrimination in their police departments, although this may be a low estimate given some officers remain closeted in policing as discussed earlier (Colvin, 2015).

Of the variety of types of differential treatment experienced by LGTBQ+ officers, biases in assignments can prove impactful in their policing experiences (Colvin, 2015). Yet there is only minimal research about discrimination in assignments experienced by LGBTQ+ officers in the UK or US. Early research on out LGBTQ+ officers found some felt they were stereotyped as amoral and even as being paedophiles, which negatively impacted their assignments (Leinen, 1993; Miller et al, 2003). Indeed, in Miller et al's study, some LGBTQ+ officers reported being cautious about being alone with children or being involved in child-facing roles for fear of being homophobically stereotyped by co-workers who might maliciously make false misconduct accusations. The periods of early research on LGBTQ+ officers reflected other types of homophobic stereotypes impacting assignments, with LGBTQ+ officers routinely stereotyped as having HIV or AIDS by co-workers, impacting both their assignments and the willingness of colleagues to work with them (RAND, 1993; Leinen, 1993; Miller et al, 2003).

When it comes to discrimination in assignments, various aspects of hegemonically masculine and heteronormative stereotypes may come into play for officers assessing whether they have been subjected to anti-LGBTQ+ discrimination. Indeed, as discussed earlier, within the street police culture which creates a dichotomous framework of masculine and feminine policing, some LGBTQ+ officers, particularly gay and bisexual male officers who are out at work, may be stereotyped as better suited to work with community members and vulnerable victims, and less well suited for the harder edged masculine policing assignments on patrol or in elite units such as firearms, narcotics or motorcycle patrols (Westmarland, 2001; Panter, 2018; Casey, 2023). Similarly, out lesbian or bisexual female officers may be assigned to masculine policing roles based on sexual orientation stereotypes, or feminine police roles with communities and victims based on gender stereotypes.

Research suggests certain policing units are still seen as more masculine policing or feminine policing than others, creating a hierarchy of gendered assignments (Westmarland, 2001; Panter, 2018). Within this hierarchy, gay men, trans women and cis women who do not appear sufficiently oriented toward masculine policing may not be given the same opportunities as straight men to join highly prestigious units such as firearms, mounted, canine or other tactical teams, or are unsupported if posted to those assignments (Westmarland, 2001; Panter, 2018; Casey, 2023). Ultimately, where LGBTQ+ officers believe they have been assigned to posts based on street police culture stereotypes, they may feel resentment about the perceived discrimination.

Naturally, there are a range of views of perceived stereotyping and bias in assignments across LGBTQ+ officers. For example, some LGBTQ+ officers in Miller and Lilley's 2014 US study enjoyed being assigned to work in traditional LGBTQ+ neighbourhoods, while others felt stereotyped by such positions, and did not want to be pigeonholed into community-facing, feminine policing roles which they perceived as low status in police institutions (Miller and Lilley, 2014).

In terms of lived experiences of discrimination in assignments for LGBTQ+ officers, surveys consistently show feelings of differential treatment in UK and US policing. For example, Colvin's 2009 survey of 66 LGBTQ+

officers from across different US police departments found 17 per cent believed they faced anti-LGBTQ+ discrimination in their assignments. Colvin's 2015 survey of 234 LGB officers found important similarities and differences between gay and bisexual men, and lesbian and bisexual female officers regarding assignments, with 12 per cent of gay male officers believing they had been discriminated against in their postings, while 9 per cent of lesbian and bisexual female officers reported the same. Interestingly, LGB officers in Colvin's study were much more likely to report discrimination experiences of LGB colleagues, with 23 per cent of gay men and 12 per cent of lesbian women reporting witnessing discrimination in the assignments of fellow LGB officers (Colvin, 2015).

There could be several reasons for the findings in Colvin's study. It is possible, for example, that the LGB officers interviewed were unaware they had experienced discrimination in their assignments or scheduling. Similarly, admitting they had been subjected to discrimination in assignments may have required respondents to acknowledge that they did not fit into their police organization as seamlessly as they believed if they were being singled out for discrimination. It could also be that it was easier to see discrimination against another LGB person than to realize they had been discriminated against themselves.

While there are very few studies of the experiences of LGBTQ+ officers of colour in relation to assignments, research suggests they may be significantly more likely to experience discrimination in roles compared to their White LGBTQ+ colleagues. For example, Jones and Williams' 2015 US survey of 836 LGB officers found LGB officers of colour were more than six times more likely to perceive discrimination in their postings compared to their White LGB counterparts. While more research is needed, the study illustrates that LGBTQ+ officers of colour have important intersectional needs when it comes to being subjected to and addressing the combination of racial and sexual orientation bias.

Promotions

Like the officers of colour and female officers subject to street police culture stereotypes discussed in previous chapters, LGBTQ+ officers similarly face challenges in relation to stereotypes and impediments to promotion to supervisory and leadership positions within UK and US policing. While there is insufficient research, it is important to consider LGBTQ+ promotions within the larger hegemonically masculine and heteronormative street policing frameworks in which they operate in policing institutions.

As discussed in Chapters 4 and 5, the police promotions process relies on candidate evaluations based on criteria which value, highlight and prioritize masculine policing traits, a process which in turn reinforces hegemonic masculinity norms (Westmarland, 2001; Miller et al, 2003; Silvestri, 2006; Rabe-Hemp, 2009; Barratt et al, 2014; Mennicke et al, 2018; Clinkinbeard et al, 2020). Even seemingly neutral promotion criteria are infused with heavily gendered and heteronormative street police culture frameworks which disadvantage those who are perceived as being incapable or ill-suited to masculinist policing priorities. Research further suggests it is at the points of greatest discretion in evaluating performance where anti-LGTBQ+ discrimination is most likely to occur (Holdaway and O'Neill, 2007; Colvin, 2009; Jones and Williams, 2015). For some LGBTQ+ officers, positive performance evaluations and promotion applications will feel elusive, or at least fraught, with potential for street police culture's homophobic influences.

The negative stereotypes about LGTBQ+ officers created by hegemonically masculine and heteronormative street police culture mean, for some seeking promotions, being out at work is perceived as a significant risk to career advancement. Indeed, studies reflect that for some officers, coming out will stall their promotion ambitions given levels of anti-LGBTQ+ discrimination. For example, 50 per cent of LGBTQ+ officers surveyed in Miller et al's 2003 US study believed that being out could have direct and likely negative impacts on their ability to achieve promotions in their department. Some believed that being closeted was the only way to achieve promotion. Others in the study believed being perceived as married or marriageable was required for promotion (Miller et al, 2003), again a reference to the heteronormative values imposed by the policing institution.

In terms of actual lived experiences or perceptions of anti-LGBTQ+ discrimination in police promotions, several studies offer insights. For example, Colvin's 2009 survey of officers from across different US police departments found 22 per cent believed anti-LGBTQ+ discrimination was a barrier to promotion. Moreover, Colvin's 2015 survey of 234 LGB officers in England and Wales found 12 per cent of gay men and 6 per cent of lesbian and bisexual women officers personally experienced discrimination in promotions. As with Colvin's 2015 findings on observed discrimination in the assignments of LGBTQ+ colleagues discussed earlier, with regard to promotions, 17 per cent of gay and bisexual men and 15 per cent of lesbian and bisexual women officers reported witnessing an LGB colleague experience discrimination in promotions. Again, it is unclear from these findings the precise reasons for these differences. While it is possible that some LGBTQ+ officers are less discriminated against than their LGBTQ+ colleagues, it is more likely that they are unable or unwilling to recognize their own experiences of discrimination out of a belief that they fit in and are accepted into their organization. Regardless of the motivations, research shows that lack of promotion and growth opportunities can negatively impact job satisfaction for LGBTQ+ officers, leading them to be more likely to seek other employment opportunities (Colvin, 2009).

Homophobic harassment

Not only do the hegemonically masculine and heteronormative tenets of street police culture impact LGBTQ+ officer promotions, but they also affect lived experiences of day-to-day discrimination and homophobic harassment in UK and US police services. Research from both jurisdictions demonstrates that many LGBTQ+ police officers have been subjected to overt and covert homophobic discrimination and harassment by fellow officers and supervisors in different forms, ranging from homophobic comments to inferior assignments to negative rumours to failures of fellow officers to provide back-up, and other homophobic behaviours (Leinen, 1993; Belkin and McNichol, 2002; Colvin, 2009).

Given the entrenched hegemonic masculinity and heteronormativity in UK and US police street police culture, it is unsurprising that LGBTQ+ officers have long been subject to homophobic comments (Leinen, 1993; Burke, 1994; Home Office, 2005; Colvin, 2009, 2012). In the UK, for example, Burke's 1994 study of LGB officers found that most, if not all, had been subjected to anti-LGB comments, jokes and information from straight colleagues. Similarly, Colvin's 2015 survey of 243 UK LGBTQ+ officers found 50 per cent reported being subjected to homophobic comments. Moreover, a UK Home Office survey of over 1,200 officers in England and Wales in 2005 found that explicit homophobic comments were routine, and even more commonplace than racist language. Interestingly, the survey found that while officers were much more aware of the disciplinary consequences for using racist language, using homophobic language did not carry the same concerns (Home Office, 2005). More recently, Baroness Casey's report on the London Met Police (Casey, 2023) found that 20 per cent of LGTBQ+ officers in the London Met Police had personally experienced homophobia, and 30 per cent reported bullying, which could range from comments to other forms of harassment and discrimination.

These findings from UK studies are consistent with US-based studies showing most LGBTQ+ officers face homophobic comments from fellow officers on the job. Belkin and McNichol (2002) found most or all LGBTQ+ officers hear or are subject to homophobic comments, jokes or graffiti. In Miller's 2003 study of LGB officers in a Midwestern US police department, 100 per cent had heard, seen or been targeted by anti-gay or lesbian jokes, comments, graffiti or cartoons. Martin and Jurik's 2007 US research found that many heterosexual male officers openly expressed overt homophobic beliefs about their LGBTQ+ colleagues, particularly gay male officers. Hassell and

Brandl (2009) also found LGBTQ+ officers had significantly more negative experiences of vulgar language than their straight colleagues. Colvin's 2009 survey of 66 LGBTQ+ officers from across different US police departments found 67 per cent reported homophobic comments were commonplace.

Again, given how established hegemonic masculinity and heteronormativity are in UK and US street police culture, it is unsurprising that studies show homophobic harassment has long been a common experience for many LGBTQ+ officers in both jurisdictions. RAND's 1993 study of LGBTQ+ officers in six of America's largest urban police departments found that some LGBTQ+ officers acknowledged enduring different forms of harassment. The study found homophobic incidents ranged from being framed by fellow colleagues for misconduct through planting false evidence to subjecting LGBTQ+ officers to false incriminating statements. Similarly, Leinen's 1993 study around the same time period involved personal observations in the NYPD and interviews with 41 LGB officers in New York City, and found more than 100 documented homophobic incidents by police toward members of the LGBTQ+ community. In that study, Leinen found that so many LGBTQ+ officers had observed harassment of LGBTQ+ colleagues and community members that many were deterred from coming out in the department. Colvin's 2009 survey of 66 LGBTQ+ officers from across different US police departments found 34 per cent had endured repeated harassment on the job, again showing the persistence of homophobia in policing.

LGBTQ+ officers' responses to harassment vary significantly, from silence to formal complaints to voluntary resignations. Given the levels of hegemonic masculinity and heteronormativity endemic in street police culture, it is unsurprising that studies have shown that LGBTQ+ officers infrequently file formal or informal complaints about homophobic harassment by colleagues compared to the numbers of race- and gender-based complaints (Belkin and McNichol, 2002). The reasons for this are multi-fold. For example, a number of LGBTQ+ officers may remain closeted at work, meaning that filing a formal or informal complaint could lead to further negative behaviours from colleagues and supervisors (Belkin and McNichol, 2002). Another reason may be driven by loyalty or the blue wall of silence among officers discussed in Chapter 2, which emphasizes unity and the informal resolution of problems among officers rather than official reporting of complaints (Belkin and McNichol, 2002). Finally, some LGBTQ+ officers perceive the punishments for homophobic behaviour to be too high for all parties involved, and require the devotion of significant time and energy to supporting the complaint (Belkin and McNichol, 2002). Whatever the reasons for the reluctance of some LGBTQ+ to file formal complaints about homophobic incidents, lived experiences of these occurences place added stresses on them that they must face alongside all the other pressures of being officers in the UK and US.

LGBTQ+ officer associations

Given the ways the established hegemonic masculinity and heteronormativity in UK and US street police culture place pressures, and create discriminatory experiences and different terms and conditions of employment for LGBTQ+ officers, LGBTQ+ officer associations have long been an important source of support in both the UK and US. LGBTQ+ officer associations generally have both internal functions supporting officers and seeking departmental change, and external functions aiming to improve police–LGBTQ+ community relations (Colvin, 2020). While many US LGBTQ+ officer associations focused on recruitment alongside other internal and external responsibilities, British and other European LGBTQ+ associations generally have not been used for recruiting purposes (Colvin, 2020). Among various accomplishments, some of the most important measurable outcomes for LGBTQ+ officer associations include providing support to LGBTQ+ officers and enhancing diversity training on LGBTQ+ issues, ranging from educating leaders to academy cadets (Colvin, 2020).

These associations first developed in the 1990s in both the UK and US. The organizations formed amid LGBTQ+ officers feeling isolated on their police forces and wanting to seek out other LGBTQ+ officers for support (Colvin, 2020). These groups were important resources for LGBTQ+ officers, offering support and camaraderie in police environments that were often openly hostile to LGBTQ+ officers. Yet the organizations were generally resisted by the police institutions from which they originated (Colvin, 2020). Similar to BAME officer groups discussed in Chapter 4, these LGBTQ+ associations were frequently viewed negatively, regarded with suspicion and hostility by their policing institutions (Colvin, 2020), presumably because they were viewed by some majority group officers and leaders as disrupting cohesion amongst officers, or drawing unwanted attention to the difficulties experienced by LGBTQ+ officers. While members of the public were generally neutral or positive about the founding of the associations, some British newspapers ran stories questioning their value (Colvin, 2020).

Studies show that even where LGBTQ+ officers were not out in their departments, some were members of LGBTQ+ officer associations (RAND, 1993). In Los Angeles in 1993, for example, only seven officers were publicly out in the force, but over 40 joined the LGBTQ+ officer association (RAND, 1993). Some officers avoid joining LGBTQ+ officer associations for fear of being outed and the negative consequences of being identified as LGBTQ+ as discussed in this chapter (RAND, 1993). Other LGBTQ+ officers declined to join perhaps because of lack of interest or lack of desire to be identified simply as 'gay cops' or 'lesbian cops' (RAND, 1993).

Interestingly, in the UK, studies show that despite the GPA being established on a national level since 1990, many LGBTQ+ police officers are not members. In 2012, there were over 5,000 members of the UK's GPA, which includes LGBTQ+ officers, community support workers and staff (Colvin, 2012). Yet in Jones's 2015 survey of 836 LGB officers in England and Wales, only 28 per cent report being members. By contrast, 44 per cent of the LGB officers in the study reported being members of their local department's Gay Staff Network, which supports LGB officers at the local level. One of the reasons UK officers may choose not to join the national GPA is the fear of stigma, discrimination and stereotyping by aligning with the interests of other LGBTQ+ officers within pressures they face within hegemonically masculine and heteronormative street police cultures which negatively stereotype LGBTQ+ officers. Indeed, officers may fear that joining LGBTQ+ associations generally will make them more visible and more likely to be targeted within explicitly or implicitly homophobic police services. These fears are borne out by some research (Jones and Williams, 2015), which shows that in the UK, members of the GPA perceive greater anti-LGBTQ+ discrimination on the job in everything from training to assignments than non-members who are also LGBTQ+.

Community engagement and community relations

The hegemonically masculine and heteronormative street police culture of UK and US policing clearly create explicit and implicit pressures for many LGTBQ+ officers. While some feel disproportionately stereotyped and steered into so-called feminine police work as discussed previously, LGBTQ+ officers' own lived experiences of bias and discrimination may make them particularly open to, or supportive of, policing approaches which reject the warrior policing model, and instead focus on guardian policing of local communities, a notion rooted in representative bureaucracy discussed further in Chapter 8.

While research is limited, some studies show that some LGBTQ+ officers see themselves as particularly able to be compassionate and understanding toward community members, given their own lived experiences of being underrepresented minorities (Myers et al, 2004). Research evidences that some LGBTQ+ officers report feeling better able to deal with the needs of traditionally marginalized communities they police than some of their straight colleagues given their own experiences of struggles, bigotry, victimization and oppression (Miller et al, 2003). For example, 50 per cent of LGB officers in Charles and Arndt's 2013 study of LGB officers in several US Midwestern police and sheriffs' departments felt their presence in policing was an asset to the way traditionally marginalized communities were policed. These LGB officers felt their own personal experiences of marginalization made them well suited to be empathetic, compassionate and supportive of a broad range of communities, and to value diversity.

This was evidenced in interviews conducted for this book. For example, Interview Subject 3, an LGBTQ+ police leader, reflected on his community engagement focused approach to his work:

> I think you have to have a top-down example of what engagement looks like. And I spent a lot of time like all my time being out in the community, building relationships, and listening to people and trying to give them a sense of hope and optimism that things could change. And then sort of spreading that as a necessary component for all the cops that work there. ... I really became one with that community and I think that engagement is about building those relationships and people can call you day and night, which they did. ... [W]e saw this as being part of a huge, exciting social change experiment that we were hugely committed to and people can sense when you're being real and when you're not and so they knew that we were working really hard to make things different and people were so incredibly grateful and cool about it, considering how hard that must be in the circumstances where I would never have the patience or the attitude to be grateful to anybody. ... But I think that engagement has to be that willingness- It goes almost against this whole cop culture [street police culture] that we've been talking about where you're trained to be so guarded.

While Interview Subject 3 did not explicitly state that his community engagement focused approach to policing was grounded in his identity and experiences as a gay male officer, his interview comments suggest as much. Indeed, some studies have illustrated that LGBTQ+ officers may feel particularly inclined toward community engagement work generally given their own personal backgrounds as LGBTQ+ people.

Regarding relations with LGBTQ+ communities in particular, recent decades have seen a number of police departments demonstrate increased awareness of the importance of building more positive relationships with LGBTQ+ communities after years of strained relations in both the UK and US, as discussed earlier in this chapter. Particularly in cities with vibrant LGBTQ+ communities, a number of UK and US police departments have endeavoured to improve relations and legitimacy in LGBTQ+ communities through a variety of institutional programmes and practices. Some police departments recruit officers in traditional or designated LGBTQ+ spaces. Others actively encourage and support LGBTQ+ officer associations. Some sponsor officers participating in annual Gay Pride events, including walking in Gay Pride parades. Other larger police departments have created LGBTQ+ liaison units to work proactively with LGBTQ+ communities to address community concerns and build better channels of communication, although some researchers are sceptical about the objectives and successes of these units (Blackbourn, 2006; Mennicke et al, 2018).

Beyond these formal UK and US departmental efforts to engage LGBTQ+ communities, some LGBTQ+ officers may have different perspectives in terms of their relationships and engagement with LGBTQ+ communities. Some officers may choose not to engage with LGBTQ+ communities out of concerns their close ties will be perceived negatively by their colleagues and supervisors (Myers et al, 2004; Jones, 2015b). Indeed, Jones's 2015 study of LGB officers in England and Wales found only 13 per cent reported coming into regular contact with LGB communities while 53 per cent reported that they rarely or never did so. Whether this lack of engagement was deliberate or due to the officers being located in police departments in communities with small LGBTQ+ populations remains unclear, and is a matter for future study.

At the individual level, LGBTQ+ officers critical of traditional street police culture stereotyping and negative framing of LGBTQ+ communities can provide much needed insights into these communities in police departments which have traditionally emphasized hegemonically masculine and heteronormative beliefs and approaches. Indeed, LGBTQ+ officers providing cultural competency on LGBTQ+ issues is an essential role in both the UK and US, as observed by LGB officers in Charles and Arndt's 2013 study of LGB officers in several US Midwestern police and sheriffs' departments.

Moreover, some LGBTQ+ officers may seek out opportunities to advocate for or support LGBTQ+ communities. As illustrated further in the representative bureaucracy discussion in Chapter 8 (Mosher, 1968; Trochmann and Gover, 2016), LGBTQ+ officers may engage in active representation of LGBTQ+ communities, seeing themselves as stewards and advocates for improved LGBTQ+ community experiences with police. However, more empirical research on LGBTQ+ officers engaging in active bureaucratic representation of LGBTQ+ communities is required.

There are also potential challenges for LGBTQ+ officers of engaging in active bureaucratic representation of LGBTQ+ communities within a street police culture that is hegemonically masculine and heteronormative. Indeed, as Myers et al's 2004 study of some US-based LGB officers found, LGB officers were already perceived by colleagues and supervisors as having inherent sympathies for LGBTQ+ communities, and as a result were perceived more negatively than their straight colleagues (Myers et al, 2004). Thus, the potential implications for LGBTQ+ officers in championing the interests of LGBTQ+ communities may carry risks of further alienation and marginalization from straight officers and supervisors who, as discussed earlier, may stereotype LGBTQ+ officers as not 'real' police and community engagement as not 'real' police work.

Police leaders and LGBTQ+ inclusion

Given the strong influence of hegemonic masculinity and heteronormativity on stereotyping LGBTQ+ people in policing, there is potentially a significant role in combatting these norms to be played by LGBTQ+ police leaders. LGBTQ+ police leaders can explicitly or implicitly not only set the tone for more fairness, equality and inclusion for LGBTQ+ officers across policing generally, including hiring, assignments and promotions, they can also signal intolerance and try to curb normalized homophobic language or practices within policing institutions.

As seen with officers of colour and female officers, research indicates that senior police department leadership setting a tone of welcoming and inclusion of LGBTQ+ officers sends a powerful message for both LGBTQ+ officers and officers with homophobic tendencies (Broomfield, 2015). Evidence suggests that the support of both visible LGBTQ+ leaders and non-LGBTQ+ leaders as allies is instrumental for LGBTQ+ officers (Charles and Arndt, 2013). This can include both directly aiding LGBTQ+ officers who confront homophobia, as well as overt expressions of respect and acceptance for LGBTQ+ officers more generally (Charles and Arndt, 2013). Some LGBTQ+ officers believe the presence of visible LGBTQ+ supervisors and leaders can discourage and reduce incidences of homophobia because they send an explicit and implicit message that homophobia will not be tolerated (Charles and Arndt, 2013). For example, Broomfield (2015: 78) observed that in one UK police department, the chief constable (aka chief of police) closed all the canteens and bars on police property as a way to eliminate the biased street police culture and discriminatory views that often flourished in those spaces. This chief attempted to create safer spaces for LGBTQ+ officers and other traditionally marginalized groups. Significantly, research suggests that police leaders can create higher levels of trust and legitimacy in police organizations for LGBTQ+ officers where they are viewed as supportive of LGBTQ+ officer concerns (Collins and Rocco, 2018). Given the entrenched nature of hegemonic masculinity and heteronormativity within street police culture in both the UK and US, this does not mean LGBTQ+ police leaders can rid policing of homophobia, but their presence, leadership and decision-making ability can lead to positive changes in the lived experiences of LGBTQ+ officers on the job, who too often face discrimination, bias and different terms and conditions of employment in both UK and US police institutions.

Conclusion

Chapter 6 examined the lived experiences of LGBTQ+ officers in UK and US police services. Situated within distinctly hegemonically masculine and heteronormative street police culture, the chapter considered the ways the tenets of this culture impact how LGBTQ+ officers see and experience their policing roles. The chapter considered how LGBTQ+ officers were historically excluded from UK and US policing and have only become more visible in recent decades. The chapter also examined the ways the quality of LGBTQ+ officers' experiences in policing may not be equivalent to those of straight officers, given the discrimination, bias, stereotyping and homophobia many LGBTQ+ officers face in both the UK and US.

Building on ideas raised in previous chapters, Chapter 6 considered the ways hegemonically masculine and heteronormative street police culture creates a false dichotomy of so-called masculine and feminine policing, and the manner in which LGBTQ+ officers are stereotyped into roles accordingly. The chapter considered how LGBTQ+ officers face significant pressures to adhere to often homophobic street police culture norms, which can impact whether LGBTQ+ officers come out at work, and how they navigate relationships with fellow officers, supervisors and the public. The chapter also considered the ways street police cultures may view and stereotype gay, bisexual, lesbian and transgender officers similarly but also quite differently, and how this impacts respective experiences on the job. Finally, it considered the impacts of LGBTQ+ police leaders in setting the tone of greater inclusion, tolerance and support for LGBTQ+ officers, and signaling intolerance for street police culture's homophobia in day-to-day policing.

7

Social class in policing

This chapter asserts that UK and US policing were created deliberately with a focus on class. Significantly, UK and US policing were founded by middle- and upper-class political leaders to employ working-class people to police working-class communities. The founding origins of UK and US policing are therefore fundamentally shaped by the class status of the officers who initially served, and continue to serve in the majority, in the policing role – officers from working-class backgrounds. UK and US policing developed an organizational culture, particularly a street policing culture, which reflects the values, norms and views of working-class men who have traditionally served as police officers. This means UK and US policing have always had street policing cultures which adopt working-class male views on masculinity, sex, gender, race, aggression, physical strength, social control, social interactions and other types of factors.

This chapter argues that many working-class officers have been able to focus on policing working-class communities that may closely resemble their own by deploying street police culture strategies to distance themselves from these populations. Alienation and dehumanization strategies have enabled many working-class officers to effectively police working-class communities without a sense of contradiction or hypocrisy in relation to their shared class status.

Awareness of the role class plays in policing is increasing, as changing social demographics, greater political power of traditionally marginalized groups disproportionately subject to policing, changing expectations communities have of police, greater publicity of police misconduct including more media and social media coverage, and greater demands for accountability, fairness, and community satisfaction with policing. UK and US policing services are under pressure to be seen to make these types of effectiveness and legitimacy changes.

One of the ways police leaders have devised to improve police–community relations is by professionalizing the police, meaning making the police more professional, transparent and accountable. Professionalizing the police seems to be an explicit or implicit effort to change the class status of policing – meaning shifting it from a working class craft to a middle class profession – to improve its image, and its operations.

But fundamentally changing policing from a blue-collar craft to a middle-class profession is very challenging. The rhetoric being used around these efforts suggests that increasing officers' education levels is the means to professionalize the police. The argument suggests that with more officers obtaining college degrees, policing can be more fair, less oppressive, and more accountable, with higher levels of community satisfaction.

Yet the suggestion that increasing officer education levels is a panacea for the problems which plague police–community relations is over-simplistic. Using police education requirements as a means to shift the class status of policing from working class to middle class is not easily accomplished. Indeed, making UK and US policing more professional requires attending to the underlying issue of the street police culture which defines policing in both jurisdictions. The realities of the embedded working-class street police culture make the success of these efforts at best fairly naive, and at worst only performative, and uncommitted to fundamentally changing policing in practice.

This chapter considers the challenges to relying on increased police education levels to professionalize the police and, in doing so, endeavouring to change the class status of a policing system that was designed for working-class officers to control working-class populations. To suggest that policing can now shift away from its explicitly stated purpose and become more accountable, less oppressive and more legitimate in the eyes of communities is a tall order.

That said, the chapter also considers how increasing the education levels of UK and US police officers may have potential to improve some aspects of police relations with communities and some aspects of policing outcomes as part of a suite of policing reforms. However, just bringing in officers with college degrees on its own, but without attending to street police culture change through a variety of measures – for example, affirmative action, early retirement, enhanced misconduct procedures and prosecutions, external oversight, and so on – cannot professionalize policing.

The chapter begins by defining policing according to its deliberately working-class roots, and the ways the majority of officers – who primarily hail from the working class – have been able to disproportionately police working-class communities. It spells out the distinctly working-class nature of UK and US street police culture, and illustrates how deeply embedded it is in police institutions in both jurisdictions. Next, it defines the challenges of defining social class, and the difficulties of measuring it among police officers. It then introduces the use of educational attainment as a proxy class measure for policing research.

The chapter next considers the origins of educational requirements in policing. It evaluates limited research linking police officers' higher levels of educational attainment to certain positive indicators of success in policing including supervisor evaluations, promotions, use of discretion, reduced authoritarianism, creativity, open-mindedness and relations with communities, and job satisfaction. Finally, it concludes by signposting to empirical evidence discussed in Chapter 8 showing correlations between officer education levels with statistically significant differences in policing outcomes including use of force and citizen complaints.

Defining class in policing

Defining social class is not straightforward. But thinking critically about class means contemplating its interconnectedness to the concept of social inequality. Class means social status divisions on the basis of wealth or income. From a critical sociological perspective, class-based social stratification is associated with 'power, prestige and control over economic resources' within a nation's social hierarchy (Reiner, 1978; Diemer et al, 2013). There is abundant evidence of UK and US class-based disparities in education, employment, housing, health and life expectancy, and other areas outside of policing (Adonis and Pollard, 1997; Horwitz and Dovidio, 2017; Friedman and Laurison, 2020). Yet in the policing context, class-based differences among police officers in terms of experiences of policing, behaviours, beliefs, opportunities or interactions with policed communities have not been sufficiently explored in theoretical or empirical research. This chapter endeavours to facilitate initial explorations of these subjects and identify areas for further study.

A thorough examination of police diversity requires considering the role of social class, and how it has shaped UK and US policing institutions, cultures, behaviours and decision-making. One of the challenges with exploring class in this context is that it is too often overlooked in theoretical and empirical policing research generally, and largely ignored in discussions of police diversity specifically.

There are many reasons class has not been heavily studied in UK and US police diversity scholarship. First, police diversity researchers often focus on visible indicators of difference among officers, such as race and gender. As discussed in Chapter 6, personal police officer characteristics which are less readily identifiable, including sexual orientation and social class, can be more difficult to observe and therefore may be studied less in terms of diversity.

A second reason for neglecting class in police diversity research may be attributable to the challenges of defining police officer class. While there are a number of indicators social scientists use to assess class status, several are not good fits for this study. For example, while father's occupation is commonly utilized to assess class on the basis that it indicates someone's social class position when they are born, this information is not consistently recorded for most UK and US police officers. Another class measure used in social science research, current occupation, is really only helpful to assess class across a broad cross-section of people in different occupations, as a way to situate individuals according to a class hierarchy. However, when studying only cohorts of police, current occupation does not readily identify class differences among officers because they all share the same occupation. Education levels are also considered by social scientists to be a reliable measure of class status. Given the limited value of father's occupation and current occupation as class measures in policing research, and given the renewed interest in police officer education as a means to professionalize UK and US policing as discussed later, this study adopts officer education level as a proxy for class because it is viewed in social science as a reliable class indicator, and given the increasing availability of police officer education data.

A final reason policing research in police diversity has often failed to adequately incorporate class analysis may be general reticence among many scholars to acknowledge the profound effects of class on the lived experiences and social and professional opportunities for individuals in both UK and US societies (Friedman and Laurison, 2020). While some researchers offer significant insights into the depths and persistence of class inequalities in the UK, US and elsewhere (Savage et al, 2013; Friedman and Laurison, 2020), much social science research continues to overlook class differences. It could be that outdated notions of meritocracy in the UK and US – that hard work determines career opportunities (McCrudden, 1998) – lull many researchers into believing that class status is irrelevant to understanding inequality and discrimination. Meritocracy arguments are particularly prevalent in UK and US policing research, (Bury et al, 2018), which likely contributes to the lack of policing research on the impact of class and the ways class differences contribute to understandings of diversity, inclusion, discrimination and inequality.

As this research will show, the role of class is fundamental to consider in relation to diversity, inequality, discrimination and lived experiences in UK and US policing. Class is a fundamental part of the ways UK and US policing developed, how they are structured and how street police culture was formed and reinforced.

While UK and US policing were once conceptualized as distinctly working-class institutions with working-class organizational street police culture, in recent decades police institutions have faced pressure to change, or give the appearance of changing, what amounts to their distinctly working-class characters. Indeed, the sense that UK and US police embody straight White working-class male views on masculinity, sex, gender, race, aggression, physical strength, social control and social interactions have been under intense scrutiny. Contemporary demands for greater police accountability, legitimacy and engagement with a diverse array of policed communities have required UK and US policing to contemplate ways to think about shifting these traditional perspectives. These pressures to change, or be seen to change, the character of UK and US police institutions not only have implications for the success of police in general, but also for individual officers and the ways they experience, perform and succeed in police services.

To the extent policing research has addressed class, it has primarily focused on the ways people from poor, lower class and working-class backgrounds and neighbourhoods are treated by police, and how policing was intended to socially control the poor and working classes (Manning, 1977; Crowther, 2000; Schafer et al, 2003; Skogan, 2007; O'Neill and Loftus, 2013). Only to a lesser extent has policing research delved into the more difficult, at times conflicting, aspects of the class backgrounds of police officers themselves, and how these impact the way they police disproportionately working-class people and communities (Reiner, 1978; Loftus, 2009). While this important topic is discussed later in relation to officers' positionality in terms of class conflict, little attention has traditionally been paid to the ways officers view themselves, experience policing and make decisions from a class perspective.

Working-class origins of UK and US policing

From the outset, UK and US policing have been deliberately crafted as working-class institutions for the express purpose of controlling working-class communities through targeted policing. This began with the purposeful recruitment of police officers from poor and working-class backgrounds in both jurisdictions in the 19th century (Robinson, 1978). In UK policing, Sir Robert Peel, the father of modern policing and founder of the London Metropolitan Police Service (London Met Police), actively recruited working-class officers believing they would readily follow the directives and authority of their leaders, unlike middle- and upper-class gentlemen (Reiner, 1978; Emsley and Clapson, 1994). Similar strategies were deployed in US policing (Miller, 1977).

For much of policing history, police officers earned very low wages, often lower than labourers in other working-class occupations (Reiner, 1978). The working-class men who traditionally comprised UK and US policing were largely seen as low-status labourers of questionable moral character (Robinson, 1978; Reiner, 1978; Emsley, 2000; Jones, 2015a). Given the working-class positionality of policing in both jurisdictions, UK and US police officers were generally viewed as closely aligned with workers from other trades, particularly in the 19th century (Reiner, 1978; Robinson, 1978; Bowling et al, 2019).

Yet the working-class nature and allegiances of UK and US officers posed problems for the state and industrialists who wanted police to protect their economic, political and social interests (Stork, 1975; Johnson, 1976; Reiner, 1978; Robinson, 1978; Bunyan, 1981; Emsley, 2000; Thomas and Tufts, 2020). Indeed, the connections between working-class police and working-class communities made social control and surveillance of the latter more difficult (Johnson, 1976; Bunyan, 1981; Williams, 2003). The *raison d'être* of policing was disrupting efforts by working-class communities to challenge their working and living conditions, assert their political rights through withdrawals of labour, strikes and protests, and engage in behaviours offensive to upper-class sensibilities (Stork, 1975; Johnson, 1976; Emsley, 1986, 2000).

By the late 19th and early 20th centuries, elites sought to sever ties between working-class officers and the working-class populations they policed using a number of strategies. For example, police institutions in both countries began actively recruiting officers from outside local areas, alienating police from local populations and making it easier for them to surveil and control local working-class communities (Miller, 1977; Emsley, 2000; Bowling et al, 2019). The US also began distributing police functions to a broader array of actors including private police such as the Pinkertons, county sheriffs and state militias, creating distance from local communities and making repression of working-class populations easier (Miller, 1977; Robinson, 1978; Emsley, 2000).

Despite the diversification of policing functions to multiple entities, UK and US police institutions have remained strongly influenced by their working-class origins. Street police culture continues to be firmly grounded in working-class conceptions of masculinity, sex, gender, race and social interactions (Miller et al, 2003; Manning, 2007; Bowling et al, 2019). These street police norms are passed down from senior to more junior officers in the police academy and field training, and reinforced on the job through performance evaluations and target metrics, indicating their deep embeddedness (Fielding, 1994; Paoline, 2003). Unsurprisingly, research suggests that working-class street police culture is so pervasive in UK and US policing that even officers who are not themselves working class readily adopt these values and ways of policing to more easily assimilate into police organizations (Martin, 1980; Manning, 2007).

Given that UK and US police institutions are, on the one hand, populated by a majority of working-class officers and, on the other hand, focus policing efforts on working-class communities, there are clear tensions and contradictions for the experiences of working-class police officers. Yet rather than create explicit problems for working-class police officers, research highlights, several conscious and unconscious strategies many working-class officers may adopt to distance themselves from the working-class communities they police in order to be socially control these populations (Banton, 1964; Robinson, 1978; Young, 1991; Loftus, 2009).

One strategy is that the socialization into street police culture helps unite officers and alienate them from policed communities (Robinson, 1978), as discussed in Chapter 2. Indeed, from the introduction to street police culture at the police academy, officers are taught to build camaraderie and loyalty with one another and not with targeted communities (Herbert, 2001). Street police culture emphasizes alienation from local populations under the guise of protecting officer safety and ensuring effectiveness (Sherman, 1980; Conti and Doreian, 2014). This street police culture-driven separation from communities is one way working-class officers might rationalize targeting working-class communities.

Another strategy illustrated by empirical research is that although most officers are traditionally from the working class, some police officers prefer to see themselves as classless. Researchers assert this strategy allows officers to rationalize being able to effectively deal with a variety of populations, from the working class to the upper class (Banton, 1964). By seeing themselves as classless, this may enable working-class police officers to distance themselves from the local working-class populations where their efforts are disproportionately concentrated.

A third strategy is for working-class officers to draw distinctions between themselves and the working-class communities they police by labelling these communities with negative moral, social and behavioural characteristics (Young, 1991; Loftus, 2009; Bowling et al, 2019). Empirical research has shown that police draw distinctions between themselves, as members of the so-called 'respectable', law-abiding working classes, and the lower working classes, often referred to as the 'underclass' or 'precariat' (Loftus, 2009). The 'underclass' or 'precariat' are framed as members of the lower working classes who are unemployed or underemployed, dependent on state benefits, spatially isolated, and are stereotyped as having a propensity for criminality and public disorder (Crowther, 2000; Savage et al, 2013). Police frequently 'other' the lower working class by removing their humanity, labelling them as unintelligent, dysfunctional, dirty, lazy, troublesome, lacking in morals and animal-like (Loftus, 2009). This approach enables working-class police officers to aggressively surveil and oppress these working-class communities without a sense of class allegiance.

This chapter argues that working-class officers have long deployed these detachment strategies to allow them to simultaneously maintain their own, personal working-class origins and identities and to be able to adhere to working-class street police culture that negatively views working-class people, and to enable them to stereotype, effectuate social control over and target working-class communities with whom they might otherwise be aligned or feel connected. While to outside observers this appears as a fundamental contradiction for working-class officers these detachment strategies enable them to operate in ways that do not encumber their policing efforts.

Class and police education requirements

Given the limitations of many existing measures of class when applied to police officers, but recognizing the need to study class as part of the robust enquiry into understanding police diversity, significant consideration was given, for this volume, to how best to measure class for UK and US police officers.

While class has been often overlooked in much policing research generally, and certainly in relation to police diversity research, it is essential to examine class as part of a comprehensive analysis of UK and US police diversity. Yet the challenges of measuring class in policing are profound, in significant part due to the challenges highlighted previously. Thus, when this volume undertook to assess class differences, class challenges and efforts to change class in UK and US policing, no measure of class was fully satisfactory. Nonetheless, a review of existing empirical literature indicates that officer education levels are the most extensively researched proxy class measure for policing, with readily available data which can be used to analyse potential class effects on individual officer behaviour.

Officer education is used in this volume as a class proxy measure for several reasons. First, education is generally considered one of the most reliable measures of individual class status in the UK and US because it is relatively stable over the life course given that it is less prone to fluctuation compared to other class measures such as income or wealth (Krieger et al, 1997). However, one limitation of using officer education as a proxy for class status in this analysis is that, in recent decades, UK and US police services have invested significantly in programmes to help officers pursue higher education, including for those currently serving. This means that while some officers obtain their final levels of education before joining the police, others obtain higher levels of education while serving. For UK and US police officers, therefore, education levels may not be as stable as in other professions. Nonetheless, for the purposes of this volume's analysis, officer education level provides a snapshot upon which to evaluate individual officer experiences and decision-making in ways that contribute to the larger discussion of police diversity.

Another reason officer education level is used as a proxy for class status in this book is that in the past few decades, and particularly in recent years, there has been significant interest in police officer education levels in the UK and US both with empirical researchers and police policy makers. Policy makers have been particularly adamant about efforts to increase officer education levels in both jurisdictions, relying on limited empirical evidence that higher levels of education can improve officer performance, legitimacy and positive policing outcomes in policed communities. While such UK and US police efforts have been in process for years, there is significant pressure on police in both countries to improve police–community relations, particularly in traditionally marginalized communities, where relations have long been strained. Indeed, police and policy makers are under increasing pressure to make police fair and more accountable to the public they serve, or at the very least be seen to be making efforts to do so.

Further, these efforts to raise officer education levels have been, explicitly and implicitly, designed to shift UK and US policing away from its origins as a working-class craft to a middle-class profession under the guise of 'professionalization'. Yet undertaking efforts to raise officer education levels as a means to change the class status of policing from its working-class origins into a middle-class profession seems fairly naive. As discussed throughout this volume, working-class street police culture is deeply embedded in UK and US policing organizations, making efforts to singularly change the class of policing institutions from working class to middle class by relying on education alone is unrealistic. Changing the class of UK and US policing away from their working-class character cannot be achieved through mere imposition of education or other requirements without attending to the larger suite of reforms to shift the working-class street police culture discussed in this volume, including increasing diversity at front-line, supervisory and leadership levels, imposing residency requirements, implementing affirmative action, lawsuits against police departments and resulting consent decrees, and a variety of other police reform tools. Indeed, imposing officer education requirements cannot be a panacea for changing policing and, on its own, certainly cannot singularly shift working-class street police culture.

That said, research suggests that higher levels of officer education are correlated with some improved aspects of greater fairness, less oppression, greater accountability and higher levels of community satisfaction with police. Yet this chapter is sceptical that introducing police college degree requirements alone, without attending to fundamental street police culture change, can have the desired effects of improving the image of policing and improving relations with communities, particularly traditionally marginalized communities.

This chapter explores the way the introduction of police college degree requirements is being explicitly or implicitly used in an effort to shift UK and US policing away from their working-class characters. Driven by strained police legitimacy, increased demands for police fairness and accountability, this chapter explores whether evidence suggests that increasing officer education levels can have the desired effects. While the empirical research suggests that increasing officer education levels is correlated with some improvements in positive policing outcomes, it remains to be seen whether increasing officer education levels can shift the working-class character of policing. The next section examines the origins and evolution of police education requirements in the UK and US.

Police education levels in the UK

In the UK, education has always been a significant topic for discussion when it comes to police services. For most of its history, UK policing did not require officers to have a college degree to join the police services. Indeed, when the UK police services were first formed in the 1820s, policing was considered a trade which did not require formal qualifications including education (Jones, 2015a). Candidates were only required to show they comprehended what they read and wrote (Miller, 1977). Policing was considered a good job for members of the working class, a majority of whom tended to lack significant educational qualifications (Lee and Punch, 2004).

In the early 20th century, concerns about police integrity prompted calls for the development of an educated 'officer class' of police (Lee and Punch, 2004). By the late 1920s and 1930s, the London Met Police sought police recruits with some level of education, which was believed could enhance the quality of police officer performance (Emsley and Clapson, 1994). By 1936, 54 per cent of London Met Police recruits had 'secondary or public school education', while 33 per cent had 'school leaving or equivalent certificates' (Emsley and Clapson, 1994: 271). Yet despite this progression, education levels remained relatively low for UK officers. Most officers had little more than basic secondary school educational qualifications well into the 1960s (Lee and Punch, 2004). Up until this time, officers with education beyond secondary school were extremely rare and seen as anomalous in UK policing (Lee and Punch, 2004). And well into the 1960s, UK policing continued to be regarded as a trade rather than a profession, meaning higher levels of education were not viewed as required for the role.

Yet the 1960s saw changes in UK policing as efforts were made to professionalize the police services. This shift was a concerted move away from policing as a trade toward making it an established profession (Jones, 2015a). During this period, education for police officers began to be seen as more valuable for numerous reasons. First, increasing the numbers of educated officers was seen as important to ensure a steady stream of qualified officers available for promotions and higher ranking

UK police positions (Wall, 1998; Lee and Punch, 2004). Educated police were also viewed as more capable of dealing with increasing pressures placed on the police by the public demanding greater accountability (Lee and Punch, 2004).

The Royal Commission on Police (1962) asserted that UK police had for too long failed to attract sufficient numbers of university graduates, and concerted efforts were required to attract a far larger share of degree holders, particularly in relation to ensuring high calibre leaders for the UK police services going forward. To support increasing officer education levels in the 1960s, UK policing launched two UK initiatives – one to allow police to be seconded to UK universities, and a Graduate Entry Scheme which allowed police institutions to directly recruit university graduates (Lee and Punch, 2004). During this period, some UK police forces enacted their own measures to increase police education levels within their ranks. For example, the chief constable of the Essex Police launched a first-of-its-kind scheme to fund two Essex Police officers to study full-time at the University of Essex, a programme which eventually resulted in most of these officers being promoted when they returned to their policing roles after earning their degrees (Lee and Punch, 2004).

By the 1970s, UK police services showed gradual increases in officer education levels. For example, Reiner's 1978 study found that the majority of UK police officers in his analysis had obtained at least one O level qualification (equivalent to some high school in the US). Wall's 1998 study of chief constables (equivalent of US police chief) found only 18 per cent of office holders in 1976 had university degrees.

The 1980s saw further increased efforts to professionalize UK policing through greater education in light of the changing nature of crime and crime fighting, including increasingly complex crimes, cross–border policing, globalization and the blurring of high and low policing functions (Lee and Punch, 2004; Brodeur, 2010). Chief constables in particular reflected stronger educational backgrounds than officers. Data show that by 1986, 70 per cent of chief constables in the UK had some education beyond high school, with 57 per cent having some university education, and the remainder having some other form of higher education, such as a certificate or a diploma (Wall, 1998). Wall found that by 1986, 22 per cent of chief constables had university degrees. Reiner's 1991 study of chief constables found that, in 1986, most had fathers who were in manual jobs. Data further show that by 1996, 93 per cent of chief constables had attended some university, and 68 per cent had earned university degrees (Wall, 1998).

In 2000, the UK government established the Foundational Degrees Pathway into policing, which combined academic and work-based learning for school or college leavers and those already in police employment (Lee and Punch, 2004). That same year, survey data of the 43 serving chief constables found 36 (84 per cent) had university degrees, five (12 per cent) had Master's degrees, and four (9 per cent) had PhDs (Punch, 2007). Beginning in 2005, UK policing introduced the Initial Police Learning and Development Programme (IPLDP) (Macvean and Cox, 2012; House of Commons Home Affairs Select Committee, 2016). The IPLDP programme required police services to train new police officers on particular topics, however the methods, structure and duration of training varied across the UK's 43 forces and depended on organizational support for the training programme and resources, among other things (McGinley et al, 2019). By 2007, 25–30 per cent of entrants to some UK police services were university graduates (Punch, 2007).

In 2016, the College of Policing (2020) announced that UK policing would require university degrees for new officers from 2020, and created a Police Education Qualification Framework (PEQF) to standardize education levels required for entry-level police officers, with three modes of entry into policing. First, the framework provides that UK police services can accept holders of Bachelor's degrees in any subject, who are then put through a two-year programme at an accredited UK university provider to earn a Professional Policing Practice graduate diploma (College of Policing, 2023). Second, applicants without university degrees can undertake a two- or three-year Professional Policing Bachelor's degree programme based on a national curriculum and delivered by a number of approved UK university providers (College of Policing, 2023). Upon obtaining the Professional Policing degree, students apply to the police service directly for the police officer position. Third, aspiring officers can join a three-year Police Constable Degree Apprenticeship where students are apprenticed with the police while also receiving instruction from a qualified university provider and earning a degree in Professional Policing Practice (College of Policing, 2023). These pathways remain in effect to the present day.

Police education levels in the US

Like UK policing, US policing began in the 1800s without any educational requirements for aspiring officers. Policing in the US was viewed as a good job for working-class men without qualifications. Requirements for departments such as the New York Police Department (NYPD) often simply required demonstrating literacy, which could be shown by just reading a newspaper title (Miller, 1977).

Early efforts to institute college education requirements for American police officers came during the first police professionalism movement in the 1910s and 1920s (Paoline and Terrill, 2007). Law enforcement pioneer August Vollmer first proposed a three-year college education programme for police officers in 1917, and believed officers should earn social science degrees rather than mere training in policing practices to make the education most valuable (Shernock, 1992). These early efforts were driven by the desire to improve the prestige of the policing profession, not necessarily to improve police behaviour (Shernock, 1992). Vollmer's work led to the establishment of a number of police education courses at US universities in the 1920s and 1930s (Shernock, 1992).

Taking forward Vollmer's work, the National Commission on Law Observance and Enforcement (1931) (aka Wickersham Commission) recommended college degrees should be required to improve police officer performance. While this recommendation was never adopted nationally, and individual departments set their education standards as they saw fit, it served as a basis for advocates to push for implementing college degree requirements to improve police effectiveness and legitimacy (Paoline and Terrill, 2007). However, these efforts led to the creation of the first two-year and four-year college degree programmes catering to police at several US colleges and universities, with 22 such programmes in place by 1954 (Goldstein, 1977).

Social changes in the 1960s, including the Civil Rights Movement and urban uprisings across American cities, ushered in renewed national interest in improving policing through education and other means (Carter and Sapp, 1990). In 1960, roughly 3 per cent of American officers had a four-year college degree (Rydberg and Terrill, 2010), while US police officers had a median of 12.4 years of education, meaning, on average, they had been educated to the level of high school completion (Katzenbach Commission, 1967). At that time, 70 per cent of US police departments required a minimum of least a high school diploma, while 25 per cent required only some elementary school education. Some departments in California proved to be outliers, with 21 police institutions requiring some college attendance (Katzenbach Commission, 1967). Contemporaneous studies at the time showed that 24 per cent of US police officers and 31 per cent of police leaders had some college attendance (President's Commission on Law Enforcement and Administration of Justice, 1967 [aka Katzenbach Commission]). By 1966, there were 152 two-year college degree programmes and 39 four-year college degree programmes for police officers (Goldstein, 1977).

As in the UK, the professionalization efforts in US policing were viewed as helping police develop stronger analytical and intellectual capacities, and build better relations with communities through increased educational obtainment, particularly through liberal arts education (Katzenbach Commission, 1967; Sherman and Blumberg, 1981; Shernock, 1992). To facilitate this professionalization, President Johnson's Katzenbach Commission recommended that all police personnel possess four-year college degrees as a minimum hiring requirement (Katzenbach Commission, 1967). It also recommended that immediate steps be taken to require four-year college degrees for all supervisory and leadership positions within policing organizations (Goldstein, 1977). But these recommendations were voluntary not compulsory, and recognized that autonomy required that individual police departments be allowed to develop and implement education hiring policies of their own.

However, with the passage of the Omnibus Crime Control and Safe Streets Act in 1968, the Law Enforcement Education Program (LEEP) was established by the federal government to incentivize police officers and candidates to attend colleges and universities by providing scholarships and loans (Goldstein, 1977; Paoline and Terrill, 2007). LEEP's creation led to unprecedented levels of funding for law enforcement education, leading American colleges and universities to greatly expand development of law enforcement and criminal justice degree programmes (Carter and Sapp, 1990). LEEP's implementation also allowed individual police departments to use federal government funds to create pay incentives, educational leave, and other programmes to reward police officers for pursuing higher education (Carter and Sapp, 1990). The impacts of LEEP were significant, as in its first year, LEEP provided financial assistance to 20,602 students (Goldstein, 1977).

Following LEEP's creation, progress in US police educational obtainment was slow and steady. By 1973, the LEEP programme financially aided 95,000 students (Goldstein, 1977). Data from that same year showed 10 per cent of US police officers possessed a four-year college degree, and 50 per cent had never attended college (National Advisory Commission, 1973; Rydberg and Terrill, 2010).

Moreover, a significant 1973 report by the National Advisory Commission on Criminal Justice Standards and Goals (1973) asserted that police officers with college degrees performed better in the role than those without, and sought to increase the educational requirements for US policing. The Commission asserted that the increased professionalization of US policing hinged on increasing officer education levels (National Advisory Commission, 1973). The Commission proposed some concrete educational goals for all US police officers: possess one year of college education within 36 months; two years of college education by 1975; three years of college education by 1978; and have an undergraduate college degree by 1982. The Commission recommended incentive pay to encourage officers to meet these education goals. Yet as with the educational requirement recommendations of prior commissions, these goals remained optional rather than compulsory.

Research shows that by 1975, only 6 per cent of American police departments required any college attendance whatsoever, while less than 1 per cent required a four-year college degree (Rydberg and Terrill, 2010). That year, there were 729 two-year policing degree programmes and 376 four-year degree programmes in policing (Goldstein, 1977). Yet, as in the UK, during this period college-educated officers remained fairly anomalous.

Indeed, a perception persisted that there was something incongruous about a college graduate becoming a police officer, and that those credentials were wasted in the police services (Goldstein, 1977).

Despite the optional nature of educational requirements recommended by the National Advisory Commission, US police departments steadily made progress in increasing hiring of officers with higher education. For example, Carter and Sapp's evaluation of data from a 1988 survey of 486 of America's medium and large police, sheriff and state trooper departments found that 86 per cent (418) required a minimum of a high school diploma or equivalent, 9 per cent required at least a two-year college degree, while 0.4 per cent required a four-year college degree (Carter and Sapp, 1990).

Carter and Sapp's survey also revealed levels of officers' educational obtainment across the 486 US policing agencies, finding that 65 per cent of officers had one or more year of college, while 23 per cent had at least a four-year Baccalaureate degree, while 4 per cent held graduate degrees. By 1990, US government data showed 6 per cent of US police departments required new officers to have some college education (BJS, 1993). By 1993, 12 per cent of US police departments required new officers to have some college education, 7 per cent required a two-year college degree, and 1 per cent required a four-year college degree (see Table 7.1; BJS, 1993).

By 2000, 6 per cent of US police departments required new officers to have some college education, 9 per cent required a two-year college degree, and 1 per cent required a four-year college degree (BJS, 2000, 2007). By 2007, research observed that most American policing agencies had never had and did not require even a two-year college degree, let alone a four-year college degree, which is repeatedly recommended as the best standard for American law enforcement education (Paoline and Terrill, 2007). Yet while the numbers of US police departments requiring some college education has steadily increased, the reality is that, for a variety of reasons discussed later in this chapter, American police departments have not required officers to undertake some college study, or earn two- or four-year college degrees as a prerequisite to hiring.

Table 7.1: US police education levels, 1960–2017

Highest education level obtained by officers	1960	1970	1974	1988	2017
High school or equivalent	80%	68%	54%	35%	
Some college	17%	28%	37%	42%	52%
Four-year college degree	3%	4%	9%	23%	30%
Graduate degree				3.7%	5%

Source: Carter and Sapp, 1990; Rydberg and Terrill, 2010; Gardiner, 2017

By the time of the 2015 President's Task Force on 21st Century Policing (White House, 2015), it was clear that increasing educational obtainment remained a priority. The Task Force emphasized the value of officers having college degrees, not only in terms of improved performance but also the broader array of languages, skills, and life experiences this provided to policing. The Task Force recommended that the US government, state, and local policing agencies should incentivize officers without college degrees to undertake college study during their careers, including through educational loan programmes. The Task Force found college degree requirements to be particularly lacking in US police training academies, with a total of only 19 per cent requiring some college education, and 11 per cent requiring instructors to have a college degree.

A 2017 Police Foundation study of 958 American policing agencies is the most extensive examination of police education levels to date. The study found 6.6 per cent of US police departments required officers to have some college education, 10.5 per cent required a two-year college degree, and 1.3 per cent required a four-year college degree (Gardiner, 2017). The study found over 55.8 per cent of US police agencies provided incentives for police officers to obtain higher education, including tuition assistance, tuition reimbursement, or 1–7 per cent pay incentives tied to having a two-year or four-year college degree (Gardiner, 2017).

In terms of officer education levels across the US, the 2017 Police Foundation survey found 51.8 per cent of US police officers had at least a two-year college degree, while 30.2 per cent had at least a four-year degree, and 5.4 per cent had a graduate degree (Gardiner, 2017). The research found police departments led by police chiefs with graduate degrees had higher percentages of officers with at least four-year college degrees. It also found 17.1 per cent of police chiefs had only a high school diploma, 19.0 per cent had a two-year degree, 28.7 per cent had a four-year degree, 32.1 per cent had a Master's degree, and 3.0 per cent had a doctorate or comparable degree (Gardiner, 2017).

Using police education requirements to shift working-class police culture

Supporters of police education requirements argue that they are integral to explicitly or implicitly shifting the working-class character of policing, and do so by offering a multitude of benefits. Proponents argue that one way police degrees can change the working-class culture of policing is that police officers pursuing full-time college degrees in university settings meet a wider variety of people on university campuses and develop greater intellectual capacity, which combats homogeneous and narrow thinking tied to working-class street police culture (Lee and Punch, 2004). Indeed, as discussed later, scholars argue police officers with university degrees perform better in the role, are more ethical, use their discretion more wisely, are less authoritarian, more open-minded, show more creative problem solving and have better community relations than their non-college-educated colleagues, as discussed further below.

A second way supporters argue that police degrees can shift the working-class culture of policing is by increasing policing's reputation, moving it away from its perceptions as a working-class craft to a middle-class, professional occupation (Shernock, 1992; Lee and Punch, 2004). Proponents assert that policing will increasingly be viewed as a middle-class profession worthy of dignity and respect with greater numbers of university graduates (Goldstein, 1977). This effort to professionalize policing through the introduction of policing degrees is an attempt to shift policing away from being perceived as a low-skill trade with low skills and low moral character, to a middle-class profession with high skills, high moral character, and one worthy of support and admiration.

Proponents argue a third way police degrees can shift the working-class culture of policing is that rather remaining homogeneous UK and US police forces comprised of straight White working-class men, degree requirements make policing more inclusive, introducing a broader cross-section of individuals to the role, with a wider array of lived experiences, beliefs and perspectives (Goldstein, 1977). As discussed throughout this volume, greater diversity in policing across race, gender, sexual orientation, class and viewpoint lines, among many other characteristics, can begin to help shift the working-class culture of policing by bringing different types of values and approaches to policing providing contrast to those embedded in working-class street police culture norms.

Finally, supporters argue that police with degrees can shift the working-class culture of policing by creating higher expectations of accountability, and lower tolerance for rule-breaking and misconduct. Supporters argue that the introduction of larger numbers of college-educated officers breaks down the blue wall of silence inherent in street police culture, which tolerates and encourages misconduct, by encouraging adherence to the law and discouraging rule-breaking. Research suggests that the more highly educated police officers become, the more police culture begins to reflect a middle-class, police managerial culture rather than a working-class street police culture (Reuss-Ianni, 1983).

Criticism of using police education requirements to shift street police culture

Yet critics, including this author, are sceptical of the ability of police degrees alone to fundamentally change policing from a working-class street police culture to a middle-class, police managerial culture. They argue that reliance on police education requirements alone is insufficient to make policing more accountable and fairer. They assert that fundamentally changing the character of policing from working-class to middle-class cannot be accomplished solely with police education requirements, and will not only be ineffective, but may in fact even be harmful to UK and US policing.

One key point is that police degree programmes do little to change street police culture, for they are often a means for early socialization and reinforcement of working-class street police culture norms. Research by Fielding (1994), Paoline (2003), Cox and Kirby (2017) and others have all found that police training is a key to early socialization into street policing culture. For police degree programmes, research by Cox and Kirby (2017) and others has found that these programmes help aspiring police officers identify with police and street police culture early, to the extent that they begin to see themselves as separate from non-policing students. Crucial to this early socialization into street police culture with police degree programmes is the fact that programme instructors are often current or former police officers, who provide police degree students with war stories – and emphasize the importance of adhering to the values of street police culture in the policing role (Young, 1991; Lee and Punch, 2004; Cox and Kirby, 2017). These police degrees thus place value in lived experiences of policing on the job rather than intellectual development or critical analysis, making aspiring police officers in police degree programmes well socialized into the values of street police culture even before setting foot in the job.

A second way police degree programmes reaffirm working-class street police culture norms is that aspiring and serving police officers tend to pursue college degrees in policing studies and criminal justice fields taught by current or former officers, rather than pursuing a broader array of degrees across disciplines, taught by scholars from a wider cross-section of class origins and lived experiences. Critics argue that the over-saturation of policing studies and criminal justice degrees among officers fails to create a sufficiently broad and varied intellectual basis for officers (Lee and Punch, 2004), which translates to officers remaining firmly entrenched in the homogeneous working-class street police culture views. As discussed above, Vollmer and others have long argued that for college degrees to shift perspectives in policing institutions and, in turn, ways of policing on the streets, police officers require broad social science and liberal arts training, not simply education in policing practices (Goldstein, 1977; Sherman and Blumberg, 1981; Shernock, 1992). This view adopts the position that criminal justice degrees catering to aspiring and serving police officers are too homogeneous, too consistent with traditional policing perspectives, and are insufficiently critical of policing and criminal justice practices to shift existing policing attitudes and practices (Goldstein, 1977; Lee and

Punch, 2004; Macvean and Cox, 2012). Critics assert that to achieve the desired effect, police education programmes must more broadly develop students' core skills and values, not simply respond to police practitioners' needs, so as to help police understand the contexts of their roles and the communities they police (Goldstein, 1977). Yet there is no consensus on this point. Paoline et al's 2015 study of 950 officers across seven US police departments who possessed Bachelor's degrees found that of the 800 who identified college majors, 50 per cent were criminal justice majors. They found there were no significant distinctions between criminal justice and non-criminal justice majors, and asserted that the socialization into street police culture was likely more impactful on police attitudes than choice of college major.

Critics of using police education requirements as a means to shift street police culture argue that policing must be learned on the street, and cannot be taught in a classroom (Bayley and Bittner, 1997; Punch, 2007). This notion reinforces the long-held belief that policing is a working-class craft where expertise is developed and reinforced on the job rather than a middle-class profession requiring education in a classroom. Proponents assert 'good' policing is the product of experience, not formal education (Paoline and Terrill, 2007). This view makes college education mostly irrelevant to being a 'good' cop, and regards police with college degrees with suspicion (Punch, 2007).

Finally, critics of using police education as a means to shift street police culture argue that the introduction of college degree requirements in UK and US policing actually further narrows the applicant pool for officers and harms diversity, which could result in policing remaining homogeneous and continuing to be comprised of a majority of White, working-class men. Indeed, these critics argue that degree requirements reduce the diversity in police applicant pools, discriminating against women and ethnic minorities, the latter of whom have lower educational obtainment compared to men and Whites (Goldstein, 1977). Such critics argue that the benefits of greater racial, ethnic and gender diversity in policing, as discussed in Chapters 4 and 5 of this book, are equally if not more important than those derived from police having degrees (Goldstein, 1977). However, the data on educational obtainment for officers of colour in more recent decades do not support concerns that educational qualifications must be sacrificed in the name of diversity. For example, evaluation by Carter and Sapp (1990) of data from national studies across 486 US policing agencies, and others, show that education levels for Black, Latino and White officers were comparable, with Black (63 per cent) and Latino (68 per cent) officers showing higher levels of college attendance compared to Whites (62 per cent). Yet it is noteworthy that Carter and Sapp's study did show that while only 45.7 per cent of female officers had completed some college education compared to 61.7 per cent of male officers, 44.6 per cent of female officers had either a four-year college degree or graduate degree compared to only 22.8 per cent of male officers.

Empirical research on officer education levels and policing outcomes

Efforts to shift policing from a working-class institution to a middle-class, professionalized institution rely on limited empirical evidence that police education requirements can improve certain aspects of fairness, tolerance, accountability and positive public perception in the eyes of communities. However, this chapter asserts that the temptation must be resisted to place all hopes for reducing, mitigating or changing the effects of working-class street police culture values in policing, and thereby hopes for reforming police, purely on imposing police education requirements. Rather, this chapter argues that while there is some promising evidence that police with higher levels of education can have better policing outcomes with communities, police education requirements are not a panacea for solving all that is flawed with UK and US policing, and that trying to magically change the class status of policing from working-class to middle-class is not readily achievable.

Existing empirical evidence about the impacts of officers' education levels on police attitudes and practices varies between the UK and the US. In the UK this research was virtually non-existent until the 2000s, when institutional police policy priorities began to shift toward increasing numbers of college-educated officers, as discussed earlier (Paterson, 2011). By contrast, in the US, empirical evidence on differences between college- and non-college-educated police officers in America began in the 1970s, again driven by changes in the policy landscape (Paterson, 2011). As a result of the relatively small amount of data compared to Chapters 4, 5 and 6, the empirical analysis in this chapter is fruitful but limited. Indeed, much more empirical research is required on individual police officer class characteristics, including educational obtainment, to develop a richer understanding of its impacts on the profession, street police culture and policing practices in the field. This chapter nonetheless seeks to contribute to the conversation, albeit in limited ways.

Police education and supervisor evaluations

UK and US police education requirements alone will not change working-class street police culture perspectives on masculinity, sex, gender, race, tolerance, aggression, community relations and social control, however there is value to exploring empirical evidence of the nuanced impacts of officer education on policing. For example, police officers with higher levels of education are perceived more positively by their superiors in UK and US policing institutions. In fact, a significant driver of efforts to impose college degree requirements on UK and US police officers may be that many police supervisors and managers in both jurisdictions view college educational obtainment positively. This may be, in part, because supervisors and police leaders tend to have higher levels of education compared to their subordinates (Reiner, 1978). For example, Reiner's study of UK police officers found that supervisors were more likely to have obtained more educational qualifications compared to other officers.

Indeed, research is fairly clear that officers with college degrees are rated more highly and perceived as better performing in the police officer role by supervisors and police leaders compared to their non-college-educated peers. This suggests that regardless of actual effects, the positive perceptions associated with college degrees bode well for the potential for career success of officers with higher education levels. For example, Carter and Sapp's 1990 analysis of data from a 1988 survey of 486 US police and law enforcement departments found that police applicants with college educations were routinely ranked highest in hiring pools, being viewed more favourably than applicants with only high school educations.

Numerous other studies have demonstrated similarly positive views from superiors of officers with college educations. For example, Smith and Aamodt's 1997 study of 299 police officers across 12 Virginia policing agencies found supervisors evaluated officers with higher levels of education significantly more favourably. Specifically, the study found officers with college or graduate degrees were evaluated by their supervisors as performing better in nearly all aspects of police work, including attitudes, report-writing, commitment to the job and communication skills, compared to officers with only high school educations. Similarly, Truxillo et al's ten-year study of 84 American police officers (1998) found statistically significant correlations between officers with two-year and four-year degrees and positive supervisor evaluations in relation to officers' job knowledge and dependability.

Along similar lines, a study by Aamodt and Fink (2001), evaluating the performance of 301 police cadets in a single US police academy training new recruits from 50 small and medium sized Virginia law enforcement agencies, found those with two- or four-year college degrees performed significantly better in the police academy compared to their colleagues with only high school diplomas or some college education. A more recent study by Marciniak and Elattrache (2020), of 98 police chiefs of small and medium sized police departments in one US state, found that 39 per cent believed officers with four-year college degrees were more effective on patrol, and 43 per cent believed their departments should give hiring preferences to candidates with at least some college education. Interestingly, the study found 59 per cent of the 98 police chiefs surveyed had at least two-year college degrees or above, which the authors believed contributed to their positive views of the benefits of officers having college educations.

These US-based studies suggest that college-educated officers are viewed as better performers by supervisors and police leaders. However, these evaluations have significant implications in relation to street police culture, as they are likely grounded in assessments of performance in relation to metrics defined by street police culture norms, such as numbers of stop and searches or traffic citations made, level of proactivity or aggression on the job, etc. Therefore, the temptation must be resisted to assume that college-educated officers are simply better in their roles without considering the ways the structural aspects of street police culture discussed throughout this book shape perspectives on the demands and expectations of those roles in policing institutions. As such, further empirical research with more detail about the criteria and metrics used to evaluate performance would be helpful to inform this discussion.

Police education and promotions

The research is also clear that college education is tied both to promotion aspirations and rates of promotion in both UK and US policing. For some departments, college degrees may be formal requirements for promotion, while in others college degrees may simply be unwritten or advantageous promotion criteria. In both jurisdictions, empirical research shows college degrees are highly valuable for climbing up the ranks in police institutions, although again it says nothing about how officers with college educations who aspire to, or receive, promotions continue to embody the street police culture values. However, as with supervisor evaluations discussed earlier, it is important to understand the ways officers with college degrees who seek promotions are being measured against promotions criteria tied to street police culture performance indicators, such as high volume of arrests and other aggressive policing measures.

For example, Reiner's 1978 UK study found that officers with higher educational qualifications were more likely to be promoted to supervisory positions than those with minimal educational obtainment. Subsequent research has found similar and fairly consistent results in the US tying promotions to educational obtainment. For example, Carter and Sapp's 1990 review of a national survey of 486 large and medium sized American law enforcement agencies found that 74 per cent (n=361) had no formal or informal requirements mandating college education for promotions, although 8 per cent did require some college education, 5 per cent had a college degree requirement and 4 per cent gave officers with some college education or degrees opportunities for early promotion. Moreover, their study showed that for sergeants, 43 per cent had no college education, 28 per cent had up to two years of college education and 30 per cent had more than two years of college education (Carter and Sapp, 1990). For officers at the rank of lieutenant and above, including police chief, 7 per cent had no college education, 23 per cent had two years of college or fewer, and 70 per cent had more than two years of college education (Carter and Sapp, 1990).

Similarly, Smith and Aamodt's 1997 study of 299 police officers across 12 Virginia policing agencies found supervisors evaluated officers with higher levels of education significantly more favourably, a key component of promotion decisions in most UK and US police departments. Along similar lines, Kakar's 1998 study of 110 patrol officers in one Florida police department found that officers with college education self-reported higher levels of leadership compared to their non-college-educated colleagues.

In 1998, Truxillo et al's ten-year study of 84 police officers in one US police department found statistically significant correlations between officers with two-year and four-year degrees and promotions/rank obtained in the police department. Truxillo et al (1998) argued that this could be because the same drivers motivating individuals to obtain college degrees could also motivate them to apply for promotions. They also posited that it could be due to the fact that officers with college degrees have developed greater skills necessary for achieving promotions. Finally, they hypothesized that officers with college degrees develop a level of professionalization that is highly valued in police departments.

Polk and Armstrong's study (2001) of 5,323 officers across 30 Texas law enforcement departments, including six large urban police departments in Houston, Dallas, San Antonio, Fort Worth, El Paso and Austin, found that those with higher levels of education were more likely to occupy higher level positions in policing. Specifically, they found those with Bachelor's degrees were better represented in supervisory (44.4 per cent) and leadership (16.1 per cent) roles than in patrol (23.4 per cent). Similarly, they found those with postgraduate level education were better represented in supervisory (41.2 per cent) and leadership (31.4 per cent) roles than in patrol (14.3 per cent). By contrast, those with high school diplomas or less were most represented in patrol (48.4 per cent) compared to supervisory (19.4 per cent) and leadership (6 per cent) roles.

Polk and Armstrong's study (2001) also considered the time it took for officers with different education levels to get promoted, and found that those with higher levels of education (a Bachelor's degree and postgraduate education), were promoted more quickly than those with lower levels of education. The study concluded that education level was one of the most significant predictors of promotion for the 5,323 officers across 30 Texas law enforcement departments.

In terms of the impacts of college degrees on promotional aspirations, the primarily US-based research suggests college-educated officers may have stronger career aspirations compared to non–college-educated colleagues, and that this may be a primary motivation for pursuing higher education. For example, Shernock's 1992 study of 177 officers across 11 Northeastern US police departments found officers' desire for higher education was related to improving their prospects for promotion, career advancement and financial status rather than tied to expectations that the degree would change how they performed their roles.

More recent US research supports these findings. Indeed, Gau et al's 2013 study of 2,109 officers across seven US police departments found that officers with a college education held greater promotion ambitions and expectations than their colleagues with high school degrees. In fact, the research found the more college education officers had, the higher their promotion aspirations (Gau et al, 2013). However, Gau et al cautioned that more highly educated officers may eventually lose motivation and become disillusioned after realizing that their promotion aspirations and goals were not tied to the realities of policing in practice. Interestingly, Gau et al found that officers with higher education did not necessarily aspire to be senior managers, but more so front-line supervisors and middle managers.

The timing of when officers obtain their college degrees may also be a factor in determinations of whether to apply for promotion. For example, Jones's self-report study of serving UK police officers enrolled in 'top up' studies for a Bachelor's degree in Police Studies (Jones, 2015a) found that, for most, higher education was an important part of preparing for promotion applications. The officers in the study saw a college-level qualification as important for a senior level police officer to possess. By contrast, Hallenberg and Cockcroft's 2017 UK-based research, examining experiences of 31 UK officers, found that half joined the police service already possessing a Bachelor's degree, while the other half obtained college-level qualifications in Police Studies while serving as police officers. The study found most believed Bachelor's degrees obtained before joining the police service were more highly valued by the police institution than degrees obtained while serving as police officers. This interesting finding would benefit from further study.

As discussed earlier in relation to supervisor evaluations, it may be that one of the drivers of college education being so closely tied to promotions in UK and US policing may be a result of police supervisors and leaders being increasingly highly educated. Limited data suggest police leaders have always had higher levels of educational obtainment compared to officers, but this trend continues to increase. Research shows police leaders are particularly well educated. A 1998 Police Executive Research Forum (PERF) survey of 358 police chiefs in medium and large cities found 87 per cent had four-year Bachelor's degrees, 47 per cent had Master's degrees and 5 per cent had doctorates or law degrees (Roberg and Bonn, 2004). Similarly, a UK study by Silvestri (2006), involving interviews with 30 top British police women at the ranks of inspector and above, found college graduates overrepresented in the sample of police leaders, with 17 of 30 female leaders having college degrees, and four having postgraduate degrees. More recently, in 2017, the Police Foundation's national study of US policing found that a college degree was very important for promotions in US policing, particularly to the rank of lieutenant (2nd-level supervisor) and above. It showed that police officers led by police chiefs with a Master's degree or higher level of education were more likely to require higher education levels to be promoted.

Taken together, these findings present fairly clear evidence that officers with college degrees not only have higher promotion aspirations, but that supervisors and police leaders in UK and US police services increasingly possess college educations. While lack of college education does not appear to be a formal prohibition on promotion in either jurisdiction, it certainly seems to be an increasingly informal requirement which increases positive perceptions of officers regardless of whether it enhances their policing performance. Yet, as discussed, more detailed empirical research is needed to assess the ways these officers are being evaluated, including how their performance according to street police culture metrics wins them accolades. From this analysis, it is unlikely that simply increasing the numbers of officers with college degrees will change policing to be more professional and middle class if the performance metrics according to which they are evaluated remain grounded in the same old street police culture norms.

Police education and ethics

Working-class street police culture is embedded with the idea of engaging in misconduct with impunity, and having little accountability to members of the public for wrongdoing. This normalization of police conduct is worsened with the blue wall of silence, which, as discussed in Chapter 2, means that officers are expected to remain silent about the misconduct of others, and alienate those who expose it. Research suggests that police education may, in fact, help mitigate this aspect of street police culture.

Specifically, research has illustrated some limited but statistically significant benefits from officers possessing college degrees in relation to police officer ethics and decision-making in relation to police misconduct. In fact, several US studies have found correlations between police officers' ethics on the job and their levels of college education. For example, Carter and Sapp's

1989 evaluation of national data from a survey of 486 US law enforcement agencies found college-educated officers were more likely to recognize and adhere to the law. Similarly, Shernock's 1992 study of 177 officers across 11 US police departments found that college-educated officers placed greater emphasis on external ethical conduct, meaning in relation to community members, compared to their non-college-educated colleagues, and that this increased as education levels increased.

One of the interesting findings of Shernock's study, however, was that there was not a similar correlation between education levels and acting ethically in relation to fellow officers' misconduct. Shernock argued that this was likely due to officers primarily seeing ethics as an issue most important in relation to communities rather than related to colleagues' behaviour. This finding is consistent with the host of research discussed in Chapter 2 about the importance street police culture places on loyalty, unity and the blue wall of silence among officers.

Subsequent studies showed positive effects in relation to college-educated officers' views of the importance of acting ethically and with integrity, again seemingly from an external perspective. For example, Kakar's 1998 study of 110 patrol officers in one Florida police department found that officers with college education self-reported higher levels of integrity and ethics, and that they were better at taking responsibility compared to their non-college-educated colleagues. Significantly, Telep's 2011 study of survey data from 925 police officers across 113 small, medium and large US police agencies found that officers with some college education and those with four-year college degrees were significantly less supportive of abusing authority in the police officer role compared to officers with only a high school diploma.

These US-based studies suggest that college-educated officers may view ethics and integrity, particularly toward communities, in ways different from their non-college-educated colleagues, and that this has potential to normalize a different way of thinking about accountability among officers, perhaps in foregrounding the importance of community relations akin to the guardian policing model discussed in Chapter 2. Taken together with the data discussed in the next section, showing lower rates of internal discipline and police misconduct complaints from communities for college-educated officers, this is a promising area for further empirical research to better understand the potential effects of college education on street police culture norms.

Police education, internal discipline and misconduct complaints

In addition to the studies relating to ethical decision-making and approaches to accountability, research also suggests that officers with college educations may also be subject to lower rates of internal discipline measures and external misconduct complaints by community members, suggesting that college education may have potential to reduce some negative aspects of interactions with the public which are normalized by street police culture. For example, an early study by Cascio (1977) of 940 US police officers found officers with higher education levels were associated with lower levels of internal discipline. Similarly, Carter and Sapp's research evaluating the 1989 national US PERF survey of 486 US law enforcement agencies found that 96 per cent reported that officers with two years or more college education were less frequently subject to internal discipline compared to their colleagues with lower levels of education. The limitations of this evidence base on this point is, of course, that it is relatively small and limited to the US, thus significantly more research in this area is needed.

However, the evidence base is significantly larger and more robust over the past few decades showing that officers with higher education levels have lower levels of misconduct complaints from members of the public. For example, Kappeler et al's study (1992) of a medium sized US police department found significant differences in the rates of complaints against officers with four-year college degrees and non-college-educated officers. They determined that officers with four-year college degrees had significantly fewer citizen complaints. Moreover, they found non-college-educated officers were responsible for 67 per cent of citizen complaints. Similarly, Carter and Sapp's (1989) evaluation of the US PERF survey mentioned earlier found that 98 per cent of responding police agencies reported that officers with two years or more college education had fewer citizen complaints than officers with less education.

Similarly, Lersch and Kunzman's 2001 study of sheriff's deputies in an American sheriff's department in the Southeastern US found 142 (61 per cent) deputies had high school diplomas or equivalent, 32 (14 per cent) had two-year college degrees, and 57 (25 per cent) had four-year college degrees. The study found deputies with only high school educations showed more departmental policy violations and received more administrative referrals compared to their better educated counterparts. Moreover, deputies with only high school educations had significantly more complaints (including both citizen complaints and internal complaints) than their college-educated counterparts.

These results are consistent with a study by Manis et al (2008) which examined 334 total complaints, including 163 formal complaints and 161 informal complaints, filed against patrol officers in a small Midwestern US police agency employing 105 patrol officers, 22 per cent of whom had studied some college without earning a degree, 13 per cent of whom had a two-year college degree, and 62 per cent of whom had a four-year college degree. They found that officers without a four-year college degree were more likely to generate a larger number of formal complaints. They further found that officers without four-year college degrees were more likely to have their complaints sustained compared to officers with four-year college degrees.

Further research by Kane and White (2009) found very similar results. They examined the personnel records of 3,085 NYPD officers: 1,543 officers fired for cause between 1975 and 1996, and 1,542 officers who had not been terminated. They found that officers who had two-year Associate's degrees or four-year Bachelor's degrees at the time of appointment to the NYPD were significantly less likely to be fired for misconduct.

The conclusions drawn from research on police misconduct suggests that there are statistically significant correlations between officers with college degrees and lower numbers of internal complaints, lower numbers of external civilian complaints, and fewer sustained complaints. These findings, particularly when coupled with the evidence on lower use of force rates for college-educated officers discussed in Chapter 8, show promise for using officer educational levels as one of many mechanisms to build better trust, confidence and legitimacy with local communities in ways more akin to the guardian policing model, and moving away from the distance and alienation street police culture promotes between officers and policed communities. Much more empirical research, however, is required.

Police education and discretionary decision-making

While street police culture normalizes intolerance, bias, aggression and stereotyping, research suggests that officers with college degrees may have different attitudes toward policing and analyse their roles differently compared to their colleagues without college degrees. This is particularly important because research shows that opportunities for discretionary decision-making are when explicit and implicit biases can activate (Correll et al, 2007; Lum, 2011), thus shifting decision-making in directions away from those street police culture norms toward less harmful exercises of discretion can potentially benefit policed communities.

The research evidence suggests that officers with higher levels of education may exhibit sounder judgment in some circumstances and use their discretion in more measured and considered ways compared to officers with lower levels of education. For example, an early study by Finckenauer (1975) of police recruits in one New Jersey police academy, 54 of whom had one or more years of college education and 44 of whom had high school diplomas, found those with one or more years of college education exercised their discretion toward the public in more creative and less punitive ways than non-college-educated officers. A later study by Carter and Sapp (1989) evaluating national survey data from 486 US law enforcement agencies found that 88 per cent reported that officers with college education used their discretion more wisely than their colleagues with lower education levels. Similarly, Smith and Aamodt's 1997 study of 299 police officers across 12 Virginia policing agencies found supervisors evaluated officers with college education as exercising better decision-making abilities compared to officers with only high school education. The studies showing positive correlations between college education and officers' discretionary decision-making abilities toward the public are bolstered by data on specific policing outcomes based on discretion, including arrests and use of force, discussed further in Chapter 8.

One caveat to the analysis of discretionary decision-making is that while the limited amount of data seems to positively correlate officer college education with exercising discretion toward policed communities in measured and thoughtful ways, it is notable that most of the research is based on impressions by supervisors and police leaders, rather than based on experiments, observations or other indicators testing officers' discretion in real-life policing scenarios on the streets. Researchers argue it can be difficult to measure discretion or to determine whether factors such as college education or others, including police training and experience, shape the way officers make decisions and exercise their discretion on the job (Mastrofski, 2004). Thus, a significantly larger evidence base drawn from studies using a variety of research methods would be beneficial to further develop this analysis.

Despite the limited amount of empirical research about officer decision-making by police with college educations, there is further potential to explore the ways university degrees could introduce more guardianship approaches to treating communities compared to the normalized, disdainful, distanced approaches street police culture dictates.

Police education and open-mindedness

As discussed in Chapter 2, street police culture embeds closed-mindedness, intolerance and prejudice, among many other characteristics. However, there is a limited body of empirical research suggesting that officer education has positive effects on indicators of police officer bias, which holds potential for further exploration.

Indeed, there is some empirical research evaluating the extent to which officers with college educations are more open-minded than those without college educations. Much of this research stems from the 1970s in the US, where researchers considered where police officers with varying education levels fell on the Dogmatism Scale (Guller, 1973). On the one hand, higher levels of dogmatism are associated with close-mindedness, rigidity, resistance to new ideas, making judgements and forming opinions with limited information, and rejecting information based on its source (Guller, 1973). By contrast, lower levels of dogmatism are associated with open-mindedness, flexibility, embracing new ideas, reduced pre-judgement and lower levels of prejudice (Guller, 1973).

Scholars argue that police with university degrees are more open-minded, more tolerant, and benefit from interactions with a wider variety of individuals while pursuing their university studies (Goldstein, 1977). While at university, students engage with a wider variety of people from different perspectives, beliefs, races, religions, sexual orientations, disabilities, and others with personal characteristics they may not have previously encountered or interacted closely with (Goldstein, 1977). The positive benefits of these increased associations among people of different backgrounds in university settings has been shown to increase tolerance and reduce levels of bias, as supported through a variety of empirical findings in relation to intergroup contact theory (Allport, 1954; Pettigrew, 1998), as discussed further in Chapter 8.

For example, Guller (1973) examined attitudes of 63 police officers in their first and final years of college, and found that officers with more college education were more open-minded and less likely to possess harsh attitudes than those with less college education. Guller asserted that the more exposure officers had to college education, the more flexible and open-minded they became. A subsequent study by Worden (1990), which analysed data from over 1,400 officers across 24 US police departments found college-educated officers to be more open-minded than their less educated supervisors. Similarly, Shernock's 1992 study of 177 officers across 11 US police departments similarly found that college-educated officers were less adherent to organizational parochialism and less insular compared to their colleagues without college degrees, suggesting they may be more open-minded.

More recent research supports these early findings. For example, Jones's UK-based study of officers pursuing 'top up' studies in BA degrees in Policing Studies found self-reporting of improved reflexivity in their interactions with members of the public. Officers reported feeling their studies had helped them consider a broad array of perspectives and viewpoints (Jones, 2015a). This research is consistent with earlier research showing officers with higher levels of education showed more open-mindedness in the workplace.

More specifically as to the issue of tolerance, a limited amount of US research has considered whether college-educated officers are more tolerant of different lifestyles, races and ethnicities compared to their non-college-educated peers. Given that intolerance, racial bias, misogyny and homophobia are core characteristics of street police culture as discussed in Chapter 2, this is a ripe area for study to determine whether college education can mitigate some of the effects of the intolerance and biases inherent in street police culture.

However, just one rigorous study reviewed for this volume looked at these effects. Indeed, Carter and Sapp's 1989 study, evaluating the 1989 national US PERF survey of 486 US law enforcement agencies, found that 88 per cent reported that officers with college education were more sensitive to racial and ethnic minority groups compared to officers with lower levels of education. Carter and Sapp (1989) reasoned that college-educated officers were better able to mediate and resolve problems and conflicts with a broader array of diverse community members. They suggested that, as a result, because college-educated officers were more tolerant and more empathetic to a wider variety of communities, they were less likely to discriminate against ethnic minorities. While these findings are promising across a fairly large, national US sample of policing agencies, far more research is needed to bolster the correlation between college-educated police officers and tolerance levels, particularly for ethnic minority communities. Thus, while the research on increased officer open-mindedness related to college education levels holds promise, the challenges of shifting street police culture normalization of stereotypes, bias and intolerance is a significant hurdle, and more studies are warranted.

Police education and authoritarian attitudes

In the same ways that street police culture normalizes intolerance and bias, it also embeds authoritarian attitudes which are largely directed at policed communities (Genz and Lester, 1976; Brown and Willis, 1985; Paterson, 2011). The limited research on police degrees suggests that they may hold potential to mitigate authoritarian attitudes and accompanying authoritarian behaviours toward communities, including violence, use of force, distance and alienation. However, much of the research is dated, and much more is needed to explore this possibility further in the UK and US.

Research from a small number of early empirical studies primarily from the US suggests that college education may help mitigate authoritarian tendencies in police officers. For example, a study by Smith et al (1967) used established psychological scales to measure authoritarianism among 226 new NYPD officers: 122 had no college education and 104 were in the first year of study at a college created to provide higher education to police officers. They found police officers with some college education showed less authoritarian beliefs than their non-college-educated counterparts. A subsequent study by Smith et al (1970) used the same psychological measures of authoritarianism in a sample of 78 officers – 39 who earned college degrees while working as NYPD officers and 39 with no college education. They concluded that officers who completed a four-year Bachelor's degree were significantly less authoritarian compared to those lacking any college education. Similar experiments by Dalley (1975) and Roberg (1978) also showed officers with college educations scored lower on scales of authoritarianism compared to their non-college-educated counterparts. These early experiments show promise, and contemporary researchers have urged further exploration of authoritarianism and other police attitudes (Paoline et al, 2015).

Yet trying to mitigate authoritarian beliefs through police education comes squarely up against the embedded street police culture which prizes authoritarianism, which is difficult to shift, particularly as research suggests officers become more authoritarian the longer they are on the job (Genz and Lester, 1976; Brown and Willis, 1985). Some scholars are therefore doubtful that college education alone can adequately mitigate authoritarian views embedded in street police culture without much more reinforcement and undertaking other measures (Paterson, 2011). This is an area where significantly more empirical research in both the UK and US would be valuable.

Police education and creative problem solving

One of the significant problems of street police culture is that it promotes officer homogeneity through a common set of norms. Rather than encouraging individualism or creativity, it facilitates collective thinking to underpin the shared police identity. This is problematic in numerous respects, including that it does little to encourage innovation in policing in areas like police relations or policing tactics. Yet there is a small amount of US policing research across several decades which suggests that police officers with college educations may be better able to adapt to different situations they encounter in policing, and arrive at more creative solutions then their less educated counterparts.

Indeed, studies indicate college-educated officers have better problem-solving skills (Worden, 1990; Rydberg and Terrill, 2010). For example, Worden's (1990) secondary data analysis of a Police Services Study from 24 urban US police departments found that officers who earned college degrees before joining the police service viewed the policing role more broadly compared to their colleagues without college degrees, which could allow a wider array of approaches and broader array of problem-solving skills. Similarly, Kakar's 1998 study of 110 patrol officers in one Florida police department found officers with college education self-reported better problem-solving skills compared to their non-college-educated colleagues. Research by Rydberg and Terrill (2010) similarly observed that college-educated officers showed greater levels of creativity and better problem-solving skills compared to their non-college-educated counterparts. These intriguing findings would be enhanced with additional empirical research.

Yet, as with other potential benefits evidenced through empirical research about police officer education, the studies are limited in number and located primarily in the US. Much more research is needed to better assess whether the creative thinking and problem-solving skills of officers with college educations exhibited in these studies could translate into policing differently in ways that better resonate with policed communities.

Police education and community relations

As discussed in Chapter 2 and throughout this volume, street police culture normalizes distance from policed communities, particularly traditionally marginalized communities including racial and ethnic minorities, women, LGTBQ+ people and the working class. While the distinctly warrior nature of street police culture foregrounds alienation from these and other communities, the guardian policing model suggests trust-building, partnerships and mutual respect between officers and policed communities is a better approach. The research discussed here suggests that officers with college degrees may have skills, or be capable of developing skills, well suited to guardianship policing.

For example, some studies indicate that officers with higher levels of education have better levels of positive engagement with policed communities. Smith and Aamodt's 1997 study of 299 police officers across 12 Virginia policing agencies found supervisors viewed officers with college or graduate degrees as better skilled at relations with communities compared to their high school-educated colleagues. Similarly, Kakar's 1998 study of 110 patrol officers in one Florida police department found officers with college education self-reported better interactions with community members compared to their non–college-educated colleagues.

Furthermore, some empirical research also suggests officers with college educations have stronger communication skills, or are perceived to have preferable communication skills, particularly when dealing with the communities they serve. The hypothesis is that college-educated officers are well socialized with the mainstream, have more positive attitudes toward communities, and may be better at interacting with them (DeJohn, 2004).

For example, Carter and Sapp's study examining the US PERF survey of 486 US law enforcement agencies across the country found that college-educated officers had better communication skills with policed communities (Carter and Sapp, 1989). An interesting observational study by Paoline and Terrill (2007), which studied 3,356 observed officer encounters with citizens suspected of wrongdoing and surveys of 398 officers in Indianapolis, Indiana and 240 officers in St Petersburg, Florida police departments found college-educated officers had preferable communication skills by relying on less verbal force. Specifically, they found that for officers with some college or a four-year college degree, encounters resulting in use of verbal force (35 per cent) were significantly fewer compared to their colleagues who only had high school educations (47 per cent).

However, such results are not consistent across all research on the communication skills of college-educated officers in terms of how they engage with community members. In fact, other research finds inconclusive or opposite evidence of police communication skills related to college degrees. For example, DeJong's 2004 study of observational and officer survey data collected from 6,135 citizens encountered by police in Indianapolis, Indiana, and St Petersburg, Florida found officers with college degrees were less likely to comfort victims. Similarly, Foley and Terrill's 2008 study, drawn from the same larger study but focused on 1,865 interactions between officers and citizens who were perceived as victims, found that where officers with college degrees engaged with victims, they were less likely to offer the victim comfort compared to officers without college degrees.

Thus, while there is some evidence that officers with college degrees may have skills toward building strong communication with policed communities, or may be inclined toward developing positive community relations in the guardianship style of policing, the hurdles posed by the working-class street police culture norms make efforts to build or improve relations with communities challenging. Nonetheless, the empirical studies discussed in this chapter suggest there is a need for further research to develop a stronger body of evidence to better assess correlations between police officer education levels and communication skills with communities.

Conclusion

This chapter examines the ways UK and US policing were long ago designed to be working-class occupations where working-class officers surveilled, controlled and policed working-class communities. This deliberately crafted working-class policing developed a very strong working-class street police culture which continues to influence policing and police behaviour in both the UK and US. Thus, the very culture of street policing is defined by working-class perspectives on race, class, gender and communities, among other factors.

Nonetheless, in recent years UK and US policing have come under increased pressure to increase scrutiny, fairness, accountability and community satisfaction with police. One of the ways police leaders have attempted to improve police legitimacy and police–community relations has been with the introduction of police education requirements, which have been designed to professionalize the police, and in doing so to shift policing from a working-class craft to a middle-class profession. But these efforts to improve policing by shifting its class status have placed too much value on police degrees as an all-encompassing fix to solve a host of police-related problems.

Empirical evidence discussed in this chapter has shown that police officers with higher education levels may be viewed more favourably by their superiors and promoted at higher rates, may use their discretion in less discriminatory ways, and may show reduced authoritarian tendencies and improved creativity, open-mindedness and relations with communities which may mean college educated officers have skills necessary to effectuate guardianship model policing. However, these correlations in a limited number of studies do not make police education degrees a panacea for implementing guardianship policing, or for shifting UK and US policing away from the deeply held working-class street police culture values. Rather than focusing only on increasing the numbers of officers with college education, policing must also focus on reforming police through other means, including residency requirements, positive discrimination programmes, more aggressive external oversight and misconduct procedures, among many other police reform tools. Without introducing a suite of police reform mechanisms, efforts to change the working-class culture of street policing with education requirements will not achieve long-term success.

8

Diversity and representative bureaucracy

One of the most important original contributions of this book to policing research is its key assertion – that officers from traditionally marginalized backgrounds may, under particular circumstances and despite street police culture pressures, engage in active bureaucratic representation, meaning in their roles as officers, representing and championing the interests of their communities of origin or other oppressed groups. While this argument has largely been explored with bureaucrats outside of policing, there is a growing body of evidence supporting the notion that ethnic minority, female and LGBTQ+ officers, among others, may explicitly or implicitly challenge aspects of street police culture and engage in policing in ways different from their straight White male counterparts.

This chapter, and this volume more generally, does not argue that all officers from historically under-represented backgrounds resist street police culture or engage in representation of their communities of origin or other oppressed groups; however, it does argue that if certain conditions described in this chapter are met, this can occur. This can partly hinge on the ways under-represented officers view themselves, view the role and experience the job, and the types of support they receive from colleagues, supervisors, their institutions and communities they serve. This is particularly important given that acting in a representative bureaucratic way for communities of origin or traditionally marginalized groups can cut against certain core tenets of street police culture, including bias against oppressed groups, distance from local communities, and loyalty to fellow officers above all others, and look more like guardian policing. Considering the ways these interconnecting theoretical frameworks might apply in practice to UK and US policing is something which has not been explored in police diversity research previously.

In analyzing how representative bureaucracy theory applies to police from traditionally marginalized groups, this volume also considers the growing body of evidence showing statistically significant differences in policing outcomes for officers from traditionally under-represented groups reflected in some studies. To date, no book on police diversity has considered the ways representative bureaucracy might hold potential to mitigate street police culture norms and move toward guardianship policing, which in turn might help reduce disparities in disproportionate policing outcomes such as stop and searches, use of force, community relations, traffic citations and other measures when officers from traditionally marginalized groups consciously or subconsciously adopt roles where they act on behalf of their communities of origin or other oppressed groups.

This chapter also examines the ways intergroup contact theory, a sociological theory with significant empirical grounding over many decades, holds much potential when applied to policing to shift street police culture norms and practices. Indeed, this chapter argues that increased intergroup contact between officers from traditionally marginalized backgrounds and straight White male officers can help the latter mitigate a host of negative effects of embedded street police culture by improving relations with officers from under-represented groups, increasing cultural competency, reducing bias, bettering relations with traditionally marginalized communities, and potentially reducing some disproportionate policing outcomes in areas such as stop and searches, arrests and uses of force, again in ways moving closer to guardianship policing.

Diversity and representative bureaucracy

This book argues that despite the homogenizing norms of street police culture, police officers are not a monolith. It asserts that in both the UK and US, there are differences in the lived experiences officers bring to the role, how they experience the position, and the ways they can conduct policing. Yet the whole of policing is not the focus of this book. Rather, it focuses on UK and US officers from traditionally marginalized or under-represented backgrounds in policing. This book asserts through application of theoretical literature, that officers from traditionally marginalized backgrounds can police in different ways from their straight White male colleagues, and potentially in more guardianship ways.

The application of these organizational culture theories to underrepresented police officers in both the UK and US has not previously been done in police diversity literature. It is based on a deep understanding of the ways people from traditionally marginalized groups experience inequality in the workplace in policing and other fields. Given the disparities in lived experiences and terms and conditions of employment faced by people from traditionally marginalized backgrounds in a variety of other professions – from banking to firefighting to the judiciary to the retail sector – it would be incongruent to believe that those inequalities did not also reach policing.

Yet even those who accept the premise that police officers from traditionally marginalized groups may experience or challenge the policing workplace differently from their straight White male colleagues are often reluctant to believe that these differences can translate into distinctions in the ways some police from traditionally marginalized groups carry out their jobs. This book makes this novel yet controversial argument, which contradicts not only street police culture's instance on officer homogeneity, but also assertions by both police supporters and detractors that police officers are a monolithic group, who have the same experiences and adhere to the same decision-making processes because they all just think and act 'blue'.

The dominant narrative from both supporters and detractors of policing is that street police culture's influence on policing is ensuring that all officers think and act the same once they put on a blue police uniform. While the majority of empirical research in this chapter has found statistically significant differences in police decision-making and outcomes from officers from traditionally marginalized groups, a minority of studies has found no statistically significant differences in police decision-making and outcomes. The application of organizational theories below to the evidence presented reflecting the data about police from marginalized groups raises provocative questions challenging police sameness which warrant further empirical study.

Representative bureaucrats

As discussed in prior chapters, one of the primary drivers of differences in policing approaches and outcomes between officers are varied lived experiences and values, which may or may not conform to established police culture norms. In the case of officers from traditionally marginalized groups, they may have lived experiences and values which differ from aspects of street police culture, and how this impacts their functioning in the role can be explained by representative bureaucracy theory.

The representative bureaucracy theory originates in public administration research, and posits that balanced representation of different groups of citizens within government agencies ensures a broader array of interests are reflected in agency experiences, policies and practices (Mosher, 1982). Passive bureaucratic representation occurs where the composition of the institution mirrors that of the community (Mosher, 1982). Research suggests that just this symbolic representation has positive effects for citizens, including improving their sense of legitimacy of the public agency (Riccucci et al, 2014; Riccucci and Van Ryzin, 2017; Keiser et al, 2022), having more positive views of local government policies (Van Ryzin et al, 2017; Lucero et al, 2022), and beliefs that government institutions were fairer (Riccucci et al, 2018; Keiser et al, 2022).

Minority groups tend to view symbolic representation positively because they perceive more inclusive public institutions, particularly local-level agencies, as better at understanding and addressing their concerns, having better communication skills with minority groups through shared values and lived experiences, and being more inclined to engage in policies and practices which support and benefit them (Bobo and Gilliam, 1990; Lim, 2006; Marks and Stout, 2011; Keiser et al, 2022). These positive perceptions make minority groups more likely to participate in public civic processes and engage with public institutions and local government initiatives (Bobo and Gilliam, 1990; Van Ryzin et al, 2017; Lucero et al, 2022).

While the benefits of these improved perceptions stemming from symbolic representation are clear for effects on activities and opinions of the public, researchers have also investigated the drivers of institutional decision-making in relation to policies and practices which benefit minority communities. This process is called active bureaucratic representation, and refers to bureaucrats from historically under-represented groups consciously or unconsciously taking an active interest in ensuring that the institutional policies and practices benefit segments of communities of which they are members (Mosher, 1982; Meier, 1993). Active representation can take numerous forms, including: (1) engaging in policy congruence, meaning making decisions in line with the policy preferences of the represented group; (2) obtaining benefits for individual members of the represented group; (3) pursuing benefits that are positive for the entire represented group; or (4) building trust and support with the represented group (Meier and Stewart, 1992).

Significant research suggests three conditions are required for a minority group bureaucrat's active representation to translate to policies and practices benefitting their group of origin: (1) adoption of organizational norms/culture; (2) opportunities for discretion; and (3) value congruence between individual bureaucrats and the communities they serve, which can mean shared socialization experiences, political attitudes or values (Meier and Stewart, 1992; Meier, 1993).

The theory of active bureaucratic representation has been empirically tested in a variety of government settings across the US, from local governments to school districts to regional offices of national agencies, with significant support in a variety of jurisdictions (Meier, 1993; Meier et al, 1999; Lucero et al, 2022). Research has tended to focus on active representation by bureaucrats of colour (Bobo and Gilliam, 1990; Meier, 1993; Meier et al, 1999; Lim, 2006; Keiser et al, 2022) and female officials (Keiser et al, 2002; Van Ryzin et al, 2017), again with clear support for the theory.

Yet active representation is not always easy even for bureaucrats who are so inclined. Bureaucrats are more likely to engage in active representation where: (1) they recognize the potential benefits for the client; (2) engaging in representation is consistent with the bureaucrat's personal values; (3) they have a high sense of salience with the identity or identities shared with the client; and (4) the benefits outweigh the costs of active representation (Meier, 2019). According to these criteria, not all bureaucrats from minority groups will decide active representation is worthwhile. Each bureaucrat makes this individual conscious or subconscious assessment for themselves on the job.

If a bureaucrat, having weighed the costs and benefits, decides to engage in active representation, there remain multiple institutional barriers that can preclude representative actions. Some of the barriers to active representation include: (1) being in positions which are unable to influence policies or practices; (2) substituting personal values for organizational values, and socialization into organizational culture, which bureaucrats are encouraged to adopt to succeed in the agency; (3) the organization may lack the jurisdiction to impact policies or practices impacting the passively represented communities; and (4) bureaucrats may lack sufficient discretion (Thompson, 1976; Meier, 1993). For bureaucrats, these obstacles can be quite significant and determinative. And for institutions with particularly strong socialization into organizational cultures like policing as discussed throughout this volume, this assessment can mean that these obstacles can make active representation off-putting for some bureaucrats. Yet, this volume argues, despite the obstacles, some bureaucrats nonetheless determine either explicitly or implicitly that they can overcome the challenges to make active representation worthwhile.

Indeed, multiple factors can be influential in helping minority bureaucrats overcome barriers and facilitate active representation. Studies indicate active representation is more likely among street-level bureaucrats than senior administrators (Meier, 1993). Research also shows minority bureaucrats are more likely to engage in active representation of their communities when they have support within their organization from other minority bureaucrats, including minority supervisors and leaders (Thompson, 1976; Henderson, 1978; Meier, 1993). Support from those outside the organization can also be instrumental in facilitating active representation, including from minority elected officials and strong minority community groups, both of whom can place pressure on agencies to address minority community needs (Thompson, 1976; Meier, 1993).

Representative bureaucrats in policing

As applied to policing, the representative bureaucracy theory suggests that police bureaucrats, both at the street level and managerial level, can under some circumstances engage in active bureaucratic representation. In policing, representative bureaucracy theory posits that police are street-level bureaucrats invested with discretion to make decisions that shape diverse citizens' experience of policing (Wilkins and Williams, 2008; Trochmann and Gover, 2016). Diversity in this regard can refer to race, ethnicity, gender, religion, social class and sexuality, among others, although empirical research most frequently examines the effects of the representative bureaucracy theory through race, ethnicity and gender lenses. The thesis suggests that, under certain conditions, police officers from traditionally under-represented groups seek, develop or create institutional policies and make discretionary decisions which benefit the minority groups to which they belong (Wilkins and Williams, 2008; Trochmann and Gover, 2016).

Yet not all officers from under-represented groups will engage in representative bureaucracy. Critics of the use of diversity as part of the police reform toolkit often point to incidents involving officers of colour or others from traditionally marginalized groups to illustrate that police are simply a monolith who all think and act the same as a result of intense socialization into street police culture. But this book offers a more complex and nuanced analysis, and argues that active bureaucratic representation can occur for minority group officers if three conditions are met: (1) adoption of organizational norms/ culture; (2) opportunities for discretion; and (3) value congruence between individual bureaucrats and the communities they serve (Johnston and Houston, 2018). When these conditions are satisfied, active bureaucratic representation is possible among police. This is particularly true for street-level officers, who tend to have the most discretion, more frequent interaction with citizens, and where their actions on behalf of communities can readily be seen (Hong, 2016).

Accordingly, the limited policing research on representative bureaucracy tends to focus on street-level officers rather than supervisors or police leaders (Wilkins and Williams, 2008; Lasley et al, 2011; Johnston and Houston, 2018). The bulk of such research is based in the US, although some important studies have been carried out in the England and Wales policing context in recent years (Hong, 2016, 2017; Johnston and Houston, 2018). As discussed earlier, representative bureaucracy research has tended to focus on racial and ethnic diversity or gender, with far less research devoted to analysing representative bureaucracy vis-à-vis social class, religion or LGBTQ+ status in policing.

Unsurprisingly, some criminal justice researchers have been particularly dubious of the role of representative bureaucracy in policing. Critics who adopt the perspective that police are a monolith argue that the aggressive socialization process into street police culture discussed in Chapter 2 limits the ability of passive bureaucratic representation to translate into active bureaucratic representation among officers from traditionally under-represented groups (Wilkins and Williams, 2008). Wilkins and Williams (2009), for example, argue that street police culture's strong socialization of officers into police camaraderie, and adversarial framing of relations with community members, supplants any affinity group identity among minority officers. According to this approach, all police, including ethnic minorities or other traditionally under-represented groups, prioritize loyalty to being 'blue' over membership in their traditionally under-represented minority group. Todak et al (2018) similarly note that evidence of the effects of representative bureaucracy in policing shows only mixed results, although they did not test the hypothesis themselves. Others, including several UK-based policing researchers, have argued against active bureaucratic representation in policing, asserting that the broad diversity in education, social class, residence for minority victims and suspects reduces the value congruence between individual bureaucrats and the communities they serve (Holdaway, 1996; Rowe, 2012).

As discussed earlier, this volume argues that representative bureaucracy in policing is not only possible, but happening routinely, although empirical research tying differences in policing outcomes to representative bureaucracy theory has been slow to make this connection, making this volume's thesis an original contribution to police diversity research. While the evidence of representative bureaucracy in policing is therefore limited, there is significant evidence that this occurs with government bureaucrats outside policing across a host of different government organizations. This volume argues for the first time in a comparative police diversity research that there is a parallel between that literature and what occurs in policing. It argues that even in policing, that under particular conditions and with appropriate support from supervisors, police leaders and communities, police may actively represent the interests of their communities of origin, and other marginalized communities, and that this may be more akin to guardianship policing.

One of the important conditions required for any bureaucrats, including police, to engage in representative bureaucracy is that they have requisite support. This is essential for police officers from traditionally marginalized groups. While research in this area is limited, some policing studies reflect how support from fellow officers and supervisors in traditionally marginalized groups can impact their approach to the role. Indeed, some research evidences that for ethnic minority officers, support organizations in both the UK and US can also play an important role in helping minority group officers resist pressures to assimilate into police culture norms and, instead, to maintain a sense of self tied to their minority group status (Holdaway and O'Neill, 2004; O'Neill and Holdaway, 2007). The importance of these types of aid mechanisms is consistent with research from Thompson (1976), Henderson (1978), Meier (1993) and others about the significant prerequisite role support plays in bringing active bureaucratic representation to fruition.

Moreover, interviews with eight police leaders conducted for this volume similarly bolster the notion from Meier (1993) and others that for active bureaucratic representation to occur, minority bureaucrats must have support from their supervisors and police leaders to resist street police culture assimilation and maintain their ties to minority communities. Indeed, all eight police leaders interviewed for this book were minority group members and all argued that, particularly for officers from traditionally marginalized groups, having the support of supervisors and leadership was essential for them to engage in active bureaucratic representation.

The nuanced argument offered in this volume is that the effects of street police culture, while significant, do not mean all officers turn 'blue' once they put on the blue police uniform. While police critics readily dismiss the possibility of representative bureaucracy in policing, such arguments lack balanced understanding of the pressures traditionally under-represented groups face, against their roles in resisting or reshaping police culture (Hong, 2017). Moreover, this volume argues for the first time in a police diversity book that the historical and structural racial, ethnic and gender-based social divisions which have shaped the lived experiences of minority group members in their experiences outside policing cannot be so easily forgotten by socialization into street police culture. Rather, this book argues that there is also a sufficient body of research showing that while officers from traditionally under-represented groups face tremendous pressure to adopt street police culture norms, they can wear pseudo-assimilation as a mask adopted out of necessity to ensure being perceived as fitting in, but in reality they are not wholly subsumed by street police culture (Holdaway, 1996). This may give them tools to be more guardian-like in their policing approaches.

While a great deal of additional empirical evidence, particularly in the England and Wales context, is necessary to more fully test the applicability of representative bureaucracy theory in policing, the evidence from the US shows the theory holds great promise for better understanding the complexities of the behaviours of officers from traditionally marginalized groups, and for a path into guardian policing. Indeed, research supports the notion that diverse officers are either consciously or unconsciously exercising their discretion in ways different from their straight White male colleagues, and often in ways which are beneficial to under-represented community members. This suggests greater diversity in UK and US police services could be a tool to help reduce disproportionate policing outcomes and taking guardian policing forward, as discussed further below.

Representative bureaucracy in practice

While the evidence of representative bureaucracy in UK and US policing is not abundant, there is a growing body of research supporting the argument made in this volume that this phenomenon does occur in practice. Indeed, this volume argues for the first time in a police diversity context that the representative bureaucracy theory helps to explain some of the statistically significant differences in policing outcomes for officers from traditionally marginalized backgrounds, including ethnic minority, female and LGBTQ+ officers, among others. This volume is the first police diversity book to offer a broad array of research to argue that representative bureaucracy occurs in policing at a fairly significant rate. This new analysis is supported by the other evidence analysed in this volume illustrating the differences in lived experiences, treatment, discrimination and terms and conditions of employment that officers from traditionally under-represented backgrounds face in UK and US policing institutions. It is when officers from marginalized backgrounds explicitly or implicitly make these connections between their own lived experiences and those of policed communities that there is potential for representative bureaucracy to operate.

Race, ethnicity and active bureaucratic representation

Critics of representative bureaucracy theory are correct that it is challenging in the policing context given the significant influence of street police culture. As discussed throughout this volume, street police culture places extraordinary pressures on all officers to conform to particular standards of behaviour which emphasize bias, aggression, violence, intolerance and alienation from police communities. As the studies analysed and the qualitative interviews conducted for this book show, street police culture norms are difficult for most officers to resist to some extent. Yet some officers do manage to reject street police culture values in whole or in part. This volume argues that evidence of this conscious or subconscious rejection of street police culture is illustrated with evidence that officers from traditionally marginalized groups, at times and under certain conditions, police differently from their majority group member colleagues. This volume is the first work on police diversity to hypothesize that rejection of street police culture norms can result in active bureaucratic representation leading to differences in some policing outcomes and lead to guardian policing, although, this hypothesis requires further testing with more empirical research.

The evidence of statistically significant differences in the policing outcomes for officers of colour continues to grow in both the UK and US. In the UK, this research is limited, but several studies show decreases in racially disproportionate policing outcomes including stop and searches, which is consistent with evidence from other jurisdictions. For example, Hong (2016) found that increased numbers of officers of colour across 43 police forces in England and Wales was associated with reductions in crime reported by citizens to the individual police forces. Similarly, Hong (2017) found that during a ten-year period across all police forces across England and Wales, an increase in the proportion of ethnic minorities in a police force was strongly associated with a decrease in the proportion of ethnic minorities subjected to stop and searches.

While more research on the impact of officers of colour on policing outcomes is needed in the UK, a significant evidence base from US police forces makes clear that often officers of colour may engage in policing in ways different from their White peers, which can positively impact communities of colour and reduce disproportionate policing outcomes, and may evidence that some officers of colour engage in active bureaucractic representation of communities of colour. For example, Black officers have been shown to better understand communication styles of Black citizens compared to their White colleagues, who can misinterpret non-verbal behaviours and communications from Black people (Vrij and Taylor, 2003). In that study, while White officers frequently misinterpreted non-verbal behaviours by Black people (including greater range of voice, raised pitch and avoiding eye contact) as suspicious, Black officers did not always reach the same conclusions. In another study, Black officers were shown to resolve conflicts with community members in ways different from their White peers (Sun and Payne, 2004).

Research has found clear differences in the treatment of people of colour, particularly Black people, by Black and White officers during police encounters. For example, Black officers have been shown to be less likely to issue traffic violations to minority citizens, while White officers have been more likely to do so (Gilliard-Matthews et al, 2008). Studies also have found White officers were more likely to initiate searches of drivers than Black officers (Lundman, 2004). Research has shown White officers to be more coercive in encounters with Black people compared to their Black officer colleagues (Paoline et al, 2018). White officers have also been shown to engage in more stop and frisks of Black and Latino people in a large-scale analysis of 4.4 million NYPD stop and frisks in New York City (where 80 per cent of stop and frisks were of Black and Latino people), compared to their Black and Latino colleagues (Fagan et al, 2015). Multiple studies have found clear differences between Black and White officers in decisions to arrest Black subjects, with White officers more likely than Black officers to arrest Black suspects (Brown and Frank, 2006; Close and Mason, 2006; Brandl et al, 2012).

In terms of racial profiling, two studies by Wilkins and Williams (2008, 2009) found no statistically significant differences in the policing outcomes of Black and Minority Ethnic (BAME) and White officers when it comes to decisions such as racial profiling. A more recent UK study by Vomfell and Stewart (2021) found no statistically significant differences in stop and searches based on officer ethnicity, which they attributed to the possibility that White officers held back from engaging in profiling because they were concerned about being perceived by researchers as racially biased. Moreover, as discussed in Chapter 4, officers of colour often feel pressure to adopt stereotyping street police cultures which racially profile people of colour as 'suspect communities' and legitimate targets for disproportionate police engagement.

Research also shows there can be significant differences in approaches to community relations and community engagement, with studies indicating that some Black officers view themselves as community stewards responsible for improving police–community relations compared to White colleagues (Kelly and Farber, 1974; Boyd, 2010), a notion consistent with representative bureaucracy theory and the guardianship model policing.

Studies have also shown Black and Latino officers may be more willing to engage in partnerships with communities of colour compared to their White counterparts (Lasley et al, 2011). In that longitudinal study of the Los Angeles Police Department, researchers found African American and Latino officers showed more desire to engage in active representation or 'partnerships' with communities than White officers, and held and retained more positive attitudes about communities of colour than their White counterparts. Research has also found that Black officers felt more connected to policed communities than White officers following the Ferguson, Missouri protests following the police killing of Michael Brown (McCarty et al, 2019). Moreover, several studies have shown Black officers more readily acknowledging systemic discrimination by police against African Americans, particularly following highly publicized police killings of Black people caught on camera, including Michael Brown, Eric Garner, Philando Castile and others (Pew Research Center, 2017; Gau and Paoline, 2017).

In terms of using physical force, some studies have shown statistically significant differences in police attitudes toward the acceptability of using force on the job, as well as racial differences in the actual use of force in practice. In terms of perceptions of racial differences in use of force against Black and White citizens, Weisburd et al (2000), for example, found in a national sample of 925 American officers that 57 per cent of Black officers believed police were more likely to use physical force against ethnic minorities than against Whites in similar situations, while only 12 per cent of non-Black ethnic minority officers and 5 per cent of White officers agreed.

Regarding use of force in practice, the Pew survey found that White officers (36 per cent) were more likely to report having physical confrontations in the past month than Black officers (20 per cent), and Latino officers (33 per cent) (Pew Research Center, 2017). Regarding frequency of use of force, 20 per cent of Black officers, 33 per cent of Latino officers and 36 per cent of White officers reported they had physically struggled or fought with a suspect who was resisting arrest (Pew Research Center, 2017). The survey further found that 31 per cent of White officers, compared to 21 per cent of Black officers and 20 per cent of Latino officers reported firing their weapon on duty (Pew Research Center, 2017).

Empirical research by Paoline et al (2018) examining 6,059 use of force incidents across medium to large urban US police agencies found that White officers used higher degrees of force compared to their Black colleagues, including using higher levels of force against Black suspects than their Black colleagues. By contrast, Black officers in the study used equal degrees of force against Black and White suspects. Paoline et al (2018) suspected the higher degree of force White officers used against Black suspects was attributable to White officers seeing Black suspects who resist during police encounters as particularly threatening, while Black officers did not necessarily view Black suspects as more threatening than White suspects. Similarly, Wright and Headley (2020) examined use of force by White, Black and Latino officers in two large American urban police departments – Indianapolis and Dallas – finding that White officers used higher levels of force against Black civilians.

However, it is noteworthy that some earlier studies found no statistically significant racial differences in officers' shootings. For example, two early 1980s studies by Fyfe (1981) and Geller and Karales (1981) found no statistically significant differences when looking at officer-involved shootings and officer race, and a subsequent study of police killing of civilians by Smith (2003) found no differences in the rates of police killings of felons in cities with higher proportions of racial minority officers. However, the more recent studies cited in support of representative bureaucracy theory discussed above involve more complex methodologies and larger sample sizes, suggesting they may be more empirically robust than earlier studies.

In terms of the impact of these physical confrontations on police legitimacy in communities, studies have shown some clear racial differences in perceptions of community trust and confidence in police. For example, the Pew survey found stark contrasts between Black and White officers in their interpretations of fatal encounters between police and Black community members. While 57 per cent of Black officers said these encounters evidenced broader problems between police and Black people, only 27 per cent of White officers and 26 per cent of Latino officers shared that view. Black female officers were particularly concerned about these incidents, with 63 per cent of Black women officers saying these incidents signalled broader problems, compared to 54 per cent of Black male officers (Pew Research Center, 2017).

The research suggests officers of colour may be particularly open to community engagement approaches in policing in the vein of guardianship policing. Black and Kari (2010), for example, examined data from 1,449 officers involved in the Impact of Community Policing Training and Program Implementation on Police Personnel in Arizona, 1995–1998 study. The study found that officers of colour, particularly male officers of colour, were most open to non-traditional, community-focused policing approaches such as community-oriented policing and problem solving, compared to their White male and female colleagues. They also found male officers of colour were best able to interact with diverse cultural groups in policed communities. That said, a minority of studies, particularly older studies, have found no statistically significant differences in citizen complaints against White and non-White officers (Pate and Fridell, 1993; Lersch and Mieczkowski, 1996; Cao and Huang, 2000).

With the majority of the empirical evidence offered here finding officers of colour engaging communities of colour in ways different from their White counterparts and aligning with aspects of guardianship policing, it is important to note that these findings clearly triangulate with qualitative interview data collected and analyzed for this book, which repeatedly found leaders of colour emphasizing the importance of community engagement-based policing approaches. For example, Interview Subject 5, an African American police leader, talked about the change in approach he instituted as police chief, which involved consistently and repeatedly emphasizing and celebrating community engagement as a priority, as opposed to simply celebrating arrest and other hard policing approaches:

[A]nd the thing we talk about is you are what you celebrate in policing. So if you are what you celebrate in policing, that means that if you're celebrating capturing the bad guy and only acts of what we call that type of typical heroism then that's all that matters, so the person that's really good at interfacing with or spending the extra ten minutes on the call with or spending extra time in the locker room with other officers helping them through a tough time doesn't get acknowledged or celebrated. That becomes a huge problem. That becomes a huge problem. So you are what you celebrate. Then it becomes, okay, how you instantiate these things into the pattern of how people interact, right? So then it really becomes how do you celebrate it? It can't be at a yearly thing. So one of the things that I did in a very tactical way, let's routinize this. ... So I would always take an example to say things that we do collectively and individually that add to the essence of what we're trying to accomplish in community. We would constantly celebrate that, and we did that. It's just another tactic. So I look at layers, so it's almost like if you have a strainer and you just overlap another strainer, another strainer, another strainer and it begins to cover up the holes so eventually less and less water leaks through, that really has to be the approach because you don't know what resonates with one person or if it will resonate with someone else on a particular approach, a newsletter or whatever but when you put information out and they hear your voice and you're present and they know you care.

Similarly, Interview Subject 6, the Latino police chief, had a parallel approach, highlighting that the importance of celebrating community-focused accomplishments rather than arrests and other hard approaches also had the impact of attracting community-focused officers to the police department:

So what we celebrate within an organization ultimately defines who we are as an organization, but it will ultimately attract who we want in the organization. It will ultimately determine who we promote within the organization and it will create a culture. So the flip example of [former department] is we are pushing away the good hearted African American young man or woman who wants to join us but who are we attracting? The abusive, aggressive individual? Because what made this even worse is the chief came out in a press conference and justified what occurred. So that level of destruction is beyond anything that we can imagine but it's directly tied in to are you creating an environment like we do here that attracts diversity? Because if you're attracting everyone you know you're doing the right thing and then the top of any particular class will come in and join us.

Taken together, the existing empirical research analysed for this book, coupled with the original qualitative interview data collected through original police leader interviews, provide both quantitative and qualitative evidence of differences in policing approaches, perspectives and outcomes for some officers of colour in the UK and US compared to their White counterparts which support the hypothesis that active bureaucratic representation is happening in policing and lends support to the guardian policing model.

Gender and active bureaucratic representation

There is also a growing body of evidence that female officers engage in policing in ways different from their male colleagues that supports the idea of active bureaucratic representation occurring in policing, and again, illustrates potential for guardianship policing. As demonstrated above in relation to officers of colour, officers from traditionally marginalized groups have potential to police in ways different from their majority group colleagues under the right set of conditions needed to facilitate active bureaucratic representation. The evidence suggests that the same holds true for female officers, who face the pressures of hegemonically masculine street police culture norms, which view women as less equipped, less competent and less able to engage in so-called masculinist policing approaches. Yet this volume argues something understudied in comparative police diversity research – that female officers may resist or push back against misogynistic street police culture norms in a number of ways, including by engaging in policing practices in ways different from their male colleagues more akin to guardian policing. This book is the first to draw attention to evidence of female officers policing differently from their colleagues and to theorize that these behavioural differences can potentially be explained by the explicit or implicit rejection of street police culture norms and embracing of active bureaucratic representation. This section analyzes statistically significant evidence of some of these tangible differences in policing behaviours of some women officers to further support the thesis that police are not monolithic, and that that police diversity is multi-layered and complicated, particularly for women and other officers from traditionally marginalized groups.

For example, a number of studies have reflected that female officers appear to possess stronger communication skills on the job. Research has shown that many female officers are more skilled at de-escalating tense situations and avoiding using violence compared to their male colleagues (Grennan, 1987; Balkin, 1988; Belknap and Shelley, 1993; Alpert and Dunham, 1997; Schuck, 2014). Moreover, studies have shown that female officers are often better at being empathetic on the job compared to their male colleagues (Seklecki and Paynich, 2007; Rabe-Hemp, 2008).

Female officers may also have the ability to develop strong rapport with crime victims, particularly female crime victims. For example, studies have found that many female officers build better rapport with, and are more responsive to, crime victims compared to their male colleagues, particularly in cases of domestic violence (Van Wormer, 1981; Homant and Kennedy,

1985; National Center for Women & Policing, 2002; Seklecki and Paynich, 2007; Schuck, 2014). Other studies found that during a period of several decades between the late 1970s and early 1990s, increases in numbers of female officers on a police force correlated with increases in reporting of serious violent crimes against women, particularly domestic violence (Miller and Segal, 2019). Similarly, Schuck (2018) examined national survey data from 315 American police departments and crime report data between 1997 and 2013, and found that police departments with more female officers saw increases in rape reports and clearance of rape cases compared to departments with fewer female officers. However, these findings raise important considerations given the significant evidence discussed in Chapter 5 that hegemonic masculinity stereotypes female officers as more desiring or more capable of working in victim-facing roles, and that they are disproportionately steered to these assignments compared to their male colleagues. The point this book makes is that rather than being steered into these roles, female officers should be given choices, not assumed to be more inclined or more interested in such roles.

Some research has also shown women victims show greater willingness to report sexual assaults to female officers (Meier and Nicholson-Crotty, 2006). Studies including Meier and Nicholson-Crotty (2006) have further found that female officers have higher arrest rates for sexual assault in the US, and higher domestic violence arrest rates across all 43 forces of England and Wales, compared to their male colleagues (Andrews and Johnston-Miller, 2013). It is noted, however, that a minority of studies have found no statistically significant differences in male and female officers' decisions to make arrests (Feder, 1997; Robinson and Chandek, 2000; Stalans and Finn, 2000; Parsons and Jesilow, 2001; Archbold and Schulz, 2012; Johnston and Houston, 2018).

In terms of use of force on the job, research primarily from the US has shown there are often statistically significant differences in the use of force between male and female officers. For example, multiple US studies have found that many female officers are less likely than their male colleagues to use physical force on the job (Brandl et al, 2001; Garner et al, 2002; National Center for Women and Policing, 2002; Schuck and Rabe-Hemp, 2005; Rabe-Hemp and Schuck, 2007; Seklecki and Paynich, 2007; Rabe-Hemp, 2008; Schuck, 2014). Regarding frequency of engaging in physical violence on the job, studies suggest female officers engage in violence less frequently than their male colleagues. For example, the national Pew survey (2017) found that male officers (35 per cent) were more likely to report they had physically struggled or fought with a suspect who was resisting arrest compared to female officers (22 per cent) (Pew Research Center, 2017). However, it is noted that a minority of studies examining gender and use of force have found no differences between male and female officers in terms of using physical force and/or coercion against civilians (Lersch, 1998; Terrill and Mastrofski, 2002; Paoline and Terrill, 2004; Hoffman and Hickey, 2005; Archbold and Schulz, 2012).

Regarding the severity of force used, studies have also shown that when female officers do use force, they may use less severe force than male officers (Schuck and Rabe-Hemp, 2005; Hoffman and Hickey, 2005; Wright and Headley, 2020). In terms of using a weapon on duty, studies have shown male officers are much more likely to do so compared to female colleagues. For example, the Pew survey found male officers (30 per cent) were nearly three times as likely as female officers (11 per cent) to say they have fired their weapon while on duty (Pew Research Center, 2017). This finding was supported by another study of a suburban US police department, which similarly found female officers were less likely to use a weapon compared to their male colleagues (Hoffman and Hickey, 2005).

Perhaps attributable to these differences in use of force on the job, research from multiple US studies has also found that many female officers are less likely to be subject to excessive force complaints compared to their male colleagues (Brandl et al, 2001; National Center for Women and Policing, 2002; Schuck, 2014). Given this, studies also reflect women are only responsible for a very small proportion of payments to settle lawsuits and claims made by victims in use of force actions compared to male officers (National Center for Women and Policing, 2002).

Studies have also reflected that female officers may be more supportive of community engagement-focused approaches such as community policing compared to their male colleagues. For example, some research has found that female officers may be more supportive of community policing and better at performing community-oriented activities (Miller, 1999; Corsianos, 2009; Schuck, 2014).

The analysis of a growing number of empirical research studies in both the UK and US comparing gender effects among officers suggests that there are important and often very significant differences in policing approaches and outcomes for female officers compared to their male counterparts. These statistically robust differences between female and male officers in some policing outcomes are fairly significant across numerous police services, and in some cases over the course of many years. Rather than ignoring this evidence, police diversity research much delve more deeply into the drivers of these differences in behaviours, and consider this book's thesis that resistance to hegemonically masculine street police culture norms and taking up active bureaucratic representation may offer some explanations.

LGBTQ+ identity and active bureaucratic representation

As discussed above, there is a growing body of empirical evidence supporting this book's hypothesis that police from traditionally marginalized backgrounds, including officers of colour and female officers, may conduct policing in ways different from their peers. Whether driven by a conscious rejection of biased street policing culture norms, or desire to actively engage in guardianship policing and represent the interests of their communities of origin, underrepresented officers hold potential to change the established ways policing is conducted in the UK and US. This analysis can similarly be applied to LGTBQ+ officers, who must navigate the complicated dynamics of hegemonically masculine and heteronormative street police culture in UK and US police institutions. However, unlike the research illustrating statistically significant differences in policing outcomes for officers of colour and female officers, the research on active bureaucratic representation for LGBTQ+ people is fairly limited generally, and virtually non-existent for policing research. Given that LGBTQ+ officer experiences are often overlooked in police diversity research, this is unsurprising. Yet this volume seeks to contribute to better understandings of the ways LGTBQ+ officers may engage in active bureaucratic representation of LGBTQ+ communities. Because LGBTQ+ research in policing is so scare, this section draws on empirical research from bureaucrats outside policing evidencing representative bureaucracy of LGBTQ+ communities to argue that LGTBQ+ police similarly have capacity to do so too.

Studies examining representative bureaucracy on the part of LGBTQ+ elected officials have found positive correlations between their presence and laws which promote equality and fairness for LGBTQ+ individuals (Haider-Markel 2007, 2010; Lewis and Pitts, 2011; Reynolds, 2013). Haider-Markel's detailed quantitative analysis of the effects of over 200 LGBTQ+ US state legislators found a positive correlation between the presence of these LGBTQ+ individuals in state legislatures and the number, type, legislative outcome and adoption of LGBTQ+ bills and policies in the correlating states (Haider-Markel, 2010). Haider-Markel attributed these effects to positive bureaucratic representation. Similarly, Reynolds (2013) hypothesized that the more open LGBTQ+ MPs there are in parliament, the more progressive a nation's legislation will be when it comes to issues of gay rights, and found support for the hypothesis, concluding that there was indeed a correlation between the presence of openly LGBT legislators and passage of progressive laws which benefit LGBT individuals/communities across 27 nations, which again was attributed to active bureaucratic representation. While these are just some of the numerous examples of legislative-based studies on LGBTQ+ representative bureaucracy, they are instructive in terms of application of the theory to other government agencies, including policing.

Despite the limited number of studies connecting representative bureaucracy to policing, interviews conducted for this volume illustrate that, at least for some LGBTQ+ officers, they engage in rejection of hegemonically masculine and heteronormative street police culture norms, and engage active bureaucratic representation of LGBTQ+ communities and other minority groups in ways consistent with guardianship policing. While much more research on

LGBTQ+ officer representative bureaucracy is required, this book highlights the potential for exciting new directions in research in this area.

Social class and active bureaucratic representation

The dynamics of representative bureaucracy and class are particularly complicated for policing. As discussed in Chapter 7, policing is a traditionally working-class occupation, giving rise to a distinctly working-class street police culture. Moreover, officers in both the UK and US were, for decades, deliberately recruited from the working class to control working-class populations. Working-class officers were deterred from actively representing the interests of their working-class communities of origin, and many have adopted a variety of mechanisms to distance themselves from the majority working-class populations they police. Adding to these complexities are the introduction of police education requirements, which seem to aim to at least superficially shift policing from a working-class craft to a middle-class profession. Nonetheless, the question of the ways social class can impact active bureaucratic representation is important, and has not been previously explored in policing literature generally, or police diversity literature in particular. This section, therefore, draws on representation bureaucracy literature on the working class from outside policing to hypothesize about active bureaucratic representation for police officers from working class backgrounds. Moreover, this section provides evidence that officers with college degrees may explicitly or implicitly feel more empowered to engage in policing in ways different from their colleagues, potentially acting in ways which can more openly represent the interests of traditionally marginalized groups, and more akin to guardian policing.

Research from outside policing has begun to explore the relationship between representative bureaucracy theory and social class, although there is a significant lack of such research in policing and other occupations (Kennedy, 2014; Vinopal, 2020; Friedman, 2023). The limited research from outside policing suggests that passive and active bureaucratic representation in public sector institutions may be more challenging for individuals from working-class backgrounds (Friedman, 2023). Friedman (2023) argues that public servants from working-class backgrounds frequently experience tremendous pressure to assimilate into organizational cultures, requiring them to code switch, meaning downplaying their working-class backgrounds, adopting the middle-class norms and signals, and assimilating into the middle-class organizational culture. Friedman asserts that this makes active bureaucratic representation for bureaucrats from working-class backgrounds more challenging and less likely, although Friedman acknowledges more empirical research is required to test this hypothesis.

This book argues that the same pressures Friedman found on working-class people in government professions outside policing applies to working-class police officers, who similarly downplay and distance themselves from working-class populations. Indeed, as discussed in Chapter 7, officers from working-class backgrounds actively police mostly working-class communities, and in doing so are compelled to adopt street police culture strategies for drawing distinctions between the working-class people they police and their own working-class backgrounds. Loftus (2009), Bowling et al (2019) and others have chronicled the ways working-class officers seek to differentiate themselves from the working-class communities where they spend a disproportionate amount of their time policing, including framing these populations negatively, painting them as ignorant, animalistic, sub-human, with propensities for violence and immoral behaviour (Young, 1991; Loftus, 2009; Bowling et al, 2019). This allows working-class officers to view themselves as different; as part of the good and respectable working class (Loftus, 2009). This suggests that representative bureaucracy for working-class officers may be more challenging than for officers of other class backgrounds because their daily lives are spent policing working-class communities with whom identification would make their jobs much more difficult. Yet this unexplored area of policing research requires much more empirical study to assess whether this is indeed occurring as hypothesized in this volume.

Moreover, the efforts to shift policing, at least in appearance, from a working-class craft to a middle-class profession with the introduction of police education requirements adds further complexity to the analysis of the ways representative bureaucracy occurs in policing. A small body of research primarily from the US discussed below suggests that officers with college degrees may feel more empowered to act as representative bureaucrats for traditionally marginalized groups than their working class counterparts. This analysis meshes with Friedman's (2023) discussion of the limitations of working-class bureaucrats in becoming representative bureaucrats, and the notion that those with education who, research suggests, become part of the middle class are more empowered to become representative bureaucrats.

This hypothesis is supported by a growing amount of empirical research, primarily from the US, which shows some statistically significant differences in policing approaches and outcomes between college- and non-college-educated police officers according to a variety of measures, including decisions to arrest, and the use and degree of force. While significantly more empirical research is required, these studies show promise for the notion that police officers with college degrees may feel more able to engage in police decision-making in ways different from their non-college-educated peers, who may feel more constrained by street police culture norms.

For example, research suggests there may be differences in decisions to conduct traffic stops between college-educated and non-college-educated officers, although significantly more empirical research is required. One such study by Rosenfeld et al (2020) examined 63,451 traffic stops conducted by 842 St Louis, Missouri police officers in 2013, and found officers with a four-year college degree conducted fewer stops than those without a four-year college degree.

Further research has found some statistically significant differences in the ways officer education impacts decisions to arrest, with some older studies suggesting officers with college education are less inclined to arrest, while more recent studies do not show any such correlation. For example, an early study by Fickenauer (1975) of police recruits in one New Jersey police academy, 54 of whom had one or more years of college education and 44 of whom had high school diplomas, found those with one or more years of college education were more likely to use their discretion to adopt non-arrest responses to scenario-based vignettes. A subsequent study by Smith and Aamodt (1997) of 299 police officers across 12 Virginia policing agencies found their supervisors did not believe that officers with college education or graduate degrees made decisions about whether to arrest differently from their high school-educated colleagues. By contrast, when Rydberg and Terrill (2010) used the same data set as Paoline and Terrill (2007) – which examined 3,356 observed officer encounters with citizens suspected of wrongdoing and surveys of 398 officers in Indianapolis, Indiana and 240 officers in St Petersburg, Florida police departments – they found no relationship between officer education and decision to arrest in encounters with citizens.

A significant body of US policing research, however, finds that college education is positively correlated with reduced use of force among US police officers. For example, Terrill and Mastrofski (2002) examined a data set containing 3,116 encounters between officers and suspects in Indianapolis, Indiana and St Petersburg, Florida police departments. They found that suspect encounters involving officers with higher levels of education were much less likely to involve force compared to those with officers with lower education levels.

Similarly, Paoline and Terrill's (2007) observational study analysing the same underlying use of force data as Terrill and Mastrofski (2002) among US officers in 12 patrol beats in each location – Indianapolis, Indiana, and St Petersburg, Florida – with different levels of education found the largest gulfs in use of force was between officers with high school education and those with four-year college degrees. The study found officers with high school education alone (46.6 per cent) were much more likely to use verbal force in citizen encounters, including giving commands, orders or threats, compared to colleagues with some college education (35.6 per cent) or four-year Bachelor's degrees (35.4 per cent). The study further found that citizen encounters with officers with some college education or four-year college degrees were significantly less likely to result in higher levels of force being used compared to their high school-educated colleagues. The study found that officers with four-year college degrees were significantly less likely to use physical force in encounters with citizens, but that that this was not the case for officers who only attended some college. The study concluded that having a four-year college degree was most beneficial in relation to officers' use of force in citizen encounters.

Ryberg and Terrill's (2010) analysis of the same underlying data set from Paoline and Terrill (2007) – this one containing 3,356 observed officer encounters with citizens suspected of wrongdoing and surveys of 398 officers in Indianapolis, Indiana and 240 officers in St Petersburg, Florida police departments – similarly found that officers with some college education or four-year college degrees were significantly less likely to use force compared to their non-college-educated colleagues. They found that officers with some college education or a 4-year Bachelor's degree were much less likely to use force compared to their non-college-educated colleagues. Moreover, they found that college-educated officers used force less frequently and were less likely to discharge their firearm.

Similar results were found by Lim and Lee (2015), who examined 2,938 use of force cases in a large, urban police department in Texas to examine the impacts of educational levels. They found that officers with Bachelor's degrees or higher were 1.6 times less likely to use higher levels of force or weapons compared to their less educated counterparts. They also observed that where supervisors had Bachelor's degrees or higher and took intermediate use of force training, officers were much less likely to use high levels of force. McElvain and Kposowa (2008) examined all officer-involved shootings in a single California sheriff's department between 1990 and 2004, finding 186 incidents involving 314 officers, and measured them against a control group of 334 officers not involved in shootings. They determined that officers with two-year Associates degrees or higher levels of college education were 41 per cent less likely to be involved in shootings than peers without college education.

Thus, the existing empirical evidence suggests that officers with college education may approach their job in ways different from their colleagues with lower levels of education. This does not mean that more educated officers do not embrace street police culture norms, but it does raise the possibility that officers with higher education levels may feel more empowered to resist or mitigate aspects of street police culture in ways less educated officers do not – either because those officers hail from the working class and want to prove their policing credentials by aggressively policing the working class, or because they embrace street police culture norms more wholeheartedly because they have not been exposed to liberal arts or other higher education environments where other types of norms such as human rights, due process, balance of powers, and so on, are highlighted as worthwhile. Nonetheless, given the limited empirical evidence studying class in UK and US policing, significantly more research in this area would be highly beneficial in strengthening these findings.

Intergroup contact theory and street police culture

While representative bureaucracy is an essential theory underlying the analysis throughout this book that officers from marginalized backgrounds can engage in policing in ways different from their majority group peers, intergroup contact theory offers insights about the ways the presence of under-represented officers can benefit those from majority groups in UK and US policing so as to mitigate some of the influence of street police culture norms.

While intergroup contact theory is well established in sociological literature, it is vastly under-researched in policing scholarship generally, and mostly overlooked in police diversity literature. Yet as discussed later, this volume offers, for the first time in police diversity scholarship, the suggestion that, because of the robust empirical underpinning of the benefits of intergroup contact theory, it is possible that the close interactions created by greater police diversity have the potential to mitigate the impacts of street police culture. Moreover, it is argued that by being in contact with a broader array of police officers from different backgrounds, the empirical evidence about intergroup contact theory suggests straight White male officers can potentially shift embedded attitudes of street police culture, including bias, intolerance, racism, misogyny and homophobia, among others. This volume hypothesizes that if intergroup contact can help straight White male officers shift away from some of the implicit and explicit biases embedded in street police culture, this could potentially be one of the ways to reduce disparities in policing outcomes such as stop and searches, arrests and uses of force.

The well-established intergroup contact theory, that is, the contact hypothesis, posits that close intergroup contact with individuals from different backgrounds can result in attitude and sometimes behavioural changes in relation to prejudices (Allport, 1954). Allport theorized four ideal conditions to reduce prejudice through intergroup contact: equal group status within the situation; common goals; intergroup cooperation; and the support of authorities, law, or custom. Pettigrew (1998) subsequently added a fifth condition – the opportunity to become friends. In the decades since Allport's pioneering research, a large number of studies have found further support for the theory that intergroup contact can lead to changes in attitudes and behaviours, even where all conditions have not been met (Pettigrew and Tropp, 2006). Thus Allport's conditions simply enhance the likelihood of seeing measurable prejudice reduction effects from intergroup contact (Pettigrew and Tropp, 2006).

Decades of empirical evidence support the viability of intergroup contact theory in reducing intergroup prejudice. In a meta-analysis of 515 studies from 38 countries, Pettigrew and Tropp (2006) found 94 per cent of studies reviewed showed discernible prejudice reduction. The analysis found even more positive prejudice reduction effects where participants could not avoid intergroup contact, such as in workplaces (Pettigrew and Tropp,

2006). Institutional support for intergroup contact was also found to further enhance positive effects across a variety of target groups, including race/ethnicity, gender, age and geography. A subsequent review by Pettigrew and Tropp (2008: 929) examined the process by which intergroup contact reduces prejudice, and found intergroup contact reduces anxiety, allowing increased 'empathy, perspective taking, and knowledge of the outgroup' to contribute to prejudice reduction.

Some studies have looked to quantify bias reduction through use of explicit or implicit measures of biased attitudes. Abserson et al (2004), for example, examined the explicit and implicit biases of Whites in interethnic friendships with African Americans or Latinos, and found that subjects who were close friends in workplaces or elsewhere with African Americans or Latinos showed less implicit bias according to the Implicit Association Test (Greenwald et al, 1998) than subjects without interethnic friendships. This study suggests that where individuals can form close intergroup friendships they can see reductions in implicit bias against other ethnic groups. Such a study would be valuable if replicated to evaluate interethnic friendships within the police services in England and Wales to compare levels of implicit and explicit bias among those with and without interethnic friendships.

Unfortunately, there are few studies examining intergroup contact theory in the context of the policing workplace, and none that make the explicit link between intergroup contact theory and mitigation against street police culture norms. But what research there is has found positive benefits for officers resulting from intergroup contact with a diverse array of work colleagues. For example, Fridell and Scott (2005) found greater diversity within a policing agency increases the chances that officers will improve their understandings and respect for differing racial and cultural views through frequent contact with diverse colleagues, which can in turn improve their interactions with an array of racially and culturally diverse communities. Similarly, Fridell (2008) found greater diversity helps officers better understand and communicate with minority communities as a result of their contact and exposure with diverse colleagues. Similarly, McCluskey and McCluskey (2004) examined the ethnic composition of law enforcement agencies in major US metropolitan areas between 1990 and 2000, with a particular interest in Latino officers. The study found that as Latino officer numbers increased the increased interactions between Latino and White officers had implications for improving police attitudes toward Latino communities and could help improve police–community relations. By extension, these findings suggest that some of the biases officers in the study had against Latinos and other minority communities may have been reduced, thus potentially mitigating the impacts of street police culture which might predispose them to bias against Latinos.

One of the most important intergroup contact theory studies in policing is Lasley et al (2011), a longitudinal study which followed 405 Caucasian,

African American and Latino male Los Angeles Police Department officers first employed between 1985 and 1991. These officers were surveyed multiple times over a 15-year period, with African American and Latino officers generally holding and retaining positive views of local communities, and significantly increasing their desire to engage community members. However, regarding intergroup contact effects, the study found White officers' attitudes toward all communities, including ethnic minority communities, became more positive over the 15-year study period. Researchers concluded that White officers benefitted from intergroup contact with African American and Latino officers, and saw changes in their attitudes and behaviours toward community members as a result. The findings of this study suggest that, over time, White officers showed less bias against African American and Latino communities as a result of working with African American and Latino officers over prolonged periods, which indicates these close working relationships may have mitigated some of the inherent street police culture biases against African Americans and Latinos.

Other studies show similar findings and lend further support to this book's hypothesis that intergroup contact theory can help mitigate the embedded racial biases in street police culture. For example, the majority of the 50 African American officers across 16 Southern US departments in Bolton and Feagin's 2004 study found that Black officers believed that increasing White officers' social contacts with their Black colleagues could help reduce tensions between White officers and Black communities, making them less reliant on stereotypes of Black people. Again, while these studies offer two examples of the positive benefits of intergroup contact theory for White officers, they suggest that greater diversity has the potential to help reduce biased attitudes these officers have been socialized into by street police culture and, in turn, change the way they conduct policing toward ethnic minority communities. Significantly more empirical research is needed to test this hypothesis in a number of jurisdictions including England and Wales, but the weight of the evidence of the prejudice reduction effects of intergroup contact theory suggests that it could be a factor contributing to mitigating street police culture effects and motivating explicit or implicit changes in police decision-making.

While the effects of intergroup contact theory in policing have been most frequently examined in the context of the impact of officers of colour, a small amount of research has also examined the intergroup contact effects of having LGBTQ+ officers in police forces. As with other contact theory studies discussed earlier, this limited amount of research about LGBTQ+ officers has found that their increased presence in police departments can diminish negative opinions of LGBTQ+ people held by some straight officer colleagues.

For example, early 1990s research by RAND (1993) on gay and lesbian officers in six of the largest US police departments found some straight officers changed their opinions of LGBTQ+ people from negative to positive after working with LGBTQ+ officers. Similarly, research by Sklansky (2006) found one-to-one interactions with LGBTQ+ officers and others could significantly improve understandings and reduce prejudices within police departments, arguing LGBTQ+ officers could help shift the hegemonically masculine and heteronormative aspect of street police culture by normalizing different policing approaches.

Taken together, this limited intergroup theory research supports this book's hypothesis about increased diversity by indicating that increased numbers of LGBTQ+ officers may be able to mitigate the homophobia inherent in street police culture by increasing positive attitudes toward LGBTQ+ people and communities. This, in turn, could reduce negative interactions or policing outcomes in LGBTQ+ communities, but further empirical testing is required.

The findings from the aforementioned studies about the ability of increased intergroup contact between straight White male officers and their non-White, female and LGBTQ+ colleagues to reduce officer biases against non-White, female and LGBTQ+ people shows another potential benefit of increased police diversity, and highlights areas for further empirical research. Yet it also meshes with the findings from the interviews conducted for this volume, where police leaders interviewed had similarly observed the ways intergroup contact among officers increased cohesion in police departments and held potential to mitigate the negative effects of street police culture biases and increase positive relations with diverse communities. For example, Interview Subject 2, a female police chief of a large, urban American police department, observed:

Q: So do you think diversity is a key component to shifting [street police] culture?

R2:   I do. I think getting people – because it forces people into the same sandbox to play and once you get people into that sandbox – maybe you have to force them into the sandbox but once you get them in there they start for the most part appreciating, oh, you know, you're not so bad. There is just a human nature element that when you start to work together and see the value that people bring to the table then you're more embracing and when you see that you start to change your thinking about stuff. That is the true culture shift there.

Thus, while there must be significantly more empirical research in the UK and US tracking the impacts of intergroup contact majority group officers, the limited evidence available suggests that increased police diversity and the resulting intergroup contact among officers can particularly benefit majority group officers by potentially increasing their cultural competency, mitigating the biases inherent within street police culture, improving relations with traditionally marginalized communities and reducing disproportionate outcomes in these communities in ways consistent with guardian policing. While more research is needed to test these hypotheses, intergroup contact theory is another theory which holds great promise for policing.

Conclusion

This chapter has challenged the widely held belief that all police are a monolith, and think and act identically. Rather, it argued that police from traditionally marginalized backgrounds can think and act in ways different from their straight White male colleagues. It asserted that despite the intense socialization into street police culture faced by all officers, that particularly intense pressure faced by officers from under-represented backgrounds can be resisted or mitigated under certain conditions. Indeed, where officers feel connection to their communities of origin or other oppressed groups, have discretion and have support from supervisors and/or police leaders, these can help empower officers from marginalized backgrounds to explicitly or implicitly act on behalf of the interests of their communities of origin or other oppressed groups along the lines of the guardianship model. While not all under-represented officers become active bureaucrats in this way, those that do can think and act in ways different from established street police culture norms which emphasize bias, oppression and distance from policed communities.

To support this hypothesis, this chapter analysed evidence of statistically significant differences in policing outcomes for stop and searches, arrests, uses of force, traffic citations and other police outcome measures, showing that ethnic minority, female and LGBTQ+ officers, and officers with higher levels of education at times conduct policing in ways different from their straight White male colleagues. This chapter offered representative bureaucracy theory as part of the explanation for these differences, which has not previously been argued in a volume about police diversity in the UK or US.

Further, this chapter posited that intergroup contact theory provides additional support for the tangible behavioural benefits of diversity, this time showing the ways officers from majority groups benefit from the presence of officers of colour, female officers, LGBTQ+ officers, among others. This section argued that regular contact with traditionally under-represented officers can potentially reduce or mitigate some of the particularly damaging aspects of street police culture, especially for majority group officers. The research discussed herein suggests this can be done by improving their attitudes toward marginalized groups – both fellow officers from these groups and community members – as well as reducing general levels of bias, and increasing cultural competency. The chapter argued that by reducing these harmful street police culture aspects, intergroup contact theory provided a basis for the possibility that diversity could lead to reduction in disproportionate policing outcomes, although this hypothesis requires further testing in UK and US police settings.

9

Conclusion

This book has considered the significance of police diversity in UK and US policing. It has defined police diversity with respect to groups traditionally under-represented in both jurisdictions – specifically racial and ethnic, gender, sexual orientation, gender identity and educational minorities. Yet in a departure from prior volumes on police diversity, it has argued that policing, and in turn police diversity, cannot be understood without considering the significant impacts of street police culture on policing institutions, police decision-making and police officer experiences. The book has argued that all police officers are impacted by the street police culture norms which set the formal and informal standards, behaviours, priorities and metrics for evaluation and agendas of police institutions. While it asserts that all police officers are forced to contend with street police culture on the job, this volume argues that for the particular experiences of officers from traditionally marginalized backgrounds – including racial and ethnic minorities, women, LGBTQ+ and those with different levels of higher education – experiences of street police culture can pose particular challenges and create additional burdens in the role.

The book asserts that the tenets of street police culture in UK and US policing are incredibly similar, which allows comparative examination of police diversity through the lens of police culture despite the different cultural contexts of policing in operation in each jurisdiction. While police institutions have multiple cultures, including street culture, middle management culture and senior leadership culture, this volume has focused particularly on street police culture given its outsized influence on UK and US policing institutions, practices and attitudes. This volume has adopted a definition of street police culture which establishes that these informal norms, attitudes and values shaping police behaviour are grounded in straight, White, working-class, male views of race, gender, masculinity, aggression, intolerance, violence, authority, dominance and related characteristics.

While the book recognizes some of the challenges of comparing UK and US policing, including different histories, laws, politics, economies, cultures and policing structures, it asserts that comparative analysis is nonetheless fruitful at the broader, overarching levels, where theories can knit together parallels in policing in both jurisdictions. In addition to the similarities in the ways street police culture shapes policing institutions and experiences in both jurisdictions as discussed earlier, other similarities provide a robust basis for comparison.

Indeed, parallels exist between the development of policing institutions in both countries, grounded in so-called Peelian principles prioritizing crime prevention, legitimacy, restraint, accountability and positive community relations. The origins of both UK and US policing in Peelian principles is one aspect that facilitates the ease of comparison. Furthermore, this volume has argued that the increasing overlap between the criminal justice rhetoric, policies and practices between the UK and US, a phenomenon scholars refer to as policy transfer, further enables robust comparison of the two jurisdictions.

This book offers police diversity as a lens through which to understand the influence of street police culture on UK and US policing and cautions against its longstanding and outsized influence on police practices. Using the illustrative examples of police officers from traditionally marginalized groups, this volume asserts that if policing is to address its host of perceived problems in the eyes of the communities they serve – over-policing and under-protecting marginalized communities, reduced legitimacy, high levels of misconduct, lack of accountability – they must address the problems faced by officers from under-represented groups. Understanding the experiences of these minority officers helps show what is wrong with policing, and gives insights about what must be changed to improve both diverse officer experiences and relations with policed communities.

This book has argued that street police culture refers to the organizational culture representing the informal norms and beliefs of patrol officers. Formed from the perspective of the straight White working-class men who have always been the majority of police officers in both nations, it is characterized by violence, aggression, intolerance, stereotypes, racism, sexism, homophobia and other traits (Loftus, 2009; Bowling et al, 2019). The volume has offered compelling evidence of the influential nature of street policing for both majority and minority group officers, and the challenges of straying from street police culture approaches to the job. Indeed, while all officers risk ostracization for resisting street police culture values, this volume has demonstrated that this is particularly acute for officers from traditionally marginalized backgrounds, including officers of colour, female officers, LGBTQ+ officers and those with college educations. This book has also asserted that street police culture is extremely difficult to change (Chan, 1997), but has asserted that significantly increasing police diversity as one way to mitigate its effects.

This book offers an important original contribution by using representative bureaucracy theory as a way to understand why increasing police diversity matters not simply on principle or for the experiences of individual officers, but also for the ways it can impact policing outcomes. First, it asserts that even passive bureaucratic representation in police institutions can have positive effects, as it can be a visual representation of diversity, something that has been shown to improve perceptions of fairness and legitimacy, particularly in marginalized communities (Riccucci et al, 2014; Riccucci and Van Ryzin, 2017; Hong, 2016, 2017; Johnston and Houston, 2018; Keiser et al, 2022). Second, it argues that when officers feel kinship to their communities of origin, have opportunities for discretion, and where benefits outweigh the costs of representing their communities, they may engage in behaviours which benefit their communities, and even extend to other marginalized communities (Mosher, 1982; Meier, 1993, 2019). Thus, this original argument offered by this volume is that where active bureaucratic representation by police occurs, this can result in reduced rates of disproportionate policing outcomes such as traffic citations, stop and searches, arrests or uses of force, which are clear and beneficial positive outcomes for policed communities. This book asserts for the first time in police diversity literature that what may, in fact, be occurring is that active bureaucratic representation may mitigate the strongly biased influences in street police culture, which then allows minority group officers to police in different ways, and potentially ways akin to guardianship policing.

Yet this volume has not offered police diversity as a singular solution to the problems plaguing UK and US policing. Rather, the book has suggested that police diversity is just one of a plethora of tools required to help shift policing from its straight, White, male, working-class traditions, norms and culture, to a more heterogeneous, more varied, more broadly thinking and more creative set of institutions.

One of the key arguments is that increasing diversity alone, without providing requisite support for officers from traditionally marginalized groups, will not succeed. It is imperative that officers who find themselves in the minority in UK and US police services have the mechanisms required to succeed in the role, and not just be left to fend for themselves. Indeed, this book has illustrated the ways traditionally under-represented officers have been heavily pressured to conform to the street police culture norms associated with negative views and treatments of historically marginalized groups, creating tremendous stress for these officers. It has argued that all officers, including those from marginalized backgrounds, should be free not to adhere to street police culture norms, and empowered to work in ways aligned with their perspectives on communities and community relations, including acting in ways which are representative of their communities of origin or other oppressed groups, and embracing of guardian policing ideals.

The book asserts that alongside increased diversity, rules-based solutions, including lawsuits, consent decrees and compulsory affirmative action programmes, are all important to changing the character of policing institutions, reducing the influence of police culture and improving the experiences of all officers, including those from traditionally marginalized backgrounds.

The book also recognizes the importance of shifting toward some non-police-led interventions, popular with the defund policing movement, to help support communities in areas such as mental health, drug consumption and domestic violence – areas that the police have traditionally led, but which pilot research suggests can be more effectively handled by first responders who are not part of the police. Below are some of the other key contributions of the book.

Unique access to police leaders

A unique contribution of this book are the in-depth interviews conducted with elite and diverse police leaders, some of which lasted many hours. Not only was it rare to have such significant access to leaders of this calibre (which was facilitated by the author's significant professional connections), but it is largely unprecedented to have the degree of frank and honest conversations about the role of street police culture, and what impacts diverse police leaders can have in policing institutions.

There was consensus among those interviewed that street police culture played a significant role, but that police leaders can also set the tone for their police organization. These leaders believed they had a duty to lead by example in their respective institutions. Most were incredibly self-reflective about having lacked power earlier on in their careers, and feeling disempowered by nature of being minorities in majority-member policing institutions. Thus, when they eventually worked their way up to supervisory and eventually leader positions within their policing institutions (although notably many did not become leaders at the same institutions where they began their careers, which is a matter for further discussion elsewhere), they often sought to model strong, ethical, conscientious leadership for their departments. As Interview Subject 1 put it:

> [T]he person at the top is really important in terms of whether they walk the talk and if they really believe in it. But what I've found [they] look to you, the person at the top and does he or she really believe in this, and they might test you out, they might push boundaries. If they see that you're consistent, that there really is genuine ... authentic in what you're saying, then they will cooperate, I think, most people. The ones who don't – you know, you deal with.

Indeed, the sense of moral responsibility to lead by positive example expressed by the police leaders interviewed for this book was significant. The extent to which their efforts to engage communities, increase diversity, change police culture or reform problematic/discriminatory police practices were supported by the officers in their departments, let alone whether they were successful, were mixed. But what is significant is that this volume has captured the desire of these diverse police leaders to engage in systemic policing change, often as a result of their direct lived experiences as diverse officers.

Moving from police warriors to guardians

Another important contribution of this book is the unique insights from police leaders about the approaches they took to navigating street police culture. Rather than adopting the warrior mentality, the majority of diverse police leaders interviewed approached policing as guardians. As discussed in Chapter 2, guardian policing focuses on police legitimacy, trust-building, developing confidence and respect, and officers feeling a sense of connection to the communities they police (Skinner, 2020; Chaffin, 2020; Eisinger, 1980; Villa, 2021). Guardianship policing aims to minimize use of violence and conflicts, and prioritizes de-escalation rather than escalation (Rahr and Rice 2015; White House, 2015). A common theme among interviewees was that they did not always feel empowered to act as police guardians throughout their careers. But once they were in positions of sufficient authority in policing institutions, they felt more agency to be able to set policies and practices designed to prioritize good relations with communities and mitigate the impacts of police warrior culture.

These leaders deployed a number of approaches to put guardianship policing into effect at the individual and institutional levels and depart from policing according to street police culture norms. Some leaders lived in the communities where they were police leaders, and believed in implementing residency requirements mandating that officers live in the police jurisdictions where they work, prioritizing community connection over alienation. Others prioritized attending community meetings and events, working very long hours into most evenings and weekends, where they could meet and develop connections with as many community members as possible, and striving to build connections to policed communities. Some distributed their personal mobile telephone numbers to community members to increase access, accountability and honest conversations. Other leaders stood side-by-side with community members protesting police injustices, such as Black Lives Matter protests.

What these police leaders had in common was that they seemed particularly dedicated to prioritizing meaningful community interactions and saw themselves as community champions, and not adhering to street police culture norms which pit officers against communities. They repeatedly expressed the significance of being leaders who could hold their departments to account for improving community relations. All of these leaders discussed the ways they set expectations for the officers in their departments to engage with, and be accountable to, the communities they served. The majority of the leaders interviewed wanted to ensure bona fide community engagement, rather than simply being able to claim they had close ties to the communities where they worked. For these leaders, connections with communities were a badge of honour, a standard by which they believed they should be measured.

Changing street police culture

This book's key argument is that there is an essential need to change street police culture given its detrimental effects for all officers, but particularly those from traditionally marginalized backgrounds. Changing or mitigating the effects of street police culture was a subject most of the leaders interviewed raised, with the vast majority expressing a desire to reshape street police culture. Rather than embracing street police culture's alienation from communities, the police leaders interviewed leaned into guardian policing, emphasizing the community engagement and partnership aspects of their work as significantly important and deserving emphasis, while acknowledging the challenges of doing so in police institutions where street police culture's distance, aggression and violence toward local communities were the norm.

Some interview subjects reflected on their particular leadership strategies for shifting police culture norms from those emphasizing policing's warrior aspects to those focused on guardianship of local communities. Interview Subject 3, for example, talked about the importance of not only leading by example in terms of taking police culture in new directions, but also ensuring that other leaders, supervisors and others within the policing organization were empowered to support this shift in police culture toward the guardianship model:

I really believe that ultimately culture change is almost like a pyramid scheme of influencers in the organization. You have to have people that feel that they have a climate that is safe and even incentivizing to influence other people to do things perhaps in a different way. Or to uphold a particular value of expectation and that is not as simple. ... I mean you promote people into the right positions and then they're just going to have influence on their particular workgroup and how hard could that be. ... [I]t's not just like a short 'You got promoted, here you go', what we're trying to really build a much broader range of skills and expectations over a much longer- like use the entire probation as a training period and not just as an evaluation period. I think that the idea is to create as much as possible a climate where people can be influencers, no matter what rank they're at and to try to incentivize an organizational culture where you try to seek out who are those people that have influence and that can have. And often, as

I said, it doesn't even involve rank but can change how other people see the job or create a climate sometimes it's as small as at a shift level on a particular geographic part of town or something.

Unsurprisingly, there was commonality across police interview subjects in how to achieve this type of police culture change, with these sentiments echoed by a number of interview subjects.

Challenges to changing street police culture

While the leaders interviewed for this book recognized the need for changing street police culture, they also discussed their frustrations with the slow pace of culture change within policing institutions. They discussed a number of barriers to making culture shifts within their police organizations. Some reflected on the lack of diversity in their police departments as impeding culture change. Others explained being hampered by external oversight mechanisms not attuned to the needs of policing organizations as slowing culture change progress. Some lamented their inability to terminate problematic police officers, including those who engaged in repeated unlawful uses of force or misconduct on or off the job, such as being involved in domestic violence incidents in their personal lives, which they viewed as reinforcing problematic street police culture. Others examined the resistance posed by police unions to street police culture changes and police reform efforts, as discussed in Chapter 2. Some talked about the difficulties of retaining good police officers similarly invested in police culture change, given that doing so meant they were out of step with status quo minded fellow officers, making them unpopular. For example, Interview Subject 3 reflected on the obstacles to police culture change this way:

I've spent now pretty much my entire career thinking I could make pretty substantive changes in this field and especially … I mean they're less than I had ever thought, because change is so incremental and tenuous in an organization like this, and particularly around culture, and so you really – it is the amount of work it takes to just create those small beacons of light throughout an organization, it's pretty substantial. You hope that then there are people starting to influence other people around them and yes, there is a certain amount of carrot and stick because you also try to find creative ways to make it harder for people that don't want to get with the programme, so to speak. … And part of, I think an interesting example of this challenge is I think one of my biggest learning experiences has been that the amount of time it takes to change organizational culture, or even introduce any of the kinds of reforms that we're talking about in a substantive way, because there are two ways to introduce reforms. You could just talk about them, which gets you actually a lot of bonus points, especially in circles of between the media and ... academics, social media on and on. I mean by promoting and talking about things that you're doing that is almost the same as doing them, except it is actually not at all the same. So if you really want to substantively try to make these things it's devilishly hard and it takes so much time to build.

Other interview subjects talked about the need to get rank and file officers to invest in police culture change by deploying a number of different strategies. There was general agreement that moving away from warrior street police culture and toward guardianship policing required leaders to show officers how it could not only improve police-community relations and legitimacy, as well as police effectiveness, but also could improve officers' own well-being on the job. Interview Subject 5 reflected on the slow process of police culture change this way:

Q: What is the process like for getting the culture change? What does that look like?

R5:   It is slow and painful. ... So it's this kind of mental, physical struggle. And it goes back also to this conversation about values. ... So I can't say I have the value until I go through the behaviours to obtain the value. So the same thing goes with any organization. The difficult thing is that undoubtedly what that means for a police organization is that you need to raise the competency level of leadership at all levels, that's the problem. ... Greatness takes work. So that's the problem. The work is to get people to aspire to the value of understanding that leadership is a skill and needs to be developed intentionally and what that means in terms of transformation inside the organization. So that's the slow process, it's a slow process of going through the discipline of what it means to get your body to perform at the next level and then embracing that value as you become adept and better at whatever you're trying to accomplish.

Some of the police leaders interviewed for this book were honest about the need to be courageous in their efforts to achieve street police culture reform, even when it made them unpopular, particularly with the rank and file police officers socialized into traditional street police culture norms. Nonetheless, the police leaders interviewed for this volume believed in the importance of street police culture change, and expressed a sense of duty to shepherd their respective police organizations toward police cultures more guardianship-oriented, focused on meaningful community engagement, and less inclined toward community hostility.

Increasing cultural competency and building bridges

One of the important findings that emerged from this research has been the intolerance inherent in street police culture, and the need for greater cultural competency and understanding of difference within police forces in the UK and US, whose ranks are increasingly diversifying, and whose departments increasingly engage with a wider variety of diverse communities. While the diverse police leaders interviewed for this manuscript recognized the importance of increasing cultural competency for these dual purposes, they were largely in the minority of police leaders in prioritizing cultural competency efforts given the inherent homogeneity emphasized in street police culture. Indeed, in this tense political climate, police institutions in the UK and US increasingly come under criticism for investing in diversity initiatives and cultural competency efforts (Bryant, 2022).

Despite street police culture resistance, all of the police leaders interviewed for this volume nonetheless took it upon themselves to use their positions as leaders from diverse backgrounds to encourage greater diversity, cultural competency and tolerance within their institutions, both in terms of dealings within their respective police services and with regards to relations with the diverse communities their departments served.

For example, Interview Subject 3, an American LGBTQ+ police leader, reflected on the internal challenges of managing diversity within his police department. He considered the ways in which his department had not handled diversity well, and required improvement. Interview Subject 3 seemed particularly attuned to the need to improve his department's handling of its increasingly diverse workforce as a matter of good and ethical leadership. He had particular empathy for the need to manage diversity well in his department given the years he spent closeted in his early police years, and later being negatively stereotyped by colleagues for being an out gay man in policing. He told one anecdote about his role as a field training officer (FTO) earlier on in his career, where he recognized that he should have attended to diversity concerns more proactively in relation to a Native American officer in his department:

> Over time, like for example when I was a field training officer, you know, I think that my first real sense of how we were really getting it wrong was with a Native American officer who was about to be thrown out, was about to fail the FTO programme and there were issues with like, you know, the favourite things that people managed to fail around were always stuff like officer presence, didn't have command presence,

weren't seen as being assertive enough in situations and things, for him it was 'Did not make eye contact and tone of voice was unacceptable for establishing command presence' and stuff. And I started to realize with this guy, who was extremely smart, and actually a really good – and still brand new officer, but that perhaps it was the bias of the programme and a complete tone deafness to cultural background and issues that would cause somebody like that to be kicked out of the programme rather than perhaps they could be really effective in communicating but maybe not in the same way that – not in this cookie cutter way that a lot of folks at the time thought you had to meet a standard around.

The experience Interview Subject 3 had in relation to his FTO role for this Native American officer impacted him significantly, and shaped how he took on his role as a police leader in several medium sized, urban American police departments. He set internal policies and procedures that he believed better attended to the diverse experiences and discrimination diverse officers might encounter on the job. Interview Subject 3's insights on how he sought to shape his police department's practices were clear reflections of his own lived experiences, and his desire to make changes to the policing institution once he had a sufficient amount of authority to do so as a police leader.

Implementing substantive equality measures to increase police diversity

Another key finding from this research is the urgency of moving beyond passive formal equality measures to substantive equality approaches to rapidly increase police diversity. Substantive equality measures such as affirmative action (that is, positive discrimination) have been instrumental in diversifying police services in the US and a variety of other jurisdictions, from Northern Ireland to South Africa to Australia, particularly in relation to increasing representation of ethnic minorities, women and religious minorities. While affirmative action remains in effect in the US in a variety of sectors, from policing to education, it remains under constant threat and has been significantly narrowed in recent decades. Research is clear that formal equality-focused programmes reliant on voluntary targets and support programmes which are commonplace in the UK and the US are significantly less effective than compulsory affirmative action programmes (Lewis, 1989; Walker, 1989). In fact, policing researchers have argued that only compulsory affirmative action programmes are capable of providing sufficient diversity gains and support mechanisms to make true differences in policing composition (Lewis, 1989; Walker, 1989).

While the current state of racial and gender diversity in US policing was only made possible as a result of affirmative action (as discussed in Chapters 4 and 5), currently in the US, affirmative action has been reduced but not eliminated across police services. One large hurdle is that US police unions have tended to oppose these programmes (McCormick, 2015; Firestone, 2015) on the grounds that hiring larger numbers of officers of colour, women, LGBTQ+ officers and others traditionally under-represented in US police departments means hiring unqualified individuals, and somehow denies opportunities to straight White male candidates. Such assertions that candidates from traditionally marginalized groups lack the skills, abilities and qualifications to be effective police officers is a type of bias referred to in the racism context as aversive racism (Turner and Pratkanis, 1994). This common criticism to deter use of affirmative action in policing was seen in Northern Ireland when affirmative action was implemented to make the Police Service of Northern Ireland more representative of the majority Catholic population, and was ultimately unsuccessful in preventing increased representation, and along with it increased perceptions of police legitimacy and fairness among not only Catholics but the wider Northern Ireland population (Northern Ireland Policing Board, 2017).

In the UK, England and Wales policing has never implemented affirmative action despite repeated and increasing calls to do so from UK police leaders and political leaders including the Morris Inquiry, the Commission for Racial Equality, the London Metropolitan Police Service, former London Met Police Commissioner Bernard Hogan-Howe, former Police Minister Damian Green, former head of the Cheshire Police Simon Byrne, former head of the College of Policing Alex Marshall, and recently the Labour Party (Morris, 2004; Commission for Racial Equality, 2005; Evans, 2013; Boffey, 2014; Dodd, 2020).

Implementing positive discrimination for UK policing would not be easy. It would face significant political opposition and challenges from rank and file UK police officers. It would also require amending the Equality Act 2010, Racial Equality Act 2000 and Human Rights Act 1998. While the UK remains covered by the EU Charter of Fundamental Rights' EU Dir 2000/43/EC of June 2000, providing for equal treatment of race and ethnicity, a derogation from this directive would also be necessary. But these hurdles to implementing affirmative action in the UK should not be the basis not to do so given the urgent need to diversify the UK police services, and the clear benefits that flow therefrom.

Lawsuits and consent decrees

Another finding identified from the research in this volume is that one of the important tools in reforming police departments and promoting greater diversity and accountability have been lawsuits brought by individuals, groups of plaintiffs or the government, which can contribute to shifting street police culture. In the US these lawsuits are more commonplace, and generally assert claims for violations of the 14th Amendment's prohibition against discrimination. Class action lawsuits against large police departments for discriminatory policing practices, including *Handschu v. Special Services Division (2016)* and *Floyd v. City of New York* (2013), have resulted in settlement agreements mandating changes in policing policies, approaches and data collection ranging from recruitment and hiring practices, to stop and search procedures, mandatory trainings, new misconduct policies, promotion procedures, among others. Interestingly, in the US, the US Justice Department also has the power to sue state police institutions under 42 U.S.C. §14141 for policing practices which constitute a pattern and practice of constitutional violations, often for discriminatory policing. These US federal government lawsuits against police departments including the New Orleans Police Department, Ferguson (Missouri) Police Department, and Oakland Police Department have all resulted in mandatory changes in policing policies and procedures, and court-mandated monitoring to ensure these changes are implemented successfully. These types of efforts not only begin to change the composition of police departments, but also the culture of the institutions themselves.

In the UK these types of lawsuits are not commonplace, although some judicial reviews brought by human rights NGOs such as Liberty, StopWatch and Joint Enterprise Not Guilty by Association (Jengba) against police services have resulted in policy changes, increased data collection and other police reforms. Yet these excellent legal actions have been limited in scope, and showcase the need for more robust UK legal avenues to compel police reforms and police culture change akin to larger-scale US pattern and practice lawsuits and private class actions with resulting long-term consent decrees.

Concluding thoughts

This volume has examined the concept of police diversity in highly original ways, offering street police culture and representative bureaucracy as theoretical lenses through which the subject should be analysed. In doing so, the book has come from a fresh perspective, arguing against the dominant narrative that all police regardless of background are first and foremost 'blue', meaning primarily loyal to and identifying with police institutions rather than their communities of origin. It has asserted that police perspectives and lived experiences, while heavily influenced by street police culture, are multifaceted not singular. It posits that understanding UK and US police diversity is complicated, and requires thoughtful, nuanced analysis drawn from robust theoretical and empirical literature.

To best understand UK and US police diversity, it has argued that police diversity be construed broadly and intersectionally. While this volume has examined in depth the experiences of officers of colour, female officers, LGBTQ+ officers and officer class, many other categories of difference could potentially have been included, including disability, religion, national origin, and age, among others. Yet this volume deliberately focused on these four particular diversity indicators for officers from traditionally marginalized groups in significant part because they were grounded in available theoretical and empirical literature, while other aspects of diversity lack much data, and require significantly more research.

While this book has been an important contribution to moving forward the discussion of UK and US police diversity, it is also a building block for future research and legal reform. This volume has pointed to a host of areas where more empirical research and legal action are required to better understand and action a host of phenomena related to police diversity. For this to be accomplished, police leaders, police institutions, academia, community leaders, NGOs and lawyers must invest more time and effort to acknowledge, support and prioritize police diversity, recognizing that it has important value for improving police legitimacy, effectiveness and outcomes.

References

A v. Chief Constable of West Yorkshire Police [1999] (IT Case No. 1802020/98) (unreported).

Aamodt, M. and Flink, W. (2001) 'Relationship between education level and cadet performance in a police academy', *Applied HRM Research*, 6(1): 75–76.

Aberbach, J., Chesney, J. and Rockman, B. (1975) 'Exploring elite political attitudes: some methodological lessons', *Political Methodology*, 2: 1–27.

Aberson, C., Shoemaker, C. and Tomolillo, C. (2004) 'Implicit bias and contact: the role of interethnic friendships', *Journal of Social Psychology*, 144: 335–347.

Acker, J. (1990) 'Hierarchies, jobs, bodies: a theory of gendered organizations', *Gender and Society*, 4(2): 139–158.

ACPO (2004) *Breaking Through Action Plan: Promoting Minority Ethnic Employment in the Police Service*, London: Home Office Communication Directorate.

Adarand Constructors v. Pena, 515 US 200 (1995).

Adonis, A. and Pollard, S. (1997) *A Class Act: The Myth of Britain's Classless Society*, London: Hamish Hamilton.

Alex, N. (1969) *Black in Blue*, New York: Appleton-Century Crofts.

Alexander, M. (2010) *The New Jim Crow: Mass Incarceration in the Age of Colorblindness*, New York: Penguin.

Allen v. City of Mobile, 331 F. Supp. 1134 (S.D. Ala. 1971), aff'd. 466 F.2d 122 (5th Cir. 1972).

Allport, G. (1954) *The Nature of Prejudice*, Reading, MA: Addison-Wesley.

Alpert, G. and Dunham, R. (1997) *Force Factor: Measuring Police Use of Force Relative to Suspect Resistance*, Washington DC: National Institute of Justice.

Andreas, P. and Nadelmann, E. (2006) *Policing the Globe: Criminalization and Crime Control in International Relations*, Oxford: Oxford University Press.

Andrews, R. and Johnston-Miller, K. (2013) 'Representative bureaucracy, gender and policing: the case of domestic violence arrests', *Public Administration*, 91(4): 998–1014.

Apuzzo, M. and Goldman, A. (2011) 'With CIA help, NYPD Moves Covertly in Muslim Areas', *The Seattle Times*, 25 August. Available at: www.seattletimes.com/seattle-news/politics/with-cia-help-nypd-moves-covertly-in-muslim-areas/

Archbold, C. and Schulz, D. (2008) 'Making rank: the lingering effects of tokenism on female police officers' promotion aspirations', *Police Quarterly*, 11(1): 50–73.

Archbold, C. and Schulz, D. (2012) 'Research on women in policing: a look at the past, present and future', *Sociology Compass*, 6(9): 694–706.

Ashton v. Chief Constable of West Mercia Police (1999) (IT Case No. 2901131/ 98) (unreported). Available at: www.yumpu.com/en/document/read/ 32083704/ashton-v-west-mercia-police

Attride-Stirling, J. (2001) 'Thematic networks: an analytic tool for qualitative research', *Qualitative Research*, 1: 385–405.

Babcock, L. and Laschever, S. (2004) 'Women don't ask: negotiation and the gender divide', *Southern Economic Journal*, 71(2). DOI: 10.2307/4135303

Bakke v. California, 438 US 265 (1978).

Balkin, J. (1988) 'Why policemen don't like policewomen', *Journal of Police Science & Administration*, 16(1): 29–38.

Banks, L., Stiff, M. and Kramer, S. (2015) 'Developing Law on LGBT Rights in the Workplace'. Presentation to the American Bar Association, Labor and Employment Law Section: National Conference on Equal Employment Opportunity Law. Available at: www.kmblegal.com/sites/default/files/ Lisa%20Banks_Nov%202015_Developing%20Law%20on%20LGBT%20 Rights%20in%20the%20Workplace.pdf

Banton, M. (1964) *The Policeman in the Community*, London: Tavistock.

Barlow, D. and Barlow, M. (2002) 'Racial profiling: a survey of African American police officers', *Police Quarterly*, 5(3): 334–358.

Barratt, C., Bergman, M. and Thompson, M. (2014) 'Women in federal law enforcement: the role of gender role orientations and sexual orientation in mentoring', *Sex Roles*, 71(1): 21–32.

Barry, D. and Connelly, M. (1999) 'Poll in New York Finds Many Think Police Are Biased', *The New York Times*, 16 March. Available at: www.ny times.com/1999/03/16/nyregion/poll-in-new-york-finds-many-think-police-are-biased.html

Barton, H. (2003) 'Understanding occupational (sub) culture: a precursor for reform', *International Journal of Public Sector Management*, 16(5): 346–358.

Bayley, D. (2002) 'Law enforcement and the rule of law: is there a tradeoff?', *Criminology & Public Policy*, 2(1): 133–154.

Bayley, D. H. and Bittner, E. (1997) 'Learning the Skills of Policing', in R. G. Dunham and G. Alpert (eds) *Critical Issues in Policing: Contemporary Readings* (3rd edn), Prospect Heights, IL: Waveland, pp114–137.

Beetham, D. (2013) *The Legitimation of Power* (2nd edn), Basingstoke: Palgrave Macmillan.

Belkin, A. and McNichol, J. (2002) 'Pink and blue: outcomes associated with the integration of open gay and lesbian personnel in the San Diego Police Department', *Police Quarterly*, 5(1): 63–95.

Belknap, J. and Shelley, J. K. (1993) 'New lone ranger: policewomen on patrol', *American Journal of Police*, 12(2): 47–75.

Bennett, R. R. (1980) 'Constructing cross-cultural theories in criminology: application of the generative approach', *Criminology*, 18(2): 252–268.

Berlant, L. and Warner, M. (1998) 'Public sex', *Critical Inquiry*, 24(2): 547–566.

Bernstein, M. and Kostelac, C. (2002) 'Lavender and blue: attitudes about homosexuality and behaviour toward lesbians and gay men among police officers', *Journal of Contemporary Criminal Justice*, 18(3): 302–328.

Berry, J., O'Connor, G., Punch, M. and Wilson, P. (2008) 'Strange union: changing patterns of reform, representation, and unionization in policing', *Police Practice and Research*, 9(2): 113–130.

Bittner, E. (1974) 'Florence Nightingale in Pursuit of Willie Sutton', in H. Jacob (ed) *The Potential for Reform of Criminal Justice*, London: SAGE.

BJS (Bureau of Justice Statistics) (1993) *Local Police Departments, 1993*, Washington, DC: US Department of Justice.

BJS (Bureau of Justice Statistics) (2000) *Local Police Departments, 2000*, Washington, DC: Department of Justice.

BJS (Bureau of Justice Statistics) (2007) *Local Police Departments, 2007*, Washington, DC: US Department of Justice.

BJS (Bureau of Justice Statistics) (2010) *Women in Law Enforcement, 1987–2008*, Washington, DC: US Department of Justice.

BJS (Bureau of Justice Statistics) (2013) *Local Police Departments, 2013: Personnel*, Washington, DC: US Department of Justice.

BJS (Bureau of Justice Statistics) (2019) *Local Police Departments, 2019: Personnel*, Washington, DC: US Department of Justice.

BJS (Bureau of Justice Statistics) (2022) *Local Police Departments, 2020: Personnel*, Washington, DC: US Department of Justice.

Black, P. and Kari, C. (2010) 'Policing diverse communities: do gender and minority status make a difference', *Journal of Ethnicity in Criminal Justice*, 8(3): 216–229.

Blackbourn, D. (2006) 'Gay rights in the police service: is the enemy still within?', *Criminal Justice Matters*, 63(1): 30–31.

Bland, N., Mundy, G., Russell, J. and Tuffin, R. (1999) *Career Progression of Ethnic Minority Police Officers*, Home Office Police Research Series Paper 107, London: HMSO.

Bloch, P. and Anderson, D. (1974) *Policewomen on Patrol: Final Report*, Washington, DC: Police Foundation

Bobo, L. and Gilliam, F. (1990) 'Race, sociopolitical participation, and black empowerment', *The American Political Science Review*, 84: 377–393.

Boffey, D. (2014) 'Police Recruiting Chief Says Force Needs Positive Discrimination', *The Guardian*, 18 January. Available at: www.theguard ian.com/uk-news/2014/jan/18/police-need-positive-discrimination-law-change

Bolton, K. (2003) 'Shared perceptions: black officers discuss continuing barriers in policing', *Policing: An International Journal of Strategies and Management*, 26(3): 386–399.

Bolton, K. and Feagin, J. (2004) *Black in Blue: African American Police Officers and Racism*, New York and London: Routledge.

Bond, M. and Haynes, M. (2014) 'Workplace diversity: a social–ecological framework and policy implications', *Social Issues & Policy Review*, 8: 167–201.

Bonilla-Silva, E. and Dietrich, D. (2011) 'The sweet enchantment of color-blind racism in Obamerica', *The ANNALS of the American Academy of Political & Social Science*, 634: 190–206.

Bostock v. Clayton County, 590 US ★ (2020).

Bowling, B. (1999) 'The rise and fall of New York murder: zero tolerance or crack's decline?', *British Journal of Criminology*, 39(4): 531–554.

Bowling, B. and Phillips, C. (2002) *Racism, Crime and Justice*, Harlow: Longman.

Bowling, B., Reiner, R. and Sheptycki, J. (2019) *The Politics of the Police* (5th edn), Oxford: Oxford University Press.

Boyatzis, J. (1998) *Transforming Qualitative Information*, London and Thousand Oaks, CA: SAGE.

Boyd, L. (2010) 'Light blue versus dark blue: attitudinal differences in quality-of-life policing', *Journal of Ethnicity in Criminal Justice*, 8(1): 37–48.

Braithwaite, J. (1982) 'Paradoxes of Class Bias in the Criminal Justice System', in H. Pepinsky (ed) *Rethinking Criminology*, Beverley Hills, CA: SAGE, pp 61–84.

Brandl, S. G. and Stroshine, M. S. (2012) 'The role of officer attributes, job characteristics, and arrest activity in explaining police use of force', *Criminal Justice Policy Review*, 24(5): 551–572.

Brandl, S. G., Stroshine, M. S. and Frank, J. (2001) 'Who are the complaint-prone officers?' *Journal of Criminal Justice*, 29: 521–529.

Brodeur, J. (2010) *The Policing Web*, Oxford: Oxford University Press.

Broomfield, J. (2015) 'Gay Men in the UK Police Services', in F. Colgan and N. Rumens (eds) *Sexual Orientation at Work*, London: Routledge, pp 73–87.

Brown v. Board of Education., 347 U.S. 483 (1954).

Brown, J. (1998) 'Aspects of discriminatory treatment of women police officers serving in England and Wales', *British Journal of Criminology*, 38(2): 265–282.

Brown, J. (2015) 'From Cult of Masculinity to Smart Macho: Gender Perspectives on Police Occupational Culture', in M. O'Neill, M. Marks and A.-M. Singh (eds) *Police Occupational Culture (Sociology of Crime, Law and Deviance, Vol 8)*, Leeds: Emerald Group Publishing Ltd, pp 205–226.

Brown, J. (2018) 'Do graduate police officers make a difference to policing? Results of an integrative literature review', *Policing*, 14(1): 9–30.

Brown, J. and Campbell, E. (1995) 'Adverse impacts experienced by police officers following exposure to sex discrimination and sexual harassment', *Stress Medicine*, 11: 221–228.

Brown, J. and Frank, R. (2006) 'Race and officer decision making: examining differences in arrest outcomes between Black and White officers', *Justice Quarterly*, 23(1): 96–126.

Brown, L. and Willis, A. (1985) 'Authoritarianism in British police recruits: importation, socialization or myth?', *Journal of Occupational Psychology*, 58(1): 97–108.

Bryant, M. (2022) 'Cut "Symbolic Gestures", Braverman Tells Police in England and Wales', *The Guardian*, 24 September. Available at: www.theg uardian.com/uk-news/2022/sep/24/suella-braverman-police-symbolic-gestures-diversity-inclusion

Bryman, A. (2008) *Social Science Research Methods* (3rd edn), Oxford: Oxford University Press.

Bunyan, T. (1981) 'The police against the people', *Race and Class*, 23(2/3): 153–170.

Burke, M. (1994) 'Homosexuality as deviance: the case of the gay police officer', *British Journal of Criminology*, 34(2): 192–203.

Bury, J., Pullerits, M., Edwards, S., Davies, C. and Demarco, J. (2018) *Enhancing Diversity in Policing: Final Report*, London: NatCen Social Research.

Byrne, J. and Monaghan, L. (2008) *Policing Loyalist and Republican Communities Understanding Key Issues for Local Communities and the PSNI*, Belfast: Institute for Conflict Research.

Cao, L. and Huang, B. (2000) 'Determinants of citizen complaints against police abuse of power', *Journal of Criminal Justice*, 28(3): 203–213.

Carter, D. and Sapp, A. (1989) 'The effect of higher education on police liability: implications for police personnel policy', *American Journal of Police*, 8(1): 153–166.

Carter, D. and Sapp, A. (1990) 'The evolution of higher education in law enforcement: preliminary findings from a national study', *Journal of Criminal Justice Education*, 1(1): 59–85.

Cascio, W. (1977) 'Formal education and police officer performance', *Journal of Police Science and Administration*, 5(1): 89–96.

Casey, L. (2023) *Final Report: An independent review into the standards of behaviour and internal culture of the Metropolitan Police Service* (The Casey Review), London.

Cashmore, E. (2000) *Ethnic Minority Police Officers: Final Report*, Stoke-on-Trent: Trentham Books Ltd.

Cashmore, E. (2001) 'The experiences of ethnic minority police officers in Britain: under-recruitment and racial profiling in a performance culture', *Ethnic and Racial Studies*, 24(4): 642–659.

Cashmore, E. (2002) 'Behind the window dressing: minority ethnic police perspectives on cultural diversity', *Journal of Ethnic and Migration Studies*, 28(2): 327–341.

Chaffin, J. (2020) 'Unorthodox Arizona Police Chief Insists Reform Can Work', *Financial Times*, 24 June. Available at: www.ft.com/content/d63f6 348-f3d8-4e0d-8d7c-64077b697721

Chan, J. (1997) *Changing Police Culture*, Cambridge: Cambridge University Press.

Chan, J., Doran, S. and Marel, C. (2010) 'Doing and undoing gender in policing', *Theoretical Criminology*, 14(4): 425–446.

Charles, M. and Arndt, L. (2013) 'Gay- and lesbian-identified law enforcement officers: intersection of career and sexual identity', *The Counseling Psychologist*, 41(8): 1153–1185.

Chavez, C. and Weisinger, J. (2008) 'Beyond diversity training: a social infusion for cultural inclusion', *Human Resource Management*, 47(2): 331–350.

Childers v. Dallas Police Department, 671 F.2d 1380 (5th Cir. 1982).

City of Richmond v. Croson, 488 US 469 (1988).

Clinkinbeard, S., Solomon, S. and Rief, R. (2020) 'Who dreams of badges? Gendered self-concept and policing career aspirations', *Feminist Criminology*, 15(5): 567–592.

Close, B. and Mason, P. (2006) 'After the traffic stops: officer characteristics and enforcement actions', *Topics in Economic Analysis and Policy*, 6(1): 1–43.

Cochran, J. and Warren, P. (2012) 'Racial, ethnic, and gender differences in perceptions of the police: the salience of officer race within the context of racial profiling', *Journal of Contemporary Criminal Justice*, 28(2): 206–227.

Cockcroft, T. (2013) *Police Culture: Themes and Concepts*, London: Routledge.

Colin, M. (2014) 'Off Duty, Black Cops in New York Feel Threat from Fellow Police', *Reuters*, 23 December. Available at: www.reuters.com/arti cle/us-usa-police-nypd-race-insight-idUSKBN0K11EV20141223

College of Policing (2014) *The Code of Ethics: Reading List*, London: College of Policing.

College of Policing (2020) *Policing Education Qualifications Framework. Initial entry routes. Learning to date: development and implementation, 2016 to 2019*, London: College of Policing.

College of Policing (2023) *Police Education Qualifications Framework (PEQF)*. College of Policing. Available at: www.college.police.uk/career-learning/policing-education-qualifications-framework-peqf

Collins, H. (2003) 'Discrimination, equality and social inclusion', *Modern Law Review*, 66(1): 16–43.

Collins, J. and Rocco, T. (2018) 'Queering employee engagement to understand and improve the performance of gay male law enforcement officers: a phenomenological exploration', *Performance Improvement Quarterly*, 30(4): 273–295.

Collins, P. (2015) 'Intersectionality's definitional dilemmas', *Annual Review of Sociology*, 41(1): 1–20.

Colvin, R. (2009) 'Shared perceptions among lesbian and gay police officers: barriers and opportunities in the law enforcement work environment', *Police Quarterly*, 12(1): 86–101.

Colvin, R. (2012) *Gay and Lesbian Cops: Diversity and Effective Policing*, London: Lynne Rienner Publishers, Inc.

Colvin, R. (2015) 'Shared workplace experiences of lesbian and gay police officers in the United Kingdom', *Policing: An International Journal of Police Strategies & Management*, 38(2): 333–349.

Colvin, R. (2020) 'The emergence and evolution of lesbian and gay police associations in Europe', *European Police Science and Research Bulletin*, 19(1): 51–70.

Commission for Racial Equality (2005) *The Police Service in England and Wales: Final Report of a Formal Investigation by the Commission for Racial Equality*, London: HMSO.

Congressional Research Service (2018) *Public Trust and Law Enforcement: A Discussion for Policymakers*, Congressional Research Service Report R43904, Washington, DC: Congressional Research Service.

Conti, N. (2006) 'Role call: preprofessional socialization into police culture', *Policing & Society*, 16(3): 221–242.

Conti, N. and Doreian, P. (2014) 'From here on out, we're all blue: interaction order, social infrastructure, and race in police socialization', *Police Quarterly*, 17(4): 414–447.

Correll, J., Park, B., Judd, C. M., Wittenbrink, B., Sadler, M. S. and Keesee, T. (2007) 'Across the thin blue line: police officers and racial bias in the decision to shoot', *Journal of Personality and Social Psychology*, 92(6): 1006–1023.

Corsianos, M. (2009) *Policing and Gendered Justice: Examining the Possibilities*, Toronto: University of Toronto Press.

Cox, C. and Kirby, S. (2017) 'Can higher education reduce the negative consequences of police occupational culture amongst new recruits?' *Policing: An International Journal*, 41(5): 550–562.

CLEAR (Creating Law Enforcement Accountability & Responsibility) Project, Muslim American Civil Liberties Coalition, Asian American Legal Defense and Education Fund (2013) 'Mapping Muslims: NYPD Spying and Its Impact on Muslim Communities'. Available at: www.law.cuny.edu/academics/clinics/immigration/clear/Mapping-Muslims.pdf

Crenshaw, K. (1989) 'Demarginalizing the intersection of race and sex: a black feminist critique of antidiscrimination doctrine, feminist theory and antiracist politics', *The University of Chicago Legal Forum*, 1(1): 139–167.

Crenshaw, K. (1991) 'Mapping the margins: intersectionality, identity politics, and violence against women of color', *Stanford Law Review*, 43(6): 1241–1299.

Crenshaw, K. (2013) 'From private violence to mass incarceration: thinking intersectionally about women, race, and social control', *Journal of Scholarly Perspectives*, 9(1): 23–50.

Crowther, C. (2000) 'Thinking about the 'underclass': toward a political economy of policing', *Theoretical Criminology*, 4(2): 149–167.

Croxford, R. (2020) 'Black Met Police Inspector "Racially Harassed" by Officers', *BBC News*, 18 August. Available at: www.bbc.co.uk/news/uk-england-london-53811375

Dalley, A. (1975) 'University vs non-university graduated policeman: a study of police attitudes', *Journal of Police Science and Administration*, 3(1): 458–468.

Daly, M. (2003) 'My Life as a Secret Policeman', *BBC News*, 21 October. Available at: http://news.bbc.co.uk/1/hi/magazine/3210614.stm

Davies, C. and Robison, M. (2016) 'Bridging the gap: an exploration of the use and impact of positive discrimination in the United Kingdom', *International Journal of Discrimination and the Law*, 16(2–3): 83–101.

DeAngelis, J. and Kupchic, A. (2007) 'Citizen oversight, procedural justice, and officer perceptions of the complaint investigation process', *Policing: An International Journal of Strategies and Management*, 30(1): 651–671.

Dejong, C. (2004) 'Gender differences in officer attitude and behavior', *Women & Criminal Justice*, 15(3–4): 1–32.

del Carmen, A., Taylor Greene, H., Nation, D. and Solomon Osho, G. (2007) 'Minority women in policing in Texas: an attitudinal analysis', *Criminal Justice Studies*, 20(3): 281–294.

Dick, P. and Cassell, C. (2004) 'The position of policewomen: a discourse analytic study', *Work, Employment and Society*, 18(1): 51–72.

Diemer, M., Mistry, R. S., Wadsworth, M. E., López, I. and Reimers, F. (2013) 'Best practices in conceptualizing and measuring social class in psychological research', *Analyses of Social Issues and Public Policy*, 13(1): 77–113.

DiSalvo, D. (2020) 'The Trouble with Police Unions', *National Affairs*, Fall 2020. Available at: www.nationalaffairs.com/publications/detail/the-trouble-with-police-unions

Dodd, V. (2020) 'Labour Backs Positive Discrimination to Close Racial Gap in Policing', *The Guardian*, 24 February. Available at: www.theguardian.com/uk-news/2020/feb/24/labour-backs-positive-discrimination-to-close-racial-gap-in-policing

Dodge, M. and Pogrebin, M. (2001) 'African American police women: an exploration of professional relationships', *Policing: An International Journal of Policing Strategies and Management*, 24(4): 550–562.

Doerner, W. (1995) 'Officer retention patterns: an affirmative action concern for police agencies?', *American Journal of Police*, 14(3/4): 197–210.

Dowler, K. (2005) 'Job satisfaction, burnout, and perception of unfair treatment: the relationship between race and police work', *Police Quarterly*, 8(4): 476–489.

Dwyer, A. (2008) 'Policing queer bodies: focusing on queer embodiment in policing research as an ethical question', *Queensland University of Technology Law Review*, 8(2): 414–428.

Eberhardt, J., Goff, P. A., Purdie, V. J. and Davies, P. G. (2004) 'Seeing Black: race, crime, and visual processing', *Journal of Personality and Social Psychology*, 87(6): 876–893.

Edwards, F., Lee, H. and Esposito, M. (2019) 'Risk of being killed by police use of force in the United States by age, race–ethnicity, and sex', *PNAS*, 116(34): 16793–16798.

Eisinger, P. (1980) *Municipal Residency Requirements and the Local Economy: Police Residency Requirements*, Institute for Research on Poverty Discussion Paper 636–80, University of Wisconsin-Madison.

Emsley, C. (1986) 'Detection and prevention: the old English police and the new 1750–1900', *Historical Social Research*, 37(1): 69–88.

Emsley, C. (2000) 'The policeman as worker: a comparative survey c. 1800–1940', *International Review of Social History*, 45: 89–110.

Emsley, C. and Clapson, M. (1994) 'Recruiting the English policeman c. 1840–1940', *Policing and Society: An International Journal of Research and Policy*, 3(4): 269–285.

England v. State of Texas, No. 484,697 (District Court of Travis County, 20th Judicial District), Plaintiff's Affidavit (1992).

Evans, M. (2013) 'Police Forces Should Use "Positive Discrimination" to Increase Diversity, Minister Tells Officers', *The Telegraph*, 11 September. Available at: www.telegraph.co.uk/news/uknews/crime/10302838/Police-forces-should-use-positive-discrimination-to-increase-diversity-minister-tells-officers.html

Fagan, J. and Ash, E. (2017) 'New policing, new segregation: from Ferguson to New York', *Georgetown Law Journal*, 106(1): 33–104.

Fagan, J., Braga, A., Brunson, R. and Pattavina, A. (2015) *Stops and Stares: Street Stops, Surveillance and Race in the New Policing*, Columbia Law School Public Law & Legal Theory Working Paper Group, Working Paper No. 14-479.

Fagan, J., Tyler, T. and Meares, T. (2011) 'Street Stops and Police Legitimacy in New York. Paper given at the Crime Decline Conference, John Jay College of Criminal Justice, 21–22 September. Available at: www.jjay.cuny.edu/Fagan_Tyler_and_Meares_Street_Stops_and_Police_Legitimacy_in_New_York.pdf

Feder, L. (1997) 'Domestic violence and police response in a pro-arrest jurisdiction', *Women & Criminal Justice*, 8(4): 79–98.

Felkenes, G. and Schroedel, J. (1993) 'A case study of minority women in policing', *Women & Criminal Justice*, 4(2): 65–89.

Feredey, J. and Cochrane, E. (2006) 'Demonstrating rigor using thematic analysis: a hybrid approach of inductive and deductive coding and theme development', *International Journal of Qualitative Methods*, 5: 80–92.

Fielding, N. (1994) 'Competence and culture in the police', *Sociology*, 22(1): 45–64.

Finckenauer, J. (1975) 'Higher education and police discretion', *Journal of Police Science and Administration*, 3(4): 450–457.

Firestone, D. (2015) 'The Rise of New York's Police Unions', *The Guardian*, 13 January. Available at: www.theguardian.com/us-news/2015/jan/13/new-york-police-unions-powerful

Fisk, C. and Richardson, L. (2017) 'Police unions', *George Washington Law Review*, 85: 712–799.

Floyd v. City of New York, Case No. 08 Civ. 1034. *Opinion and Order*. United States District Court, Southern District of New York (2013).

Foley, T. and Terrill, W. (2008) 'Police comfort and victims', *Victims and Offenders*, 3(2–3): 192–216.

Forman, J. (2017) *Locking Up Our Own*, New York: Farrar, Straus and Giroux.

Francis, J., Johnston, M., Robertson, C., Glidewell, L., Entwistle, V., Eccles, M. P. et al (2010) 'What is an adequate sample size? Operationalising data saturation for theory-based interview studies', *Psychology & Health*, 25(10): 1229–1245.

Fredman, S. (2008) *Human Rights Transformed: Positive Rights and Positive Duties*, Oxford: Oxford University Press.

Fredman, S. (2016) 'Substantive equality revisited', *International Journal of Constitutional Law*, 14(3): 712–738.

Fridell, L. (2008) 'Racially Biased Policing: The Law Enforcement Response to Implicit Black-Crime Association', in M. Lynch, B. Patterson and K. Childs (eds) *Racial Divide: Racial and Ethnic Bias in the Criminal Justice System*, Monsey, NY: Criminal Justice Press, pp 39–59.

Fridell, L. and Scott, M. (2005) 'Law Enforcement Agency Responses to Racially Biased Policing and the Perceptions of Its Practice', in R. G. Dunham and G. P. Alpert (eds) *Critical Issues in Policing* (5th edn), Prospect Heights, IL: Waveland Press, pp 304–321.

Friedman, S. (2023) 'Climbing the velvet drainpipe: class background and career progression within the UK Civil Service', *Journal of Public Administration Research and Theory*, 33(4): 563–577. https://doi.org/10.1093/jopart/muac045

Friedman, S. and Laurison, D. (2020) *The Class Ceiling*, Bristol: Policy Press.

Fuller, M. (2019) *Kill the Black One First: A Memoir of Hope and Justice*, London: Blink Publishing.

Fyfe, J. (1981) 'Who shoots? A look at officer race and police shooting', *Journal of Police Science and Administration*, 9(4): 367–382.

Fyfe, J. and Kane, R. (2006) *Bad Cops: A Study of Career-Ending Misconduct Among New York City Police Officers*, National Institute of Justice Grant No. 1996-IJ-CX-0053, Washington, DC: United States Department of Justice.

Galvin-White, C. and O'Neal, E. (2016) 'Lesbian police officers' interpersonal working relationships and sexuality disclosure: a qualitative study', *Feminist Criminology*, 11(3): 253–284.

Garcia, V. (2003) '"Difference" in the police department: women, policing, and "doing gender"', *Journal of Contemporary Criminal Justice*, 19(1): 330–344.

Gardiner, C. (2017) *Policing around the Nation: Education, Philosophy, and Practice*, National Policing Institute and California State University, Fullerton.

Garland, D. (2001) *The Culture of Control: Crime and Social Order in Contemporary Society*, Oxford: Oxford University Press.

Garner, J. H., Maxwell, C. D. and Heraux, C. G. (2002) 'Characteristics associated with the prevalence and severity of force used by the police', *Justice Quarterly*, 19(4): 705–746.

Gau, J. and Paoline, E. (2017) 'Officer race, role orientations, and cynicism toward citizens', *Justice Quarterly*, 34(7): 1246–1271.

Gau, J., Terrill, W. and Paoline, E. (2013) 'Looking up: explaining police promotional aspirations', *Criminal Justice and Behavior*, 40(3): 247–269.

Gaub, J. (2020) 'Understanding police misconduct correlates: does gender matter in predicting career-ending misconduct?', *Women & Criminal Justice*, 30(4): 264–289.

Geller, W. and Karales, K. (1981) 'Shootings of and by Chicago police: uncommon crises, Part I: Shootings by Chicago Police', *Journal of Criminal Law and Criminology*, 72(4): 1813–1866.

Genz, J. and Lester, D. (1976) 'Authoritarianism in policemen as a function of experience', *Journal of Police Science and Administration*, 4(1): 9–13.

Gilliard-Matthews, S., Kowalski, B. and Lundman, R. (2008) 'Officer race and citizen-reported traffic ticket decisions by police in 1999 and 2002', *Police Quarterly*, 11(2): 202–219.

Gilroy, P. and Sim, J. (1985) 'Law, order and the state of the left', *Capital & Class*, 9: 15–54.

Giordano, M. A. (1981) 'I Am Proud of Being Gay: Cop', *NY Daily News*. Available at: www.goalny.org/our-history

Glaser, J. (2014) *Suspect Race*, Oxford: Oxford University Press.

Goldstein, H. (1977) *Policing a Free Society*, Cambridge, MA: Ballinger.

Green v. County School Board. of New Kent County, Va., 391 U.S. 430, 437–38 (1968).

Green v. City of Saint Louis, No. 4:19 CV 1711 DDN (E.D. Mo. Dec. 2, 2020).

Greene, J. (2007) 'Make police oversight independent and transparent', *Criminology & Public Policy*, 6(4): 747–754.

Greenwald, A., McGhee, D. and Schwartz, J. L. K. (1998) 'Measuring individual differences in implicit cognition: the implicit association test', *Journal of Personality and Social Psychology*, 74(6): 1464–1480.

Grennan, S. A. (1987) 'Findings on the role of officer gender in violent encounters with citizens', *Journal of Police Science & Administration*, 15(1): 78–85.

Griffith, D., Mason, M. A., Yonas, M. A. Eng, E., Jeffries, V., Plihcik, S. and Parks, B. A. (2007) 'Dismantling institutional racism: theory and action', *American Journal of Community Psychology*, 39: 381–392.

Griggs v. Duke Power Company, 401 U.S. 424, 432 (1971).

Grutter v. Bollinger, 539 US 306 (2003).

Grynbaum, M. M. and Connelly, M. (2012) 'Majority in City See Police as Favoring Whites, Poll Finds', *The New York Times*, 20 August. Available at: www.nytimes.com/2012/08/21/nyregion/64-of-new-yorkers-in-poll-say-police-favor-whites.html

Guajardo, S. (2014) 'Workforce diversity: ethnicity and gender diversity and disparity in the New York City Police Department', *Journal of Ethnicity in Criminal Justice*, 12(2): 93–115.

Guajardo, S. (2015) 'Women in policing: a longitudinal assessment of female officers in supervisory positions in the New York City Police Department', *Women & Criminal Justice*, 26(1): 1–17.

Guest, G., Bunce, A. and Johnson, L. (2006) 'How many interviews are enough? An experiment with data saturation and variability', *Field Methods*, 18(1): 59–82.

Guller, I. (1973) 'Higher education and policemen: attitudinal differences between freshman and senior police-college students', *Journal of Criminal Law, Criminology and Police Science*, 63(3): 396–401.

Gustafson, J. (2008) 'Tokenism in policing: an empirical test of Kanter's hypothesis', *Journal of Criminal Justice Reform*, 36(1): 1–10.

Gustafson, J. (2013) 'Diversity in municipal police agencies: a national examination of minority hiring and promotion', *Policing: An International Journal of Police Strategies & Management*, 36(4): 719–736.

Haarr, R. and Morash, M. (1999) 'Gender, race, and strategies of coping with occupational stress in policing', *Justice Quarterly*, 16(2): 303–336.

Hager, E. and Li, W. (2020) 'White US Police Union Bosses Protect Officers Accused of Racism', *The Guardian*, 10 June. Available at: www. theguardian.com/us-news/2020/jun/10/police-unions-black-officers-white-leaders

Haider-Markel, D. (2007) 'Representation and backlash: the positive and negative influence of descriptive representation,' *Legislative Studies Quarterly*, 32(1): 107–133.

Haider-Markel, D. (2010) *Out and Running: Gay and Lesbian Candidates, Elections and Policy Representation*, Washington, DC: Georgetown University Press.

Hall, S., Critcher, C., Jefferson, J. and Roberts, B. (1978) *Policing the Crisis: Mugging, the State, and Law and Order*, London: Palgrave Macmillan.

Hallenberg, K. and Cockcroft, T. (2017) 'From indifference to hostility: police officers, organizational responses and the symbolic value of "in-service" higher education in policing', *Policing*, 11(3): 273–288.

Handschu v. Special Services Division, Case No. 71 CIV. 2203. Ruling on Proposed Settlement Agreement. United States District Court, Southern District of New York (2016).

Harvey, W. (2010) 'Methodological approaches for interviewing elites', *Geography Compass*, 4(1): 193–205.

Hasan, M. (2021) 'Racist bullying of BAME (Black and Asian Minority Ethnic) women within police services in England: race, gender and police culture', *International Journal of Police Science & Management*, 23(2): 182–195.

Hassell, K. and Brandl, S. (2009) 'An examination of the workplace experiences of police patrol officers: the role of race, sex, and sexual orientation', *Police Quarterly*, 12(4): 408–430.

Hassell, K. D., Archbold, C. A. and Stichman, A. J. (2011) 'Comparing the workplace experiences of male and female police officers: examining workplace problems, stress, job satisfaction and consideration of career change', *International Journal of Police Science and Management*, 13(1): 37–53.

Headley, A. (2022) 'Accountability and police use of force: interactive effects between minority representation and civilian review boards', *Public Management Review*, 24(11): 1682–1704.

Headley, A., D'Alessio, S. and Stolzenberg, L. (2020) 'The effect of a complainant's race and ethnicity on dispositional outcome in police misconduct cases in Chicago', *Race and Justice*, 10(1): 43–61.

Heidensohn, F. (1992) *Women in Control? The Role of Women in Law Enforcement*, Oxford: Clarendon Press.

Henderson, L. J. (1978) 'Administrative advocacy and black urban administrators', *The Annals of the American Academy of Political and Social Science*, Vol 439, Urban Black Politics, pp 68–79.

Hennink, M., Kaiser, B. and Marconi, V. (2016) 'Code saturation versus meaning saturation: how many interviews are enough?', *Qualitative Health Research*, 27(4): 591–608.

Henry, T. and Franklin, T. (2019) 'Police legitimacy in the context of street stops: the effects of race, class, and procedural justice', *Criminal Justice Policy Review*, 30(3): 406–427.

Herbert, S. (2001) '"Hard charger" or "station queen"? Policing and the masculinist state', *Gender, Place and Culture: A Journal of Feminist Geography*, 8(1): 55–71.

Herz, M. and Johansson, T. (2015) 'The normativity of the concept of heteronormativity', *Journal of Homosexuality*, 62(8): 1009–1020.

Hickman, M., Piquero, A. and Greene, J. (2000) 'Discretion and gender disproportionality in police disciplinary systems', *Policing: An International Journal of Police Strategies & Management*, 23(1): 105–116.

HM Government (2021) 'Confidence in the Local Police, by Ethnicity', HM Government website. Available at: www.ethnicity-facts-figures.serv ice.gov.uk/crime-justice-and-the-law/policing/confidence-in-the-local-police/latest

HMIC (Her Majesty's Inspectorate of Constabulary) (1997) *Winning the Race: Policing Plural Communities – HMIC Thematic Inspection Report on Police Community and Race Relations 1996/97*, London: Home Office.

HMIC (Her Majesty's Inspectorate of Constabulary) (2001) *Winning the Race: Embracing Diversity*, London: HMSO.

HMIC (Her Majesty's Inspectorate of Constabulary) (2016) *PEEL: Police legitimacy 2015: A National Overview*, London: HMIC.

Hoffman, P. and Hickey, E. (2005) 'Use of force by female police officers', *Journal of Criminal Justice*, 33(1): 145–151.

Holdaway, S. (1996) *The Racialisation of the Police*, Basingstoke: Palgrave Macmillan.

Holdaway, S. (1997a) 'Responding to racialized divisions within the workforce: the experience of black and Asian police officers in England', *Ethnic and Racial Studies*, 20(1): 69–90.

Holdaway, S. (1997b) 'Constructing and sustaining race within the police workforce', *The British Journal of Sociology*, 48(1): 19–34.

Holdaway, S. (2010) 'Understanding "trust" and "confidence": problems within and out with constabularies', *Policing*, 4(3): 258–264.

Holdaway, S. (2013) 'Police race relations in the Big Society: continuity and change', *Criminology & Criminal Justice*, 13(2): 215–230.

Holdaway, S. and Barron, S. (1997) *Resigners? The Experience of Black and Asian Police Officers*, London: Palgrave Macmillan.

Holdaway, S. and Parker, S. (1998) 'Policing women police', *British Journal of Criminology*, 38(1): 40–60.

Holdaway, S. and O'Neill, M. (2004) 'The development of black police associations', *British Journal of Criminology*, 44(1): 854–865.

Holdaway, S. and O'Neill, M. (2007) 'Where has all the racism gone? Views of racism within constabularies after Macpherson', *Ethnic and Racial Studies*, 30(3): 397–415.

Holder, K., Nee, C. and Ellis, T. (2000) 'Triple jeopardy? Black and Asian women police officers' experiences of discrimination', *International Journal of Police Science & Management*, 3(1): 68–87.

Homant, R. and Kennedy, D. (1985) 'Police perceptions of spouse abuse: a comparison of male and female officers', *Journal of Criminal Justice*, 13(1): 29–47.

Home Office (1999) *Dismantling Barriers to Reflect the Community We Serve: The Recruitment, Retention and Progression of Ethnic Minority Officers: Action Plan*, London: HMSO.

Home Office (2005) *Assessing the impact of the Stephen Lawrence Inquiry*, Home Office Research Study 294, London: HMSO.

Home Office (2010) *Police Service Strength England and Wales, 31 March 2010*, London: HMSO.

Home Office (2014) *Police Workforce, England and Wales, 31 March 2014*, London: HMSO.

Home Office (2016) *Police Workforce, England and Wales, 31 March 2016*, Statistical Bulletin 05/16, London: HMSO.

Home Office (2017) *Police Workforce, England and Wales, 31 March 2017*, Statistical Bulletin 10/17, London: HMSO.

Home Office (2019) *Police Workforce, England and Wales, 31 March 2019* (2nd edn), Statistical Bulletin 11/19, London: HMSO.

Home Office (2020) *Police Workforce: England and Wales, 31 March 2020*, London: HMSO.

Home Office (2021) *Police Workforce, England and Wales: 31 March 2021* (2nd edn), London: HMSO.

Home Office (2022) *Police Workforce, England and Wales, 31 March 2021* (2nd edn), London: HMSO.

Home Office (2023a) *Police Workforce, England and Wales, 31 March 2022* (2nd edn), London: HMSO.

Home Office (2023b) *Police Workforce, Ethnicity Facts and Figures.* Available at: www.ethnicity-facts-figures.service.gov.uk/workforce-and-business/workforce-diversity/police-workforce/latest/

Home Office (2024) *Police Workforce, England and Wales, 31 March 2023* (2nd edn). Available at: www.gov.uk/government/statistics/police-workforce-england-and-wales-31-march-2023/police-workforce-england-and-wales-31-march-2023#diversity

Hong, S. (2016) 'Representative bureaucracy, organizational integrity, and citizen coproduction: does an increase in police ethnic representativeness reduce crime?', *Journal of Policy Analysis and Management*, 35(1): 11–33.

Hong, S. (2017a) 'Black in blue: racial profiling and representative bureaucracy in policing revisited', *Journal of Public Administration Research and Theory*, 27(4): 547–561.

Horwitz, S. and Dovidio, J. (2017) 'The rich—love them or hate them? Divergent implicit and explicit attitudes toward the wealthy', *Group Processes & Intergroup Relations*, 20(1): 3–31.

Hough, M., Jackson, J., Bradford, B., Myhill, A. and Quinton, P. (2010) 'Procedural justice, trust and institutional legitimacy', *Policing*, 4(3): 203–210.

House of Commons (2001) *Police Service Strength England and Wales 31 March 1977 to 30 September 2000*, London: HMSO.

House of Commons Home Affairs Select Committee (2008) *Macpherson 10 Years On*, London: HMSO.

House of Commons Home Affairs Select Committee (2013) *Third Report: Leadership and Standards in the Police*, London: HMSO.

House of Commons, Home Affairs Select Committee (2016) *Police Diversity: First Report of Session 2016–17*, London: HMSO.

Hsieh, H. and Shannon, S. (2005) 'Three approaches to qualitative content analysis', *Qualitative Health Research*, 15: 1277–1288.

Huang, W. and Vaughn, M (1996) 'Support and confidence: public attitudes toward the police', in T. J. Flanagan and D. R. Longmire (eds) *Americans View Crime and Justice: A National Public Opinion Survey*, Thousand Oaks, CA: SAGE, pp 31–45.

Huber, L. and Gunderson, A. (2023) 'Putting a fresh face forward: does the gender of a police chief affect public perceptions?', *Political Research Quarterly*, 76(3): 1418–1432.

Hunt, J. (1984) 'The development of rapport through the negotiation of gender in field work among police', *Human Organization*, 43(4): 283–296.

Hunt, J. C. (1990) 'The logic of sexism among police', *Women and Criminal Justice*, 1(2): 3–30.

Independent Commission on the LAPD (Christopher Commission) (1991) *Report of the Independent Commission on the Los Angeles Police Department*, Los Angeles.

Irlbeck, D. (2008) 'Latino police officers: patterns of ethnic self-identity and Latino community attachment', *Police Quarterly*, 11(4): 468–495.

Jackson, J., Bradford, B., Hough, M., Myhill, A., Quinton, P. and Tyler, T. (2012) 'Why do people comply with the law? Legitimacy and the influence of legal institutions', *British Journal of Criminology*, 52(6): 1051–1071.

Jacobs, P. (1966) *Prelude to Riot*, New York: Vintage.

Johnson, B. (1976) 'Taking care of labor: the police in American politics', *Theory and Society*, 3(1): 89–117.

Johnston, K. and Houston, J. (2018) 'Representative bureaucracy: does female police leadership affect gender-based violence arrests?', *International Review of Administrative Sciences*, 84(1): 3–20.

Jollevet, F. (2008) 'African American police executive careers: influences of human capital, social capital, and racial discrimination', *Police Practice and Research: An International Journal*, 9(1): 17–30.

Jones, D. (2004) 'Screwing diversity out of workers? Reading diversity', *Journal of Organizational Change Management*, 17(3): 281–291.

Jones, D. and Stablein, R. (2006) 'Diversity as Resistance and Recuperation: Critical Theory, Post-Structuralist Perspectives and Workplace Diversity', in P. Prasad, J. K. Pringle and A. M. Konrad (eds) *Handbook of Workplace Diversity*, London: SAGE, pp 146–167.

Jones, M. (2015a) 'Creating the "thinking police officer": exploring motivations and professional impact of part-time higher education', *Policing*, 10(3): 232–240.

Jones, M. (2015b) 'Who forgot lesbian, gay, and bisexual police officers? Findings from a national survey', *Policing*, 9(1): 65–76.

Jones, M. and Williams, M. (2015) 'Twenty years on: lesbian, gay and bisexual police officers' experiences of workplace discrimination in England and Wales', *Policing and Society*, 25(2): 188–211.

Jones, S. (1986) *Policewomen and Equality*, London: Palgrave Macmillan.

Jones, T. and Newburn, T. (2006) *Policy Transfer and Criminal Justice: Exploring US Influence Over British Crime Control Policy*, Milton Keynes: Open University Press.

Jones, T. and Newburn, T. (2021) 'When crime policies travel: cross-national policy transfer in crime control', *Crime and Justice*, 50(1): 115–159.

Kakar, S. (1998) 'Self-evaluations of police performance: an analysis of the relationship between police officers' education level and job performance', *Policing: An International Journal of Police Strategies & Management*, 21(4): 632–647.

Kane, R. and White, D. (2009) 'Bad cops: a study of career-ending misconduct among New York City police officers', *Criminology and Public Policy*, 8(4): 737–770.

Kanter, R. (1977) 'Some effects of proportions on group life: skewed sex ratios and responses to token women', *American Journal of Sociology*, 82(5): 965–990.

Kappeler, V., Sapp, A. and Carter, D. (1992) 'Police officer higher education, citizen complaints and departmental rule violations', *American Journal of Police*, 11(2): 37–54.

Keiser, L., Haider-Markel, D. and Darolia, R. (2022) 'Race, representation, and policy attitudes in U.S. public schools', *Policy Studies Journal*, 50: 823–848.

Keiser, L., Wilkins, V., Meier, K. and Holland, C. (2002) 'Lipstick and logarithms: gender, institutional context, and representative bureaucracy', *American Political Science Review*, 96(3): 553–564.

Kelley, T. (2000) 'Call for Calm after Shooting of Policeman by Colleagues', *The New York Times*, 30 January. Available at: www.nytimes.com/2000/01/30/us/call-for-calm-after-shooting-of-policeman-by-colleagues.html

Kelly, R. and Farber, M. (1974) 'Identifying responsive inner-city policemen', *Journal of Applied Psychology*, 59(3): 259–263.

Kerner Commission (1967) *Report on the Causes, Events, and Aftermaths of the Civil Disorders of 1967*. National Advisory Commission on Civil Disorders. Available at: www.ojp.gov/ncjrs/virtual-library/abstracts/national-advisory-commission-civil-disorders-report

Kleinfeld, N. (2009) 'A Final Farewell for a Slain Police Officer', *The New York Times*, 4 June. Available at: www.nytimes.com/2009/06/05/nyregion/05funeral.html

Klockars, C., Kutjnak Ivkovich, S. and Haberfeld, M. R. (2004) 'The Contours of Police Integrity', in C. Klockars, S. Kutjnak Ivkovich and M. R. Haberfeld (eds) *The Contours of Police Integrity*, Thousand Oaks, CA: SAGE, pp 1–18.

Knapp, W. (1973) *Report of the Commission to Investigate Allegations of Police Corruption and the City's Anti-Corruption Procedures*, New York.

Konrad, A., Richard, O. and Yang, Y. (2021) 'Both diversity and meritocracy: managing the diversity-meritocracy paradox with organizational ambidexterity', *Journal of Management Studies*, 58(8): 2180–2206.

Krieger, N., Williams, D. and Moss, N. (1997) 'Measuring social class in US public health research: concepts, methodologies, and guidelines', *Annual Review of Public Health*, 18(1): 341–378.

Krimmel, J. and Gromley, P. (2003) 'Tokenism and job satisfaction for policewomen', *American Journal of Criminal Justice*, 28(1): 73–88.

Kringen, A. and Novich, M. (2017) 'Is it "just hair" or is it "everything"? Embodiment and gender repression in policing', *Gender Work and Organization*, 25(2): 1–19.

Kurtz, D. L. (2008) 'Controlled burn: the gendering of stress and burnout in modern policing', *Feminist Criminology*, 3(3): 216–238.

Kuykendall, J. and Burns, D. (1980) 'The black police officer: an historical perspective', *Journal of Contemporary Criminal Justice*, 7(4): 4–12.

Lacey, N. (2008) *The Prisoner's Dilemma: Political Economy and Punishment in New Democracies*, Cambridge: Cambridge University Press.

Lammy, D. (2017) *Outcomes of BAME in UK Criminal Justice System* (The Lammy Review), London: HMSO.

Lasley, J., Larson, J., Kelso, C. and Brown, G. (2011) 'Assessing the long-term effects of officer race on police attitudes towards the community: a case for representative bureaucracy theory', *Police Practice and Research: An International Journal*, 12(6): 474–491.

Lawrence v. Texas, 539 US 558 (2003).

Lea, J. and Young, G. (1984) *What Is to Be Done about Law and Order?* London: Penguin.

LeCount, R. (2017) 'More black than blue? Comparing the racial attitudes of police to citizens', *Sociological Forum*, 32(S1): 1051–1072.

Lee, M. and Punch, M. (2004) 'Policing by degrees: police officers' experience of university education', *Policing and Society*, 14(3): 233–249.

Lehr, D. (2009) 'The Blue Wall of Silence', *The Boston Globe*, 21 June. Available at: http://archive.boston.com/bostonglobe/magazine/articles/2009/06/21/the_blue_wall_of_silence/

Leinen, S. (1993) *Gay Cops*, New Brunswick, NJ: Rutgers University Press.

Lentz, S. and Chaires, R. (2007) 'The invention of Peel's Principles: a study of policing "textbook" history', *Journal of Criminal Justice*, 35(1): 69–79.

Lersch, K. M. (1998) 'Police misconduct and malpractice: a critical analysis of citizens' complaints', *Policing: An International Journal of Police Strategies & Management*, 21(1): 80–96.

Lersch, K. and Kunzman, L. (2001) 'Misconduct allegations and higher education in a southern sheriff's department', *American Journal of Criminal Justice*, 25(2): 161–172.

Lersch, K. and Mieczkowski, T. (1996) 'Who are the problem-prone officers? An analysis of citizen complaints', *American Journal of Police*, 15(3): 23–44.

Lewis, G. and Pitts, D. (2011) 'Representation of lesbians and gay men in federal, state, and local bureaucracies', *Journal of Public Administration Research and Theory*, 21: 159–180.

Lewis, P., Newburn, T., Taylor, M., Mcgillivray, C., Greenhill, A., Frayman, H. and Procter, R. N. (2011) *Reading The Riots: Investigating England's Summer of Disorder*, London: London School of Economics and Political Science.

Lewis, W. (1989) 'Toward representative bureaucracy: blacks in city police organizations, 1975–1985', *Public Administration Review*, 49(3): 257–268.

Lilleker, D. (2003) 'Interviewing the political elite: navigating a potential minefield', *Politics*, 23(1): 207–214.

Lim, H. (2006) 'Representative bureaucracy: rethinking substantive effects and active representation', *Public Administration Review*, 66: 193–204.

Lim, H. and Lee, H. (2015) 'The effects of supervisor education and training on police use of force', *Criminal Justice Studies*, 28(4): 444–463.

Little, C., Stephens, P. and Whittle, S. (2002) 'The praxis and politics of policing: problems facing transgender people', *Queensland University of Technology Law Review*, 2(2): 226–243.

Lock, J. (1979) *The British Policewoman: Her Story*, London: Robert Hale Ltd.

Loftus, B. (2009) *Police Culture in a Changing World*, Oxford: Oxford University Press.

Logan, L. (2020) *Closing Ranks: My Life as a Cop*, London: SPCK Publishing.

Long, C. (2013) 'Federal Trial Provides Insight into NYPD Practices', *Associated Press*, 26 March. Available at: https://apnews.com/article/cefc6776b0de4115bc36a50a1a7a39ec

Longhofer, J., Floersch, J. and Hoy, J. (2012) *Qualitative Methods for Practice Research*, Oxford: Oxford University Press.

Lott, J. (2000) 'Does a helping hand put others at risk? Affirmative action, police departments, and crime', *Economic Inquiry*, 38(2): 159–367.

Low, J. (2019) 'A pragmatic definition of the concept of theoretical saturation', *Sociological Focus*, 52(2): 131–139.

Lucero, E., Trounstine, J., Connolly, J. and Klofstad, C. (2022) 'A matter of life or death: how racial representation shapes compliance with city disaster preparedness orders', *Journal of Urban Affairs*, 44(8): 1168–1185.

Lum, C. (2011) 'The influence of places on police decision pathways: from call for service to arrest', *Justice Quarterly*, 28(4): 631–665.

Lundman, R. (2004) 'Driving while black: effects of race, ethnicity, and gender on citizen self-reports of traffic stops and police action', *Criminology*, 41(1): 195–220.

M v. Chief Constable of West Midlands Police [1996] (IT Case No. 08964/96) (unreported).

Macpherson, W. (1999) *The Stephen Lawrence Inquiry: Report of An Inquiry*, London: HMSO.

Macvean, A. and Cox, C. (2012) 'Police education in a university setting: emerging cultures and attitudes', *Policing*, 6(1): 16–25.

Mallory, C., Hasenbush, A. and Sears, B. (2013) *Discrimination against Law Enforcement Officers on the Basis of Sexual Orientation and Gender Identity: 2000 to 2013*, Los Angeles, CA: UCLA Williams Institute.

Manis, J., Archbold, C. and Hassell, K. (2008) 'Exploring the impact of police officer education level on allegations of police misconduct', *International Journal of Police Science and Management*, 10(4): 509–523.

Manning, P. K. (1977) *Police Work: The Social Organization of Policing*, Cambridge, MA: MIT Press.

Manning, P. (2001) 'Theorizing policing: the drama and myth of crime control in the NYPD', *Theoretical Criminology*, 5(1): 315–344.

Manning, P. (2007) 'A Dialectic of Organisational and Occupational Culture', in M. O'Neill, M. Marks and A.-M. Singh (eds) *Police Occupational Culture (Sociology of Crime, Law and Deviance, Vol 8)*, Bingley: Emerald Group Publishing Limited, pp 47–83.

Marciniak, L. and Elattrache, A. (2020) 'Police chiefs' opinions on the utility of a college education for police officers', *Journal of Criminal Justice Education*, 31(3): 436–453.

Marks, M. and Stout, C. (2011) 'Rating Los Angeles' top cop: descriptive representation and support for the police chief', *Race and Justice*, 1(4): 341–361.

Marschall, M. and Shah, P. (2007) 'The attitudinal effects of minority incorporation examining the racial dimensions of trust in urban America', *Urban Affairs Review*, 42(5): 629–658.

Marshall, B., Cardon, P., Poddar, A. and Fontenot, R. (2013) 'Does sample size matter in qualitative research? A review of qualitative interviews in IS research', *Journal of Computer Information Systems*, 54(1): 11–22.

Martin, C. (1996) 'The impact of equal opportunities policies on the day-to-day experiences of women police constables', *British Journal of Criminology*, 36(4): 510–528.

Martin, S. (1980) *Breaking and Entering: Police Women on Patrol*, Berkeley: University of California Press.

Martin, S. (1989) 'Women on the move? A report on the status of women in policing', *Women & Criminal Justice*, 1(1): 21–40.

Martin, S. (1991) 'The effectiveness of affirmative action: the case of women in policing', *Justice Quarterly*, 8(4): 489–504.

Martin, S. (1994) '"Outsider within" the station house: the impact of race and gender on black women police', *Social Problems*, 41(3): 383–400.

Martin, S. and Jurik, N. (2007) *Doing Justice, Doing Gender*, London: SAGE.

Mastrofski, S. (2004) 'Controlling street-level police discretion', *The Annals of the American Academy of Political and Social Science*, 593(1): 100–118.

May, T. (2011) *Social Research: Issues, Methods and Process*, Buckingham, UK: Open University Press.

McCarty, W., Aldirawi, H., Dewald, S. and Palacios, M. (2019) 'Burnout in blue: an analysis of the extent and primary predictors of burnout among law enforcement officers in the United States', *Police Quarterly*, 22(3): 278–304.

McCluskey, C. and McCluskey, J. (2004) 'Diversity in policing: Latino representation in law enforcement', *Journal of Ethnicity in Criminal Justice*, 2(3): 67–81.

McCormick, M. (2015) 'Our uneasiness with police unions: power and voice for the powerful? *Public Law Review*, 35(47). Available at: https://ssrn.com/abstract=3285422

McCracken, G. (1988) *The Long Interview*, London: SAGE.

McCrone, B. (2017) 'Police Union President Calls Black Lives Matter Protesters Outside Philadelphia Officer's House "a Pack of Rabid Animals"', *NBC Philadelphia*, 1 September. Available at: www.nbcphila delphia.com/news/local/police-union-president-calls-black-lives-mat ter-protesters-outside-philadelphia-officers-house-a-pack-of-rabid-anim als-report/26796/

McCrudden, C. (1982) 'Institutional discrimination', *Oxford Journal of Legal Studies*, 2(3): 303–367.

McCrudden, C. (1998) 'Merit principles', *Oxford Journal of Legal Studies*, 18(1): 543–579.

McElvain, J. and Kposowa, A. (2008) 'Police officer characteristics and the likelihood of using deadly force', *Criminal Justice and Behavior*, 35(4): 505–521.

McGinley, B., Agnew-Pauley, W., Tompson, L. and Belur, J. (2019) 'Police recruit training programmes: a systematic map of research literature', *Policing*, 14(1): 52–75.

Meier, K. (1993) 'Latinos and representative bureaucracy: Testing the Thompson and Henderson hypotheses', *Journal of Public Administration, Research and Theory*, 3: 393–414.

Meier, K. (2019) 'Theoretical frontiers in representative bureaucracy: new directions for research', *Perspectives on Public Management and Governance*, 2(1): 39–56.

Meier, K. and Nicholson-Crotty, J. (2006) 'Gender, representative bureaucracy, and law enforcement: the case of sexual assault', *Public Administration Review*, 66(6): 850–860.

Meier, K. and Stewart, J. (1992) 'The impact of representative bureaucracies: educational systems and public policies', *American Review of Public Administration*, 22: 157–171.

Meier, K., Wrinkle, R. and Polinard, J. (1999) 'Representative bureaucracy and distributional equity: addressing the hard question', *Journal of Politics*, 61: 1025–1039.

Mennicke, A., Gromer, J., Oehme, K. and MacConnie, L. (2018) 'Workplace experiences of gay and lesbian criminal justice officers in the United States: a qualitative investigation of officers attending a LGBT law enforcement conference', *Policing and Society*, 28(6): 712–729.

Messner, S. (2014) 'Social institutions, theory development, and the promise of comparative criminological research', *Asian Criminology*, 9: 49–63.

Miller, A. and Segal, C. (2019) 'Do female officers improve law enforcement quality? Effects on crime reporting and domestic violence', *Review of Economic Studies*, 86(5): 2220–2247.

Miller, S. (1999) *Gender and Community Policing: Walking the Talk*, Boston, MA: Northeastern University Press.

Miller, S. and Lilley, T. (2014) 'Proving themselves: the status of LGBQ police officers', *Sociology Compass*, 8(4): 373–383.

Miller, S., Forest, K. and Jurik, N. (2003) 'Diversity in blue: lesbian and gay police officers in a masculine occupation', *Men and Masculinities*, 5(4): 355–385.

Miller, W. (1977) *Cops and Bobbies: Police Authority in New York and London, 1830–1870*, Chicago, IL: University of Chicago Press.

Mitchell, C. (2015) *The transformation of gay life from the closet to liberation, 1948–1980*. Unpublished PhD thesis, Rutgers University.

Mollen, M. (1994) *Report of the Commission to Investigate Allegations of Police Corruption and the Anti-Corruption Procedures of the Police Department*, New York.

Morash, M. and Haarr, R. (2012) 'Doing, redoing, and undoing gender: variation in gender identities of women working as police officers', *Feminist Criminology*, 7(1): 3–23.

Morris, F. (2002) *Report of the Tribunal of Inquiry Set up Pursuant to the Tribunal of Inquiry (Evidence) Acts 1921–2002 into Certain Gardaí in the Donegal Division, Report on Explosives 'Finds' in Donegal*, Dublin: Ireland.

Morris, W. (2004) *The Report of the Morris Inquiry: The Case for Change*, London: The Morris Inquiry.

Mosher, F. (1968) *Democracy and the Public Service*, Oxford: Oxford University Press.

Mosher, F. (1982) *Democracy and the Public Service* (2nd edn), New York: Oxford University Press.

Muibu, D. and Olawole, I. (2022) 'Does representation matter? Examining officer inclusion, citizen cooperation and police empowerment in a divided society', *Conflict, Security & Development*, 22(2): 191–220.

Muir, R. (2001) *The Virdi Inquiry Report*, London: Metropolitan Police Authority.

Murji, K. (2014) 'A representative workforce: the BME police recruitment target and the politics of enumeration and categorization', *International Journal of Sociology and Social Policy*, 34(9/10): 578–592.

Murji, K. and Culter, D. (1990) 'From a force into a service? The police, racial attacks, and equal opportunities', *Critical Social Policy*, 10(29): 92–99.

Myers, K., Forest, K. and Miller, S. (2004) 'Officer Friendly and the tough cop: gay and lesbians navigate homophobia and policing', *Journal of Homosexuality*, 47(1): 17–37.

Namako, T. (2015) 'Police Union Compares Baltimore Protests to a "Lynch Mob"', *BuzzFeed News*, 23 April. Available at: www.buzzfeednews.com/article/tomnamako/police-union-president-compares-baltimore-protests-to-a-lync

Nanes, M. (2018) 'Policing in divided societies: officer inclusion, citizen cooperation, and crime prevention', *Conflict Management and Peace Science*, 37(5): 580–604.

National Advisory Commission on Criminal Justice Standards and Goals (1973) *Report on Police*, Washington, DC: U.S. Government Printing Office.

National Center for Women & Policing (1999) *Recruiting & Retaining Women: A Self-Assessment Guide for Law Enforcement*, Washington, DC: Feminist Majority Foundation.

National Center for Women & Policing (2002) *Men, Women, and Police Excessive Force: A Tale of Two Genders*, Washington, DC: National Center for Women & Policing.

National Commission on Law Observance and Enforcement (1931) *Report on the Police*, Washington, DC: U.S. Government Printing Office.

National Institute of Justice (2019) *Women in Policing: Breaking Barriers and Blazing a Path*, National Institute of Justice Special Report, Washington, DC: Department of Justice.

Nelken, D. (2010) *Comparative Criminal Justice*, London: SAGE.

New York Attorney General's Office (2000) *An Investigation into the NYPD's Stop and Frisk Practices*, New York: New York Attorney General's Office.

Newburn, T. and Jones, T. (2007) 'Symbolizing crime control: reflections on zero tolerance', *Theoretical Criminology*, 11(2): 221–243.

Nicholson-Crotty, S., Nicholson-Crotty, J. and Fernandez, S. (2017) 'Will more black cops matter? Officer race and police-involved homicides of black citizens', *Public Administration Review*, 77(2): 206–216.

Niederhoffer, A. (1967) *Behind the Shield: The Police in Urban Society*, Garden City, NY: Doubleday and Company Inc.

Noaks, L. and Wincup, E. (2004) *Criminological Research: Understanding Qualitative Methods*, London: SAGE.

Nolan, H. (2020) 'Police Union Denies Racism, Calls AFL-CIO President "Disgraceful" in Irate Letter', *In These Times*, 30 June. Available at: https://inthesetimes.com/article/police-union-racism-afl-cio-trumka-cabral

Nolan, T. (2009) 'Behind the blue wall of silence', *Men and Masculinities*, 12(2): 250–257.

Noon, M. (2010) 'The shackled runner: time to rethink positive discrimination?', *Work, Employment and Society*, 24(4): 728–739.

Northern Ireland Policing Board (2017) *Public Perceptions of the Police, PCSPs and the Northern Ireland Policing Board*, Belfast: Northern Ireland Policing Board.

Novak, K., Brown, R. and Frank, J. (2011) 'Women on patrol: an analysis of differences in officer arrest behaviour', *Policing: An International Journal of Police Strategies & Management*, 34(4): 566–587.

NPCC (National Police Chiefs' Counsel) (2019) *Understanding Disproportionality in Police Complaint & Misconduct Cases for BAME Police Officers & Staff*. Available at: www.npcc.police.uk/SysSiteAssets/media/downloads/publications/publications-log/2020/npcc-understanding-disproportionality-in-police-complaint-misconduct-cases-for-bame-police-officers-and-staff-2019.pdf

NYS (2010) *Reducing Inherent Danger: Report of the Task Force on Police on Police Shootings*, Albany: New York State Task Force on Police-on-Police Shootings.

Obergefell v. Hodges, 576 US 644 (2015).

O'Neill, M. and Holdaway, S. (2007) 'Examining "window dressing": the views of black police associations on recruitment and training', *Journal of Ethnic and Migration Studies*, 33(3): 483–500.

O'Neill, M. and Holdaway, S. (2015) 'Black Police Associations and the Police Occupational Culture', in M. O'Neill, M. Marks and A.-M. Singh (eds) *Police Occupational Culture (Sociology of Crime, Law and Deviance, Vol 8)*, Leeds: Emerald Group Publishing Ltd, pp 253–274.

O'Neill, M. and Loftus, B. (2013) 'Policing and the surveillance of the marginal: everyday contexts of social control', *Theoretical Criminology*, 17(4): 437–454.

Oakley, R. (1996) *Race and Equal Opportunities in the Police Service: A Survey Report*, London: Commission for Racial Equality.

Opotow, S. (1997) 'What is fair? Justice issues in the positive discrimination debate', *American Behavioral Scientist*, 41(2): 232–245.

P v. S and Cornwall County Council ECJ [1996] IRLR 347.

Panter, H. (2018) *Transgender Cops: The Intersection of Gender and Sexuality Expectations in Police Cultures*, London: Routledge.

Paoline, E. (2003) 'Taking stock: toward a richer understanding of police culture', *Journal of Criminal Justice*, 31(1): 199–214.

Paoline, E. and Terrill, W. (2004) 'Women police officers and the use of coercion', *Women & Criminal Justice*, 15(3–4): 97–119.

Paoline, E. and Terrill, W. (2007) 'Police education, experience, and the use of force', *Criminal Justice and Behavior*, 34(2): 179–196.

Paoline, E., Gau, J. and Terrill, W. (2018) 'Race and the police use of force encounter in the United States', *British Journal of Criminology*, 58(1): 54–74.

Paoline, E., Terrill, W. and Rossler, M. (2015) 'Higher education, college degree major, and police occupational attitudes', *Journal of Criminal Justice Education*, 26(1): 49–73.

Parsons, D. and Jesilow, P. (2001) *In the Same Voice: Women and Men in Law Enforcement*, Santa Ana, CA: Seven Locks Press.

Pate, A., Fridell, L. and Hamilton, E. (1993) *Police Use of Force: Official Reports, Citizen Complaints, and Legal Consequences*, Washington, DC: Police Foundation.

Paterson, C. (2011) 'Adding value? A review of the international literature on the role of higher education in police training and education', *Police Practice and Research*, 12(4): 286–297.

Paul, J. and Birzer, M. (2017) 'The experiences of black police officers who have been racially profiled: an exploratory research note', *Journal of African American Studies*, 21(1): 567–584.

Payne, B. K. and Cameron, C. D. (2010) 'Divided Minds, Divided Morals: How Implicit Social Cognition Underpins and Undermines Our Sense of Social Justice', in B. Gawronski and B. Keith Payne (eds) *Handbook of Implicit Social Cognition: Measurement, Theory, and Applications*, New York: Guilford Press, pp 445–460.

Pettigrew, T. (1998) 'Intergroup contract theory', *Annual Review of Psychology*, 49(1): 65–85.

Pettigrew, T. and Tropp, L. (2006) 'A meta-analytic test of intergroup contact theory', *Journal of Personality and Social Psychology*, 90(5): 751–783.

Pettigrew, T. F. and Tropp, L. R. (2008) 'How does intergroup contact reduce prejudice? Meta-analytic tests of three mediators', *European Journal of Social Psychology*, 38(1): 922–934.

Pew Research Center (2017) *Behind the Badge: Final Report*, Washington, DC: Pew Research Center.

Pincus, F. (2003) *Reverse Discrimination: Dismantling the Myth*, Boulder, CO: Lynne Rienner Publishers.

Pogrebin, M., Dodge, M. and Chatman, H. (2000) 'Reflections of African-American women on their careers in urban policing: their experiences of racial and sexual discrimination', *International Journal of the Sociology of Law*, 28(1): 311–326.

Police Federation of England and Wales (2022) *Police Federation Website: About Us*. Available at: www.polfed.org/about-us/aims-objectives/

Polisar, J. and Milgram, D. (1998) 'Recruiting, integrating and retaining women police officers: strategies that work', *Police Chief*, 65(10): 42–52.

Polk, E. and Armstrong, D. (2001) 'Higher education and law enforcement career paths: is the road to success paved by degree?', *Journal of Criminal Justice Education*, 12(1): 77–99.

Potts, L. (1983) 'Equal employment opportunity and female employment in police agencies', *Journal of Criminal Justice*, 11: 505–523.

Prasad, A. (2001) 'Understanding workplace empowerment as inclusion: a historical investigation of the discourse of difference in the United States', *The Journal of Applied Behavioral Science*, 37(1): 51–69.

Prasad, P., Pringle, J. K. and Konrad, A. M. (2006) 'Examining the Contours of Workplace Diversity: Concepts, Contexts and Challenges', in A. M. Konrad, P. Prasad and J. K. Pringle (eds) *Handbook of Workplace Diversity*, London: SAGE, pp 1–22.

Pringle, J. and Ryan, I. (2015) 'Understanding context in diversity management: a multi-level analysis', *Equality, Diversity and Inclusion: An International Journal*, 34(6): 470–482.

Prokos, A. and Padavic, I. (2002) ' "There oughtta be a law against bitches": masculinity lessons in police academy training', *Gender, Work and Organization*, 9(4): 439–459.

Punch, M. (1979) 'The Secret Social Service', in S. Holdaway (ed) *The British Police*, London: Edward Arnold, pp 102–117.

Punch, M. (2007) 'Cops With Honours: University Education and Police Culture', in M. O'Neill, M. Marks and A. Singh (eds) *Police Occupational Culture (Sociology of Crime, Law and Deviance, Vol 8)*, Bingley: Emerald Group Publishing Limited, pp 105–128.

Punch, M. (2009) 'Why Corporations Kill and Get Away with It: The Failure of Law to Cope with Crime in Organizations', in A. Nollkaemper and H. van der Wilt (eds) *Systemic Criminality in International Law*, Cambridge: Cambridge University Press, pp 42–68.

Quinlan, T. (2021) 'Field, capital and the policing habitus: understanding Bourdieu through the NYPD's post-9/11 counterterrorism practices', *Criminology and Criminal Justice*, 21(2): 187–205.

Quinlan, T. (forthcoming) 'Positive action has failed: why positive discrimination must be used to diversify police in England and Wales'.

Quinnipiac University Polling Institute (2000) 'Race Divides New Yorkers' Attitudes on Police, Mayor, Quinnipiac College Poll Finds; Vallone, Green, Hevesi All Get 50 Percent Approval', Quinnipiac University Polling Institute, 15 March. Available at: https://poll.qu.edu/Poll-Release-Leg acy?releaseid=627

Quinnipiac University Polling Institute (2013) 'Support for Kelly, Cops at New High, Quinnipiac University New York City Poll Finds; Voters Give Mayor A 'b' as in Bloomberg'. Available at: https://poll.qu.edu/poll-rele ase-legacy?releaseid=1832

Rabe-Hemp, C. (2007) 'Survival in an "all boys club": policewomen and their fight for acceptance', *Policing: An International Journal of Police Strategies & Management*, 31(2): 251–270.

Rabe-Hemp, C. (2008) 'Female officers and the ethic of care: does officer gender impact police behaviors?', *Journal of Criminal Justice*, 36(5): 426–434.

Rabe-Hemp, C. (2009) 'POLICEwomen or PoliceWOMEN? Doing gender and police work', *Feminist Criminology*, 4(2): 114–129.

Rabe-Hemp, C. and Schuck, A. (2007) 'Violence against police officers: are female officers at greater risk?', *Police Quarterly*, 10(4): 351–471.

Raganella, A. J. and White, M. D. (2004) 'Race, gender, and motivation for becoming a police officer: implications for building a representative police department', *Journal of Criminal Justice*, 32(6): 501–513.

Rahr, S. and Rice, S. (2015) 'From warriors to guardians: recommitting American police culture to democratic ideals', *New Perspectives in Policing Bulletin*, Washington, DC: National Institute of Justice.

Rambaut, R. and Bittner, E. (1979) 'Changing conceptions of the police role: a sociological review', *Crime and Justice*, 1(1): 239–288.

RAND (1993) *Sexual Orientation and U.S. Military Personnel Policy: Options and Assessment*, Santa Monica, CA: RAND.

Ray, V., Ortiz, K. and Nash, J. (2017) 'Who is policing the community? A comprehensive review of discrimination in police departments', *Sociology Compass*, 1–34. DOI: 10.1111/soc4.12539

Raymond et al v. The City of New York et al, No. 15-CV-6885-LTS-HBP (Southern District of New York) (2017).

Reaves, B. and Hickman, M. (2002) *Police Departments in Large Cities, 1990–2000: Bureau of Justice Statistics Special Report*, Washington, DC: Department of Justice.

Reiner, R. (1978) 'The police in the class structure', *British Journal of Law and Society*, 5(2): 166–184.

Reiner, R. (1991) *Chief Constables: Bobbies, Bosses or Bureaucrats?*, Oxford: Oxford University Press.

Reiner, R. (1992) 'Policing a postmodern society', *Modern Law Review*, 55(6): 761–781.

Reiner, R. (2010) *The Politics of the Police* (4th edn), Oxford: Oxford University Press.

Reuss-Ianni, E. (1983) *Street Cops and Management Cops: The Two Cultures of Policing*, London: Routledge.

Reynolds, A. (2013) 'Representation and rights: the impact of LGBT legislators in comparative perspective', *American Political Science Review*, 107(2): 259–274.

Riad, S. and Jones, D. (2022) 'Approaching intersectionality through metonymy: coloniality and recursion at work', *Gender, Work and Organization*. https://doi.org/10.1111/gwao.12828

Riccucci, N. and Van Ryzin, N. (2017) 'Representative bureaucracy: a lever to enhance social equity, coproduction, and democracy', *Public Administration Review*, 77(1). DOI: 10.1111/puar.12649

Riccucci, N., Van Ryzin, G. and Lavena, C. (2014) 'Representative bureaucracy in policing: does it increase perceived legitimacy?', *Journal of Public Administration Research and Theory*, 24(3): 537–551.

Riccucci, N. Van Ryzin, G. and Jackson, K. (2018) 'Representative bureaucracy, race, and policing: a survey experiment', *Journal of Public Administration Research and Theory*, 28(4): 506–518.

Richards, D. (1990) 'Elite interviewing: approaches and pitfalls', *Politics*, 16(1): 199–204.

Richardson, L. (2015) 'Police racial violence: lessons from social psychology', *Fordham Law Review*, 83(6): 2961–2976.

Rivera, L. (2012) 'Hiring as cultural matching: the case of elite professional service firms', *American Sociological Review*, 77(6): 999–1022.

Roberg, R. (1978) 'An analysis of the relationships among higher education, belief systems, and job performance of patrol officers', *Journal of Police Science and Administration*, 6(1): 336–344.

Roberg, R. and Bonn, S. (2004) 'Higher education and policing: where are we now?', *Policing: An International Journal of Police Strategies & Management*, 27(4): 469–486.

Robinson, C. (1978) 'The deradicalization of the policeman: a historical analysis', *Crime and Delinquency*, 24(2): 129–151.

Robinson, A. and Chandek, M. (2000) 'The domestic violence arrest decision: examining demographic, attitudinal, and situational variables', *Crime & Delinquency*, 46(1): 18–37.

Rojek, J. and Decker, S. (2009) 'Examining racial disparity in the police discipline process', *Police Quarterly*, 12(4): 388–407.

Rosenfeld, R., Johnson, T. and Wright, R. (2020) 'Are college-educated police officers different? A study of stops, searches, and arrests', *Criminal Justice Policy Review*, 31(2): 206–236.

Rowe, M. (2004) *Policing, Race and Racism*, Cullompton: Willan Publishing.

Rowe, M. (2012) *Race & Crime (Key Approaches to Criminology)*, London: SAGE.

Roy, K., Zvonkovic, A., Goldberg, A., Sharp, E. and LaRossa, R. (2015) 'Sampling richness and qualitative integrity: challenges for research with families', *Journal of Marriage and Family*, 77(1): 243–260.

Rumens, N. and Broomfield, J. (2012) 'Gay men in the police: identity disclosure and management issues', *Human Resource Management Journal*, 22(3): 283–298.

Runnymede Trust (2009) *The Stephen Lawrence Inquiry 10 Years On: An Analysis of the Literature*, London: Runnymede Trust.

Rydberg, J. and Terrill, W. (2010) 'The effect of higher education on police behavior', *Police Quarterly*, 13(1): 92–120.

Sass, T. and Troyer, J. (1999) 'Affirmative action, political representation, unions, and female police employment', *Journal of Labor Research*, 20(4): 571–587.

Savage, M. and Williams, K. (2008) 'Elites: remembered in capitalism and forgotten by social sciences', *Sociological Review*, 56(1): 1–24.

Savage, M., Devine, F., Cunningham, N., Taylor, M., Li, Y., Hjellbrekke, J., et al (2013) 'A new model of social class: findings from the BBC's Great British Class Survey experiment', *Sociology*, 47(2): 219–250.

Scarman, L. (1981) *The Scarman Report*, London: Penguin.

Schafer, J. A., Huebner, B. M. and Bynum, T. S. (2003) 'Citizen perceptions of police services: race, neighborhood context and community policing', *Police Quarterly*, 6: 440–468.

Schuck, A. (2014) 'Gender differences in policing: testing hypotheses from the performance and disruption perspectives', *Feminist Criminology*, 9(2): 160–185.

Schuck, A. (2018) 'Women in policing and the response to rape: representative bureaucracy and organizational change', *Feminist Criminology*, 13(3): 237–259.

Schuck, A. and Rabe-Hemp, C. (2005) 'Women police', *Women & Criminal Justice*, 16(4): 91–117.

Seklecki, R. and Paynich, R. (2007) 'A national survey of female police officers: an overview of findings', *Police Practice and Research*, 8(1): 17–30.

Sherman, L. (1980) 'Perspectives on police and violence', *The Annals of the American Academy of Political and Social Science*, 452(1): 1–12.

Sherman, L. and Blumberg, M. (1981) 'Higher education and police use of deadly force', *Journal of Criminal Justice*, 9(4): 317–331.

Shernock, S. (1992) 'The effects of college education on professional attitudes among police', *Journal of Criminal Justice Education*, 3(1): 71–92.

Shjarback, J. and Todak, N. (2019) 'The prevalence of female representation in supervisory and management positions in American law enforcement: an examination of organizational correlates', *Women & Criminal Justice*, 29(3): 129–147.

Shoenfelt, E. and Mendel, M. (1991) *Gender Bias in the Evaluation of Male and Female Police Officer Performance*. Paper presented at the 37th Annual Meeting of the Southeastern Psychological Association (New Orleans, LA, 20–23 March).

Silvestri, M. (2006) 'Doing time: becoming a police leader', *International Journal of Police Science and Management*, 8(4): 266–281.

Sim, J. and Tombs, S. (2009) 'State Talk, State Silence: Work and "Violence" in the UK', in L. Panitch and C. Leys (eds) *Socialist Register Vol 45, Violence Today*, London: The Merlin Press, pp 88–104.

Skinner, P. (2020) 'I'm a Cop. I Won't Fight a "War" on Crime the Way I Fought the War on Terror', *Washington Post*, 3 June. Available at: www.washingtonpost.com/outlook/2020/06/03/beat-cop-militarized-policing-cia/

Sklansky, D. (2006) 'Not your father's police department: making sense of the new demographics of law enforcement', *The Journal of Criminal Law and Criminology*, 96(3): 1209–1243.

Sklansky, D. (2007) 'Seeing Blue: Police Reform, Occupational Culture, and Cognitive Burn-In', in M. O'Neill, M. Marks and A. Singh (eds) *Police Occupational Culture: New Debates and New Directions (Sociology of Crime, Law and Deviance, Vol 8)*, Bingley: Emerald Publishing Group, pp 19–45.

Sklansky, D. (2022) 'Police reform in divided times', *American Journal of Law and Equality*, 2(1): 3–35.

Skogan, W. (1994) *Contacts Between Police and Public: Findings from the 1992 British Crime Survey*, London: Home Office.

Skogan, W. (2007) 'Asymmetry in the impact of encounters with police', *Policing and Society*, 16(2): 99–126.

Skogan, W. and Hartnett, S. (1997) *Community Policing, Chicago Style*, New York: Oxford University Press.

Skolnick, J. (2002) 'Corruption and the blue code of silence', *Police Practice and Research: An International Journal*, 3(1): 7–19.

Skolnick, J. (2008) 'Enduring issues of police culture and demographics', *Policing and Society*, 18(1): 35–45.

Smith, A., Locke, B. and Fenster, A. (1967) 'Authoritarianism in policemen who are college graduates and non-college police', *The Journal of Criminal Law, Criminology, and Police Science*, 61(2): 313–315.

Smith, A., Locke, B. and Walker, W. (1967) 'Authoritarianism in college and non-college oriented police', *The Journal of Criminal Law, Criminology, and Police Science*, 58(1): 128–132.

Smith, B. (2003) 'The impact of police officer diversity on police-caused homicides', *Policy Studies Journal*, 31(2): 147–162.

Smith, G., Johnson, H. and Roberts, C. (2015) 'Ethnic minority police officers and disproportionality in misconduct proceedings', *Policing and Society*, 25(6): 561–578.

Smith, S. and Aamodt, M. (1997) 'The relationship between education, experience, and police performance', *Journal of Police and Criminal Psychology*, 12(2): 7–14.

Somvadee, C. and Morash, M. (2008) 'Dynamics of sexual harassment for policewomen working alongside men', *Policing: An International Journal of Police Strategies & Management*, 31(3): 485–498.

Stalans, L. J. and Finn, M. A. (2000) 'Gender and socialization: how women and men police officers handle domestic violence', *Women and Criminal Justice*, 11(3): 1–24.

Stauffer, K., Song, M. and Shoub, K. (2022) 'How police agency diversity, policies, and outcomes shape citizen trust and willingness to engage', *Policy Studies Journal*. DOI: 10.1111/psj.12479

Stokes, L. and Scott, J. (1996) 'Affirmative action and selected minority groups in law enforcement', *Journal of Criminal Justice*, 24(1): 29–38.

Stone, V. and Tuffin, R. (2000) *Attitudes of People from Minority Ethnic Communities towards a Career in the Police Service*, London: Home Office.

Stork, R. (1975) 'The plague of the blue locusts: police reform and popular resistance in northern England, 1840–57', *International Review of Social History*, 20(1): 61–90.

Stoughton, S. (2014) 'Law enforcement's "warrior" problem', *Harvard Law Review Forum*, 128(6): 225–234.

Stroshine, M. and Brandl, S. (2011) 'Race, gender, and tokenism in policing: an empirical elaboration', *Police Quarterly*, 14(4): 344–365.

Sullivan, P. S. (1989) 'Minority Officers: Current Issues', in R. G. Dunham and G. P. Alpert (eds) *Critical Issues in Policing: Contemporary Readings*, Prospect Heights, IL: Waveland Press, pp 331–345.

Sun, I. and Payne, B. (2004) 'Racial differences in resolving conflicts: a comparison between black and white police officers', *Crime & Delinquency*, 50(4): 516–541.

Swerling, J. B. (1978) *A study of police officers' values and their attitudes towards homosexual officers*. PhD Dissertation, Los Angeles, CA: California School of Professional Psychology.

Syed, J. and Ozbilgin, M. (2009) 'A relational framework for international transfer of diversity management practices', *International Journal of Human Resource Management*, 20(12): 2435–2453.

Taylor Greene, H. (2000) 'Black females in law enforcement a foundation for future research', *Journal of Contemporary Criminal Justice*, 16(2): 230–239.

Teahan, J. (1975) 'A longitudinal study of attitude shifts among black and white police officers', *Journal of Social Issues*, 31(1): 47–56.

Telep, C. (2011) 'The impact of higher education on police officer attitudes toward abuse of authority', *Journal of Criminal Justice Education*, 22(3): 392–419.

Terrill, W. and Mastrofski, S. (2002) 'Situational and officer-based determinants of police coercion', *Justice Quarterly*, 19(2): 215–248.

Terrill, W. and Paoline, E. (2015) 'Citizen complaints as threats to police legitimacy: the role of officers' occupational attitudes', *Journal of Contemporary Criminal Justice*, 31(2): 192–211.

Texeira, M. (2002) ' "Who protects and serves me?" A case study of sexual harassment of African American women in one U.S. law enforcement agency', *Gender & Society*, 16(4): 524–545.

The President's Commission on Law Enforcement and Administration of Justice (Katzenbach Commission) (1967) *Task Force Report: The Police*, Washington, DC: U.S. Government Printing Office.

The Royal Commission on Police (1962) *Final Report*, London: Royal Commission on Police.

Theobald, N. and Haider-Markel, D. (2009) 'Race, bureaucracy, and symbolic representation: interactions between citizens and police', *Journal of Public Administration Research and Theory*, 19(2): 409–426.

Thomas, M. and Tufts, S. (2020) 'Blue solidarity: police unions, race and authoritarian populism in North America', *Work, Employment and Society*, 34(1): 126–144.

Thomas, R. R. (1992) 'Managing Diversity: A Conceptual Framework', in S. E. Jackson (ed) *Diversity in the Workplace: Human Resource Initiatives*, New York: Guilford, pp 306–318.

Thompson, F. (1976) 'Minority groups in public bureaucracies: are passive and active representation linked?' *Administration & Society*, 8(2): 147–272.

Thompson, R. and Nored, L. (2002) 'Law enforcement employment discrimination based on sexual orientation: a select review of cases', *American Journal of Criminal Justice*, 26(2): 203–217.

Toch, H. (2002) *Stress in Policing*, Washington DC: US Department of Justice. Available at: www.ojp.gov/ncjrs/virtual-library/abstracts/stress-policing

Todak, N., Huff, J. and James, L. (2018) 'Investigating perceptions of race and ethnic diversity among prospective police officers', *Police Practice and Research*, 19(5): 490–504.

Todak, N., Leban, L. and Hixon, B. (2021) 'Are women opting out? A mixed methods study of women patrol officers' promotional aspirations', *Feminist Criminology*, 16(5): 1–22.

Townsey, R. (1982) 'Black women in American policing: an advancement display', *Journal of Criminal Justice*, 10(1): 455–468.

Trautman, N. (2000) 'Police code of silence facts revealed'. In Annual Conference of the International Association of Chiefs of Police. Available at: www.aele.org/loscode2000.html

Trochmann, M. and Gover, A. (2016) 'Measuring the impact of police representativeness on communities', *Policing: An International Journal of Police Strategies & Management*, 39(4): 773–790.

Truxillo, D., Bennett, S. and Collins, M. (1998) 'College education and police job performance: a ten-year study', *Public Personnel Management*, 27(2): 269–280.

Turner, M. and Pratkanis, A. (1994) 'Positive discrimination: insights from social psychological and organizational research', *Basic and Applied Social Psychology*, 15(1–2): 1–11.

Tyler, T. (2003) 'Procedural justice, legitimacy, and the effective rule of law', *Crime and Justice*, 30: 283–357.

Tyler, T. and Fagan, J. (2008) 'Legitimacy and cooperation: why do people help the police fight crime in their communities?', *Ohio State Journal of Criminal Law*, 6(1): 231–276.

Tyler, T. and Wakslak, C. (2004) 'Profiling and police legitimacy: procedural justice, attributions of motive, and acceptance of police authority', *Criminology*, 42(2): 253–280.

UK Police Foundation (2018) *A Diversity Uplift? Police workforce gender and ethnicity trends from 2007 to 2018 and prospects for the future*, Perspectives on Policing: Paper 6, London: Police Foundation.

United States v. Windsor, 570 US 744 (2013).

USCCR (US Commission on Civil Rights) (1981) *Who Is Guarding the Guardians?*, Washington, DC: US Commission on Civil Rights.

Van Ryzin, G., Riccucci, N. and Li, H. (2017) 'Representative bureaucracy and its symbolic effect on citizens: a conceptual replication', *Public Management Review*, 19(9): 1365–1379.

Van Wormer, K. (1981) 'Are males suited to police patrol work?' *Police Studies*, 3: 41–44.

Villa, D. (2021) *Measuring the impact of residency requirements and the relationship with the citizens in the community*. Unpublished PhD dissertation, DePaul University.

Vinopal, K. (2020) 'Socioeconomic representation: expanding the theory of representative bureaucracy', *Journal of Public Administration Research and Theory*, 30(2): 187–201.

Vitale, A. (2017) *The End of Policing*, London: Verso.

Vomfell, L. and Stewart, N. (2021) 'Officer bias, over-patrolling and ethnic disparities in stop and search', *Nature Human Behavior*, 5(5): 566–575.

Vrij, A. and Taylor, R. (2003) 'Police officers' and students' beliefs about telling and detecting little and serious lies', *International Journal of Police Science and Management*, 5(1): 41–49.

Waddington, P. (1999) 'Police (canteen) sub-culture: an appreciation', *British Journal of Criminology*, 39(2): 287–309.

Walker, S. (1983) 'Employment of black and Hispanic police officers', *Review of Applied Urban Research*, 11(06), Omaha: Center for Applied Urban Research.

Walker, S. (1989) 'Employment of black and Hispanic police officers, 1983–1988: a follow-up study', *University of Nebraska Occasional Paper No. 89–1*, Omaha: Center for Applied Urban Research.

Walker, S. (2007) 'Police accountability: current issues and research needs'. Available at: https://samuelwalker.net/wp-content/uploads/0201/05/NIJResearchNeeds2006.pdf

Walker, S. (2008) 'The neglect of police unions: exploring one of the most important areas of American policing', *Police Practice and Research: An International Journal*, 9(2): 95–112.

Walker, S., Spohn, C. and DeLone, M. (2017) *The Color of Justice: Race, Ethnicity, and Crime in America*, Belmont, CA: Wadsworth.

Wall, D. (1998) *The Chief Constables of England and Wales: The Socio-Legal History of a Criminal Justice Elite*, London: Routledge.

Wang, L. (2003) 'Race as proxy: situational racism and self-fulfilling stereotypes', *DePaul Law Review*, 53(3): 1013–1109.

Washington Post (2023) *Police Shootings Database*, Washington, DC: *Washington Post*. Available at: www.washingtonpost.com/graphics/investigations/police-shootings-database/

Webster, C. (2007) *Understanding Race and Crime*, London: McGraw Hill.

Weisburd, D., Greenspan, R., Hamilton, E. E., Williams, H. and Bryant, K. A. (2000) *Police Attitudes Toward Abuse of Authority: Findings from a National Study, National Institute of Justice Research Brief*, Washington, DC: Department of Justice.

Weiser, B. and Goldstein, J. (2014) 'Mayor Says New York City Will Settle Suits on Stop-and-Frisk Tactics', *The New York Times*, 30 January. Available at: www.nytimes.com/2014/01/31/nyregion/de-blasio-stop-and-frisk.html

Weitzer, R. (2002) 'Incidents of police misconduct and public opinion', *Journal of Criminal Justice*, 30(1): 397–408.

Weitzer, R. and Tuch, S. (2006) *Race and Policing in America*, Cambridge: Cambridge University Press.

Weitzer, R., Tuch, S. A. and Skogan, W. G. (2008) 'Police–community relations in a majority-black city', *Journal of Research in Crime and Delinquency*, 45(4): 398–428.

Welch, K. (2007) 'Black criminal stereotypes and racial profiling', *Journal of Contemporary Criminal Justice*, 23(3): 276–288.

Wertsch, T. (1998) 'Walking the thin blue line: policewomen and tokenism today', *Women & Criminal Justice*, 9(3): 23–62.

Westmarland, L. (2001) *Gender and Policing: Sex, Power and Police Culture*, New York: Willan.

Westmarland, L. (2017) 'Putting their bodies on the line: police culture and gendered physicality', *Policing: A Journal of Policy and Practice*, 3(1): 301–317.

Westmarland, L. and Conway, S. (2020) 'Police ethics and integrity: keeping the "blue code" of silence', *International Journal of Police Science & Management*, 22(4): 378–392.

Westmarland, L. and Rowe, M. (2018) 'Police ethics and integrity: can a new code overturn the blue code?', *Policing and Society*, 28(7): 854–870.

Whetstone, T. (2001) 'Copping out: why police officers decline to participate in the sergeant's promotion process', *American Journal of Criminal Justice*, 25(2): 147–159.

Whetstone, T. and Wilson, D. (1999) 'Dilemmas confronting female police officer promotional candidates: glass ceiling, disenfranchisement or satisfaction', *International Journal of Police Science and Management*, 2(2): 128–143.

White House (2015) *Final Report of the President's Task Force on 21st Century Policing*, Washington, DC: The White House.

Whitfield, J. (2004) *Unhappy Dialogue: The Metropolitan Police and London's West Indian Community*, Cullompton: Willan.

Wilkins, T. (2022) 'Prince George's Settles Lawsuit with Family of Detective Killed by Fellow Police Officer', *NBCWashington*, 10 May. Available at: www.nbcwashington.com/news/local/prince-georges-county/pri nce-georges-settles-lawsuit-with-family-of-detective-killed-by-fellow-pol ice-officer/3047839/

Wilkins, V. and Williams, B. (2008) 'Black or blue: racial profiling and representative bureaucracy', *Public Administration Review*, 68(1): 652–662.

Wilkins, V. and Williams, B. (2009) 'Representing blue: representative bureaucracy and racial profiling in the Latino community', *Administration and Society*, 40(1): 775–798.

Williams, R. (2003) 'A state of permanent exception: the birth of modern policing in colonial capitalism', *Interventions*, 5(3): 322–344.

Wilson, C. and Wilson, S. (2014) 'Are we there yet? Perceptive roles of African American police officers in small agency settings', *Western Journal of Black Studies*, 38(2): 123–133.

Wilson, C., Wilson, S. and Thou, M. (2015) 'Perceptions of African American police officers on racial profiling in small agencies', *Journal of Black Studies*, 46(5): 482–505.

Wilson, J. and Kelling, G. (1982) 'Broken Windows', *The Atlantic Monthly*, 1 March. Available at: www.theatlantic.com/magazine/archive/1982/03/ broken-windows/304465/

Wilson, S. and Buckler, K. (2010) 'The debate over police reform: examining minority support for citizen oversight and resistance by police unions', *American Journal of Criminal Justice*, 35(1): 184–197.

Woodeson, A. (1993) 'The first women police: a force for equality or infringement?', *Women's History Review*, 2(2): 217–232.

Worden, A. (1993) 'The attitudes of women and men in policing: testing conventional and contemporary wisdom', *Criminology*, 31(2): 203–242.

Worden, R. E. (1990) 'Badge and Baccalaureate: policies, hypotheses, and further evidence', *Justice Quarterly*, 7(3): 565–592.

Wrench, J. (2005) 'Diversity management can be bad for you', *Race & Class*, 46(3): 73–84.

Wright, J. and Headley, A. (2020) 'Police use of force interactions: is race relevant or gender germane?', *American Review of Public Administration*, 50(8): 1–14.

Young, D. and Casey, E. (2019) 'An examination of the sufficiency of small qualitative samples', *Social Work Research*, 43(1): 53–58.

Young, J. (2003) 'Winning the Fight against Crime? New Labour, Populism and Lost Opportunities', in R. Matthews and J. Young (eds) *The New Politics of Crime and Punishment*, London: Routledge, pp 33–47.

Young, M. (1991) *An Inside Job*, Oxford: Oxford University Press.

Zempi, I. (2020) '"Looking back, I wouldn't join up again": the lived experiences of police officers as victims of bias and prejudice perpetrated by fellow staff within an English police force', *Police Practice and Research*, 21(1): 33–48.

Zhao, J. (1998) 'Determinants of minority employment in American municipal police agencies: the representation of African American officers', *Journal of Criminal Justice*, 26(4): 267–277.

Zhao, J., He, N. and Lovrich, N. (2005) 'Predicting the employment of minority officers in U.S. cities: OLS fixed-effect panel model results for African American and Latino officers for 1993, 1996, and 2000', *Journal of Criminal Justice*, 33(1): 377–386.

Zimring, F. (2006) 'The necessity and value of transnational comparative study: some preaching from a recent convert', *Criminology & Public Policy*, 5(1): 615–622.

Index

References to tables appear in **bold** type.